Anthony Smith is Director of the British Film Institute and a former Fellow of St. Antony's College, Oxford. His previous books include *The Shadow in the Cave: The Broadcaster, His Audience, and the State; Geopolitics & Information: How Western Media Dominate World Culture;* and *Goodbye Gutenberg: The Newspaper Revolution of the 1980s.*

Newspapers and Democracy

Newspapers and Democracy

International Essays on a Changing Medium

Edited by Anthony Smith

The MIT Press ^{OO}
Cambridge, Massachusetts,
and London, England

This book was set in VIP Century Schoolbook by Grafacon, Incorporated and printed and bound by The Murray Printing Company in the United States of America.

Library of Congress Cataloging in Publication Data

Main entry under title:
Newspapers and democracy.

Includes bibliographical references and index.
1. Government and the press—Addresses, essays, lectures.
2. Journalism—Political aspects—Addresses, essays, lectures.
3. Newspapers—Addresses, essays, lectures. 4. Newspaper
publishing—Technological innovations—Addresses, essays, lectures.
I. Smith, Anthony, 1938–
PN4735.N46   070   80-15665
ISBN 0-262-19184-9

Contents

Acknowledgments

This volume of essays is the result of a project commissioned by the German Marshall Fund of the United States, Washington, D.C., to investigate the ways in which the familiar medium of the newspaper is altering in the closing decades of the century in the countries of the developed world. The underlying purpose was to see how changes in technology and in the economic organization of the medium are affecting the historic purposes of the newspaper in those societies that, broadly speaking, have accepted the basic tenets of a free press. I am deeply indebted to Benjamin Read, who was president of the German Marshall Fund at the time the project was conceived, and to his successor, Robert Gerald Livingston, who has supported and encouraged it almost week by week from June 1977 until its completion two years later, and who has been adviser, critic, and friend. The project will result in two volumes, the other published by Oxford University Press.

It is impossible to thank the hundreds of people who have given me information, hospitality, and encouragement. They are spread over twenty countries. All I can do is to single out those who have made a specific contribution toward the construction of this volume. First among these is Pauline Wingate, who has been researcher, manuscript editor, and general consultant over the course of many months. I wish to thank Jackie Lebe and Yvonne Richards who have typed the many manuscripts at various stages of the work, often under great pressure. Peter Langdale translated the Italian and French chapters. Idwall Jones translated the Norwegian chapter. John Howkins edited and published an earlier version of chapter 1 in *InterMedia*. Eddi Ploman, Robert

Tritt, Joanna Spicer, Andrea Seimsen, and Jack Rich of the International Institute of Communications have been constant sources of loyal encouragement. I am indebted to the Acton Society for the generous loan of secretarial aid and equipment.

Introduction

In the last decades of the twentieth century, the newspaper is going through a transformation in technology and internal organization, in its structure as an industry, in its generally accepted social and political purpose, in its whole stance toward society. This historic convulsion is taking place internationally as the result of the convergence of a series of changes in society and demographics, in the economics of advertising, and in technical possibility. At the same time changes are taking place in the demarcations between the newspaper and other printed forms as newspaper editors and publishers search for new types of content and new ways to hold together their dual market of readers and advertisers. On the horizon a far greater transformation looms, one in which the newspaper might even disappear, giving way to new electronic devices for circulating similar material at lower cost and at greater convenience than the cumbersome method of transporting large quantities of heavy newsprint once or twice a day.

Historians of newspapers are by no means short of comparable moments in the past history of the form when the destruction of an old press order gave way to a new one and familiar journals and styles disappeared from the scene. The newspaper has undergone a cataclysmic change roughly once a century, in fact. The stylish gazette of the 1660s took over from the cruder corranto and mercury of the early seventeenth century in many of the European nations that had pioneered printed news, and it was this smart double-columned sheet that a British emigrant publisher attempted unsuccessfully to establish in the American colonies in the 1680s. In the mid-eighteenth century a whole industry of thrice-a-week papers flourished on the boulevards and in the salons of European society until a new kind of daily publication drove them out of business toward the end of the century. Before World War I Britain witnessed the "Harmsworth Revolution" and America the impact of Pulitzer when a new popular newspaper form brought about a widespread alteration in publishers' and journalists' attitudes and seemed at the time (possibly rightly) to be a destructive technological and financial upstart, based upon the degeneration of traditional standards and the abandonment of the newspaper's role as the engine of coterie politics. Today's changeover from late-Victorian mechanical technology to computerized printing is taking place at a time when local monopoly is becoming the standard form of distribution, and the average reader in the Western democracies is ceasing to have daily access to a series of competing examples of the newspaper form. This shift represents a drastic change in the political role of publishers and in the editorial purposes of the newspaper. The problem is how to relate the various changes taking place in roughly comparable societies to the central public purpose with which the newspaper is associated: the linking of the individual to the political realities of society. The changes are related and are being generated by the same forces throughout the countries of North America, Australia, New Zealand, Japan, and Western Europe. All of the previous changes in the evolution of the newspaper took place convulsively and simultaneously across a large area of the globe, and this one is no exception.

In the last quarter of the twentieth century, important transformation in the form of the newspaper is occurring as a result of the convergence of a series of changes in industry, in the organization of production, in the demands of advertisers, in the interests of readers, in the demarcations between the roles of the newspaper and other (largely electronic) media, and also because of other financial and organizational constraints.

To many people who read (in the press) of the death of certain newspapers and the tribulations of others, it seems that the press as we know it is dying. One of the things that concerns them most is the fear that, with the death of a medium that has traditionally been the carrier of many forms of political comment, a vital dimension will soon be absent from our political and civic life. The issue is an important one.

What most Europeans think of as a newspaper is something that emerged with the 1848 revolution and the struggle for primary nationhood and that was inseparable from the struggle for the establishment of separate political parties, each of which, in expressing its view of the coming nationhood, found it necessary to appeal to the whole of a population or a class. Many of the most powerful papers of today were founded in the aftermath of that heady year of change: *Die Presse* of Vienna, *Figaro* of Paris, the many *Tagesanzeigers* of Germany, the *Telegraph* of London.

Until the 1870s, papers were founded to express a certain set of expectations of the nature of the new civic life. Even in England, which had not experienced any social cataclysm, there were new social movements at work in mid-century that fought hard (and won) a battle for easing newspaper taxes, thereby strengthening the lines of party difference and enabling the press to reach out into the society at large to spread "opinion."

In 1872 Walter Bagehot, editor of *The Economist,* called the new age the Age of Discussion and described with pride the way in which the battle over the Corn Laws had been fought out in dignity on the platform and in the newspaper, without riot or bloodshed—quite in contrast with the battle over the Great Reform Bill only fifteen years before, when the newspaper was not yet a major instrument of official formal political life. Until the 1920s, the newspaper remained associated with that view of political life. All of the European nationalist movements began life with their own newspapers. Papers that arrived first stood the best chances of survival; those that arrived with the newer parties (the Social Democrats, the Communists) have not survived as well as those that came with the Liberals or Radicals or Agrarians in the mid- to late nineteenth century (even where the later parties became electorally the stronger).

The late twentieth century has developed a strange and paradoxical problem: powerful parties with weak newspapers. Economic forces also enforce this paradox. Advertisers now want to reach not small groups of a population that subscribe to certain party papers, but whole demographic groups. Those papers that address a median audience (often politically of the center) stand greater chances of survival and prosperity; papers that cannot manage to reach a majority of readers of a given age group or income group are under pressure. They have ways of fighting back, but they are under pressure. Efforts are being made of many kinds to overcome the new facts of economic life. In many countries (a majority of those in Western Europe) newspapers are now eligible for various kinds of subsidy, especially papers that represent opinion or are the direct spokesmen of specific political causes. Subsidy has reached very high levels in some countries (10 percent of the total income of the press in Norway, 15 percent in France, probably 20 percent in Italy).

The reader can choose whether to treat this volume as a connected survey of the state of the art in various parts of the world or as a series of separate glimpses at the presses of different countries. Each country has been selected as a case study of a special problem or situation, but all of the thirteen topics raised are relevant, to one extent or another, to all of the countries of the developed world.

There is a scramble for new technology in many countries. The United States has undergone the most advanced technical transformation, and West Germany, Sweden, and Japan are moving very rapidly to computerized typesetting and low manning levels. The newspaper may be a labor-intensive mechanical industry of Victorian times that survived long beyond its true era; it is becoming a less labor-intensive electronic product in the late twentieth century. That, however, is the beginning rather than the end of its problems. A computerized newspaper is different as a form from its mechanical forebear; its internal structure of command finds itself under very different pressures; all sorts of demands for control and democracy assert themselves in a context where these claims are organizationally much easier to satisfy than in the past. In some countries (such as Italy and several Scandinavian countries) the issue of subsidy, the problem of new technology, and the institution of new kinds of press freedom (within the newspaper and between the government and the newspaper) have all become fused into one problem: the question of the future of the press.

It is possible to look at the newspaper as if it were one single object, a product made in a certain way and financed through sales and advertising, a receptacle for certain categories of information labeled news and comment. The newspaper cannot, however, be studied as if it were an automobile or a house. It does not have a single historical line of growth, and therefore to examine its future one must search in many different places. Newspaper owners tend to think of the newspaper as a unitary product since it issues forth from their premises; newspaper employees have very much the same perspective. More detached observers, however, may find it useful to deal with the problem in a different way.

The newspaper is a dual medium; it serves readers and consumers, it spreads information and commerce. Changing needs within commerce affect it as much as changing needs for information. Thus the tendency of the post-1960 era for display advertising to shrink as a proportion of total available advertising and for classified advertising to grow will cause a fundamental shift in the viability of certain categories of newspaper. The big national dailies of Britain are very hard pressed indeed. Manufacturers can reach their consumers through the flexible, attractive, colorful medium of television, and retailers can reach their buyers through regional or local or evening papers.

At the same time, the new consumer-citizen has acquired different interests and loyalties than the old voter-citizen. His relationship with political parties is much looser. The readers of today in Europe (and perhaps Japan and the United States also) do not define themselves in terms of their adherence to political causes. We are all less conscious of ourselves as members of a class. We are also less conscious of ourselves as members of a nation, as the new supranationhoods and fissiparous regional nationhoods become stronger. The content of the newspaper, therefore, appeals to readers at different levels and in different ways. Certain categories of material, and therefore certain kinds of newspapers, are growing in importance. Newspapers with a high content of sexual stories and pictures are increasingly popular, as are papers that concentrate on financial and industrial news. People require forms of entertainment and diversion that cannot be obtained easily elsewhere, and kinds of information that cannot be found elsewhere in sufficient detail.

The most important issue concerns the new electronic media. There has been an important (and far too little studied) rearrangement of types and categories of information between radio, television, weekly magazine, and newspaper. Some of the changes are obvious; for instance, a newspaper movement toward investigative stories or stories that appear to be the result of some special inquiry. Television news increasingly takes over the role of the town crier, providing the main stories of generally agreed-upon high news value. The shifts are so subtle that to discover them one must interview news editors in great depth. Even they may not always be aware of the changes taking place in their hour-to-hour judgments.

On the horizon is a series of further changes in production, content, internal editorial control, forms of advertising, and competition from even newer media. We are seeing many new kinds of papers being tried out, and some are prospering (one is a new financial daily in Lyon). We are also seeing many old kinds of papers being tried out again and failing (a new self-consciously left-wing daily in Paris, for example). We are seeing the new media of teletext and videotex starting up in Britain and, very soon, in France, Germany, and Sweden. When it develops further, it will tend to unpack various categories of information from the existing press and repackage it in its own screen-delivered form direct to the home.

Newspapers themselves, having computerized their production and composition methods, may prefer to deliver themselves to readers via a telecommunicated device (facsimile or teletext) rather than through newsstands or home delivery. This category of change is part of the present transformation, not of the distant future. The pressure of change on the newspaper is coming through many separate channels. Some changes will arrive because existing newspaper owners are acquiring interests in electronics, telecommunications, free-sheets, television, and radio, which may enable their enterprises to diversify in outlets and make better use of the information input of their businesses. Such developments, of course, raise the question of whether monopoly is a justified fear in the field of information.

At the heart of the study is the realization that there is a late-century swing within the whole of the media from the private to the public sectors. It is government everywhere that is having to make the decisions affecting the future of the media. Although the newspaper—once the dominant information medium—is still largely in the private sector and still lives by the traditional fourth estate ethic, it is necessarily being dragged along, in form and content, by public-sector decisions. Government is now a major press advertiser; government decides the pace of growth in radio and television provision; government (in the smaller territorial countries) acquires the frequencies that must be used for transmission; ultimately government must decide at what level society will refuse the further growth of intermedia ownership. The newspaper is thus at the mercy of government, though it continues to see its role within society as a mediator of public opinion, as a broker of information between authority and society, and as an inciter of public sentiment when governmental action appears misjudged.

What happens, therefore, to the fourth estate notion in the new information environment? At the end of our study, what may be said about the ethic of the press, about its role within the body politic? In the late century, must we begin to construct a new doctrine for the press, one that delineates the new role of government (or society as a whole) within the sphere of the media? The answer to all these is almost certainly yes, although to answer in that manner must entail some careful statement about what the state actually is in this new context.

Perhaps the whole press ethic must be restated on the basis of new sociology of the press, which has been in the process of development over the 1970s. By means of informed discussion, society arrives at a view of what type of provision should exist within the media, and this the government has to guarantee or provide. Only government can make the decision as to how many stations or channels should exist in television, whether advertising should appear on teletext services, whether value-added tax should be charged on newspapers. Government decides, willy-nilly, on the range of media that may exist.

The independence of the information media can be maintained in these circumstances only through society's vigilance or through the construction of institutions that undertake this function of vigilance. The First Amendment of the American constitution may not be sufficient to guarantee in a public-sector-dominated media system the freedoms from restraint that the press requires. Certainly a new series of questions and problems arise in the field of press freedom as a result of the realization that the environment of information is changing. The end product of this study could be and should be a restatement of this problem in the light of the information acquired.

The entire nexus of relationships within which the editorial practices of the newspaper have evolved is altering. This book is designed as a synoptic and international study that aims to answer a simple question: What is happening to the newspaper; is it dying or being reborn?

Newspapers and Democracy

I

Technology and the Press

The chapters in this section examine some of the "cost-push" and "technology-pull" factors that have been responsible for the great self-examination that newspaper publishers have been obliged to conduct in the 1970s. Chapter 1 starts by looking at the way in which the internal economies of American newspaper management have been placed under considerable strain as a result of demographic changes and alterations in the structure of cities. The changing market structure led to the cost crisis and panic of the 1960s, when the newspaper seemed to be in the midst of a permanent decline and when publishers reached out for new technological solutions to problems of marketing and production. The new technology, which is now passing into editorial and production areas of newspapers throughout the world, was the outcome of this reappraisal. The newspaper emerged from the process as a series of local "monopolies" poised to benefit from greatly improved financial circumstances. What we are now observing, however, in the American newspaper industry is perhaps the opening phase of a more far-reaching alteration in the informing processes of society: The newspaper industry, with its new electronic apparatus, is becoming just one of a series of information-providing devices, all of which depend upon computerized storage and advanced telecommunications.

Japan provides some of the most dynamic examples of the implications of computerized information storage for postindustrial society. The Japanese have constructed much of their economic and industrial miracle on information technology, and thus are deeply concerned about how the next generation of electronic equipment may suit the information needs of the next generation of consumers. Tetsuro Tomita's chapter emphasizes looking at social habit and need before deciding which of the new devices will be most appropriate. The 1990s will offer the real opportunity for these new domestic information systems, although the 1980s are witnessing the pioneering of dozens of incompatible experiments around the globe in electronic storage of information with simple retrieval. Perhaps toward the end of the century, it will be possible for one or more of these to act as substitutes for the traditional newspaper. For the foreseeable future, however, these devices will develop (if at all) along with the newspaper, complementing it without displacing it.

Tomita's approach to this phenomenon may startle some readers in the Western world. He starts by looking at all of the information flowing in society between individuals and between individuals and audiences and creates a system for analyzing this vast flow, showing which forms of communication appear most urgently capable of development: those that link small groups of citizens to individually selected areas of information. Only then is the new medium of CAPTAINS, a push-button domestic device similar to Prestel, Telidon, Antiope, and other systems being pioneered in Europe and North America, introduced and analyzed as a possible filler of the discovered gap in information provision. The phenomenon he identifies—the public need for nonstandardized information, responsive to the receiver's individual wants—is certainly the same as that identified by the institutions that have pioneered the rival systems to CAPTAINS. What is of very considerable interest in the Japanese approach is the way it has been tackled and analyzed. It has taken many decades for the West to comprehend the limitations imposed upon all information fashioned for the mass market. Repeatedly in this volume readers will notice how all of the new technologies (those inside the newspaper business, as well as those attempting to circumvent the newspaper) are trying to meet in different ways the late twentieth-century reluctance to enforce the economies of mass marketing any further in the realm of culture and information. Where the nineteenth and early twentieth century were concerned to transmit material to the whole of the new mass audience, which technology had identified, the new age is obsessed with the countervailing problem of how to break down the wedge of material and offer it to the individualized tastes of smaller publics. It is as if society, in its search for new media, is trying to break free of the bonds of class and mass, without abandoning the economies of scale in the collection and dissemination of information. At the same time, of course, the phenomenon may be envisaged in more negative terms, as an attempt on the part of a media colossus, aided in most cases by the state, to reach into the private areas of taste and life-style, to dominate parts of individual life and culture, which had previously been outside the organized context of the media.

Underlying all discussion of the plight or supposed plight of the newspaper industry has been the fear that it has been growing out of its own basic raw material: newsprint. The belief, widely held in the 1970s, that the newspaper was in a terminal crisis arose partly because of the spiraling price of this commodity. Pauline Wingate analyzes the causes of the newsprint crisis and shows how the unstable market for newsprint and newspaper publishers' insistence on short-term contracts and rock-bottom prices have led to sharply declining profits in this industry and therefore to inadequate investment in modernized mills, recycling processes, and new ways of production. Newsprint thus is weighed down with its problems of access to raw materials, labor intensiveness, pollution control, and energy cost. There is some hope that newsprint may break out of this destructive cycle through the arrival of nonwood sources of cellulose, plants that grow faster and in more geographical zones than the trees of the northern forests. There were some Victorians who despaired of ever finding a practical substitute for the increasingly expensive rag paper, even though chemical and mechanical methods of turning wood to pulp had already been invented and cheap newsprint (and therefore the cheap press of the 1880s and 1890s) was about to burst upon the world. The 1980s will discover whether there will be a real commercial breakthrough into a new raw material for making newsprint, which could extend indefinitely the life of the traditional newspaper. The failure to supply such a commodity could lead to an acceleration in the development of electronic substitutes for the newspaper.

The Newspaper of the Late Twentieth Century: The U.S. Model

Anthony Smith

In the office of the *Times* in downtown Los Angeles, the janitor will show you a Mergenthaler linotype machine made in 1949. It sits behind a glass panel, its brass accoutrements gleaming, its maker's name plate painted smartly in silver and blue. The exhibit bears a chilling legend: "Los Angeles Times. A Corner of the Composing Room, 1881–1974." After all, we are only very late Victorians, it reminds us, with one foot still in the age of California's robber barons; we have lived only to see the beginning of the printing revolution.

Next to the linotype lies a carefully preserved collection of hand tools, the defining equipment of generations of typesetters, the survivors of whom today pass the exhibit on their way to the preternaturally clean composing room to which they have been transplanted: mallets and makeup rules, composing sticks and type gauges, a table saw for cutting leads, steel V-joints for measuring the angle line of type, an old "hell-box" for rejected spacing leads, unused lengths of metal, a printer's apron, and a pair of green eyeshades.

If you look at the hands of the printers still working in the building, you can still see the impressions made by decades of the use of this equipment in their roughened skin, hardened to the touch of hot metal, calloused from the pains of apprenticeships served in that dark age, which lasted from 1881 to 1974. Indeed if you stare at the old Mergenthaler No. 61295 long enough, it will suddenly seem to emit that distinctive sound of newspaper composing rooms made by the clatter of brass matrices slipping through metal channels.

The familiar smells, noises, and vibrations of the traditional newspaper industry have disappeared from a large proportion of the American press in the course of the last half-decade. It was only in 1970 that the first computers began to operate, rather bulkily and clumsily, in pioneer newspapers, embarrassedly experimental, ambassadors of NASA's space activities to the medium of print.

The first electronic editor's terminal was put on the market by the Harris Corporation in 1973. The company made the ingenious transition from being a medium-sized manufacturer of printing equipment (founded in 1895 as the Harris Automatic Press Company) to an electronic conglomerate by way of merging with the Intertype Corporation (the great rival of Mergenthaler) and acquiring a series of firms operating in space communications.

Renamed plain Harris in 1974, it is one of a leading group of organizations that have brought about a computer and electronic revolution in American newspaper typesetting almost overnight. Raytheon, which has designed the custom-built electronic newsroom for the *Washington Post* (at a cost reputed to be in the region of $7 million to $8 million), only started thinking of newspapers as potential purchasers of electronic equipment in 1973, having built its business on microwave ovens and guided missiles. In these few years every company operating in the field of newspaper printing equipment has had to move through mergers or reeducation in the medium of computer-based engineering. For students of the impact of the computer on society, the American newspaper industry offers an instant laboratory.

The advent of the computer in newspapers has been part of a total transformation of an industry. To understand the role of the computer, one must look comprehensively at the position of the newspaper in American economics and American society. The interconnection of computers with information may be the great contribution of the late twentieth century to the evolution of human knowledge and consciousness, although it is too soon to discover just how this computer storage of information is changing the intellectual environment.

The newspaper industry, with highly organized internal communications, has reached out for the computer as part of its response to the problems of its own internal economy. It has been brought in as a new tool to perform traditional tasks, and, by examining its effect upon the newspaper, one may perhaps discern something of the larger shifts that may come about in society as more and more of its processes become computer based.

It is useful to compare the present situation to the days when printing first appeared in Europe in the late fifteenth century. At that time the system for copying manuscripts, already organized commercially, was unable to fill the demand for texts. By the thirteenth century, the monastic scriptoria had lost their monopoly over copying ancient texts when groups of craftsmen joined the bands of clerics in the newly founded universities to produce reading material for an increasingly educated laity. The universities needed texts to assist in the process of teaching, but texts had to be made from good exemplars, perfect manuscripts that were kept under the control of university or monastic authorities and rented out, section by section, in quires for skilled copyists to handle. All copying entailed error, and the exemplars on which copies were based were precious because they were often the only source of pure, uncorrupted text. A series of specialist divisions of labor evolved. Specialists prepared the skins for parchment before the copyists could start their work, rubricators added the elaborate capital letters and chapter heads, illuminators filled in the illustrations according to the marginal notes of the scribes.

What Gutenberg wrought was a means for speeding up one of these processes, the copying of the basic text with the use of moving letters. To make these letters accurate, metalwork was necessary, and goldsmiths, bringing their special tools and skills, moved into the business of copying manuscripts. Tracing paper had already been developed by which each scribe could duplicate and triplicate his work, but printing quickly transformed the system within which texts were produced and distributed. It created fixed texts that were as good as the exemplars; it made possible the accumulation of material in libraries in which different communities of scholars could have access to identical material; it carried the exemplar across time and space, and with the exemplar came the author, previously of little account in the process once his first text had been taken from him. The author became the authority over the text. But it should be remembered that the purpose of printing was far from being to change the nature of intellectual authority. Its object was simply to satisfy an enlarged demand for traditional texts. By 1520 the entire corpus of classical literature had been put into print; forty thousand works were turned out in over 250 different towns. The new technology had first gone through the process of finishing a task that had defeated the old skills and techniques.

We must expect the computer in our day to concentrate on solving the problems of disseminating printed forms as we know them before it transforms our consciousness and releases us from customary attitudes toward authorship, toward the control of text. The computer must first work at closing the gaps in our existing print-based industries before the opportunities it offers can be more profoundly explored.

The technology of the computer, considered abstractly, could do much more than assist printing machinery to smear a fifth of an ounce of ink across a kilo of paper more cheaply than before, and so perpetuate the traditional newspaper form. No doubt, in the course of time, its greater potential will be realized. In examining the industrial conditions that have given rise to the remarkably widespread and sudden adoption of electronic editing in the American newspaper, one can descry some of the characteristics of an altogether different mode of information dissemination.

As we shall see, the crisis that appeared to be about to engulf the American newspaper industry in the 1960s arose from fundamental changes in the demographic organization of American society, in the structure and formation of the family, in the relation of city, suburb, and country, and in the organization of work and commuting. A retailing revolution occurred partly to take account of these changes. Increasingly television seemed a more convenient means for organizing the market for consumer goods.

Everything about the newspaper suddenly began to seem wrong: its readers lived in the wrong places and were in the wrong age groups; it was sold in placed where readers were ceasing to go; home delivery depended upon an army of increasingly truculent teenagers; it was manufactured in places from which it was difficult to reach the readers at the time when they were free to read it. It was a labor-intensive medium at a time when skilled labor was becoming well organized and very expensive. Its raw material, newsprint, was extremely heavy to truck around thousands of miles of countryside and hundreds of miles of congested urban areas but at least was cheap until a last straw seemed to break the newspapers in the early 1970s; that advantage too was lost, and newsprint prices rocketed.

A complete revolution in technology and an intense period of self-examination was required for newspapers to find a route out of this enveloping crisis. The new technology had to cater to at least four separate parts of the newspaper process: it had to speed up the process of getting the copy from the reporters and editors to the pressmen and cut down the costs of setting type, laying out pages, and making plates; it had to print the paper more cleanly and efficiently; it had to help the newspaper reorganize its marketing, so that readers who actually wanted the paper would get it where and when they wanted it; and finally, it had to improve the expensive internal processes of a paper, the collection and billing of classified advertising (a growing sector of newspaper advertising), and the storage of records. The printing equipment industry was ready to help with the improvement of web-offset presses, which accomplished the second of these tasks. But all the others required still-undeveloped sophisticated computer techniques. All of the improvements, however, necessitated a complex overhauling of job demarcations, not only in production but in the newsroom and in sales and advertising.

The newspaper had to look very deeply into its own traditional functions. The American Newspaper Publishers Association (ANPA), with its Research Institute, had already set about an overt and systematic preparation of their hundreds of members to reverse the apparent tides of history. Together with the Newspaper Advertising Bureau, an offshoot of the ANPA, a corpus of research findings was developed and endless internal propaganda activity undertaken to get publishers, large and small, interested in the new equipment. It was clear that what helped one newspaper could help them all. Few newspapers in America now operate in direct daily competition with others, and anything that reeducated the public into newspaper reading, any new de-

8

vice that simplified or cheapened production, any fresh statistic that brought advertisers to one newspaper, would be of assistance to all.

The first offset presses were bought in the 1960s. Today, 1,250 out of 1,764 dailies are printed offset. Fewer than 90 papers continue to use hot metal. The first front-end system (a newsroom where reporters key their material through video display terminals into computers that set the type) was established in 1973. Today roughly half of the U.S. press has at least some of its copy being set by computer. At the level of management and circulation, the computer is more of a novelty, but several newspapers already have their entire list of subscribers' names and addresses on line.

Hundreds of newspapers have organized special zoned editions of local information so that each separate pocket of readers has more material, editorial as well as advertising, targeted at it. Audiences, of course, can be targeted through internal reorganization and reconstruction of the product; but the computer can help refine this task downward to smaller and smaller groups, as revenue permits, guaranteeing that articles find their way only into selected copies of the paper. The computer is assisting the tailoring of the paper to very small groups of readers. What is now visible to anyone who observes this industry today are the segments of a comprehensive reconstruction of the newspaper as a form, each layer of change being associated with a new stratum of technology directed at a different layer of problems. The technical and managerial overhaul of this industry needs to be set inside the framework of where the newspaper found itself at the end of the first era of television competition in American society.

A New Form of Competition

When Frank Munsey, owner of the *New York Sun*, looked around the city in 1920 for papers with which to merge his war-weakened journal, there were fourteen from which to pick. He acquired three of them and constructed his *Herald Tribune*, which survived until 1958. In 1963 there were still twelve newspapers in New York; today there are three. But the city is still the wealthiest in America in its number of titles. Only 185 towns and cities in America, out of more than 1,544 in which newspapers are published, have more than one paper; of these only 40 have papers with competing owners.

To some this statistic is synonymous with the partial death of the newspaper as a form. Yet the total number of papers in the United States has not dropped significantly for a generation. The *Ayer Directory of Publications* lists 2,154 titles in the year 1900, a peak of 2,461 in 1916, 2,015 on the outbreak of World War II, and a low of 1,792 in 1972, since when there has been a steady but slow expansion. *Editor and Publisher* presents slightly different figures, following the same pattern but ending up with 1,764 at the end of 1977.

9

What has taken place is a reorganization of newspaper markets. The new geographical areas contain a pattern of publication quite different from the street-by-street competition of the late nineteenth and early twentieth centuries. Zonal monopoly has become the natural condition of the newspaper. Where competition does exist, there tends to be (as in Chicago and New York) a fairly clear separation between the papers, based on class or economic differences. Market differentiation does not take place nearly as completely or dramatically as in the United Kingdom or in so politically clear-cut a fashion as on the European continent, however.

The localization that has been the basic characteristic of the American press determines the voice and the power of a given paper. The *Sacramento Bee* speaks to and for the politically minded population of California's capital city, while the *San Francisco Chronicle* and *Examiner* represent the broader, more cosmopolitan interests of a much larger community. Even the international papers of America, the *New York Times* and the *Washington Post,* are primarily local media of very powerful cities in whose suburbs competing newspapers circulate.

No major American newspaper finds itself competing cheek by jowl with another comparable paper, although as a paper's circulation fans out more thinly toward the peripheries it usually finds other medium-sized and small but successful papers standing in its path. One should, therefore, look at the American newspaper map as a many-layered table. Half of the total daily circulation of 61.7 million copies belongs to 125 newspapers, most of them based in cities with populations above a quarter of a million.

In San Francisco, the morning *Chronicle* and its evening half-sister the *Examiner,* which are under different ownership but cooperate in production, the collection of advertising, and distribution, dominate the city center and are available throughout northern California. These two represent the first layer of daily publications. Next, each of the region's satellite cities (such as Oakland and San Jose) has its own newspaper that circulates thickly at the center and more thinly in the surrounding area, though never intersecting with the circulation area of another comparable paper. All of these satellite papers exist within the orbit of the San Francisco papers and act as major obstacles to their growth.

Next is a string of more than a dozen suburban papers, including several that cater to the Berkeley and Stanford academic communities. The suburban papers do not have overlapping circulation areas either, but cover all areas that are not the epicenter of papers on the first and second layers. Fourth, there is an enormous—indeed uncountable—group of weekly and thrice-weekly papers, many of them distributed without cover prices or delivered free. Some of these, such as the Harte-Hanks–owned *Progress,* reach into the San Francisco central area and contain a great deal of local news, some of it of an investigative kind.

Others in this category are mere "shoppers" or throwaway material, with very little aspiration toward journalism.

The fourth-layer papers are often at their most influential in the central zones of the first- and second-layer papers, since they can deal more wholeheartedly with local affairs while the bigger papers have to emphasize state, national, and international news. This structure is repeated in virtually every major newspaper market of America; it is an organic structure in that changes in one sector will lead to changes in another. Nothing is fixed or static about it; it is merely where the newspaper system has arrived in its evolution away from the era of internal city competition.

The sense of crisis that has developed around the newspaper's current market system arises from the tremendous shift in population settlement in the 1950s and 1960s. The fifty main metropolitan centers of the United States now contain half of the total population. From 1970 to 1974, the population of the U.S.A. grew more slowly than at any time this century except during the 1930s and World War II. The growth rate was a mere 4.8 percent. In the formation of households, however, the country grew very rapidly in that same period; the rate was 11 percent, almost the highest for any other five-year period this century. The average American household has now shrunk from 4.76 persons in 1900 to 2.95 in 1975 and is still falling.

Publishers have been troubled by the fact that the number of copies sold per household has dropped below one. In 1960 the figure was 1.12 newspapers per household; in 1974 it was 0.88. Multiple newspaper readership has statistically disappeared as demands upon leisure time have increased and populations have shifted from the city centers and other places where there is easy access to a diversity of titles. Total circulation kept pace with the increase in the proportion of 21-year-olds within the U.S. population, but a small decline in the mid-1970s has begun to erode optimism based upon that index also. Throughout the country, newspapers published in urban centers have felt a certain stress, amounting in some cases to panic. Both afternoon and evening papers have lost circulation. Morning papers have had something of a revival, but even that has not affected the diminishing number of purchases per household.

In the largest fifty metropolitan areas, the population has grown by 20 percent since the beginning of the 1960s, but morning newspaper circulation has dropped by nearly 1 percent. Afternoon circulations have lost 10 percent of their sales in the same period. Suburban papers have increased accordingly. Most seriously of all, it has been discovered that when a newspaper in a major metropolitan area has ceased publication, as thirty-two have since 1960, the bulk of the readers either lose the habit of purchasing newspapers daily or, if they were multiple-newspaper readers, keep the benefits of the saving in weekly household costs.

11

The Decline of the City

For a hundred years the newspaper has belonged to the American city, providing its imagery, attracting residents and employers to it, and filled with its gossip. The stories the paper told were drawn from the streets in which its readers lived; the decision-making elite of the city heard the same newsboys' cries as did the masses of the immigrant population. City life defined the nature of the "event," the raw material of newspaper journalism. The newspaper presented in its pages images of success and failure, the nirvana of society prestige juxtaposed with accounts of the abyss of crime into which the city dweller could fall. Max Weber wrote that the newspaper was the intellectual instrument of the modern city.

The American city in the present century has grown into an interlinked network of town and suburb. Long trunk routes for fast automobiles have been cut through the rectangles of streets, breaking up neighborhoods, dividing some communities and linking others into a total megalopolitan construct that contains within it all that the inhabitants seem to require for work, leisure, business, education, and culture. The suburb of the interwar years has been knitted inextricably into this whole complex, although important class and race differences separate the old downtown from the newer residential zones.

"Inner city" has become one of the modern euphemisms for the black population. Nearly 30 percent of the population of the inner cities of the fifty largest metropolitan areas in America is black, compared with only 5 percent in the suburbs of the same cities. The old city centers have become alien, frightening places, avoided at night by the white population. More often than not, the downtown area is entered and left by car rather than by bus or subway. New shopping centers have opened up at the edges of megalopolis, with rows of chain motels and eating places, all reached directly by automobile. Much of the old central city is derelict; large parking spaces, empty at night, take the place of former movie houses or shops.

The old social and business elites have moved out of many of the major cities, taking their social life and talk of city politics with them. They feel little loyalty toward these concentrations of crime-ridden rooming houses, as they travel in and out every day to go to work. They pay taxes on their suburban dwellings and think of themselves as citizens of those other townships in which they vote and educate their offspring. To this elite the city seems to consist of a series of problems of race, housing, crime, and poverty. The metropolitan areas are irreversibly bifurcated socially, intellectually, fiscally, racially, and culturally.

When most of the voters and the leaders lived in the city, newspapers had a clear set of duties, each presenting its own moral perspective in contradistinction to that of competing papers. As the population grew so did retail outlets, all of which needed newspaper space to announce their wares. The papers outside New York, Washington, Philadelphia,

12

Chicago, and Boston were the familiar parochial bulletin boards of their respective communities, each of them representing a set of interests within a given city and utterly committed to it.

The whole concentration of the paper's editor was on the internal affairs of the city in which he distributed his paper and where it was read in homes and factories and streetcars. A downtown store could advertise its wares knowing that people would travel into the center to do their shopping. The city's major stores and manufacturers could use the newspaper to reach out to the suburbs, a valuable and growing market. But the small neighborhood shopkeeper who advertised in the same paper had no way of exploiting the extra coverage.

By the late 1970s the vast majority of all retail sales in the United States were captured by the large chains that made such great headway after the end of World War II. Every year now, for a generation, they have replaced tens of thousands of one-branch retail establishments. The growth of the chain store has been an integral part of suburban development. The new chains are highly professional in management and in their attitudes to retailing and advertising. Where the seller of newspaper space had been occupied mostly with the thousands of small retailers who needed to advertise, today the retail chains can command the kind of space they require, and the connections on both sides between press and advertiser are far less personal, more functional, and more career oriented. When chain stores choose locations for new outlets, they examine the kinds of advertising media in the communities concerned. Even the companies with large stores in the city centers find it more and more important to have large establishments in every major suburb well represented in the appropriate print and electronic media.

Free newspapers known as "shoppers" have offered instant, total household coverage in given areas coterminous with those served by a given group of stores; editorial material is fitted into the space left by the advertisements. Other forms of advertising have grown up around the new retailing revolution; printed leaflets are sent through the mail, and preprints are inserted into the Sunday editions of large newspapers.

The U.S. postal authorities introduced the zip code in the 1960s, facilitating the distribution of advertising material through the mail. Local television stations have provided an ideal medium for retail advertising, each signal covering a suitable marketing area and putting out programs that appeal to that audience. In contrast, the newspaper has to cover the news in its outer areas in a haphazard town-by-town way, never certain that its material dovetails with the interests of its readers and the material of its advertisements.

The television signal, efficient though it is for an advertiser trying to reach a circle of readers defined purely in geographical terms, tends to blot out distinctions between small communities. Nielsen's neat definition of the designated market area (DMA) simplified the tasks of media

13

planners by dividing the whole of the United States into contiguous regions, without population overlaps, but in so doing overrode the historical subtleties of the American newspaper map, with its countless overlapping areas of coverage. Increasingly, media planners base their decisions upon a Nielsen perspective of America, drawing sales territories to follow the lines of the DMAs; often they also use a parallel system, designed by the American Research Bureau, of areas of dominant influence (ADIs).

Both advertising and selling thus acquired, within their own professionalism, a built-in bias against newspapers. Television always looks like a better buy for advertisers if the newspaper's influence on readers is measured with the geographical and statistical tools of television time salespeople. What is more, advertisers tend to treat newspapers as if they were television stations and place advertisements only in the paper that dominates the DMA or ADI concerned irrespective of the differentiation of groups of readers in the print media of the area concerned.

A new generation of advertising persons has created a newer and cruder human geography with which to work, one that ignores the traditional civil loyalties and other sectional demarcations out of which the newspaper slowly evolved. The retail revolution and the attendant change in advertising and sales management were silent collaborators in the death of the American city and in the creation of megalopolis.

Other aspects of this same change in demographic organization (and in the perception of the change) further undermined the established newspaper industry. Among daily papers, an important differentiation took place between mornings and evenings. After 1960 morning papers became progressively stronger, if less numerous, than the afternoon and evening papers.

The change in population covered was much larger than the mere change in the total number of titles. The decline in the use of streetcars, buses, subways, and trains and the popularity of automobiles meant that there were fewer street sales of afternoon papers. Home delivery became ever more important for afternoon papers yet much harder to achieve. Among blue-collar workers, television was becoming the main source of afternoon news. The effective management of an afternoon paper necessitated delivery to the home well before the beginning of peak-hour television, something that the newspaper, on the whole, was not geared to achieve, either in its production or circulation departments. Research indicates that the period between 4 and 4:30 P.M. is the peak time for newspaper reading, but to deliver afternoon papers at this time entailed a drastic overhaul of editorial and production deadlines, as well as changes in local agents and distributors.

Newspapers could try to run after their commuting readers into the suburbs, but the delivery trucks were stuck in the same traffic jams as were their readers, who would arrive home fully informed from their car radios about the main news developments of the afternoon and in

14

time to watch up-to-the-hour pictures on the local television news. The newspaper was already many hours old before the reader picked it up.

The crisis of the central area of U.S. cities was thus at the core of a crisis in the newspaper industry, although for many years the newspapers ignored these changes editorially or managerially (or both). "We watched Chicago rot away right up to our loading bays, before we actually realized what the death of the central city meant to us," is how one of the two remaining Chicago newspaper publishers puts it. The newspaper found that it had to redefine its relationship with its city market and to undergo the major expense and reorganization entailed in that exercise. Meanwhile many continue to lament the death of the old journalistic traditions of the city press and feel that it leads to a kind of betrayal of citizenship.

Leo Bogart, an advertising researcher and a principal intellectual of the medium who has played a major role in restoring much of the newspaper's faith in its economic future, still believes in the possibility of reforging the links between editorial content and the residents of the central core of the cities. "Only when the city is synonymous with the market can there be an identity between citizenship and the sense of belonging in a place, and thus between the audience and the medium."

For the majority of publishers, the medium in the 1970s became considerably more profitable than it ever had been in the past but considerably more risky. The vast majority of publishers found themselves with local monopolies, often tied to radio and television outlets (although no newspaper in the future is permitted to acquire major electronic franchises in the same geographical area, under new rules promulgated by the Federal Communications Commission and backed by the courts). These monopolies became increasingly profitable, stacked though they are with hazards. Newsprint costs doubled to more than $300 per ton in the early years of the decade, and though the newsprint industry accepted the lighter-weight newsprint manufacturers had developed as a partial solution to their own problems and thus reduced the total weight that newspapers needed to bundle and truck every day, still the truck drivers had to go farther each year, using larger quantities of valuable energy ("If the U.S. government removed our exemption from newsprint tariffs, the sheer cost of the stuff would drive scores of papers over the edge" is a typical publishers' cry). Many papers continued to try to rely upon young teenagers to carry the much heavier papers to the front porches ("If the U.S. government ceased to provide the newspaper industry with exemption from the Child Labor Act, half of us would be finished"). The sheer growth in the number of pages delivered began to attract the attention of conservationists ("If the U.S. government succumbed to the pressure for a really strong antilitter act, we could be made responsible for collecting tens of millions of tons of used newsprint"). But most newspapers have exploited the rapidly growing total volume of additional advertising to reach new readers. They have learned to envelop their readers, changed though

15

their life-styles are, with a whole range of special material. Many papers now produce supplements on food, recreation, hobbies, sports, and business affairs, each with complementary advertising. Many are putting out zoned supplements of local news, financed with full-page advertisements from local stores eager to attract relatively tiny pockets of households. There has been a tremendous growth in the delivery of preprinted advertisement sheets inside the newspaper proper (15 percent of the total retail advertising of the *Washington Post* now consists of preprints).

The *Chicago Tribune* has started a string of seven (soon to be nine) suburban supplements, which are really free local papers inserted into the main journal. The paper has thus thrown a noose around the city, basing its future on its ability to reach its readers with material relating to their new suburban lives. Inside the city, the *Sun-Times*, having ceased publishing its companion afternoon paper, the century-old *Daily News*, is preparing to break out of the noose with a brighter, more popular paper. Its readership has been substantially increased by survivors from the now-defunct *Daily News,* which still bases itself on the inner city but also provides material for long-distance commuters.

At this stage of history, newspaper competition within a single market can be enormously expensive. In Chicago, the costs of the fight between the *Sun-Times* and the *Tribune* to reconstruct stable markets suggests that it must be a fight to the death. Both papers must offer advertising space at lower prices than either of them would if it had a monopoly, and both must expand their total pages and thereby raise their delivery costs much more than they would do merely to satisfy a captive Chicago readership.

To the outside critic, the average U.S. metropolitan newspaper publisher appears to be sitting on an easy monopolistic gold mine. All he has to do is get the paper to his readers and pocket the advertising revenue. To the publisher the picture looks rather different: He has a gold mine, yes, but a gold mine that is constantly in danger of flooding. He has to thicken his paper considerably in order to embrace the full range of tastes and life-styles of his widespread audience. He has to bundle and truck his papers to reach the farthest suburbs, which in the case of the *Los Angeles Times* are 400 miles away.

Typically the newspaper has to distribute over a distance of up to one hundred miles from the central printing plant. The cover price must not rise or readers will turn to cheaper and more local papers. (Most U.S. newspapers are sold on subscription, and the aggregate sum paid monthly or weekly simply cannot be allowed to rise dramatically. When the paper reaches the suburbs, it has to meet the competition of the small city papers, with their more concentrated, easier-to-reach markets. Inside the central area it must cope with the fact that street sales must be from vending machines, which are easy to rifle, and that a large section of residents may be unable to read English or may belong to a racial group that feels alien to the society to which the newspaper is addressed.

16

The great metropolitan dailies today are spread very thinly across their target areas. The immensely rich *Los Angeles Times* reaches only 10 percent of its total potential market, not very much for a paper that is competing, formally, only with the Hearst-owned *Herald-Examiner,* which has a tiny circulation. The *New York Times,* too, reaches only 10 percent of the households in its enormous region, which contains about 18 million people, depending on where you choose to draw New York's boundaries. The *Louisville Courier-Journal* provides a fine example of the sort of calculation that has to be made. It has traditional pockets of readers up to 150 miles from the city and, as it contemplates the half-million dollars a year spent on local distribution, it often thinks of ignoring some of these groups of readers and cutting its losses. To do so, however, would automatically make it very worthwhile for several local weeklies to turn into dailies and establish a comfortable base for a gradual encroachment on a larger segment of the *Courier-Journal* market.

It seems prudent for the newspaper to keep these groups of readers— some of whom have taken the paper for 70 years—in the fold. But the paper is rather larger than it was 70 years ago. Since 1950, in fact, the average American newspaper has increased from 34 to 60 pages, and despite the drop in the average weight of newsprint the total bulk of paper in some places is now too heavy for children to be used for home delivery. Moreover, the average reader looks at only one-tenth of the total material that finally reaches him. And yet, to instance the *Courier-Journal* again, only one-tenth of the editorial material available in its computer on any one day actually gets printed at all.

The newspaper wastes most of the material it collects, then wastes most of the material that it prints and delivers. It is not surprising that the more forward-looking publishers are beginning to wonder whether there lies, in the very long run, a technological barrier that, when broken, might give the daily newspaper a wholly new form and a new content. But the problems of the present crowd upon him. One must look at the technologies now being put in use before envisaging those that might take the newspaper into a wholly new phase of its history.

Newspaper Technologies

It is convenient to look at the contrast between the traditional and the new technologies in diagrammatic form. Figure 1.1 divides the main operations into compartments that in most plants tend to correspond to craft groupings. Several of these activities are eliminated in the transition from old to new. The composing room of the newspaper, which is the most thoroughly transformed division of all and is extremely labor intensive in the old system, is almost eliminated by the new technology.

In the old system the copy emerges from reporters (who use traditional typewriters) and advertisement takers and passes to an editor

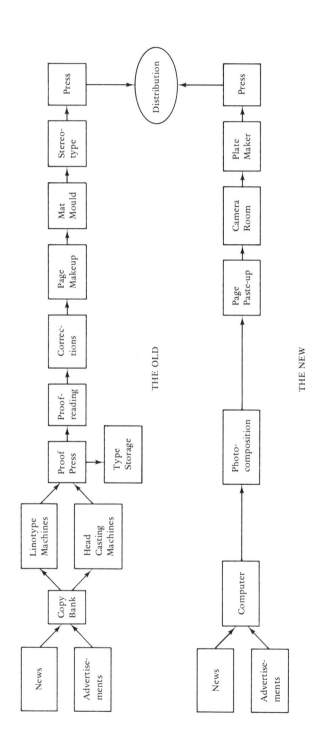

THE OLD

THE NEW

Figure 1.1

or manager, who attaches a heading. The copy then goes (often through a pneumatic tube) to the copy-cutting desk, the first stage of the composing room. Here it is sliced into sections, which are handed out to different typesetters whose work afterward has to be reassembled in the correct order. The text and the headlines go to different operators, each specialized in the kind of type (the metal letters and signs) and the size and style required.

The linotype machines, which set the text in type, have keyboards like typewriters which assemble rows of matrices or metal molds. The operator creates his text in lines of type, adding hyphens and spacers where necessary to justify the lines. He then strikes a key that causes molten lead to be poured into the lines of the matrices, which are then automatically lifted and deposited in a metal case (the whole process is characterized as hot-metal typesetting). The original matrices are later redistributed and used again. The headlines are set by a similar process, although the very large type sizes are done by hand.

An average typesetter can set about five lines of type per minute, with an error appearing roughly every two minutes. Soon after World War II typesetting was greatly speeded up by the introduction of paper tape. The operator uses a keyboard to punch holes in a paper tape, which is then used to drive the linotype machine; hyphenation and justification are performed automatically. By using tape a linotype operator can produce ten to fifteen lines per minute, reducing the labor involved in the whole process by some 40 percent.

When the story is set in lead it goes to a proof press, where a pressing is made for the proofreaders; the type, meanwhile, goes into a type-storage area. The proofreaders look for errors, mark them, and send the marked proof back to the line-casting area for changes. Simultaneously the original writer and/or subeditor—indeed a variety of people who are involved in the editorial process—may read the proof and make editorial corrections. Lines with errors or corrections are removed and replaced. This entire process may have to be repeated several times.

The corrected type is next sent to page makeup, where it is cut into pieces and locked into metal page forms. Makeup is a very skilled and time-consuming activity. It is at this stage that the zinc engravings of photographs and display advertisements are fitted into the page and final corrections inserted. The page form is a mirror image of the actual printed page.

The next step is the mat-making process where, by application of enormous pressure, a mold of the page is made in a kind of papier-mâché. The mold is curved to fit the rollers of the printing press and then dried and trimmed.

The mat goes into the stereotype machine, which forces molten lead under pressure into the mold and makes a heavy cylindrical lead plate (where more than one press is used, duplicates must be made). The making of plates by this method involves much heavy labor but uses very cheap materials, all the lead being recyclable.

19

In traditional printing the cylindrical plates are fitted onto the rollers of a letterpress machine, which feeds a continuous roll of paper across the raised letters of the plate at high speed and produces a continuous sheet of printed pages. Modern letterpress machines can print up to seventy thousand copies per hour. The process of cutting and folding, stacking and bundling, completes the cycle of work.

Three general observations about this traditional process must be made at this stage of the description. First, the production processes consume enormous quantities of labor, even in the smallest newspapers, and are cumbersome, dirty, and unhealthy. Second, the rigid division of the work into a series of specialist crafts has led to the growth of powerful labor organizations, often disunited but capable of disruption through local disputes. Third, the basic material—the editorial copy— has to be laid out again and again at the different parts of the process. The reporter or advertising salesman, the typesetter, proof operator, editor, and all the others are essentially going through the same material, copying the text or type again and again on different kinds of keyboards.

The defining object that causes the newspaper to be this miscellaneous form is the stereotype plate; it is the plate that fuses all of the different elements of the newspaper's content onto a single variegated page. The new technology has thus concentrated on improving the processes for making plates and on improving the plate itself. But the methods by which it does this could be preliminary to the abolition of the plate altogether as a means of producing newspapers. It is at this point that the newspaper could begin to change its form and cease gradually to be necessarily as miscellaneous as it has been. Indeed these problems of the American newspaper industry that are reaching out for computer-based technologies for their solution may, through these very solutions, lead the newspaper toward a wholly new definition of itself.

One must remind oneself of the ways in which printing first arose in Western culture. It was developed to solve the production problems of the manuscript copiers and scribes. Then the new technology introduced the era of the printed book and led the business of copying toward a kind of self-negation. Completely new kinds of written culture emerged as necessary corollaries of the new equipment.

The essence of the new newspaper technology is cold type and the elimination of the processes of hot lead. The new print images are generated photographically. The computer emerges as the most obvious means of achieving faster speeds.

Figure 1.1 shows that the basic copy, news and advertisements, flows from reporters and advertising people to a computer by means of video display terminals (VDTs). These units, basic to the entire process, have keyboards similar to the traditional typewriter, but there the resemblance ends.

Reporters using a VDT see their copy emerge on a screen instead of on paper, and can correct their own material before pushing the button that passes the whole packet or file into computer storage. In some systems reporters type out their copy on an ordinary electric typewriter, and the paper is then scanned by an optical character reader (OCR), which codes the copy for the computer. This process requires that the journalist or a secretary produce a perfect version of the copy on paper and so has not proved popular in most newsrooms, except as an interim stage of familiarizing the plant with computer typesetting. It is kept in most modern newsrooms, however, for special functions (such as taking in syndicated material). Its great advantage is that the editors and managers can summon from the computer any text that pertains to their particular department and edit it on a screen.

All VDT users must register with the computer before it will offer them a window on the text it holds, and each layer of the hierarchy in a newsroom has access only to those parts of the text that it is entitled to see. The electronic newsroom is a great stickler for rank and a meticulous observer of security.

The computer can be fed with material from outside the newsroom without any human intervention. The wire services, for example, can feed their material straight to the computers of all their clients, who may then select and edit the texts with great ease and with no further copying or keyboarding. The proofreading processes cease to constitute a specialized craft, since corrections are made as the material itself develops in the computer. The computer automatically hyphenates and justifies according to the practices of the newspaper concerned; it can also be programed to choose an appropriate typeface.

The computer sends out a continuous stream of type. The simplest versions achieve twenty-five lines per minute. The very fastest machines can now turn out two-thirds of a mile of a column of type in one hour. The type that the computer produces is laid out and pasted up on boards; unlike hot metal, which is made up in a mirror image, cold type is laid out to look exactly as it will on the printed page. The makeup person arranges the columns, adds the advertisements, and photographs the completed page. The negative is used to expose a photosensitive printing plate, a thin sheet of metal, which replaces the heavy lead stereotypes.

Offset printing is based upon the fact that ink (which contains oil) and water are mutually repellent. Those areas of the photosensitive layer that contain type and have been exposed attract the ink, while areas that do not contain type repel the ink and attract water. In traditional letterpress printing the raised type is smeared with ink and held under enormous pressure against a sheet of paper, and an impression is made. The new offset process uses a flat rather than raised plate and requires much less pressure. It is called offset because the litho plate and the paper never actually touch. Instead a blanket roller takes an impression from the plate and then presses it onto the paper. It is possible to print directly from a photosensitized plate, however, and traditional letterpress machines can be adapted to take such di-litho plates, saving the enormous expense of purchasing completely new presses. Both offset and di-lithography have the disadvantage that, each time the press is started, the ink-and-water system takes some time to adjust itself and many copies are wasted. Newspaper managements have to balance the odds: a certain amount of built-in wastage against savings in labor and some materials. The new plates are not recyclable and cost more to produce than do lead stereotypes, but they consume less labor time. In the past the small-circulation paper has reaped the most rapid advantages from the offset method of printing. A paper that produces a million copies of each edition will require many hundreds of plates per day, even thousands for the Sunday editions. This new expense, added to the cost of the unavoidable wastage and the cost of compensation that must be paid to redundant manpower, deterred the larger newspapers from using the new technology until very recently. But now the manufacturers are promising models that will be cheaper and less wasteful, and the trade unions have either fought or made agreements over the phasing out and retraining of displaced labor.

In a number of newspapers, a new type of raised-surface plate is being used: a floppy but hard-wearing photopolymer product created from the photocomposed page but mounted in place of the old lead stereotype. The polymer plate gives a new lease of life to the old presses, which have always had the advantage (or disadvantage) of extremely long life (up to fifty years, in most cases). These plates can be made from a photographic system of typesetting and can be recycled. The modern newspaper is very conscious of the need to save scarce energy when introducing new equipment and, sometimes, to avoid using products that are neither biodegradable nor recyclable.

The *Los Angeles Times* has developed a wholly different method for cheapening and yet modernizing its platemaking system. It uses the enormous number of twenty-five thousand plates every week. But the high cost of the materials in most modern plates deterred the management for several years from introducing any new techniques. Its own experts then devised a system of injection molding, which made printing plates in plastic. A full-page engraving is made of every page; a mold is taken and used to make a plastic plate. The plastic plates cost about thirty-three cents each, compared to two or three dollars for most modern relief printing plates. The system has other advantages. The capital cost of the basic equipment to make the plates was surprisingly cheap (about $125,000 at 1972 prices), and the whole system takes less than a half-minute to make a plate, compared with several minutes for offset and di-litho systems. The *Times* has thus avoided the longer deadline times between page makeup and platemaking that have bedeviled most other newspapers that have crossed from the old to the new technology.

However, no satisfactory method has been devised for composing an

22

entire page on a screen (as of this writing). In a sense, the whole development of the newspaper technology is now slowing down, awaiting this next step of full pagination. Until then, the process of cutting and pasting every single page will remain slow and labor-intensive. Compared with the automation now practical in other stages of production, manual paste-up feels irritatingly old-fashioned. Full pagination is spoken of by the aficionados of the new technology as a kind of promised land, an ultimate destination in the evolution of the automated newspaper.

Many papers have improved their typesetting to the point at which the paste-up stage is really becoming a paste-in stage; almost everything except the transfer of photographs to the page is done electronically. But to find a cheap, easily adaptable, and marketable full pagination system may still take a year or two.

By a strange paradox, when managements reach the point of being able to set pages (and therefore make plates) directly by computer, without the intervention of manual operations, the way is open to printing without plates at all. Ink-jet and other forms of nonplate printing are being developed quickly, and the way is open, via full pagination, to the making of a newspaper that is actually printed directly by a computer (or, at least, to stereotypes that are made directly by the computer).

It is at this stage that the newspaper can begin to think about tailoring itself to the requirements of individual readers. The computer already has access to most of the wanted facts about readers and their needs. It is conceptually possible for the computer that prints the paper to also separate readers into groups or even to pinpoint individuals.

Computer-based plateless printing implies a gradual evolution away from the historic generalized, miscellaneous form of the newspaper. This process has already begun, as we have seen, under the old technology. The newspaper has been zoned and split into physically separate sections, and preprinted materials are inserted into the finished package. Here, again, we see the configurations of a future technology being built into the struggles of the traditional system to cure its problems with traditional tools.

All transformation of the newspaper industry must begin with pioneers and individual prototypes. Every individual newspaper is singular. There are very few common modular elements. The diversity means that change is never sweeping but slow and painstaking. Every innovation is seen to have a clear set of drawbacks, or comcomitant changes in style or content, which are deemed unacceptable.

The three-days-a-week boulevard paper of the late eighteenth century built up a complex set of relationships among the rural postal services, the country printers who copied its material for smaller papers, the flow of high society news, and the systems by which advertisers chose to organize their own markets. With the arrival of improved postal services, bigger newspaper markets, and slightly faster presses, younger editors were anxious to explore the six-day-a-week publication, and they had the capital with which to start. The old managements preferred to watch their markets dissolve before their eyes rather than undergo the disruption of their traditional operations.

The introduction of the teletypesetter in the 1920s meant that the same story could arrive simultaneously in newspapers all over the country. It was an important technical advance, but one that seemed at first to threaten the individuality and uniqueness of the city newspaper. The arrival of the computer as a tool of both the newsroom and the composing room at the same time was immediately seen as a similarly radical transformer of habits.

The newspaper has always been late to enter new technological eras; it is linked to society in so many ways that change always appears as a trap. The frequency of publication, the types of information collected, the arrangements of the page, the size and number of pages, the layers of personnel taken on, the system by which the product is delivered to the reader—all these have depended upon simple technologies that are interdependent and highly durable. They have become so familiar as to appear almost natural.

The newspaper is more than ordinarily conservative. Its complex linkages to society force it to change its structure and system only when it is absolutely obliged to do so, and then it tends to do it in something of a rush. It is continually being posed with the problem of simple survival. The offset press was introduced in the late 1930s, but only thirty years later did it become the accepted new system of printing. Even today less than 40 percent of all newspaper copies (but the majority of titles) in the United States are printed by offset.

It was the same with phototypesetting. The American Newspapers Publishers Association (ANPA) demonstrated the first machine back in 1950, and four years later the *Quincy Patriot-Ledger* in Massachusetts installed some photocomposition equipment at its small plant. By 1960 only a score or so of plants used these nonmanual forms of typesetting. The extremely fast rise in typesetting costs (caused by the upswing in newspaper advertising in the 1960s) had a great deal to do with the search for nonmanual systems.

Two things had to happen before the newspaper industry accepted the inevitability of this latest and most major round of changes. The first was the determined approach of the computer industry in search of new fields to conquer. The second, and perhaps more important, was the creation within the newspaper industry of a publisher-led organization, sponsored by government and private enterprise, that was dedicated to studying how to exploit the valuable spinoffs of the new technology developed in the American public sector. That organization was the Research Institute of the ANPA, which was set up in 1958 from the earlier Mechanical Committee. The institute had and has its own laboratories for testing equipment, and also makes use of the Electronic Systems Laboratory of the Massachusetts Institute of Technology in the

24

field of computer techniques. The MIT research was particularly responsible for the adoption by the main wire services of computerized data-processing methods, which is steadily transforming the intake of news.

The ANPA Research Institute is more than a neutral assignee of research problems. It is a dedicated and deliberate propagandizer, energetically persuading its members to experiment with the new methods. It provides them with software packages of many kinds, ranging from the automatic detection of spelling errors to automatic sub-editing systems. It has developed a slot machine that will sell one newspaper at a time instead of making the whole stack available to pilferers. It provides consulting facilities and trains personnel for its member newspapers.

Behind the consultative strike force of the ANPA Research Institute lies a more powerful force. In the 1960s, radio and television showed themselves able to supply audiences to advertisers at a lower unit cost than did newspapers. It was therefore a matter of survival for the newspaper to reduce its production costs while turning out a product that could compete in sheer attractiveness with the two rival media. A great problem since the early 1970s has been the price of newsprint. It is perhaps the greatest cause of internal crisis, and is on the whole out of anyone's control. What is more, the improvements being made in this area would be accepted and adopted without much individual choice. The ANPA Research Institute has mounted research projects in conjunction with the U.S. Department of Agriculture to find new sources of newsprint pulp that are cheaper and politically less sensitive than the forests of Quebec, but no one expects great cost reduction in the short term.

The fastest way to save labor costs and the fastest route to the improved appearance of the newspaper happened to coincide in the composing room. It is here that the revolution has been taking place. In the late 1960s it was calculated that the publishers (mainly wire services) that had adopted computers for the simple tasks of hypenation and justification were already cutting labor time by 40 percent. The figures encouraged a number of new companies to challenge IBM, Mergenthaler, and the other giants for this new and expanding market. They began by supplying peripheral equipment, but gradually they began to broaden their attention to all areas of the newspaper enterprise. Machines were supplied to the front end of the newspaper (as computer languages described the newsroom and advertising sections) to link their activities directly to the composing room. Seven thousand such video display terminals were installed between 1971 and 1976, a fraction of the total to be employed by the end of the decade.

The reintegration, after many years, of the functions of content (journalism) and presentation (typesetting) mirrored similar changes in many other businesses. Both newspapers and other similarly complicated business organizations chose the same system based on the new concept of time-sharing. Without time-sharing, many of the advantages of putting computers in the composing room were negated by the need to rekey all of the text. This problem was solved when VDTs were put directly in front of reporters. It was a technical and bureaucratic breakthrough.

In the newspaper the process of technical development was hastened by the multifaceted nature of computers and related equipment, but it was not always so. In the early days, IBM had been asked by one or two papers to devise a vast unified system. One huge computer, it was hoped, would perform every task from copy-taking to wire services, typesetting, the control of laser platemaking, business management, and circulation. But no such system was ever completed (some newspapers to this day blame their late involvement in computers on the fact that they waited for this development, which never took place). Instead minisystems became as valuable as macrosystems.

The new electronic circuitry was incorporated into the design of photocomposers and presses and machinery for bundling and tying; the reporter's VDT had built into it microcomputers that helped him handle his relatively small amount of information before it was offered to a central store. The many functions of the newspaper were remodeled for the computer and the computer for them, so that dozens of functions could be carried out in real time without reference to the central processor.

Today human action intervenes at many stages to pass from one computer to the next a completed piece of work that is geared to the taste of the individual. Design has become more sensitive and much more flexible. Experience has shown that every computer spends a certain amount of time in breakdown, however well designed the system. It is possible today for all of the component activities of a complex newspaper plant to continue during periods of maintenance.

The bureaucratic changes have been no less significant. Scores of newspapers in the United States (and many in Europe and Japan) have undergone a democratic design process in which representatives of many departments have worked with the equipment suppliers for months until acceptable terminals have been created. In the process of creating a new system, the computer has often served to suggest methods of internal reorganization and the reassessment of hierarchy.

The classified advertising section provides a good example. The work involves transcribing the text, checking the client's credit, billing, placing the advertisement in the correct classification, and ordering repeats. With a computer, all functions can be done simultaneously. Once the information has passed from the "intelligent" terminal into the general data base, the various departments within the classified section are simultaneously serviced. A variety of different users of the same material can have access to it, for their different reasons, and within the scope of each person's different authority. At the same time, the newspaper can plan the overall work load of the computer and establish priorities according to its own deadlines.

The newspaper is developing into a congeries of processing facilities of growing complexity and intelligence. Essentially a range of smaller systems is linked to an integrated central information-processing system, and the benefits of centralization and decentralization are reaped at the same time. Most newspapers acquire their technology in a modular fashion, first introducing photocomposition, then VDTs for editors, then VDTs for reporters and the people handling classified advertisements, and then finally VDTs for display and composition. Many of today's oldest systems are the result of a series of constant modifications and wholly unlike their original design. Very few newspapers have purchased all of their equipment from one supplier, although many total systems are on the market.

The Case of the Los Angeles Times

The case history of the *Los Angeles Times* is a remarkably clear example of the gradual building of a complex system over many years. This paper has a special flexibility stemming from the fact that it has never been unionized. Its workers have long been paid somewhat above the average in exchange for a willingness to cooperate with constant change and development.

In 1962 the *Times* joined with the RCA Corporation to develop a computer program for hyphenating and justifying text. An RCA 301 computer read the text from paper tape and then created a justified text, also on paper tape, which drove a hot-metal line-casting machine. The system, which was used for both editorial and classified material, required a good deal of manual assistance (especially when handling lines of type of different sizes). Three years later it was improved by switching to an IBM 360/30 computer, which received multiple tapes simultaneously. The paper also integrated its business and production computer operations into a single department. By 1968 the typesetting system was expanded to include the disc storage of news stories, and the classified advertising department started using small screens for checking the credit of advertisers.

At the end of the 1960s, the *Times* formed its own Research and Development Committee, which started to prepare a grand design for a new publishing system. The first stage consisted of creating a system that would recall news stories for checking on video terminals; the terminals were large and showed text in both lower case and upper case. The committee also started at this point, rather precociously, to plan a method of handling the photocomposition and even pagination of classified and display advertising and news.

By 1970 a display and layout system had been created (DAL I). It was rather complex, using magnetic tape (instead of the more usual paper

27

tape) to drive the photocomposition equipment. A year later the committee worked on an improved system (DAL II), based on a new command language for laying out each advertisement, which went into operation in 1973. In a separate development, some news pages were photocomposed by a range of new equipment that was driven by paper tape but that then controlled hot-metal line-casters. The next step was the introduction of a larger IBM computer that controlled all of the new systems. Simultaneously the Research and Development Committee started the design of a whole new system, DAL III.

By 1974 hopes of a system for full pagination were abandoned, and the committee concentrated on introducing photocomposition to the whole paper as quickly as possible. An IBM 370/158 was acquired for all of the paper's publishing work. Classified advertisements were completely transferred to photocomposition, and a hybrid system was used for news sections and display advertisements. By the end of the year, the entire paper was being photocomposed, although VDTs capable of performing graphics did not arrive for a further year.

When they did turn up and were added to DAL III, a whole series of new facilities were introduced, involving great flexibility in the newsroom. Environ/1, a comprehensive on-line control system that had been running since 1971, took command of the whole publishing system. New photocomposers (APS-4), which could cope with full-page widths and could perform logo generation together with the text, were added and formed an interface on-line with the publishing computer.

In 1977 the *Times* came closer to its goal of full automation than many had believed possible. All of its pages of classified advertisements are now laid out by computer in all weekday editions and in most of its Sunday pages. New control mechanisms in the photocomposer subsystem can add complex graphics to the text. Stock tables supplied by Associated Press are fed into the news system by high-speed transmission links and then typeset and paginated. Meanwhile a new system is being designed that will enable four hundred terminals to be linked to a news editing system, which will put large numbers of outside correspondents in direct touch with the publishing system.

At the same time as this long evolution has been taking place, the *Times* has been developing its unique injection-molded platemaking unit and, in parallel to the main plant in downtown Los Angeles, opening a new plant in Orange County. The EOCOM corporation has constructed a facsimile platemaking network, using lasers, which consists of two transmitter-receivers at each plant. The film negatives are imaged by the laser and automatically processed. They are next exposed to a plastic master and then set into a plastic matting process. The resulting matrix is used to make plastic printing plates simultaneously at both plants (through a 375-ton Cincinnati injection-molding press). The *Los Angeles Times* has thus created a kind of Siamese twin of itself, which multiplies its potential access to audiences and enables it to

28

compete in certain of the outermost commuter suburbs with the second- and third-layer papers in southern California.

Changing Internal Relationships

The costs of setting up this sort of system vary enormously. Every newspaper has gone through the experience of discovering that similar functions can be achieved by a myriad different means and devices at wildly different costs. And every newspaper goes through the process, during the following years, of justifying the costs it has actually incurred. It is as difficult to cost such a system as it is to cost the tasteful furnishing of a room. Both benefits and prices are very hard to calculate.

After the introduction of computers and cold type, the whole atmosphere of the newspaper is different. Old equipment, not included formally in the scheme, may have to be thrown away before full amortization because the general mood has changed. The process of wage bargaining is thoroughly altered. There are, of course, considerable redundancy and retraining costs (in-house training is in general the cheapest and best method). But new demands arise. Employees have to be set aside for showing the new equipment to parties of schoolchildren and other visitors. The staff may raise complaints about humidity, dirt, and other discomforts which they formerly ignored. The insurance can also be expensive, and minor delays and legal costs tend to be omitted in the estimates.

It is similarly hard to calculate the advantages. Wire-service material no longer has to be expensively reset. Many internal message-sending functions are eliminated. Far more labor time is often saved in proofreading than calculated in advance. Storage space for many commodities is saved. The elimination of printing errors is perhaps the greatest saving; it renders the product as a whole more convenient and satisfying to its readers. This aspect is difficult to calculate in money terms.

The new technologies have been a battleground of the most variegated kind. Some of the most active and contentious protagonists have been the trade unions. In the United States, as in other societies, powerful craft unions grew up in the printing industry in the late nineteenth century. Their traditions harked back to ancient craft-based guilds, many hundreds of years old. The Typographical Union, founded in Cincinnati in 1852, covered the whole spectrum of skills. Then as printing and engraving developed the 1880s on, the union lost many groups of members. The pressmen left in 1886, the engravers went at the turn of the century, and the stereotypers and electrotypers departed a matter of months later. Fourteen unions were involved in American newspaper publishing by the end of World War II. Then the process started to reverse itself, especially after it became clear that new composing machinery was going to reduce severely the number of members of the parent union, the International Typographical Union (ITU). In the early 1980s, if all the present negotiations are successful, the ITU will join forces with the Newspaper Guild, which organizes all reporters as well as other newspaper employees, and may even reunite with the pressmen's union, which has already relinked with other specialist processes. In a totally computerized newspaper there could be a single industrial union, but that lies far ahead, perhaps to be resolved only after many bloody battles.

Within the newspaper industry at present, the position is utterly different in different states, regions, and newspapers. The powerful labor organizations of the East Coast have been severely dented after important disputes with the *Washington Post* and *New York Times*. In many parts of the South, the unions have failed to mount any serious offensive against the new technology. Many newspapers' disputes over the new equipment have led to management's simply employing nonunion labor and continuing operations without ever resolving the original dispute. In some veteran papers, like the *Quincy Patriot-Ledger,* union organization has simply died away.

Today members of the Newspaper Guild cross the picket lines of the ITU in Sacramento, and the reverse occurs in other disputes a thousand miles away. Everywhere the printing worker has to reckon with the fact that the computer-based technology can be operated by entirely unskilled people. He may find that fact difficult to accept in an industry whose whole labor organization has been founded upon the preservation of crafts deliberately wrapped in mysterious private words and jargon phrases and protected by age-old customs, traditions, and even rituals. But the old craft skills are being swept away.

At first, many local branches of the ITU tried to keep the new equipment out of newspaper plants. When that proved entirely ineffective, they gained guarantees of lifetime employment for their members. But some of these guarantees have proved extremely fragile. Many ITU typesetters who believed their papers had promised them a new job after their typesetting functions had disappeared instead discovered that, after they had taken part in a strike on some other issue, their so-called permanent contracts were declared null and void.

American management often gives the appearance, in its private meetings and conventions, of waging a deliberate war against union organization. Many American publishers actually welcome the new technology simply as a weapon to destroy the unions. Very often nonunionized workers are deliberately trained in one plant in order to be moved into another where a dispute threatens (or has even been engineered by management).

The atmosphere was soured early when several attempts to introduce labor-saving composition methods within the compass of the old technology led to disasters (for instance, in the 1950s, some papers tried to float lead type directly in the forms and to print without plates), and the unions were blamed for inefficiency or even sabotage. Management seldom blamed itself for riding roughshod over the traditional, safer methods. From the perspective of the unions, many publishers—sometimes quite famous ones—seem to be determined to override rather than work with the labor organizers.

The unions themselves are staring at one another across a great series of historic battlefields. Their leaders are certain that strength lies only in reunification, but they are unable as yet to find the way or to take their members with them. The ITU has watched its membership shrink from over a hundred thousand after the war to about sixty thousand now and hopes that the figure will settle at fifty thousand. But the arrival of full pagination and the elimination of page paste-up will open the way to a further round of redundancies.

Since 1967 the ITU has been intent on training its own members to use the new equipment and thereby to save many of their jobs. It took the view that typesetters, if properly trained, could learn to use the new keyboards and service a wide range of computer-based equipment and that management would have less excuse for eliminating them. From 1969 on, the ITU started to acquire examples of each stage of the new equipment and to run training courses, both independently and with managements. Equipment manufacturers and the publishers themselves, of course, train large numbers of people, but many do not and many are glad to share the costs with the union. Today the ITU headquarters at Colorado Springs has a virtually complete chronological museum of computer printing, going back for more than a decade, and featuring some extremely modern devices.

Experience varies wildly across the United States, but it is obvious that the present computer-led convulsion in the evolution of the newspaper has been dictated to a great extent by the politics of the labor market. It is perhaps one of the few instances in industrial history when technical transformation has proceeded at a pace so heavily influenced by the sometimes subtle, sometimes violent pattern of management-labor relations.

The patterns of the new technology are being worked out in a jungle of choice. It is becoming evident that the modern newspaper is the testing ground of something wholly new in human communication systems. A major priority has been to render the modern newsroom as serviceable and flexible as the mechanical one that it replaces. Manufacturers are therefore making their terminal equipment ever more "intelligent." Groups of journalists in paper after paper have brought about a progressive upgrading of the services built into their terminals. With the coming of the portable, remote, feed-in, stand-alone unit, the newspaper becomes a network of minicomputers with a wide repertoire of skills.

The Teleram VDT, which resulted from research conducted by ANPA, the *New York Times,* and the Teleram Communications Corporation, is a fine example. It will fit under an airline seat, although it

31

accommodates 616 characters on its small 4 by 3 inch screen; its display memory has 2,048 characters; it records data on a 300-foot cassette, which can hold 1,600 words; and it works on a car battery. Reporters can use a Teleram to collect information for their background research from remote, computerized data banks. They can then transmit completed copy at three hundred words per minute through a telephone wire or at twelve hundred words per minute if they have access to a high-speed model. The Teleram is merely the first of a new series of competing models. Its market exists because it can help to extend news deadlines. It transmits, even in this early version, six times as fast as a facsimile system and six times as fast as a person dictating copy to a secretary. Given a distance of fifty miles from the publishing center, the unit cost of transmitting copy is reduced to one-quarter.

Facsimile systems are also being improved and, for some time to come, will be a powerful competitor to remote VDTs. An advanced piece of facsimile equipment can scan a page every fifty seconds. This output is transmitted and scanned again at the publishing end by an optical character reader. The problem with OCRs in general is that they often reject material that has been folded in the mails, and they restrict the newspaper to a limited range of type fonts.

Another major innovation is the high-speed wire used by the AP and UPI agencies. AP's Datastream and UPI's DataNews transmit material at twelve hundred words per minute straight into the computer of each individual newspaper; security precautions protect the privacy of each client. The material is geographically coded, and local computers can automatically monitor the input and exclude whole sections of out-of-region material. The coding system also enables each individual newspaper to route the material to its own specialist staff, story by story. UPI now allows its client newspapers direct access to its wire. At the 1976 political conventions, for instance, the clients were allowed to use UPI's VDTs, operated by UPI staff, to send material directly into their own computers.

The Intelligent Terminal

It is important to see the level of sophistication to which today's intelligent video display terminals now aspire. They all consist fundamentally of a cathode-ray tube, which displays text on a screen. The screens vary in size depending on whether the unit is to be used simply for verifying the material being entered by a reporter into the photocomposition system or whether it is being used for more complex processes of text editing. The early keyboards were complex and cumbersome. Today they are much simpler and provide single keys carefully labeled for single functions. Terminal users do not need more than a few hours' training. The more experience they have in interfacing with the computer, however, the more sophisticated and elaborate are the operations they can perform; it is the same with operators at an airline ticket booking terminal.

The most important group of keys are those that move the cursor (flashing dot) which indicates where the operator is working at a given moment on the screen (that is, the copy, the page). By manipulating the cursor, the reporter-editor can delete characters, words, lines, and whole paragraphs; add material; move blocks of text around the page; or cancel any of these changes. Many terminals are stand-alone units with their own storage devices, where text can be manipulated privately and then fed, when completed, into the central processing unit (CPU). Stand-alone units are also capable of conducting on-line functions with the CPU, such as asking for special files (stories) to be displayed or transmitting commands concerning the typefaces or design of the printed text.

The larger terminals designed for editors have more elaborate facilities for arranging the layout of text. They can give certain groups of words a bolder, brighter prominence or underline them; cause stories to be stacked in order of priority; and perform many other organizational tasks. The built-in minicomputer makes these larger terminals fundamentally different from a mere peripheral terminal on a large system. They can store a great deal of material; they have a number of command functions; they can receive magnetic tape; and they can connect directly with a photocomposition machine. Some models can even obtain hard copy of their output by means of a small printing device.

Both kinds of terminal, of course, can review the contents of the common data base for background research, for wire reports, and for stories on the subject that have been previously published in the newspaper. In some newspapers, the reporter's terminal can even provide all of the index information of the newspaper's own library (known as the morgue).

The reporter's terminal, with its limited memory store, has to be cleared every so often of unwanted journalistic clutter, although it will hold on to a number of stories on which current work is underway for any length of time required. The supervisor or editor has access to any of this material over the head of the reporter. The terminals have their rules, and each knows its place in the system.

The *Washington Post* has designed a particularly versatile system with Raytheon, which it is now marketing to other papers. It enables reporters to use the machine as a note taker and to retain collections of notes for all the stories on which they are working at a given moment. The terminal may in time also be able to record telephone messages and signal that it is holding them. Over the whole newsroom (which holds 250 terminals in all), there presides a production manager, independent of the editors, whose job it is to act as a traffic manager, prodding reporters to complete work and reminding editors of the priority of various items.

The problems of the *Post* are particularly taxing for an electronic

33

system. It has 300 reporters (two-thirds of them working at peak times), 19 remote bureaus in the United States, and 13 abroad. Its reporters have to be able to file copy from anywhere in the world; they are responsible for a larger proportion of the material printed in the average issue of 66 pages per day (174 on Sundays) than the staffs of most other papers.

Material from the wire services passes from hand to hand on the *Post* rather than to a single editor. Indeed many editing processes take place in the *Post* in a more complicated and interactive way than in most other newspapers. The specifications designed by the paper's special task force for Raytheon reveal complexities of internal interaction that defy brief description. The full system uses 15 wire services and 46 typefaces, and the terminal equipment has taken two years to design.

The entry of the *Washington Post* into the era of the new technology was delayed partly as a result of a bitter and prolonged industrial dispute in 1975, which involved the deliberate sabotage of the press machinery. As a very large newspaper (600,000 copies on weekdays, and rising) with an enormous number of pages to produce daily (and therefore a large number of stereotype plates), the *Post* has found it economic to use offset, photocomposition, and a front-end system only in very recent months, as unit costs have begun to fall.

Its existing stereotype platemaking equipment has to produce 400 pages an hour during peak time (9 plates for each of 45 pages) and extra plates at other times. The *Post* has not felt absolutely secure, even now, in making its decision to acquire offset equipment when its letterpress machinery is still in excellent working order (the sabotage having been long since fully repaired). Presses are normally amortized over 25 years, although if they are looked after, their working life can be double that. The price explosion of the 1970s has sent up the cost of new offset presses of the size required (and the *Post* needs nine of them) to something approaching $3 million each. The paper's last purchases of letterpresses were made only in 1970, and the arguments for keeping the whole hot-metal process have seemed overwhelming until now. The introduction of the computerized newsroom is costing $7 million (but will save the cost of a hundred printers, $2 million a year).

It has been hoped that before the presses wore out, the much-debated and researched plateless printing would arrive, which would enable the *Post* to throw away stereotypes and presses forever, in favor of a computer that would print directly. However, the best forecasts now available (from Arthur D. Little, Inc.) suggest that no usable form of plateless printing will arrive before the mid-1980s. Reluctantly, therefore, the *Post* is planning a slow move into offset, as are most other major American papers in the early 1980s. But it is keeping one eye on the 1979 round of wage negotiations and the other on the latest developments in platemaking.

The classified advertisement section of the *Post* is so great that another lengthy round of research and development has to be under-

34

gone. The management has to find a suitable system for an intake desk with 150 telephone input points. The editing systems for classified advertisements can, of course, be much simpler than those for newsrooms, but the sheer quantity of the intake and business management functions is so complex that the study of how to deal with them has alone cost over $2 million.

The introduction of new technology in so large an organization as the *Washington Post*, where every separate shop has come to think of itself as a special craft, is rather like trying to introduce social reform into a whole society. Management can only build slowly from what is already there, making tentative plans for the future year by year in the knowledge that they can very easily be blown away. If a newspaper does not publish at all, the loss is total and irrecoverable. Each paper has to proceed in the knowledge that major industrial upheavals, or the total failure of equipment, are normally more costly than any good that can be derived from new systems. The case of the *Washington Post* reminds one that the determinants of the format of any new technology are the ways in which it is actually used. The complexities that the *Post* has forced into its own system are much greater than those of nearly all other newspapers. These complexities relate directly (and, in the case of the *Post*, consciously) to the kind of modern journalism practiced at the paper.

In the hundreds of pages of specifications offered by the *Post* to Raytheon, there appears a detailed analysis of the origins and process of a number of recent stories. They range from a brief foreign report of a few lines, which originated in wire service copy 27 times as long, to the coverage of the Hanafi Muslim siege, which took place in Washington in March 1977 when three buildings were invaded by bands of gunmen and hostages taken and held for several days. All of the stories involved the assimilation into the (human) editing system of a large quantity of material. This material had to be manipulated rapidly but skillfully, in many complicated ways, by a large number of people before it could be finally fixed as editorial copy, as text. The story of the Hanafi siege received special treatment. In the era of television, newspapers have to complement television service (and vice versa). The basic stories and pictures are quickly fed by the broadcasters into each home. The newspaper has had to develop a much more detailed and investigative type of coverage. The audience (readers, viewers, and listeners) has a much larger capacity for detail than has been supposed, but the organization of the reportage required to satisfy its varied demands is equally more difficult than it ever has been.

The Hanafi siege involved 134 hostages, two black Muslim sects, hundreds of policemen, FBI agents and other officials, three Arab ambassadors (all trying to persuade the gunmen to surrender), and 28 *Washington Post* reporters. Information had to be collected from dozens of different points within Washington. While reporters roamed the city for coverage of the events, others did background research on the personalities and organizations involved. All reporters on the street were under instruction to telephone every thirty minutes to describe what was happening; thus their material appeared as a stream of memorandums.

Each memo was copied six times and all copies were given to a single editor, who sorted them according to the different aspects of the story. Piles of memos went to different writing groups, who had to seize upon the information they needed, write their copy in sections, and send it for editing at various levels of coordination. Different sections of the *Post* were concerned with the story from completely different points of view; the "national" reporter wrote an essay on terrorism, while the "style" team produced a piece about television coverage of the siege.

Sixty people were involved in handling the text of the story: 12 writers in teams, six individual writers, three writers in the "style" and "national" sections, 11 originating editors, 2 screening editors, 6 copy editors, 12 dictationists, and 8 senior editors. The grand total of employees concerned comes to 96: 28 reporters, 21 writers, 35 editors, and 12 dictationists. They contributed 330 columns of copy, consisting of 92,400 characters. A further 90 transcript pages of material had been written in the newsroom, and a great deal of wire service copy taken in and read, as well as handouts by most of the institutions and organizations involved in the siege. Much of the material moved not along a single line but by six different locations within the office.

Most of the Hanafi activity was crowded into three hours toward the end of the first day of the siege (March 9). The management had to decide whether to add extra pages or to drop a number of advertisements to increase the "news hole." Because a great deal of the other news of the day was important, it was decided to add four extra pages. A complicated run of decisions then had to be made concerning the positioning in the paper of the material emerging from the siege.

The dummy of page 1 of the first edition was ready only at 8 P.M., two hours later than planned. Three extra columns on the story were added for the second edition, which started to move through the composing room at 8:56. Replating and additional typesetting continued in three further bursts of activity, the final press run taking place at 4:29 A.M. By that time the staff was planning the coverage of the next day's edition, which followed a similar pattern, except that the hostages were freed the following night, at 2 A.M., just after the second edition had been completed. The main story became immediately useless, and something more drastic than a replating had to take place. By 2:44, eleven new pages had been prepared and were through the composing room. The management had decided to stop the presses; otherwise the entire run would have been complete before the new plates had been mounted. As it turned out, the paper produced 159,000 copies with the revised copy.

This greatly shortened account of the activities entailed in a single major story illustrates the ways in which modern journalism taxes the existing technology (of input, composition, and printing) to the bursting point. The newspaper is no longer a monopoly medium in the field of news; it is obliged to compete with the faster media of radio and television, and it has to do so in terms of the quantity of information, as well as speed. Multiple input journalism (the term given to operations like that of the *Post*) requires the kind of flexibility that only electronic composition can provide; but it requires foolproof systems, vast quantities of redundant storage, and processes that allow the text to be manipulated very easily.

One can see in the modern newsroom the configuration of circumstances that necessitate central processing units and intelligent terminals. The pattern is highly symbolic. It is the old technology that is piloting the new. Multiple authorship replaces the eponymous author of personal journalism. The newspaper's computer contains what amounts to a mediated and filtered social memory of the affairs of an entire community. The transformation of newspaper technology represents a kind of prefiguration from scribal to print culture.

The editorial process turns into a kind of instant librarianship as the functions of research and writing become the input of a collectivized process of text selection and text manipulation. The computerized newsroom helps us to observe the results of the important change that has come over written journalism in the age of television. The editor becomes a commentator (in the old word, glossator); the reporter, in taking over some of the functions performed in the past by printers, becomes a scribe.

In the past the newspaper regarded itself as a rapidly made throwaway product, broadly competitive with other similar entities. Today the newspaper is a monopoly product collecting information at the heart of a community. With computerized storage and retrieval of information it can begin to see the practicality (cheapness) of acting as a librarian of the society it serves. If it categorizes the material it has accumulated and then transfers the information into a computer, the newspaper creates a new asset, which can be resold and reused. The problem is how best to organize this new function. In the past, the newspaper's collection, processing, and distribution of information were inextricably intertwined; they were seen as one continuous process. Today the new technologies, directly and indirectly, are making the activity of collecting information increasingly separate from the newspaper's activities as an information factory and as a system of distributing information.

Many newspapers have substantial repositories, constantly updated, of information. The New York Times Information Bank has been in operation since 1973 and consists of an index to the whole corpus of work that has appeared in the newspaper since 1969, as well as information from many other publications and from eight wire services. Through a VDT and keyboard, the user (who may be a paying member of the public) may search the files under various key words (persons, organizations, geographical place names, subject areas, and so forth). Once material has been identified from the bibliographic references on the VDT screen, it can be retrieved from its microfiche storage. The problems with the system are as interesting as they are serious. The cost of storage is still so great that the Information Bank is too expensive for the staff of the *Times* to be permitted to use it for free. What is more, the problems of deciding on systems of access, categories, keyboards, and other facets are so great that the researcher has to be extremely skilled and patient to use the bank effectively.

Several other newspapers, with smaller data banks of their own, have now produced more serviceable systems than the Information Bank. Perhaps the best known is the system operated by the *Louisville Courier-Journal*, called Info-key, which links the newspaper's library with other libraries in the same city. The microfiche storage, VDT, and keyboard are convenient and comfortable, and searching the index and reading the chosen clippings on microfiche takes a matter of seconds. One minicomputer drives the whole double system.

Other systems provide complete on-line directories of newspaper libraries. NewsMeadia is one new marketed system for an electronic library that can hold several years' worth of information and make it directly accessible by a VDT. The journalist enters key words, which set up research routines into the complete texts of all articles held. Every word in every article is scanned for an exact match. The reader is then told the number of articles containing the key word and offered a variety of options for selection and display.

The material chosen may be had in hard copy (on paper) or on the VDT. A newspaper possessing an IBM 360 or 370 may acquire the software of NewsMeadia and build its own electronic library. Alternatively it can store its material remotely and retain on-line access; and for an additional fee, the newspaper can join its own electronic library with that of other subscribing newspapers. There are other systems. To help newspapers choose the most appropriate for their needs, the ANPA has devised a simple Newspaper Morgue Directory System software package, which is available at a cost of $100.

Despite the wealth of models, newspapers are being relatively slow to use computers to organize their libraries. There are, indeed, problems in choosing the input system, in training enough personnel to exploit the system, and in devising markets for external services. However, it is evident that the larger regional papers that have installed these systems are beginning to see a new source of revenue, an altogether novel function, in selling their backlogs of information. There is an obvious commercial asset in an information bank that in a single city can draw on the energies of scores of trained reporters. The city's newspaper, of course, can publish only a tiny fragment of its reporters' combined knowledge.

Distribution

In the era of the computer, the newspaper's distribution system also has possibilities of commercial exploitation. The United States has 1.25 million full- or part-time newspaper carriers. They are increasingly difficult to find and expensive to employ. Today many are only marginally employable and often unreliable. Therefore a whole range of new equipment is being rapidly introduced for the stacking, tying, and bundling of the finished newspaper. Managements that have acquired a great deal of computer expertise can now transfer to the computer many of the tasks of distribution, circulation, and sales. The computer can stack the newspapers in amounts that correspond to the different orders for agents and retailers, it can print the destination on each bundle, and it can produce them in the correct order for delivery. The delivery driver merely has to stick a special key into a slot at the loading bay to tell the computer his intended route. The machine selects a number of bundles, according to route priorities, and shoots them into the waiting trucks.

The computer's sphere of competence is being progressively extended. Most circulation departments have tended to keep lists of the hundreds or thousands of local carriers, but not of the hundreds of thousands of individual subscribers. Today several papers have on line the names, addresses, and route numbers of every subscriber. One operation in Michigan has reduced the time taken to get a new subscriber into the system from three days to several minutes. The computer knows who has not paid his bill on time and the reasons given by each individual for cancelling his subscription. It informs the local carrier automatically of a new subscriber or of a complaint. This particular paper has also acquired from a regional mailing company a complete list of names and addresses in its target area. Of those who might subscribe, it knows who has so far failed to do so, an invaluable service for the circulation department. One added advantage is that the newspaper can put a free "shopper" into the homes of all who are not subscribers to the newspaper and guarantee its advertisers penetration into all households. And this vastly improved management information has been achieved with a very large decrease in complex paperwork.

The long-term potential for the editorial department is not overlooked. With pinpoint knowledge of each group and pocket of readers, the editors of the paper can provide information services of ever-increasing exactitude and usefulness.

Newspapers as General Carriers

Many newspapers have improved their local distribution system by taking the carriers, previously hired on a contract basis, into direct employment. But this extension of the traditional arrangements, even if computerized, does not take full advantage of the new opportunities. Many publishers wish to go much farther. They believe that the increasing speed and sophistication of their delivery mechanisms enable them to operate as general carriers and to offer, on contract, to carry other companies' printed matter.

In the United States, the home delivery of print is very big business indeed. In 1970, 8 billion preprints were delivered; by 1980 there are expected to be 18 billion. Meanwhile the magazine industry is deeply affected by the rising cost of postage. Both sectors could switch part of their business to the newspaper's computerized newspaper operations if methods could be devised to insert automatically, inside the local morning or afternoon newspaper, the right magazine or the right preprint into the right household.

The issue here is the ever more precise pinpointing of tiny pockets of readers with specialist interests. Plateless printing or cheap platemaking solves the production problems of satisfying these small markets. As soon as automated stuffing machines can move at the same speed as the printing press, selecting the bundles and individual homes for chosen specialist items, the problems of distribution will be solved as well. This kind of machine has been the object of a good deal of experimentation, much of it successful (in Louisville especially). But advance in this area depends upon technologies that are not yet on the market; indeed they are still at the margins of publishers' concern. It is likely, however, that when they are implemented, they will have enormous social impact.

The fundamental problem of the newspaper has been the varying geographic and demographic formation of its market. Audiences have spread out and thinned; some have partly disappeared. There are also a variety of specialist audiences that have never been satisfied by the available media. The American business community has an insatiable appetite for detailed information about itself and about all industry. The diplomatic and scientific communities are also eager for continuous streams of highly detailed information. Groups of people, scattered throughout the United States, while not identical to the academic audience with its overfull supply of monthly and quarterly journals, are anxious to be brought up to date in specific areas of interest, and so willing to subscribe to a newspaper with a substantial information content.

The *Wall Street Journal* is one paper that uses advanced technology to identify and reach that audience. The *Journal* and COMSAT devised in 1974 a system of facsimile printing that has today developed into a national system of facsimile, covering almost every population center in the United States. The *Journal* has become the country's first really national paper. The paper is actually produced on a local basis. Stories, headlines, and advertisements are collected at centers throughout the country and assembled into pages in each region. The pages are photocomposed and the negatives wrapped around a transmitting drum. This high-speed drum scans each page at 6,000–8,000 lines per inch and transmits digital pulses at 75,000 bits per second to a geosynchronous satellite, Comstar, which sends them down again to receiving plants where they are reconverted to light and reexposed. The pages are then printed from lithographic plates. The entire process takes three minutes.

The satellite costs are not related to distance and can undercut the equivalent terrestrial microwave service (which is rigidly costed by distance) by nine-tenths. The newspaper is offered the opportunity of linking specialist audiences without much extra charge. This could lead to a thorough reorganization of the conventional marketing practices based on a regional monopoly. But the satellite is worthwhile only with newspapers whose advertising space is very valuable. Even if the satellite can offer cheap trunk rates, local distribution is still expensive.

This kind of fascinating historic switch in the structure of the newspaper's information base can be achieved only if the newspaper possesses a daily content that is equally attractive to an audience in all parts of a large land mass. Everyone is waiting to see whether the *New York Times* can use similarly advanced telecommunications to spread its very large audience. In France, meanwhile, managements are starting to use similar facsimile systems to extend politically oriented Parisian newspapers into the provinces.

An important related development is the plan for a U.S. satellite network to book and transmit national and regional newspaper advertising throughout the entire country. The newspaper has lost a great deal of national advertising to television. In spite of fighting hard for this important slice of revenue, newspapers only had 21.1 percent of all U.S. national advertising revenues in 1960, and by 1976 the figure had dwindled to 14.8 percent (although in terms of volume, the newspaper experienced a 55 percent increase between 1972 and 1976). The newspaper now looks to the satellite (and its own computers) to provide a cheap, convenient, and instant system for collecting national advertising. It is already possible, even without the development of automatic full-page composition, to send display advertisements in facsimile directly into the computer storage of several papers.

In the early 1980s, there is likely to be a national distribution service, by satellite, of display advertisements. The service will greatly help media planners of large corporations to run advertising campaigns across selected areas of the country. They will no longer have to go through the complicated business of booking separate advertisements one at a time in hundreds or thousands of publications. The implications for the pattern of U.S. marketing and advertising campaigns, and of retail distribution, are very great.

It is obvious that the new technology is assisting the newspaper in the United States to adopt a more flexible policy toward its market. As the market's geography changes, so does the newspaper's size, shape, and content. The attention of the audience is being recaptured. Total

41

daily circulation rose by 700,000 in 1977; the share of total national advertising revenue is moving up toward 30 percent again. This recent upswing is the result of the work and experimentation of the last decade.

The opportunities for expansion are very large. A newspaper can be produced in twin plants as in Los Angeles; or spread itself across the entire society, like the *Wall Street Journal*; or simply grow solidly into the lives of a city's expanding population, as does the *Washington Post*. Tiny papers can cull high-quality information from an increasing variety of wire services and sell that information again to specialized audiences of individuals, firms, or geographical areas.

The newspaper is now becoming conscious of its new roles as specialist carrier, as data base, as information processor, and as communal memory. Many papers are watching the development of the various teletext services in Europe and Japan with a combination of hope and fear. They realize that this extension of computer technology into the field of information might threaten their own system for marketing information and oblige them to invest heavily in a new system of dissemination. The U.S. authorities cannot yet decide whether these new devices are common carriers, which are not allowed to process information, or data processors, which must be regulated and cannot be common carriers, a complexity posed by America's twin desires to bust monopolies and to separate powers. The very flexibility offered by the new services and technologies offers both opportunities and confusion.

There is now a feeling that a certain standardization is necessary within the territory already gained (in photocomposition and cold type) before further major advances can be considered. An advance to automated full-page composition could entail so great a leap forward in the sophistication of equipment and in new job routines that many publishers are feeling that they ought now to sit back and wait a bit before attempting it. After all, the newspaper has only just realized the proper nature of its four-layer market, and it has its work cut out to get back into the lives of the twenty-year-olds who have been eschewing it in recent years. The industry wants time to absorb the changes brought by the first stage of computerization and to exploit them in the cause of consolidation.

The Customized Newspaper

Hitherto the newspaper in America rushed into innovation in an attempt to remain on the same spot, so to speak, in an attempt to recover from the chronic problems that had been plaguing it. An important turning point lies ahead. The next round of changes in the speed of production and the size of each issue will begin to produce changes in kind.

Steadily over the course of four centuries, the newspaper has developed by adding material to itself. Every new group of readers acquired, every new territory of distribution, every new tool for the collection of news and advertisements, has generally meant that a new section could and would be added. Some things have been lost along the way, including serial fiction and certain kinds of shipping and trade news that were too specialized for the general market. But overall the newspaper has grown more and more miscellaneous. Even now, when the newspaper is almost too big to distribute, let alone read, it is still growing in volume as it tries to serve the varied new life-styles of its successive layers of audience. But the same computer that is helping the newspaper to grow, and to grow as efficiently as possible, has several fundamental tendencies of its own that point in the reverse direction. The computer can assist a mass manufacturer to economize by making more copies of a repeated product, but it can as easily help him to individualize his product. The new computer-driven plants can achieve variety as well as speed, and the more sophisticated computers can narrow their focus upon markets in dozens of ways. Viewdata is a very good example of this trend toward the detailed tailoring of information. The hardware that newspapers are progressively accumulating (and the expertise they have gained) will enable the newspaper to grow out of its basic miscellaneity. The computer can bring about—either across the whole market or in special sectors of it—a kind of Hegelian negation of the newspaper. It could change from being a general hold-all to something custom-designed. What is more, the change could occur quite rapidly. Many current tendencies point in this direction.

The way in which newspapers have been gradually extending themselves into the distant suburbs (through zoning and special supplements) has taught them a great deal about how to deal with tiny groups of readers. The increased spending power of most Americans, and their apparently limitless ability to absorb more information, has made these extensions very worthwhile. Second, newspaper audiences are no longer being counted only as accumulations of individuals but in terms of the percentages of households within a zone. This new concept is a vital step toward the identification of special audiences for special products—of the kind that the computer can supply with relative ease. Finally, the newspaper has increasingly become a carrier of material produced by syndication agencies and wire services (the *Washington Post* excepted). The sharp end of the newspaper is no longer editorial singularity but marketing efficiency.

43   It is impossible to speculate on how or when a new form could emerge in the newspaper industry. Plateless printing, which one may presume is the *sine qua non* of an individualized newspaper, will probably not arrive until the late 1980s, although the Mead Corporation and others are now experimenting with ink-jet equipment as a newspaper-printing method. The idea of paperless newspapers delivered direct to the home, which has been discussed since the 1930s, seems to fade away into futurist mists the more one examines the problems. The arrival of view-

data and other teletext systems is, in the view of some people, more likely to postpone the home-delivered facsimile newspaper rather than advance it. New semiconductors are needed, as well as much greater transmission bandwidth, a new nonglare screen larger than the cathode ray tube, and a form of strong erasable paper, before the home facsimile newspaper is viable. The last is often forgotten but especially important. Without it large amounts of paper would have to be delivered to each home regularly—a cumbersome and expensive business—whereas the saving of paper could be the new device's greatest boon. Perhaps the most important element in home-facsimile newspapers that still needs to be discovered is the audience. The transformation of reading habits entailed in the concept is scarcely imaginable at this stage.

Such skepticism can be tarred as a simple failure of imagination. Every development in the field of computers since World War II has taken place a decade or so earlier than expected by the boldest predictions, and so might home facsimile. But nothing that has happened in the various Japanese experiments leads one to suppose that a market trial would establish a service as viable. Certainly the amount of investment that has been irrevocably sunk in the existing newspaper system constitutes a tremendous pressure against the rapid development of facsimile alternatives.

Much more fruitful are the developments in the field of fiber optics and the mushroom growth of the new transactional and recreational services that depend upon the television screen and the telephone wire. It is possible that developments in the field of entertainment (as in Home Box Office and other similar pay-television networks) will encourage the audience to feel at home when it uses the telephone, a television screen, and perhaps a minicomputer for a variety of other services. Changes in U.S. public policy to permit telephone companies to take over cable enterprises and transfer them gradually onto optic-fiber networks could quite quickly turn the improbable into the possible. The capacity for home facsimile newspapers might indeed develop as an offshoot of other strands of computerization in entertainment and commerce.

History seems to suggest that the computer, once summoned to redress the balance of traditional media, will stay to transform them. Perhaps the center of that transformation, as it affects print, lies in a paradox. The newspaper is changing. It has been a medium written by individuals for general audiences. It is now achieving specialist status in which an amalgam of semianonymous written services are provided for individualized audiences. The change signals the route away from the glorification of eponymous authorship toward the collectivized holding of information under the sovereignty of a librarian-editor.

It is difficult to make moral judgments about these changes, although much shrill advice is offered to and by politicians, social critics, pressure groups, and the like. The reason for the difficulty is partly that the moral attitudes of the past toward such things as chain ownership, cross-ownership, and monopolistic practices are not relevant in many of the new circumstances. The United States will be obliged to change its stance (for example, on the ownership or control of cable installations by telephone companies) when optic-fiber transmission, with its vast capacities, becomes widespread. It will also have to change its position on the activities of common carriers in the field of processing; at least it will if the United States is ever to have viewdata services.

Many people involved in U.S. and Canadian telecommunications must be watching with interest the versatility now being demonstrated by the European public telecommunication monopolies. The Europeans seem to suffer from no inhibitions concerning the separation of functions. Telephones, television, decoders, physical mail services, electronic message services—all are being constructed in hybrid fashion without fear of breaching some great juridical or jurisdictional frontier.

The values associated with the image of the fourth estate have been steadily eroded over the past decades as fewer and fewer owners control more and more newspapers. Newspaper chains and groups have spread and have been lamented since the days of Hearst and Scripps, although some kind of ceiling now seems to have been reached.

Today 71 percent of the United States' daily circulation is controlled by sixteen ownerships; there has been a parallel growth in local monopolies. The chains range from Gannett's seventy-nine papers and Thomson's fifty-seven to the Times/Mirror syndicate in Los Angeles, which owns a small group of papers with the huge total circulation of nearly two million. The larger chains are now buying up the smaller chains. The Newhouse group now owns the Booth group, and Gannett owns both Speidel and Combined Communications' radio and television outlets. Many of the larger groups own valuable subsidiary utilities, such as publishing houses, timber plantations, magazines, radio and television stations, and cable systems.

What is often not recognized is the extent to which economic pressures have been increasing the pace of conglomerate growth in the last few years. The spread of local monopolies has meant that large sums of cash pile up in the publishers' accounts. If they are not used for fresh acquisition within the financial year, these cash reserves are taxed. The result is that newspaper utilities (especially local monopolies) may be valued at thirty and forty times their annual earnings. The historical patterns of ownership are another contributing factor. Most papers that are still independent or tied to one or two local subsidiaries are family owned and subject periodically to inheritance takers. The Internal Revenue Service assesses these duties on the basis of market values (that is, the value that an existing chain will pay at that moment). Families may be asked to pay inheritance taxes that are extremely (even artificially) large in relation to the actual earnings of the enterprises they have inherited. Some papers have been left to their employees in an

45

attempt to prevent their acquisition by chains. In many cases, however, the value of the asset has grown so rapidly that the new owners have been tempted by lucrative offers. The *Kansas City* newspaper, which was owned by its workers, recently sold out to make fifteen people into overnight millionaires and scores of other individuals very wealthy indeed.

In these fiscal circumstances the temptations to sell are overwhelming, and the large chains are growing accordingly. As professionalized management teams, with one eye permanently on the stock exchange, move into the desks vacated by the scions of great families, the notion of a fourth estate is further weakened. Often, of course, the families remain. They train a new generation in the skills of modern management, obtain a stock exchange quotation, and prepare themselves for growth on a twentieth-century scale. But by the mid-1980s many observers and participants expect to see most of the American daily and Sunday press in the hands of eight to ten large groups. The new technology contributes to this development because it facilitates cost cutting (and profit growth) and requires large sums of capital.

Newspaper publishers are beginning to see that their whole development in the late twentieth century is more severely affected by decisions taken by the federal and state governments, the courts, and regulatory agencies than would have seemed conceivable in the past. In the past, the idea of the fourth estate has been very important in the American context. It still is. Press freedom is so trenchantly guaranteed in the U.S. Constitution as to make the press virtually a protected industry. The principle will die hard.

But it is clear that the newspaper, as a form, is now utterly dependent upon decisions that can only be taken at the level of society as a whole. These decisions now completely control its evolution as a carrier of commercial and social information. Public policies on planning and transportation affect the modern retailing revolution, which is itself strongly determining the development of newspaper supplements and other matters. But regulations on a whole variety of matters, including litter and child labor, as well as all those affecting the future of telecommunications, are also major determinants of newspaper governance.

The growth of chains and conglomerates is also one aspect of the way in which previously separate technologies are converging to create new configurations of media linkages. These linkages are creating entirely new opportunities for the dissemination of information and entertainment throughout any society with a high level of technological and social development. But they are also creating new divisions. They do this because of their efficiency. They create the divisions precisely between those groups whose information desires can be so accurately pinpointed and satisfied. In its traditional patterns of ownership and distribution, the newspaper seemed to guarantee the information flows that were required by Western democracies. The mass electorate sup-

46

posedly formed the basis of public opinion and therefore of social decisions.

The newspaper and attendant information media are now being locked into patterns of advertising and distribution that make large quantities of information available to small elites. The information is much more substantial and perhaps better than ever before. But those sections of the audience who do not demand to be informed (and who, in practice, perhaps never were) are now much more completely cut off. The *San Francisco Chronicle*, for example, which has never been quoted as being among the United States' high quality papers, now provides a variety of special supplements with carefully zoned advertisements for each sector of the Bay Area community. The "Briefing" section contains excellent material, culled from other newspapers and information services, on foreign affairs and public policy matters. The newspaper simply acts as a conduit for this externally generated material. The *Chronicle* appears to symbolize the way in which the newspaper is becoming a deliverer of specialized information to relevant groups.

The functions of the press as a fourth estate demand that the newspaper be a complete social presence, not just a channel for someone else's information. The new technology, and the new perceptions that surround it, are preparing mass society for important and perhaps undesirable internal partitions, which may place great strains upon the self-image of democratic societies. The new technology itself does not change social formation. It merely brings home to us some unpalatable truths about the kind of social dividing lines we already have.

References

Eisenstein, Elizabeth. "Some Conjectures about the Impact of Printing on Western Society and Thought: A Preliminary Report." *Journal of Modern History* 40 (1968): 1–57.

American Newspaper Publishers Association, *Facts About Newspapers, 1978.* Reston, Va.: ANPA, 1978.

Febre, Lucien, and Martin, Henri-Jean. *The Coming of the Book: The Impact of Printing, 1450–1800.* Translated by David Gerard. London: New Left Books, 1976.

John Fleischman, various articles contributed to the *Newsletter* of the Alicia Patterson Foundation, 1977.

Graphic Arts Marketing Information Service, Arlington, Virginia.

Grundfest, Joseph, and Baer, Walter. "Regulatory Carriers to Home Information Services." Paper presented to the Sixth Annual Telecommunications Policy Research Conference, Warrenton, Virginia, May 1978.

Moghdam, Dineh. *Computers in Newspaper Publishing: User-Oriented Systems.* New York: Marcel Dekker, 1978.

Rosse, James N. *Economic Limits of Press Responsibility.* Studies in Industry Economics, No. 56, Department of Economics, Stanford University, 1972.

Rosse, James N.; Owen, Bruce M.; and Dertouzos, James. *Trends in the Daily Newspaper Industry, 1923–1973.* Studies in Industry Economics, No. 57, Department of Economics, Stanford University, 1977.

Sterling, Christopher H., and Haight, Timothy R. *The Mass Media: Aspen Institute Guide to Communication Industry Trends.* New York: Praeger, 1978.

Udell, Jon G., ed. *Economic Trends in the Daily Newspaper Business, 1946–70.* Madison, Wis.: Bureau of Business Research and Service, 1979.

Winsbury, Rex. *New Technology and the Press.* Royal Commission on the Press Working Paper No. 1. London: HMSO, 1975.

2

The New Electronic Media and Their Place in the Information Market of the Future

Tetsuro Tomita

The Position of the Newspaper in Japanese Society

According to UNESCO statistics of 1970 the diffusion rate of Japanese newspapers was 537 copies per thousand persons, slightly surpassing Sweden's 535 copies per thousand and making Japan the top newspaper-reading nation of the world. (It ranks unexpectedly low, however, in terms of television and books.) In 1974, this rate dropped to 526 copies per thousand because of a contraction of the economy following the oil crisis. This rate was lower than Sweden's 536 copies but still gave Japan a wide lead over the country in third place, Great Britain, with 443 copies per thousand. Moreover, all five of Japan's national newspapers have circulations of well above a million copies, and the *Yomiuri Shimbun* and the *Asahi Shimbun* have circulations of more than 7 million.

The Japanese newspaper industry has unmistakably exerted a great effort to establish its present position. The newspaper companies have spent a great deal of manpower and money in consolidating their reporting systems; it is believed that Japanese newspapers have the largest number of correspondents stationed overseas. In addition, the Japanese public has also played a role in promoting the development of the mass media as a whole, since, with a homogeneous population and a single language, they are more inclined than other nations to accept standardized information or information from a central source. Newspapers enjoyed a predominant position in Japanese society until the advent of television, which has had an impact on the newspaper that radio failed to exercise. In recent years the enormous influence of the newspaper has begun to wane. At the same time, it has been challenged in its field by television, weekly news magazines, and now new forms of technology.

The census of information flow in Japan carried out by myself and others for the Ministry of Posts and Telecommunications has revealed that newspapers recorded little growth between 1965 and 1975.[1] Our study charted the increases and decreases in the production of the volume of words used in various media and forms of discourse, and we calculated the varying amounts of time the population dedicated to its various information pursuits. We were thus able to make statements about the way the production of media content related to the actual use of the media concerned, and in the case of the newspaper it was evident that while the total volume of words on paper had increased considerably the per capita consumption of such material had declined appreciably. Furthermore, a survey conducted by NHK (Japanese Broadcasting Corporation) also shows that there has been practically no change in the average newspaper reading hours of twenty minutes per day per person since forty years ago when the first records of newspaper reading hours were logged. The volume of information supplied by the television media for public consumption, however, is now about sixty to eighty times that of the newspaper.

In the last decade, the news function of the newspaper was thought to be substantially greater than that of television. Television news as compared to newspaper news lacked analytical comment. Moreover it was difficult to evaluate the relative importance of items of television news, whereas in newspapers the value of news could be judged by the layout of the paper. Also newspapers normally carried more detailed reports than television news did. In recent years, however, television has begun to adopt a new style in news reporting, and even the newspaper companies do some of their reporting over television news programs under their company names. There is now intense competition between the two media.

The weekly magazine industry also poses a threat to newspapers. Although there are only fifty-six weeklies out of a total of 39,337 publications in Japan, they have a combined circulation of 1,163 million copies (compared with 598 million in 1960), or about 40 percent of the circulation (3,000 million) of all publications (in 1977). Over the last twenty years, weekly magazine publishing has been booming, partly because these publishing firms broke the newspaper companies' monopoly in this field. *Shukan Shincho,* inaugurated in 1956, was the first weekly magazine to be issued by an ordinary book publisher rather than by a newspaper company.

In terms of news reporting and commentaries, the quality of weekly magazines is about on par with that of newspapers, and in recent years they have begun to check the excesses of the newspapers. But twenty years of publishing experience can hardly compete with the newspapers' tradition, dating back a century. The weekly magazine simply does not have the influence on society that the newspaper has, nor does it offer serious competition to the newspaper as an industry. Indeed the most powerful challenge to the newspaper could be from new forms of technology.

Recent Developments in Technology

More than ten years have passed since the addition of the words *information* and *information society* to the Japanese vocabulary signaled the impact of information technology. In the meantime, there has been steady progress in the development of new technology and a rapid upsurge in the volume of information centering around the data communications industry. Moreover, information media themselves are becoming more sophisticated and diversified.

The Ministry of Posts and Telecommunications has been conducting the Information Flow Census since fiscal 1973 in order to make a comprehensive survey of the level of diffusion of information in Japanese society. The study has attempted to grade the flow of information by using a common yardstick, the word, as a measure cutting across all types of media. Three figures are calculated in regard to each medium: the number of words carried, words times distance (the word-kilometer), and cost times words times distance (yen per word-kilometer). These measures can be applied to messages sent and to messages received. By making a comprehensive and quantitative study of the present state of information flow, the census hopes to provide useful data for predicting the development trends of each medium and for making indexes for gauging the degree of informatization.

Figure 2.1 depicts the trend of total supply and consumption of information from fiscal 1960 to fiscal 1975. The supply of information has expanded remarkably, about eightfold, in the fifteen-year period because of the explosive expansion of television, followed by the switch from monochrome to color broadcasting. On the other hand, the volume of information consumption showed a relatively stable growth, roughly a twofold increase over the same period. The reason is that the consumption of information is regulated by factors that have changed comparatively little, such as increases in leisure time and in population. As a result, the rate of consumption of information had decreased by 1975 to an average of 9.9 percent of total media as compared to 40.8 percent in 1960. It was this disparity of supply and demand that created an era of excess information, sometimes called the "flooding of information" or "information pollution." Because of this excess, demand has grown for more detailed information that meets individual requirements rather than the standardized information provided by present television and newspaper media, and so information media that can supply inexpensive information designed for individual needs have been developed and consolidated.

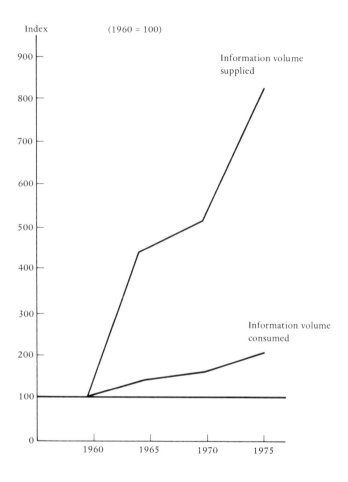

Figure 2.1

In today's society much information required for individual living and corporate activity can be obtained from the communication media. However, they are not able to supply specific information to meet the needs of anybody, at any time, anywhere, at inexpensive rates. In mass communications media, such as television, there are certain restrictions in terms of broadcasting hours of news, for example, or in the content of general information. Thus it is impossible to set up an adequate information supply system that could provide news desired outside the time frame of broadcasting hours or could respond to individual needs. In the case of personal communications media, such as the telephone, the restriction is one of cost when a person tries to obtain necessary information immediately. Figure 2.2 shows the number of recipients of information supplied by present media and the time it takes for the information to reach them. The blank zone in the diagram could possibly by filled by the new information media that can meet a demand for individualized information.

Figure 2.3 indicates the trends from fiscal 1960 to 1975 of information flow and distribution costs. It suggests that consumers select information distribution media by considering the cost and volume of the information to be received. This is apparent from the fact that the media are positioned along the vicinity of the regression line of the chart. For example, let us assume that a businessman in Tokyo has an assignment that would require about two hours of conversation with a party in Osaka. Whether he will travel all the way to Osaka by bullet train or finish his business by long-distance telephone depends on how he selects the alternatives, taking into account the cost of the media and the quantity of information he hopes to get. If the cost of the long-distance call is less than 10,000 yen, he may use the telephone; if the expense of traveling by bullet train is about 20,000 yen and there is virtually no difference between that and the cost of calling long distance, he may choose to travel to Osaka. It was previously thought that people would select the most convenient medium even if it meant paying a little more. But the figure shows that cost is more important than convenience. It also shows that the media that have registered the most rapid growth in the past ten years are data and facsimile communications. This change cannot be attributed simply to the fact that they are convenient. There has been growth in these sectors because their costs were competitive.

Figure 2.3 also indicates a widening gap between the economically weak and strong media. In the diagram, the media whose vectors are pointing to the left are those whose unit costs are declining year by year. Vectors pointing up indicate that the volume of information handled by that particular medium is increasing. Thus those media (such as data communications) where the vectors are slanted to the left and up have a promising future. Conversely the media with vectors slanting to the right and down are those that are on the decline. A striking example of such a decline is telegram service.

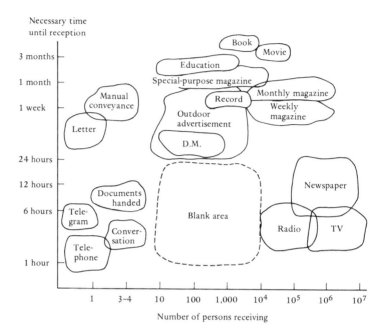

Figure 2.2

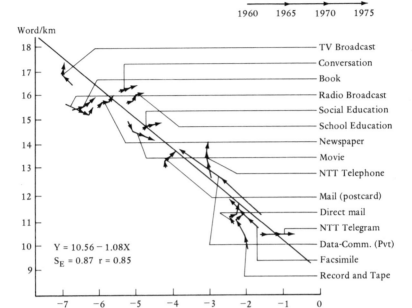

Yen = log word/km cost (cost to transport one word one km)
Word/km = log distance volume of consumption (annual total words
　　　　　multiplied by distance in km)
Source: "Information Flow Census," Ministry of Posts and
　　　　　Telecommunications

Figure 2.3

What future, then, is in store for those media that have vectors shifting merely to the right but not down? In spite of the annual rise in costs, these media are handling the same amount of information as in the past, in violation of economic principles, but it is unlikely that this can continue very long, because it is impossible for a medium to exist inside the area far from the linear regression line that governs all media. Still because of the limitations in evaluating the macrocosmic figures of the present census, it is impossible to forecast when these media will reach the watershed that will signal their permanent decline. In any event, the nontelecommunications media such as the newspaper must pay close attention to the evolution of the new information media, which may offer them serious competition in the future as the demand for individualized information increases.

Aware of this situation, the Japan Newspaper Association in November 1974 published a report, *The Possibilities of the New Telecommunications Media*, which included a compilation of opinions from some 132 experts in the fields of newspaper, broadcasting, and publication; a study on three new services and six transmission lines such as character display service; still-picture transmission service; facsimile service; utilization of off-air time frames for television broadcasting and television multiplex broadcast; FM multiplex broadcast; usage of independent broadcast waves; coaxial cables and telephone lines; and also a study of television sound multiplex broadcast and direct broadcasting services by communications satellite.

The report concludes that three services should be in commercial use by the latter half of the 1980s (figure 2.4). The character display service provides a form of written information available instantly on a normal domestic television receiver, very similar to the videotex services currently operating in various parts of Europe and North America. Still-picture transmission is a means by which visual information can be fed onto the same kind of receiver with a soundtrack and in color, rather like an illustrated slide lecture; the service can be supplied without the use of the very wide bandwidth required by an ordinary television channel. The facsimile service enables pages of written material to be sent to and received from the home. In the evaluation of transmission lines, the report has great expectations for the utilization of radio waves, including coaxial cables, and a rather low evaluation of the future usage of telephone lines. It appears, however, to be unable to estimate the prices of terminals and the possibilities of their expansion, primarily because the study was made when a proper appraisal of the value of LSI (large-scale integration) technology could not be had. In other words, the report pays little attention to the most important aspect of the possible expansion of this medium: cost.

Since January 1976, the Ministry of Posts and Telecommunications has been conducting experiments on the newly developed consumer information system involving five hundred residents of the Tama New Town outside Tokyo. There have been experiments with ten types of

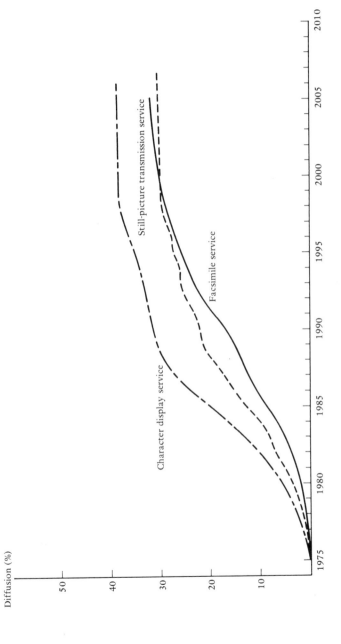

Figure 2.4

services, some closely related to newspapers, including the newspaper-size, facsimile newspaper service and the still-picture request service, which is a data-bank type service, while the center's information storage system employs a microfiche. Although they were all successful technically, the experiments were not necessarily successful from the commercial standpoint. One of the reasons was that the development of experimental equipment was completed in 1973 when the technology of the application of LSI was not firmly established.

It appears unlikely that these new services will be commercially viable on the coaxial cable network in the near future, so new systems—the television character multiplex broadcasting system and the character and pattern telephone access information network system (CAPTAINS)—have now been devised that use existing broadcasting frequencies and telephone networks, which cost less. A field test to determine the optimal system for the first was conducted in the fall of 1978. Experiments in the second are continuing into the early 1980s.

CAPTAINS is a new medium devised against the background of progress in communications technology, the existence of a telephone network servicing 35 million subscribers, and the spread of television sets, which are now owned by more than 90 percent of households. It is designed to offer an information service to individual customers and uses the ordinary home television and telephone. Through a special adaptor, the television receiver is hooked to the telephone line, allowing the subscriber to request information, such as news or consumer information, which is relayed in written or graphic form and displayed on the television screen (figure 2.5). The Prestel system in Britain and the Bildschirmtext of West Germany are similar to CAPTAINS. But while the British and German systems use a coded transmission system, CAPTAINS employs a facsimile-type pattern transmission system because of the special problems involved in using the thousands of kanji characters in Japanese script. In the British and German systems, the character and graphic generators are incorporated into the home terminals, whereas in CAPTAINS this device is located at the control center.

During 1979, the Ministry of Posts and Telecommunications and Nippon Telegraph and Telephone Public Corporation (NTT) jointly conducted an experiment with about 1,000 telephone subscribers in Tokyo using an information bank carrying about 100,000 pages (one page incorporating 120 characters). The purpose of the experiment is to confirm the technical possibilities of CAPTAINS and see whether such a service meets the needs of consumers. More than 100 companies have volunteered to provide information for the system during the experimental period, among them 10 newspaper firms, including major newspapers.

Previous experiments have tended to ignore operating costs, but this new experimental service will give this full consideration since the objective is to introduce a commercial public service in the near future.

58

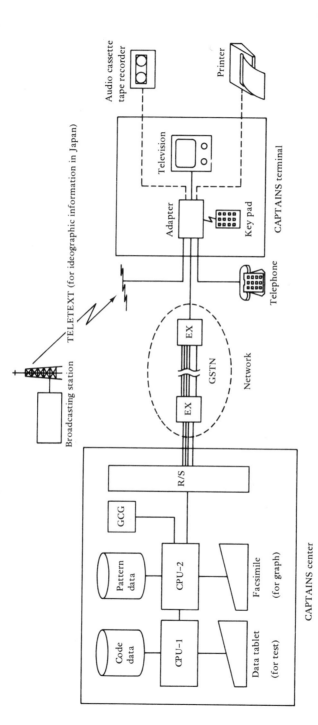

Broadcasting station

TELETEXT (for ideographic information in Japan)

Audio cassette tape recorder

Printer

Television

Adapter

Key pad

CAPTAINS terminal

Telephone

EX

GSTN

EX

Network

R/S

GCG

Pattern data

Code data

CPU-2

CPU-1

Facsimile (for graph)

Data tablet (for test)

CAPTAINS center

CPU-1 : processor for information retrieval CPU-2 : processor for image conversion GCG : graphic character generator equipment
R/S : receive/send control unit EX : telephone exchange GSTN : general switching telephone network

Figure 2.5

Moreover, an adaptation of CAPTAINS could be used for television character multiplex broadcasting. For example, in newscasts, it will be possible to offer a simple news flash over the television character multiplex broadcasting system and then follow up with a more detailed report through CAPTAINS.

An Evaluation

Newspapers as a mass medium offer immediacy, a permanent record, periodicity, and diversity. But they also have the disadvantage common to all printed media: the information they offer and the material they print have to be delivered by physical transportation. Rapid progress in the field of wideband transmission technology and information-processing technology could bring about a revolution both in newspaper production and in the biggest newspaper bottleneck, distribution. The route this revolution could take is toward the fully electronic newspaper, which would directly transmit printed papers into the home.

On the other hand, with increasing demand for individualized information and with rapid progress in information processing, the public is reaching a stage where it may no longer be content with standardized, conventional, one-way information traffic from newspaper company to reader. The new information media, in these circumstances, could become a threat to existing media.

How might newspapers cope with such new information media as CAPTAINS and television character multiplex broadcasting? Could these new services actually turn into electronic newspapers? In the past, one of the prime requisites of an electronic newspaper seemed to be the production of hard copy, but under present circumstances, when advanced LSI technology becomes available such a requirement becomes superfluous. Once information in electric signal form is temporarily stored in the terminal, it is a simple matter to give subscribers the choice of displaying the information through the cathode-ray tube display or through the printer. It is no longer such an expensive proposition to produce hard copies, but, considering that the subscriber to the Prestel- or CAPTAINS-type services could also request a retransmission of information, hard-copy availability is hardly an essential requirement.

Nevertheless, neither CAPTAINS nor television character multiplex broadcasting could in the immediate future become electronic newspapers. Certainly by 1990 there will be a considerable expansion of both of these services, and as a result it is anticipated that a considerable volume of classified advertisements will shift from newspapers to CAPTAINS service. It is also conceivable that because of its speed in reporting, the television character multiplex broadcasting system might eliminate the demand for conventional evening newspapers—a development that could deal a heavy blow to the newspaper industry. But it is unlikely that the current form of newspapers will have disappeared by the 1990s. First, CAPTAINS and television character multiplex broadcasting do not have the means to lay out news. Of course, this can be done, in a sense, through a changing time frame (the news stories would succeed one another, as in a radio bulletin); but to effect a spatial layout would be impossible, and it would also be extremely difficult to combine the news deftly with commentary. Second, there is doubt whether the functioning of a free press could take place satisfactorily within the new media. This is a weighty consideration, since normal demographic political processes depend on free access to the press, which is not in itself dependent on a state-owned resource as the new media are.

Many people think it unlikely that critical discussion and subjective reporting by journalists can adequately take place in the new media. If that proves to be the case, it is thought that the public after the 1990s will continue to demand newspapers that feature reporting by free journalists but are not necessarily in the form of today's newspaper. Japanese newspapers today are involved in various activities, having entered the fields of entertainment, publishing, and broadcasting. There is a fundamental difference in the question of whether newspaper companies involved in these areas will survive and whether free journalism will survive. In any event, rapid progress in communication technology based upon computers and electronics will bring about competition with established media such as broadcasting and printing, and, under mutual influence, they will identify areas of possible cooperation and areas where their roles in the information industry of the future will divide. Concrete examples of this convergence of mode have already appeared in the new information media. Such developments will undoubtedly pose problems of coexistence and competition to the newspaper industry.

The newspaper industry has shown great interest in the experiments that led to CAPTAINS. And since the new media will rest upon telecommunications, the newspaper industry of the future will assuredly pay even closer attention to the development of Japan's national communication policy. They cannot survive without the telecommunications systems of the future, and some fear they cannot survive with them. The strongest force supporting the traditional newspaper, however, as it interacts with the new media, must surely be its dominance in the political field and its deep roots in social custom.

Notes

1. "The Volume of Information Flow and the Quantum Evaluation of Media," *Telecommunication Journal* 42 (1975): 339–349; "Volume of Information Flow: Quantum Evaluation of Media," *Dentsu's Japan Marketing Advertising* (1972–1973), pp. 100–107. The full report is a ministry document of 1974 and an earlier one, *Is Information Exploding: Report by Information Circulation Census Study*.

3

Newsprint: From Rags to Riches— And Back Again?

Pauline Wingate

Newsprint is the generic term for the distinctive type of paper used in the printing of newspapers. Before newsprint, newspapers used the same very high-quality, very expensive, and at times rather scarce paper that everyone else used. After newsprint, they had a medium tailor-made exactly to their requirements: "strength to run under tension very fast; opacity; the ability to accept one or more colours in solid areas for text and headlines, as well as having a fine enough surface to reproduce photographs and half tones acceptably; and the lowest possible price."[1] Abundant supplies of very cheap paper: it was like finding the goose that laid the golden eggs, and for the next nearly 100 years, supplies of newsprint kept on coming, unchanging in quality, hardly at all in price, as reliable as a natural element and as taken for granted. This was the circulation medium that was the foundation of the transformation of the newspaper into the first of the mass communication media.

In recent decades, newspapers have kept their golden goose on very short commons, starving it of healthy profits so that it has become less and less a strong and profitable industry. As outside forces have come into play— worldwide inflation and escalating energy costs, among others—there have inevitably been radical changes in quality, price, and security of supply. At a time when the newspaper has been weakened by the competition of broadcasting (whose medium is scarce but free as air), it now has to face the grim prospect that newsprint may never again be abundant or cheap. This fact must fundamentally affect the newspaper's chance of survival in an electronic age, at least in its present form. What hope is there that this perilous position may be retrieved?

Raw Materials

Traditionally newsprint's prime raw material is the long-fibered softwood of coniferous trees (particularly the spruce), which grow abundantly in the northern forests of Europe, Asia, and America. It makes very good quality mechanical or groundwood pulp, which is conventionally the cheap basic furnish (80 to 88 percent) of a newsprint paper. The mechanical pulping process grinds logs at high speed in a stream of water or defibers wood chips with revolving knives. The fibers are torn out rather than pulverized in order to preserve the length that will give strength to the paper finally produced, but the main object is to achieve a high yield, better than 90 percent, rather than fiber in as pure and undamaged a state as possible. Groundwood pulp, therefore, contains all of the vegetable constituents of wood, including nonfibrous substances and lignin (which binds the cellulose fibers together and gives the tree its rigidity). Because of these impurities and because the mechanical pulping process cannot avoid damaging some of the cellulose fibers, groundwood pulp paper has excellent opacity and printability but relatively poor color and cleanliness, is not long lasting, and to make newsprint, it is normally reinforced by the admixture of about 12 to 20 percent coniferous chemical pulp. In the chemical pulping process, where chemicals are used to dissolve away lignin and other substances and release the cellulose fiber, removal of impurities is at the maximum and damage to the fiber at the minimum so chemical pulp paper is very strong. But chemical pulp costs much more than groundwood pulp because the yield from the chemical process is much lower (45 to 55 percent) and chemicals are expensive.

The manufacture of pulp into newsprint uses methods that in principle have hardly changed since the technique of papermaking was invented nearly a thousand years ago. Cellulose fibers are dispersed in a great volume of water; they are fibrillated so they retain more water, swell, and become gelatinous; the water is then removed by drainage, compression, or evaporation; and as they dry, the fibers' surfaces bond together to form the sheet of paper, which is then finished to the standards required. The difference today is that newsprint is not made by hand but by highly automated machines operating at great speed, machines that can now be up to 10 meters wide, running at 60 kilometers per hour.

A very small proportion of the world's newsprint, mainly in regions where coniferous trees do not grow, is made from raw materials other than softwood. For over thirty years, there have been experimental papermaking ventures using the hard, short-fibered wood of deciduous trees, like the birch, which abound in temperate regions, and the tropical and equatorial hardwoods, like eucalyptus. These can now produce excellent chemical pulp and are increasingly used in the manufacture of other papers. But hardwood makes a very poor quality mechanical pulp, and this has so far limited its use in newsprint manufacture.

However, when economic realities demand, its use can be very worthwhile. In Japan, which is the world's second largest newsprint consumer and depends on imports for about half of its pulp supply for papermaking, newsprint is made with an admixture of 30 to 40 percent short and brittle hardwood fibers. It is of inferior quality, but waste is kept to a minimum by careful computer and human control. Experiment in the use of hardwood continues as it does also into ways of using the possibly much cheaper raw materials, the annual plants like bamboo, or the by-products of annual crops, like sugar cane bagasse. Technical progress in making paper from these sources has to some extent already relieved the pressure on the northern coniferous forests as historically the only suppliers of wood pulp. But world demand for newsprint is still expanding, particularly in the developing countries, and with the continuing rises in world prices inspires greater efforts to find alternative, possibly cheaper, raw materials and methods of manufacture.

Since newsprint is an internationally traded commodity, prices everywhere keep in step. The sudden rise between 1972 and 1974 happened worldwide and was a wrenching shock to newspaper finances. Since then prices have gone on rising and are expected to continue to rise by rather more than prices generally at least for a time.[2] This is the most radical of all the recent changes in the newsprint world. The traditional, profligate evaluation of newsprint as a very cheap product in practically unlimited supply no longer holds good and may never do so again.

A Brief History of Prices

Paper . . . so cheap that, supposing you are interested in proving that circulation of your newspaper is something immense, enormous, you can do it for certain with slight expense . . . you can print a couple of hundred thousand extra papers at a cost which is almost nothing compared to the advertising you may get from it; and then, instead of a circulation of 500,000 every morning, you can show a circulation of 700,000. The utility of that mass of printed papers is not destroyed. They are not sold to be sure, but the printing is recorded truthfully by the presses, and they show in the figures of your circulation, which advertisers love to examine.[3]

That was the euphoria of the wood pulp revolution of the late nineteenth century when the invention of the mechanical grinding process had made possible the commercial production of paper from cheap and plentiful wood and had brought newsprint into being.

"At the turn of the century the pulp-paper industry found itself in the enviable position of making money at a tremendous rate, with seemingly no end in sight."[4] From 1890 to 1900 the value of wood pulp in the United States quadrupled, while its price fell by over a third. Most of it was made into newsprint, which also became cheaper and cheaper.

Newspapers cut their cover charges: "the period of the 1880s and 1890s . . . was when newspapers sold for 4, then 3, 2 and sometimes 1 cent per copy."[5] They also grew in size: "*The World* which was a 5 cent paper in 1866, sold for 2 cents in 1882, and this for a paper which had doubled its size to 8 pages in the same year."[6] And they enormously increased their circulation (2.4 times in 20 years).

Far more familiar to contemporary ears are the cries of anguish from newspapers in the period before the introduction of wood pulp. The following statements were made in 1866:

We have been fighting hard for the past year against a rise in the price of the *Daily Argus* . . . had hoped to get paper at the old price . . . it now costs almost double.[7]

In consequence of the enormous increase in the cost of white paper within a short time over its previous rates, and the increased cost of every article entering into the composition of a daily newspaper, including labor, the *Boston Post, Advertiser, Journal* and *Traveler* have increased their costs.[8]

At that time paper was made primarily from old rags but also from any other waste material that would serve and had no use elsewhere. This had been so from the time of its first invention ascribed to T'sai Lun, god of the papermakers, in China in 105 A.D. The Arabs discovered the secret of papermaking when, in repelling an invasion of Samarkand in 751 A.D., they captured some Chinese prisoners who knew the art. They were able to use abundant local crops of flax and hemp as raw material. But as the demand for paper increased and its manufacture spread through Islamic lands, papermaking again became a recycling activity. It was as such that Europeans eventually learned its technique when they had overcome their strong prejudice against all things Islamic and the opposition of the guilds of parchment makers. A license to make paper issued in England in 1589 to Sir John Spilman, jeweler to Queen Elizabeth, was also "to gather for the purpose, all manner of linen rags, scrolls or scraps of parchment, old fishing nets et cetera."[9]

Paper was essential for the new European invention of printing, which opened the floodgates to an insatiably growing demand for knowledge, news, and ideas. As the demand for paper increased, there were recurrent crises of shortages of rags with accompanying rises in prices, which were a constant inspiration to find some new raw material. In 1781, the Royal Society of Arts, noting that the consumption of paper was "every day increasing" (and the price of rags every year higher), offered a reward for the making of paper from vegetable substances that had not previously been made into cloth. Nearly a hundred years later, the *London Times* was again offering a reward (of £1,000) for a new and readily available material that would bring down the price of paper. It was well known in principle that paper could be made from any cellulose-containing substance, but no technique for doing so had been commercially successful. The example of the wasp (who makes paper rather like newsprint, nearly as firm and made essentially of the same material—woody fibers) had not gone unnoticed. In 1719, Réaumur, the French scientist, had written:

Wasps make a very fine paper. . . . They extract the fibre of common wood and teach us that one can make paper from the fibres of plants without using rags or linen. They seem to invite us to try whether we cannot arrive at making fine and good paper by the immediate use of certain wood.[10]

In England in 1800, Matthias Koops had published his *Historical Account of the Substances Which Have Been Used to Describe Events and to Convey Ideas from the Earliest Date to the Invention of Paper.* He had earlier taken out patents for making paper from straw, hay, thistles, and other vegetable substances and for a process of extracting ink from old paper, repulping the paper, and using it again, and his book put his ideas into practice, being printed on paper made from straw, from nettles, and seven pages in the appendix from wood. He invested a large fortune in a well-equipped paper mill, but within three years he was bankrupt.

In the next 150 years there were many improvements in the technology of making paper from rags (chlorine bleaching, for example) and the mechanization of the papermaking process, but papermakers appeared to close their eyes to the possibility of using a different raw material. Meanwhile the demand for paper escalated, and the supply of rags dwindled. England, Europe, and then the United States fought for rags in a market still basically organized by the local rag and bone man and wholesale rag merchant. New sources were opened up in Alexandria, Smyrna, and Trieste and then India, China, and Japan. But in London in 1861, giving evidence to a Parliamentary Select Committee, the papermakers were pessimistic about the future. John Evans noted that "upwards of 100 patents had been taken out for different materials for the manufacture of paper," but "I think there is no probability of any substitute for rags being discovered."[11] The appetite for books and newspapers was insatiable. How could it possibly be fed?

In fact, esparto grass in England and straw in America were already being used successfully as sources of pulp and were beginning to cause the price of rags to fall from the peak in 1860. And although the Parliamentary committee never mentioned it, both the mechanical and chemical processes of pulping wood were already being developed. By 1900, Britain's paper manufacturers were importing 16,000 tons of rags, 194,000 tons of esparto grass, and 448,000 tons of wood pulp.[12] All concern about high costs and shortages had been obviated, and newspapers were luxuriating in an abundance of cheap paper, newsprint, for them the lifeblood of a revolution. Many restrictions had been laid on newspapers as they had struggled into existence in Europe in the previous two hundred to three hundred years. Governments had not viewed their development with wholehearted enthusiasm but rather had sought to restrain it by licensing laws, censorship, taxation, and other restrictions. And always there had been the high cost of paper to keep the price of a newspaper high and circulation therefore limited. Despite these constraints, such was the universal passion for news and opinion that newspapers survived and, in the end, flourished. Copies were widely read, if not widely bought, and demand rose as population and literacy grew. With the advent of newsprint, the last serious restriction was removed: the newspaper tiger was out of the cage. The price of a newspaper came within the reach of almost everyone, and almost everyone took advantage of this and bought at least one, and often more than one, every day. The mass communications industry had been born, and newspapers were holding a monopoly in it.

In the long history of the press, this period of preeminence was comparatively short-lived before what may in the end be a losing battle began with broadcasting and, later, the new electronic information media as competing purveyors of news, ideas, entertainment, and advertising space. Competition has brought changes, not least in newspapers' own methods of production, which have to change to encompass and take advantage of the new technology. Newsprint as a circulation medium is now in competition with the electromagnetic spectrum, which costs nothing. But until the 1970s, newspapers found no cause to worry and went on taking newsprint very much for granted.

Changes in the Product

It used to be said that newsprint is newsprint, meaning that newspapers the world over wanted the same basic commodity manufactured to agreed standards of moisture content, print quality, brightness, opacity, and weight and knew they could expect the standard product from the newsprint mills.

Until the 1970s the only changes in the industry were in patterns of production and consumption. For the first years of the century, the biggest producers of wood pulp were North America, Sweden, Finland, and Norway. In 1949 they accounted for 81 percent of world production. But by 1974 their share had dropped to 69 percent. North America remains the largest producer, but second and third now are the Soviet Union and Japan.[13] More than half of the present world output of newsprint is in the United States and Canada, a little less than a quarter in Western Europe (three-quarters of that in Finland, Sweden, and Norway), and the remaining quarter in Japan, the Soviet Union, and South America. The biggest consumer of newsprint is the United States, 10.2 million tons in 1977, more than four times as much as Japan (2,290,000 tons), the second largest consumer. California alone uses more newsprint than do France, Italy, and Greece combined. Of the 92 percent of total production that Canada exports, 65 percent goes to the United States. Thus North America is almost an autonomous economic unit.

The biggest consumers in Western Europe—West Germany, Britain, and France—are supplied mainly by the Scandinavians.

In recent years, however, there have been far more radical changes. Newspapers have changed their requirements. They are no longer all produced by standard methods, and production innovations—the changes from mechanical to electronic composition—require different qualities in newsprint.

Whether the individual newspaper has elected to remain with either letter press using plastic plates, converting the existing unit to some form of direct lithography, or to replace the entire press line with new offset units, the effect on newsprint has been to tighten the requirements the publisher has placed on the supplier.[14]

Newsprint mills, while struggling with the problems of adapting to these new and often conflicting demands, are in turn asking newspapers to accept innovations in newsprint, which pressrooms have to find new techniques for handling.

Newsprint used to be the one grade of paper to which a single quality standard applied and was internationally understood, but this is no longer true. One worldwide change in the definition of newsprint already widely accepted is the introduction of newsprint of significantly lighter paper weight than the traditional 52 grams per square meter (g/m^2 or gsm). Until recently it would not have been possible to use such paper for newspapers, but improved technology has made it so. The United Nations Food and Agricultural Organization now defines newsprint as weighing "usually not less than 40 gsm and generally not more than 60 gsm" and reported in its 1975–80 survey that

among the countries which now report their newsprint capacity in tonnages corresponding to the actual grammage expected to be made and which is normally lower than 52 gsm are Finland, Sweden, France, UK, USA and Australia. In New Zealand and Chile most production will be 48.8 gsm newsprint instead of 52 gsm as in the recent past.[15]

It expects that in the future more countries will use lightweight newsprint and weights even lower than 48.8 gsm will prove acceptable. Table 3.1, from the report of the British Royal Commission on the Press illustrates this trend.

Not only are there the new weights of paper but also newsprint made from new mixtures of pulps—from 100 percent recycled waste paper, from pulps made by new pulping processes, or from different kinds of wood fiber, or from nonwood fiber. These new technologies are all part of the constant battle to produce newsprint at a price that newspaper publishers will accept as reasonable. In the 1970s it has been a battle against increasing odds: the end of the era of unlimited, cheap fuel; inflationary rises in the costs of raw materials and labor; new governmental policies enforcing conservation and penalizing pollution of the environment. Profits from the manufacture of newsprint have been cut to the minimum and below, but, even so, prices of newsprint have increased (by double between 1972 and 1974) and gone on increasing.

Table 3.1 *Weights of Newsprint Supplied to the United Kingdom Market, 1972–1975*

	50–52 gsm	48.8 gsm	45 gsm
1972	81.2%	0%	18.2%
1973	77.0	0	23.0
1974	22.2	37.0	40.7
1975	12.5	44.0	43.5

Source: Royal Commission on the Press, *Final Report* (London: HMSO, 1977), table D4.

Note: Information relates to newsprint supplied by those companies approached for information by the commission. Between them they account for about 70 percent of the U.K. market. The commission's survey covered the suppliers of 97 percent of Swedish and Norwegian newsprint to the U.K. market; 59 percent of Finnish newsprint; and 48 percent of Canadian newsprint.

Table 3.2 shows how this happened in the United Kingdom.

The staggering rises in newsprint prices between 1972 and 1974 caused a radical change in newspapers' careless attitude to newsprint. Great efforts have been made in Europe and America to use it more economically and to cut down on waste. The interim report of the British Royal'Commission on the Press summed up the new situation, which affects newsprint consumers everywhere:

The proportion of operating expenditures taken up by newsprint costs has increased from 26.6% in 1970 to 31.4% in 1975. The total tonnage of newsprint used in 1975 was 530,000 tonnes (7½%) less than that used in 1970 but the total cost of the 1975 tonnage was £113 million as against £50 million in 1970, an increase of 126%. . . . At current prices a 1% reduction in usage achieves a saving of over £1 million. The savings would be significantly greater if prices increase.[16]

Agreeing with similar European and U.S. policy directives on waste control procedures, the report states: "In practice, newsprint waste can be reduced to a minimum by the imposition of and adherence to strict rules. Waste reduction can be achieved by i) effective reporting procedures; ii) attention to detail; iii) discipline in newsprint handling; iv) and selling all waste."[17]

Economy measures include using narrower reels (rolls) of newsprint, a change made practicable if the format of the newspaper is altered—cutting down margin and column width, having nine narrower columns on a page instead of eight with a margin, for example. The greatest single economy, though, has resulted from the use of lighter weight newsprint. Pressrooms initially had problems adapting to its use and there have been complaints about its quality, but its acceptance has meant lower distribution costs (which are based on tonnage), fewer reels to handle annually, storage of more days' supply in the same storage area, and longer reels with therefore fewer reel changes on the press, reducing web-break risk and wastage. All of the measures have

Table 3.2 *Price per Tonne of 50 gsm Newsprint*

	Price per tonne	Index (1970=100)
July 1957	£ 59.06	84.8
July 1963	55.85	80.2
July 1966	55.85	80.2
July 1970	69.63	100.0
July 1971	73.08	105.0
July 1972	76.25	109.5
July 1973	88.60	127.2
July 1974	154.37	221.7
July 1975	165.19	237.2
July 1976	184.28	264.7
May 1977	229.36	329.4

Source: Royal Commission on the Press, *Final Report* (London: HMSO, 1977), p. 118.
Note: The prices shown are those charged by Reed Paper and Board (U.K.) Ltd. There has been some tendency for the prices charged by the two U.K. producers and by overseas importers to differ in recent years, but the general trend has been the same whatever the source.

resulted in substantial savings. Some newspapers at least have been able to beat rising newsprint costs. The 1975 annual report of the *New York Times* showed that, compared with 1969, it was using less newsprint and making more money (table 3.3).

An Unstable Market

It has been said that in the United States the acceptance of lighter grammages did for wood fiber in newsprint what the nation had failed to do with oil: decreased the annual requirement by over 6 percent. However, the high price that newspapers are paying for their paper is not, as in the nineteenth century, caused primarily by a shortage of its raw material, wood, but much more by the escalating costs of the labor and energy needed to get the wood out of the forest, process it into pulp, and manufacture the pulp into paper. Demand for softwood has grown steadily since World War II at about 5 percent a year and, around 1972, outpaced supply, causing an increase in prices. But there are further resources of softwood that can be exploited if higher prices make it profitable to do so. The main determinants of prices of wood, pulp, and paper are demand and production costs. Strong demand enables the producer to raise prices. Newspapers have reacted to higher newsprint prices by cutting their demand for it. Their success is of real, if necessarily short-term, value to them, but it does very little to solve the problems of the newsprint manufacturers, who need higher prices

Table 3.3 *Response of* New York Times *to Rising Newsprint Costs,*
1969–1975

	1969	1975
Newsprint use (tons)	385,000	267,338
Newsprint expense	$57 million	$66.4 million
Advertising revenue per ton of newsprint	$476	$730
Circulation (weekday)	940,000	828,000
Annual circulation revenue per ton of newsprint	$121.60	$265

Source: *Newsprint Facts* (May–June 1976): 1.

to meet soaring production costs and higher profits to finance investment in new technology and mechanization, the only hope of putting a
brake on those costs.

Newspapers make unreliable customers. Their consumption of newsprint can fluctuate wildly because it is closely related to the cycle of
advertising expenditure, which in turn is extremely sensitive to the
national economic cycle. If a country's economy is flourishing, newspapers can sell more advertising space, increase editorial content to
balance it, and thus expand the number of their pages and use more
newsprint. In a slump the reverse happens, and also a paper may lose
readers who may give up buying a newspaper as part of their attempt to
economize. Thus circulation drops, and the demand for newsprint is cut
again. But in good times and bad, newspaper publishers demand short-
term contracts and rock-bottom prices, and the unsteady market makes
it very difficult for newsprint mills to resist these demands. In the
1960s and early 1970s, the real price of newsprint was actually declining. From 1960 to 1972, the cost of newsprint and ink to British national newspapers decreased as a proportion of total costs and even in
1975, after the big jump in newsprint prices, it had not returned to 1960
levels (table 3.4). Similarly figures for a typical daily paper of 700,000
circulation in the United States show newsprint as 32.5 percent of total
publishing cost in 1958, 26.05 percent in 1975, and 26.90 percent in
1976.[18]

There is international agreement among newsprint manufacturers
that the effects of this long period of static pricing were bad for
everyone in the newsprint world, as the following quotes from Sweden,
Canada, and the U.K. show:

I would not say that the newsprint industry gave away the products but
in any event we spoiled the publishers by absorbing all price increases
on raw materials, wages and on investment. This had to come to an end
and we all know when and how it happened.[19]

(Swedish mill executive Olle Lundqvist)

One of the root causes of the abrupt upward climb of the '70s was the
long price plateau extending from 1953 to 1965 inclusive. Over those 13
years newsprint price increases totaled $8. The "unduly low" levels of

Table 3.4 *Newsprint and Ink as a Proportion of Total Costs of British National Newspapers, 1960–1975*

	"Quality"		"Popular"	
	Dailies	Sundays	Dailies	Sundays
1960	33%	29%	42%	38%
1966	29	n.a.	33	n.a.
1970	24	23	30	29
1971	23	22	31	26
1972	24	24	30	25
1973	25	25	32	28
1974	29	29	37	33
1975	28	28	36	34

Source: Royal Commission on the Press, *Final Report* (London: HMSO, 1977), table D6.

Note: The Royal Commission adopted the convention of classifying national newspapers in the U.K. as "qualities" or "populars," which refers primarily to content. Quality papers devote less editorial space to pictures and more to political, social, and economic features than the populars. Populars are read by many more people and cost less than the qualities.

newsprint cost made it a bonanza era for newspapers. They enabled publishers to keep ad. rates relatively low. "Cheap" ad. space and rapid expansion of retail sales caused ad. volume to swell. Newsprint consumption grew tremendously . . . then the '70s brought inflationary acceleration of costs . . . the accumulated need for a better price had to be met head-on. . . .[20]

(a Canadian mill economist)

The producers . . . had to suffer returns that were insufficient to encourage new investment in what is a highly capital intensive industry. In consequence, during the exceptional economic boom of 1973 and 1974, there was insufficient capacity to meet the rapid increase in demand for newsprint—both for immediate use and for building up stocks against a future shortage of supply. Prices rocketed and newspaper economies were shaken to their foundations.[21]

(Alex Jarratt of Reed International Ltd.)

By 1972 a North American paper company operating worldwide could expect only a 4.7 percent return on capital investment, as compared with 15.6 percent in 1950.[22] In the United Kingdom, most newsprint makers were accepting less.

In 1967 a study by the Paper and Board Industry Economic Development Committee noted paper mill returns on capital (at replacement value) mostly in the 0 to 10 percent range (before tax and dividends) and commented: "It is difficult to see how mills which return so little in the way of depreciation or plough back capital can provide or raise the necessary financial resources to perpetuate even the present output levels, let alone expand or engage in major modifications."[23] British

73

paper manufacturers have come to concentrate on the more profitable papers; production of newsprint declined from 17 percent of the total in 1964 to 8 percent in 1974 to 7.9 percent in 1976. Statistics show a decline in newsprint production in other European countries, notably France, where it has fallen steadily since 1964 (table 3.5).

The increasing difficulty of making any profit out of newsprint has resulted in the concentration of its production in forest-rich countries where production costs are lowest. Large, integrated Canadian and Scandinavian mills benefit from economies of scale and, because they are located in or near forests, have the advantages of owning their supplies of raw material and paying minimum costs for handling it. If they run on hydroelectricity, their energy costs also will be comparatively low. British producers' evidence to the Royal Commission on the Press suggested that

the cost of producing newsprint in Canada has been almost half the cost of UK production. Even allowing for the higher delivery costs of an overseas producer, a UK price which scarcely covers the costs of UK produced newsprint will give a substantial margin of profit on newsprint produced overseas.[24]

Integration of all stages in the production of newsprint, from wood to pulp to paper, has obvious benefits, and the number of integrated mills is increasing, but for those newsprint producers who cannot integrate, it results in a further handicap: increasingly high prices for wood pulp. It has been estimated that integrated mills now absorb 87.5 percent of the world's production of pulp. This inflates the price of the 12.5 percent that is available on the world market, and nonintegrated mills find themselves, in the words of Hans Gorsler, president of the European Confederation of Pulp, Paper and Board Industries (1977), "trying to compete against imported paper that sells for barely more (or even less) than the per tonne cost of imported market pulp."[25]

Even the largest integrated mills suffer from the low levels of profitability forced on them. A Canadian analyst calculated that newsprint prices rose at an average rate of 3.3 percent a year from 1956 through 1974, although the actual prices remained static until 1973 and then skyrocketed. Cheap newsprint helped newspapers to finance new plants, new processes, and "a wave of corporate acquisitions that enhanced the newspapers' future," but he questions whether newspapers and mills would not be better off today if actual pricing had followed the average increase year by year: "Of course, it's an impossibility. Prices are a function of supply and demand, expenses and revenues, and the market place. But the exercise illuminates some aspects of the relationship between mills and newspapers."[26]

At present, newspapers have succeeded in economizing on newsprint, but they cannot do without it, and in time demand will rise again. And, to quote an American former large-scale newsprint buyer,

When demand does tighten up, some people will find there isn't as much newsprint around as they thought. . . . It is a common mistake to

74

Table 3.5 *Worldwide Paper Production Data*

	Total Paper and Board Production (tonnes × 10³)		Newsprint Production (tonnes × 10³)		As % of Total Production		
	1970	1977	1970	1977	1970	1977	% Difference
United Kingdom	4,903.9	4,077.8 (4,152.1 1976)	757	326.2 (1976)	15.4	7.9 (1976)	− 7.5
France	4,134	4,719.8	430	219.3	10.4	4.6	− 5.8
Germany	5,516	6,603.2	408	5,441	7.3	8.2	+ 0.9
Netherlands	1,596	1,625	167	123.2	10.5	7.6	− 2.9
Italy	3,451	4,288.4	273	234.5	7.9	5.5	− 2.4
Austria	1,017	1,424.4	155	131.6	15.2	9.2	− 6.0
Spain	1,280	2,160	115	106	9	4.9	− 4.1
Turkey	118	388 (1976)	10.7	79.6 (1976)	9.1	20.5	+11.4
Sweden	4,358	5,059.9	1,030	1,110.7	23.6	22.0	− 1.6
Norway	1,421	1,518	554	537	39	35.4	− 3.6
Finland	4,260	4,622	1,305	978.8	30.6	21.1	− 9.5
Canada	11,137	12,138	7,814	8,154	70.2	67.2	− 3
United States	46,117	52,611	3,035	4,385	6.6	8.3	+ 1.7
Japan	12,973	15,702.8	1,917	2,369.8	14.8	15.0	+ 0.2
Australia	109,212 (1972)	1,210 (1976)	181.9 (1972)	220 (1976)	16.6	18.2	+ 1.6
New Zealand	447.4 (1973)	647	47.7 (1973)	282	47.7	43.5	− 4.2

Source: Pulp and Paper Quarterly Statistics 1978/2 (Paris: Organisation de Co-opération et de Développements Economiques, 1978).

think that paper producers are locked into the production of newsprint. . . . Mills will close down machines or switch to other grades in order to stay in business if their newsprint return on investment is not adequate.[27]

Against this background of low profits, newsprint manufacturers are battling with soaring production costs unprecedented in their history, the result of escalating oil prices and worldwide inflation.

Production Costs

The major components of production costs are raw materials (such as wood and chemicals), labor, energy, and transportation. In evidence to Canada's anti-inflation board, one company president said in justification of a newsprint price increase that in the period 1973–1976 the cost of wood, depending on the area, increased 36 to 40 percent, mill labor about 40 percent, and freight rates 30 percent. Electricity costs had jumped as much as 70 percent, with further rises to come, while steam generated from oil or natural gas was costing 110 percent of the 1973 rate.[28]

Raw Materials

World consumption of wood has grown steadily in the last quarter century. In 1949 output of wood pulp was 20 million tonnes; in 1974, a peak year, it was 120 million tonnes, which required an input of 435 million cubic meters of wood. This is only a small part of all the wood growing in the world, much of which has so far been unexploited (for example, there is unexploited wood in North as well as South America and in the Soviet Union).[29] But the commercial forests in the industrialized countries, which supply the traditional raw material for newsprint, coniferous wood (softwood), have raised their level of production to or near to the maximum sustainable level of forest output. Sweden, Finland, and Norway were exporters of wood in 1949. They are now dependent on imported wood for an increasing proportion of pulp production.

Economic and commercial factors determine the survival or expansion, and the value, of forest land in competition with roads, houses, dams, lakes and other industries. The unlimited timber era is finished in the United States, as in Europe, and increasing demand for softwood must be met by more intensive management of existing forests. Improved forestry practices have increased the rate of tree growth, and improved tree breeding may increase it considerably more. There has also been rapid development in maximizing the use of the wood harvested. Industrial wood residues (such as slabs, chips, and sawdust) are an added source of raw material and make no additional drain on the forest. This and increased recycling of waste paper has made possible the expansion of pulp and paper production at a much higher rate than the production of round wood pulp wood from the forest. But increasing supplies of wood from the forest will in the end be the critical factor in the future availability and cost of wood pulp.

Canada has large reserves of unexploited forest, possibly nearly as much again as is now being cut. But much of it is relatively inaccessible and therefore considerably more costly to harvest. There are also increasingly strict environmental restrictions on timber cutting, which add to its costs. The Soviet Union may double its forest product exports from 1970 to 2000 but is likely to absorb all the surplus. Half of the world's wood volume is in the tropical forests of developing regions, but this is not the coniferous wood traditionally used for newsprint. As these regions develop culturally and economically, their demand for newsprint increases. In 1975, 63 percent of their then requirement had to be imported, with a subsequent strain on foreign exchange resources. As a result there has been some development of unconventional newsprint manufacturing techniques in these countries using furnishes of, for example, hardwood, bamboo, and cane bagasse. These countries are expected to become increasingly self-sufficient in this area (table 3.6).

In the industrial countries the emphasis has been on increasing production by increased mechanization of wood harvesting. In a brief to the Quebec provincial government, a newsprint company said that the company's forest operations productivity had increased fourfold between 1951 and 1976; direct logging productivity had grown by 50 percent between 1968 and 1976. Without this improvement in productivity, it calculated wood costs would have been $14 a cunit higher in 1976. (One cunit is 100 cubic feet of solid wood, approximately enough to make one ton of newsprint.) The cost of this mechanization program was $10.8 million.[30]

Labor
Another company report said that over fifteen years, investment of $147m to improve productivity, although necessary to reduce costs to

Table 3.6 *Rate of Self-Sufficiency in Developing Countries*

Year	Newsprint	Paper for Other Printing	Other Papers and Boards
1960	0.21	0.68	0.66
1965	0.34	0.76	0.77
1970	0.36	0.64	0.78
1975	0.37	0.74	0.81
1980	0.59	0.80	0.95
1985	0.70	0.85	0.95

Source: *Tendences et perspectives de la demande de l'offre et du commerce de la pâte et du papier jusqu'au 1990* (Rome: FAO, 1977), quoted in *Paper* 190, no. 6 (1978).
Note: The rate was determined by dividing production by consumption.

meet competition, returned less than 2 percent annually.[31] Although capital costs of mechanization are high (the newer woods machines cost up to $250,000), new equipment can halve the number of man-hours needed to produce a ton of newsprint. This is a useful saving if, as has been calculated, wood costs in Canada are made up of 65 percent labor and that cost is increasing at a compound annual rate (1971–1977) of 13 percent a year.[32] In 1967, Canadian logging employed 51,000 at average hourly earnings of $2.69. In 1977 it employed 40,000 at average earnings of just over $7 an hour.[33] At a management symposium in Switzerland, the substantial increases in wages and lower productivity rates than in the United States were given as reasons for production costs in most industrialized Western European countries, catching up with 1972–1973 U.S. levels and now exceeding them.[34]

Inflated labor costs may be reduced by mechanization, which needs fewer workers, and modernization to increase productivity, since labor and other costs are less if output per hour is greater, but the investment necessary is often prohibitive and, at the least, a very heavy burden in an industry that has been starved of profits over many years.

Energy
Another large question in the future of an industry as energy intensive as newsprint is how it will cope with spiraling fuel costs. Awareness of the finite nature of oil and coal resources and high and constantly increasing costs of all forms of energy have generated a great deal of research into new techniques and processes that use energy less or use it more efficiently. At the Centre Technique Papetier in Grenoble, serious consideration has been given to the development of small, specialized newsprint machines that would use far less energy. One technique (being developed also in the United States and the United Kingdom) that might make this more possible abandons the traditional papermaking process for one that joins fibers together in a dry state, replacing the direct fiber-to-fiber attraction, which happens when the fibers are immersed in water, with indirect binding (fiber-binder-fiber). Such a process should require only 70 to 75 percent of the energy used in a conventional system.

In use already are new kinds of furnaces and boilers developed to burn new kinds of fuel, particularly the wastes generated in the production process (hog fuel, for example, which is composed of bark and sawmill wastes like sawdust and shavings). The cost of such a development is very high—for one Canadian mill $13 million, nearly as much as the company's total earnings in that year—but it should cut production cost of newsprint by several dollars a ton.[35]

High energy costs could drive out of the market a new pulping process that has been the brightest hope in the newsprint industry. Known as thermomechanical pulping (TMP), this is a process of refining wood chips, or even just sawdust, under pressure. Conventional mechanical

78

pulp, the main furnish of newsprint, has strength and quality limitations and has to be improved by the addition of the more expensive chemical pulp; and the lighter the grammage of the newsprint, the more chemical pulp is needed. Newsprint profitability is very sensitive to changes in the cost of chemical pulp, and in recent years this has inceased sharply with simultaneous shortages. TMP produces mechanical pulp with far superior properties in burst, tear, breaking strength, and tensile energy absorption so that it can be directly substituted for chemical pulp. Very satisfactory newsprint can already be produced from 100 percent TMP, and research is succeeding in still further improving its strength and quality (treating the wood chips with chemicals before refining—chemithermomechanical pulp, for example). But all mechanical pulping processes use a lot of energy, and the energy consumption of TMP is about 50 percent higher than for stone groundwood, and 50 percent higher again if any other but coniferous wood is used. Even so TMP has been accepted and commercialized extraordinarily quickly. At the end of 1976 the annual capacity for TMP in the world was around 2.4 million tons and orders had been placed that would take the total to 5.2 million tons. An annual growth is expected between 1975 and 1980 of 38.5 percent in Europe and 86 percent in North America.[36] Most of the TMP produced is used for newsprint.

Thermomechanical pulp could reduce capital outlay. For mills of equivalent size, capital cost for mechanical pulp is only about 20 percent that of chemical pulp; and where increased pulp mill capacity is required, TMP obviates the need to expand chemical pulping facilities, which would in turn require expansion of the cooking, brownstock washing, screening, bleaching, liquor recovery, and lime kiln and/or recovery boiler systems. It also improves yield from wood resources by between 10 and 15 percent.

Research is in progress into ways to reduce TMP's energy consumption. In Finland energy is recovered from TMP systems in the form of low-pressure steam to be used for paper drying, with consequent energy savings of some 15 percent. However, fuel costs could rise so much that the economic value of TMP might be totally eroded except in Scandinavia, which has the best raw material and comparatively high wood costs.

Environmental Costs

One of the many advantages of TMP is that it creates fewer environmental problems than do conventional groundwood and chemical pulp, no light consideration since government regulations in Canada, the United States, and Europe are becoming increasingly strict about the disposal of the vast quantities of liquid and solid wastes left behind when newsprint is shipped off to newspapers. "Polluter pays" policies can mean closure for older mills. Antipollution systems mandatory by government regulations in Canada are estimated to account for 25 percent of the capital required for a new mill. Continuing investment in pollution control is a heavy cost on existing mills. As an example, a Canadian mill estimated that it had spent $25 million in the decade 1966–1976, enough to pay for half a 100,000-ton-per-year newsprint machine, half the annual production of which (50,000 tons of newsprint) would have meant an annual gross revenue of over $15 million.

Successful development of pollution control techniques can create useful economies of production if it involves recycling mill wastes and more efficient use of raw materials. Water, a vital constituent in the papermaking process, can now be reused a number of times. It is purified each time within the mill, and during the process fibers and other materials are recovered; 128,861 tons of pulp, worth £8 million to £10 million, were recovered in the United Kingdom in 1974 by the use of such devices as disc filters, floculators, and flotation units.[37] Steam can be raised by chemical recovery boilers, which burn the spent liquid (rich in lignins and chemicals) from the cooking of wood chips in chemical solution to produce chemical pulp. Wood wastes now sometimes burned as an alternative to oil were formerly buried at some expense (incineration outside the mill is forbidden for environmental reasons).

Raw materials, labor, energy, pollution control—the best hope of beating rising costs in all areas lies in research and development of new technology and in modernization of existing mills to increase productivity. Many technological innovations are being developed, but they need investment of costly capital, which for a long period profits from newsprint have not been providing.

Cost of Capital

Pulp and papermaking is a capital-intensive industry, and the soaring costs of capital have made the cost of constructing a new mill impossibly high. Richard Mazer of Hudson Pulp and Paper Co., explaining why his company abandoned a new newsprint mill in Florida, said, "The capital cost kept growing every time we studied the matter more closely. It reached a magnitude that entailed the kind of risk we didn't think we could take. The numbers just didn't work out."[38] The mill would have cost something like $130 million. The resultant capital cost was therefore about $1,000 per annual ton of production. This would mean interest and amortization charges alone on each roll produced of about $90 compared to about $10 at typical existing installations. Such newsprint would have to sell at over $100 a ton more than the 1977 market price. Similarly in 1977 Anthony H. Tyrell of Pitfield Mackay, Ross and Co. saw the possibility of a newsprint supply shortage in the near future and costs of $50 to $100 more per ton if investment in new mill capacity were to be justified. In 1978 a Canadian mill executive said that because the cost of constructing a newsprint plant today is close to $300,000 per daily ton as against $130,000 in 1972, there is no chance of new units being built in Canada in the near future. He predicted, "There will be some additional Canadian capacity from relatively inexpensive speed-up programmes but this will probably be offset by some obsolete plant and/or machine shutdowns."[39] The cost of investment in the developing countries is 50 percent higher even than in industrialized nations because of the infrastructure costs.

Worldwide growth of pulp and paper products, as shown in the FAO 1977–1978 survey, has declined in the last three five-year periods. This will not be reversed quickly. Mills take 3 to 5 years to build, and the time needed to plan them is considerably longer. The head of the FAO's Policy and Planning Service of the Forestry Department believes that "In spite of the reduced rate of expansion in pulp and paper mill capacity, it appears that it may be adequate to match the more moderate demand level now foreseen to the beginning of the 1980s."[40] But if demand does increase to exceed supply as it did in 1973–1974 and push newsprint prices up steeply, will the manufacturers have the capacity to take proper advantage of this?

From the point of view of the manufacturer, newspapers must now accept a steady and continuing rise in the cost of newsprint:

We are selling our product too cheaply. We cut down the trees, truck them to the mill, put them through an expensive pulping process, and then across a high-capital-cost and high-energy-consuming paper machine. We wrap the paper and ship it 500 miles or more and land it in a newspaper pressroom at about 15 cents a pound.[41]

(Canadian mill executive, 1977)

Unless newsprint prices are maintained at a sensible level, there could be contraction of supply. Replacement of old or construction of completely new newsprint capacity is an extremely costly business at any time and has become particularly so in these recent inflationary years. . . . Major oscillations in price help neither the producer nor the user since neither is sufficiently flexible in its operations to survive effectively in such an environment. Clearly there has to be sufficient competition to encourage efficiency both in the production and use of newsprint. But over the years, it will be essential to ensure that the general level of newsprint prices is sufficient to sustain adequate production capacity. If not, it will be the publishers—who have no alternative but to use paper—who will be the ultimate sufferers.[42]

(Alex Jarratt, Reed International Ltd.)

For two years now, selling prices have been extremely unfavourable as compared with production and other costs, such as pulp, pollution control, investments and energy. Therefore paper prices should as soon as possible reach an acceptable level. In the absence of sufficient profits, there is scant chance for any meaningful capital projects.[43]

(Hans Gorsler, 1977)

From the point of view of the newspaper publisher, an inexorable rise in the price of newsprint may be hard to take, as the British Royal Commission on the Press reported in 1977:

Publishers can respond in a variety of ways to continuing increases in newsprint prices. They can absorb them in lower profits or bigger losses or reduce the amount of newsprint they use or try to generate more revenue to cover higher costs by raising cover prices or advertising rates. . . . Some publishers of national newspapers are already making losses or such small profits that they cannot carry the whole cost of further increases in newsprint prices without raising cover prices further, as happened in January 1977. They will also have to charge more for advertising space. But it seems unlikely that they will all be able to produce sufficient additional revenue to meet the higher bill for newsprint since, at a given level of demand for advertising space, higher rates tend to drive some advertisers to other outlets.[44]

Also after a certain level of increase in newspaper price, circulation drops. Between 1965 and 1975, prices of national newspapers in Britain increased by over 300 percent, twice the rate of increase in the retail price index, and in that period, sales per day of national weekday newspapers dropped from 15.5 million to 14 million and those of Sunday newspapers from 24 million to 19.5 million. Before the era of cheap newsprint, demand for printed news was such that it overcame high prices. But now, in the industrialized world at least, the value of the newspaper, both to reader and advertiser, has declined in the face of competition from the broadcasting media.

Possible Remedies

The largest Canadian newsprint producers (members of the Newsprint Information Committee) have long been concerned with the health of their newspaper customers. Since the 1950s they have been sponsoring large-scale national advertising research on the newspapers' behalf. In 1977 they financed the most comprehensive readership research ever conducted in North America, the first step in the American Newspaper Publishers Association's Newspaper Readership Council's massive industry-wide effort to increase newspaper readership. Also the Canadian newsprint industry, through the Canadian Pulp and Paper Association, has joined with ANPA, through its newsprint committee, to consider seriously a systems approach to newspaper problems, recognizing that the primacy of the newspaper medium is now at stake. As Derek Page of the Pulp and Paper Research Institute of Canada explains,

The paper machinery manufacturer supplies paper machines to the paper maker; the paper maker sends his paper via the transporter to the publisher; the publisher, who gets his presses from the press manufacturer, his advertising from the advertiser, his news from the news editor, his ink from the ink manufacturer, puts this all together and ships his product to the customer. . . . We can no longer survive by ensuring the viability and efficiency of our own immediate operation. We must see what's happening to other segments of the system with which we interact. It is a false economy to take steps to increase the efficiency of our own operation if by doing so we seriously upset the efficiency of another segment. . . . Let us look cooperatively at the efficiency of the total system and move in a direction that will maximise it.[45]

82

In Europe, IFRA (The Research Association of the International Newspaper Colour Association and the Fédération Internationale des Éditeurs de Journaux et Publications) is also working along these lines. In the words of Gerard Martin, former vice-president of IFRA,

The doubling of the price of newsprint in the course of a few years, and the almost certain continuation of rising prices when the economy of the western world recovers, makes it necessary for producers and consumers to cooperate, since the measures envisaged by the producers to put a brake on rising rates have important repercussions on the consumers. If this cooperation is to be fruitful it must be accompanied by a clear understanding of the difficulties encountered by all parties.[46]

Governments of countries that are net importers rather than producers of newsprint and are therefore facing increasingly heavy import bills (sometimes made heavier by unfavorable currency exchange rates) are beginning to pay attention to the state of their own newsprint industries. The United Kingdom Newsprint Users' Committee, representing all of the major domestic users of newsprint, told the Royal Commission of the Press that further reductions in home production "would be unfortunate." It should be maintained to preserve employment, ensure a strategic reserve for emergencies, and make savings in the balance of payments.[47] It has been calculated that by 1977 the U.K. wood products import bill had risen to £2,340 million, this sum almost exactly matching the import savings from North Sea Oil; and that in 1974 the European Economic Community (EEC) imported about 60 percent of its consumption of wood products at a cost of about £5,000 million per year, second only to petroleum products.[48]

The European Confederation of Pulp, Paper and Board Industries (CEPAC) was founded in 1963; its members are Germany, Belgium, France, Italy, the Netherlands, the United Kingdom, Denmark, and Eire. Its role is to study all economic problems of interest to the industry. Hans Gorsler, a past president, characterized it thus:

Its "basic mission" is to collect, "comprehensive, readily available and harmonised statistical data between our various countries . . . on consumption, production, imports and exports . . . as would make it possible for us . . . to gain a better insight into current situations, the prospects for our industry and the orientations we should take for our own sake and in the general interest."

There is also an embryonic EEC common policy for the pulp, paper, and board industries of member countries since they were taken as a test case when the European Commission was considering the desirability of a common industrial policy (like the common agricultural policy). In 1974 the commission recommended to the Council of Ministers programs of afforestation; improved collection and processing of waste paper; specialization in areas of expertise; extended research and development into the technologies of raw materials, the manufacturing process, and the finished product, the environment, the strategy of the industry, and overseas commercial policy. This communication, not approved, was to be superseded by directives in each of the areas covered.

83

Continental Europe was once a heavily forested area and could certainly grow more of its own wood if this were economically desirable. The yield of wood per hectare is higher than in Scandinavia and the average harvesting age is much lower, around 50 years as against 100 years in the far north. Unexpectedly substantial current reserves of timber sources have been revealed by EEC paper industry surveys. It is estimated that present commercial forests could improve production by at least 30 percent in the next 15 years and be up to about 200 million m^3 by the first half of the next century.[49] There is no chance of the EEC's achieving self-sufficiency in wood or wood products, nor does the commission see this as a desirable aim for a trading community. But every tonne of home-grown pulp wood decreases the strain on the EEC balance of payments, so improvements in forest policies and more economical use of indigenous timber are being encouraged.

Improving the supply of home-grown wood fiber is necessarily a long-term policy. A more immediate measure of protection for the newsprint industries of member countries has been the introduction of tariff regulations. Each year the EEC estimates the amount by which home production of newsprint will fall short of consumption and that amount (the duty free quota, or DFQ) may be imported free of duty. But on any imports newspaper publishers make over their country's allocated share of the DFQ, duty must be paid. If this quota can be fairly fixed, it should restrain publishers from buying imported newsprint when their home producers have spare capacity, even in times of depressed world demand when the larger foreign newsprint mills are more able to reduce prices.

Other government interventions that can help their own newsprint industries are to give subsidies related to newsprint usage, as in Sweden, for example, and to encourage the greater use of recycled waste paper in the manufacture of newsprint. In June 1976, the U.K. government made £23 million available to help the papermaking industry to utilize greater quantities of indigenous fibers, hoping "to bring about a substantial increase in waste paper usage and hence a more assured demand for waste paper in the future."[50] Holland has given direct financial aid to mills using waste paper; Norway has offered subsidized loans to companies storing waste paper; and Sweden has passed legislation to oblige householders to segregate newspapers and magazines from other waste.

The technology of recycling waste paper is well developed. The deinking process (washing the print from products like once-read newspapers and computer paper) has improved so much that good-quality newsprint can be made from 100 percent recycled fiber. It is a costly process because the waste has to be sorted into grades by hand and because it creates large amounts of effluent, which are expensive to treat, but these are not the problems for which political help is needed. The stumbling block to the proper exploitation of recycled fiber is the difficulty of collecting the waste paper. This is still done mainly by

84

voluntary groups, one-man businesses, and local authorities, a structure hardly more sophisticated than the rag and bone man and rag merchant of the rag paper era. The business has not been attractive to large, commercial enterprises because prices for waste paper are tied to the cyclical swings of the paper market and therefore fluctuate wildly. The economic boom of 1973 sent waste paper prices up and stimulated its collection, but in 1974,

newsprint consumption declined owing to economy measures and shrinking advertising sections, so that the re-use of waste paper also went down. However, it was not till later that falling prices put a stop to waste paper collection, with the result that today, at least in Europe, thousands of tons of it are piled up unwanted.[51]

European governments know that this problem must be overcome. Even in wood-rich Scandinavia and Finland, waste paper as a fiber resource is being seriously considered. For Common Market newsprint manufacturers, recycled fiber is the one bright hope of a secure future. The Royal Commission on the Press in the United Kingdom quoted the report of the Waste Management Advisory Council, "Collectors, especially local authorities, need assured outlets, while the paper industry needs assured supplies if it is to invest in new plant and machinery to use more waste paper," and hoped that the WMAC "will keep the supply of waste paper under review in view of the importance of indigenous raw materials to the newsprint industry of the United Kingdom."[52]

The biggest consumer of newsprint in the world is the United States. It has large timber resources and in the first decades of wood pulp paper produced almost all of the newsprint that was used. However after 1913, when an act of Congress allowed newsprint to enter the country duty free, newsprint production declined as the American newspaper publishers turned to importing nearly all of their supplies from the rapidly expanding Canadian industry, which, with its natural advantage of vast forests of spruce, could offer lower prices. Some measure of independence was regained around 1936 when industrial leaders and newspaper publishers began to promote the manufacture of newsprint from rapid-growing southern pine. This was successful, and commercial production of newsprint in the South has flourished. However the greater part of the U.S. newsprint requirement today is still supplied by Canada. Canadian labor problems (which led to long strikes between 1973 and 1976), the political unrest in Quebec, the steep increases in newsprint prices, which seem bound to continue, and possible future shortages have again turned newspaper publishers' minds to the possibility of improving home supplies. At the very least, this would cut transportation costs by bringing newsprint manufacturers closer to their principal customers. And some have considered reversing the present-day trend to larger and larger mills with their huge capital and energy costs and building instead numerous small mills. The potentialities of improving indigenous forest output and of using recycled fiber are being fully explored. Serious consideration is also being given to the development of a new papermaking fiber, kenaf (*Hibiscus cannabinus*), a fast-growing annual or biennial plant similar to cotton, hemp, and sisal. When cultivated in suitable climatic conditions, it is capable of a yield 3 to 5 times that of softwoods and can also be produced at about half the cost.

The successful use of this new raw material for newsprint developed out of a U.S. Department of Agriculture project started in the 1950s to try to increase the relatively few plants (of the more than 250,000 species known) that are cultivated by man. It was thought that non-woody cellulose sources might one day become important to the paper industry, and, after appraisal of some 500 species, kenaf was chosen for development as the best prospect for a new source of paper pulp. Experimental work has been going on since the 1960s, making kenaf into chemical pulp, blending it with wood pulp, both hardwood and softwood, and making it into different grades of paper. Then in 1977, with the cooperation of the ANPA and the *Peoria Journal Star*, newsprint made from 100 percent kenaf pulp processed thermochemically was used in an experimental commercial press run.

The test was an unqualified success. The newsprint proved to have nearly the same bursting pressure level as commercial newsprint with only 5% less tensile strength. It was also somewhat stronger . . . was nearly identical to the commercial newsprint in brightness; opacity was similar for both. . . . Under close visual inspection, the newspaper pages printed on the kenaf-made paper compare favourably with the regular newsprint run.[53]

In 1978 more kenaf was grown to produce a further one hundred tons of newsprint and was effectively tested in commercial press runs. The team that developed this new fiber source feel that it is now ready for exploitation. They are, however,

acutely conscious that the real economic potential can only be gauged by the future course of demand and supply conditions in the pulp and paper industry; not so much the actual course as revealed in time, but the course expected by pulp and paper industry management. Kenaf's economic potential resides in the pulp and paper industry's strategy adopted to cope with the future. Perhaps the relevant question is at which point in time will pulp mill management decide that the tree supply is becoming sufficiently scarce and that Kenaf's cost and capability are sufficiently strong to bring it on stream.[54]

Newsprint Facts reported in January 1978 that some analysts of the North American newsprint situation felt that 1978 was a year of decision for future supply since it takes two or three years to build a new mill and "the statistical lines of supply and demand intersect in 1980. In other words, current reserve capacity of about a million tons in Canada plus new tonnage coming on stream in the next two years will be fully employed in that year should growth continue at the expected rate."

How many manufacturers will think it worthwhile to continue their fight to keep newsprint a viable industry; to develop new technology and build new mills in the belief that the present increasing costs of producing the traditional newsprint paper can be checked and that demand for it will be steady and expanding; or to step into the relative unknown and develop new resources that will bypass old problems?

The firm that is mainly concerned about its present operations and economic survival will make different decisions than the firm whose present security is established and its plans are to provide for continued operation of the firm 50 or even 100 years into the future.[55]

If newsprint looks like becoming an uneconomic proposition, there will be no new ventures, and production of it will inevitably shrink; there are already more profitable uses for groundwood pulp. Governments may intervene to encourage and protect, but in the end everything depends on the behavior of customers. If newspapers in their present form disappear, there could be no demand for newsprint. If newspapers continue but cannot or are unwilling to pay an economic price for newsprint, manufacturers will stop making it. If, however, newspapers' demand for newsprint is strong and profit on it assured, new technology and new resources will be developed as wood pulp was developed a century ago, and that demand will be met.

Notes

1. British Paper and Board Industry Federation, *Facts*: "Newsprint."

2. Royal Commission on the Press, *Final Report* (London: HMSO, 1977), p. 58, paragraph 7.6.

3. Charles A. Dana, "Newspaper Making, the Conditions, Usefulness and Future of the Press" (address to Cornell University, 1895).

4. David C. Smith, "Wood Pulp and Newspapers 1867–1900" *Business History Review* 38 (Autumn 1964).

5. Ibid.

6. Ibid.

7. Ibid.

8. Ibid.

9. Dunkin, History of Dartford (Harleian manuscript 2296 f. 124b) (London: British Library), p. 305.

10. René de Réaumur, French naturalist and physicist, 1683–1757, quoted by Harrison Elliott, "The Evolution of Newsprint," *Papermaker* 23 (1954):45–49.

11. Select Committee (1861), p. 9.

12. D. C. Coleman, *The British Paper Industry, 1495–1860* (Oxford University Press, 1958).

13. S. L. Pringle, "Future Availability of Wood Pulp—A Global Picture." *Paper*: World Development issue, 1978:11.

14. Malcolm A. Borg, quoted in *Pulp and Paper* (September 1977):105.

15. United Nations Food and Agricultural Organization, *Pulp and Paper Capacities Survey, 1975–1980* (Rome, 1976), pp. 1–10.

16. Royal Commission on the Press, *Interim Report,* Appendix B, p. 83.

17. Ibid., p. 83.

18. *Newsprint Facts* (May–June 1977):6.

19. Ibid. (January 1976):2.

20. Ibid. (September 1976):4.

21. Alex Jarratt, Livery Lecture to the Worshipful Company of Stationers and Newspaper Makers, January 1977.

22. British Paper and Board Industry Federation, *Facts*: "Newsprint."

23. Quoted in Christine Thomas, *Paper Chase* (Earth Resources Publication, London 1977).

24. Royal Commission on the Press, *Final Report*, Appendix D, p. 115.

25. Interview with *Paper* 187 (April 1977):343.

26. *Newsprint Facts* (September 1976):4.

27. Peter B. Hickey, ex-newsprint buyer of Gannet Newspapers, now publisher of the *Ithaca Journal,* quoted in ibid. (September 1977):2.

28. *Newsprint Facts* (March 1977):3.

29. The FAO has estimated that the world's standing timber volume was so vast at 300 b m³ that a doubling of the pulp wood required for all uses by 1985 would represent only an additional 0.1 percent drawn on existing sources.

30. *Newsprint Facts* (March 1978):3.

31. Ibid. (January 1978):4.

32. Data from Abitibi-Price mills in Canada reported in *Pulp and Paper* (September 1977).

33. Canada Pulp and Paper Association estimate, reported in *Newsprint Facts* (November 1977):4.

34. European Management Symposium, Davos, Switzerland, 1977. Quoted by Hans Gorsler, who chaired the paper and wood industry branch discussion.

35. *Newsprint Facts* (November 1976):2.

36. *Pulp and Paper* (August 1977):111.

37. British Paper and Board Industry Foundation, *Facts:* "Water."

38. *Newsprint Facts* (May–June 1977):3.

39. Ibid. (January 1978):4.

40. S. L. Pringle, "Future Availability of Wood Pulp," *Paper* (1978):11.

41. *Newsprint Facts* (January–February 1977):2.

42. Jarratt, Livery Lecture, January 1977.

43. Hans Gorsler in an interview with *Paper*, April 4, 1977.

44. Royal Commission on the Press, *Final Report,* p. 61.

45. At a seminar in Toronto sponsored by the Canadian Pulp and Paper Association, May 1976.

46. Gerard Martin, "Can Technology Overcome the Newsprint Problem?" *Newspaper Techniques* (April 1975):4–12.

47. Royal Commission on the Press, *Final Report,* p. 59.

48. R. M. Cumming, "Fibrous Raw Materials and the Pulp and Paper Board Industry—Part II," *Paper*, June 19, 1978.

49. Ibid.

50. Hansard (HC), November 18, 1976, vol. 919, col. 717.

51. "Waste Paper Recycling as an Economic Barometer," *Newspaper Techniques* (April 1975):1–2.

52. Royal Commission on the Press, *Final Report*, p. 62.

53. *Inland Printer/American Lithographer* (January 1978):48–50.

54. C. A. Moore, W. K. Trotter, R. S. Corkern, and M. O. Bagby, "Economic Potential of Kenaf Production," *Tappi* 59 (January 1976).

55. Ibid.

II

The Press and the State in Established Democracies

The public in all of the democratic societies of the world accept as a general principle that government must be kept out of the press's finances and out of its editorial policies. The conditions of the last two decades, however, have forced practice to diverge from theory. In almost every European society, government has been obliged to take on a new role, intervening in the management of the press. The purpose has not been to direct editorial policy but to help a given newspaper structure to survive in a society in which the needs of advertisers have not been identical with the audiences of given newspapers. The Scandinavian press, for example, has evolved around the political parties, and the basic public of a given newspaper has consisted of the supporters of a specific ideological approach. The consumer economy has developed advertiser needs that are in conflict with this established pattern of readership. At the same time the newspaper industry has been affected by the general range of raw material and distribution problems, and a pattern of local monopoly has started to emerge, arrested only by the creation of a system of public subsidy in Sweden, Finland, and Norway. Denmark eschewed subsidy and has lost a far higher proportion of its newspapers than its Scandinavian colleagues. We are therefore witnessing a new doctrine in these and other countries with firmly established democratic parliamentary institutions; it holds that the state may acquire a special enabling role, a duty of guaranteeing the existence of a certain pattern of information media in a society, without necessarily arousing fears of a government-dominated press.

Of course, throughout the age of broadcasting, the role of the state in the media has been a growing one, partly because of its necessary function as a regulatory mechanism, partly as a protector of national cultures against domination from foreign powers. For many European societies, the cultural content of mass society has been imported; the sheer profusion of American material has become a subject of political concern, even of despair. In the 1970s, the world has come to understand the tremendous dangers of media imperialism in the context of North-South relationships in the world, and it is sometimes overlooked that the smaller countries of Europe have been obliged to cope with the same problem since the end of World War I that vexes the third world today. European societies benefited from a well-established institutional base from which to conduct their struggle for cultural autonomy, which many of the third world nations do not yet enjoy. Hans Dahl, in his chapter on Norway, shows how the indigenous popular press was the bulwark against the imported mass culture; for this reason it was the press that attempted, with varying success, to provide the capital basis for the modern electronic media. Dahl's argument is one with resonances in many other societies: the press may demand to be protected by the state against newer electronic media, which may be dominated by foreign capital, and in so doing play the role of protecting a native culture and language. The Scandinavian countries have thus become foremost among those where the state is expected by the public in general to play a complex guaranteeing role in the media, even though that same public is vehement in its disapproval of state control over the flow of information. How far the state's provisioning of society with media can be kept apart from the state's control of content is a question that time will answer.

Karl-Erik Gustafsson's chapter shows how a large and complex body of doctrine and experience has now emerged in Sweden after more than a decade of state subsidy. Sweden realized that for subsidy to achieve the purpose of preventing the death of minority newspapers, or newspapers with a small section of a geographically defined market, cash had to be distributed selectively and deliberately to help the weaker papers that were losing the competitive struggle. The Swedish subsidy scheme is far more interventionist than those of other European nations. The importance of Gustafsson's account of the evolution of the scheme lies in the articulation of the underlying doctrine that seems to reverse traditional ideas about the maintenance of a free press.

Most countries have attempted to achieve similar results with nonselective subsidies. France, as we see from Antoine de Tarlé's chapter, has constructed an elaborate and informal system of intervention alongside its formal subsidies, which alone would not have sufficed to preserve newspaper competition. Some readers may find this article disturbing in its implications. The French government has become far more active than any other in the democratic world in manipulating the internal affairs of the newspaper dynasties, even though the French press remains one of the liveliest in Europe. Even state intervention of

92

the massive and complex kind described here does not appear to as-
phyxiate dissent, although many would expect it to do so if practiced in
most other societies. The basis of the crisis of the French press is financial. Between 1935 and 1970, the price of an average newspaper in
France consumed five minutes' labor time of an average worker, but in
the 1970s it doubled to ten minutes and cost the lives of a large group of
French newspapers, including several new titles bravely pioneered. De
Tarlé argues that state intervention, unless applied with extreme sub-
tlety and dexterity, causes more damage than benefit. What compli-
cates the problem is that it is the state that is today providing the
newspapers with their greatest potential source of competition in cable,
satellite, and local radio, all of which are searching for advertising
revenue and all of which are being researched and developed by departments of the same government that seeks to aid its defeated subject
and rival.

4

The Press, Most National of Media: A Report from Norway

Hans Dahl

Currently there is talk, and considerable evidence to justify it, of a world media imperialism, an electronic imperialism that subtly forces poor countries into dependence on the rich countries' multinational concerns. Foreign electronics creates a market to which an endless stream of programs can be exported. The pattern is comparable with classical raw-material-market imperialism, and it is said that American capital plays the same role in the twentieth century's media imperialism that British capital did in the nineteenth century's classical system.

Something that is often forgotten in the discussion of such concepts is the intermediate type, the country or market that may ironically warrant the definition underdeveloped but at the same time may enjoy the status of being itself a producer of mediaware. Such countries are often no less interesting than the pure type, and there are certainly many, the Scandinavian ones among them.

The Scandinavian countries import both hardware and software from multinational media companies. But they do have something that has allowed them to stand up against media imperialism: their press.

By means of data from Norway, but with a glance at the other Scandinavian countries, I shall endeavor to show that the role that the press plays within the total media in such an intermediate kind of country is something more and greater than simply the production (in this case, of a great number) of newspapers. The press as an institution has had a very great deal to do with how such a country has met the flood from the international media industry.

The Scandinavian Press

Available production capacity in the book and general print industry provides the usual starting point for the establishment of the press in Scandinavia, where the modern newspaper market was first opened up in the 1870s and 1880s. Newspapers were to be found before that date also, but it was at this time that establishments came so thick and fast that one can talk of a breakthrough. This breakthrough accompanied the extension of the vote and the consequent mobilization of the electorate through the comprehensive formation of political parties in the 1880s. The Scandinavian press became a party press, intimately connected to a political public of the classical democratic type. It also became a local phenomenon, an indigenous institution. New papers were established, and they were economically and technically independent of each other. They were oriented toward something that virtually no longer exists, the wholly local market. There are few institutions as decentralized as the press. The economic basis of this is clear. Experience in the pioneer period emphasizes that there is practically no bottom limit to how small a public a paper can have or to how many papers can be set up. It was so then because the local units in this part of the world were already small when the newspaper came into being. The reason was not the topographical wealth of mountain and fjord, as one might easily be led to believe, for the situation was the same in flat Denmark. Rather it must be attributed to many traditional factors, of which topography is only one.[1]

As well as its foundation on a very sparse population, the Scandinavian press before World War I was noteworthy for the large number of papers in each locality. Not only were the markets small, but in each one of them competition was great. The typical Danish town with its surrounding district had four papers right up to World War II: a conservative, a liberal, an agrarian, and a social-democratic one. Sweden and Norway had a less even structuring, but the three-paper market was the most typical. Several had more. A town such as Stavanger in Norway, with its 45,000 inhabitants, had five newspapers from the beginning of the century until World War II.

Press and Film

A powerful party press closely bound to local politics characterized the media structure that was dominant when film stormed in over the Scandinavian societies. It was a structure that proved itself comprehensive enough to imprint a decided character upon the new medium.

Film began, as in other countries, as a sort of curiosity about the turn of the century and gained a firm and lasting hold in the years between 1910 and 1920. It is not at all difficult to imagine what a chasm separated the celluloid world in the early days of the silent film from the pattern of daily life in a poor provincial country as strongly agricultural and pastoral in character as all Scandinavia then was. The generation of around the time of World War I was exposed to a cultural shock that can clearly be compared to, though by no means equaled by, that experienced when television erupted upon the third world in the 1960s.

The Scandinavian countries each responded differently to this development. In both Sweden and Demark, national film production was set up and entered what was soon to prove a phase of development that demanded little capital. This early wave in Danish and Swedish film was by no means uneventful and evoked such producers as Dreyer and Stiller. The development in Norway is more interesting from the point of view of the press. In this country, cinema became a public and official monopoly under the Cinema Law of 1913. The presentation of cinematographic pictures was defined as the sole right of the community. Most town councils chose not to distribute concessions to others but to establish an official municipal company that would be responsible for all presentation of film.

There has still not been any reliable investigation of the driving powers behind this extraordinary legislation, which in fact created an official media monopoly ten years before radio broadcasting came on the scene.[2] All the same, data from several towns seem to indicate that the local press people, especially the editors who also had seats on the municipal councils, provided something of a driving force behind the whole process. Their intention was not to prevent competition in the media market; rather they saw the financial possibilities that film offered. The reform was simply of a fiscal nature, even though the justification for it given in the press—and there was widespread newspaper controversy over these matters—for the most part concerned itself with the need for public control of a medium that through its intimacy and extensive infiltration threatened harm to children and the defenseless. A law of official film censorship was consequently passed simultaneously with the monopoly law of 1913.

The municipal cinema monopoly has thus always been supported by the press in Norway. The newspaper editor normally sits on the board of cinema directors, and the newspapers regard the local monopoly as something to be taken for granted. Attacks on this arrangement have come not from the press but from film people, the profession that has suffered in that the ticket income from movies never recirculates back to the production side, generating capital for future films. Film presentation does not provide the economic foundation for the production of new films. There is in that respect no film market in Norway, nor is there traditionally any real film production to speak of. Only within the last fifteen years or so has state support of film production been substituted for the box office income as a secure financial foundation.

It may well be asked what the press and the municipal treasury have gained, culturally, from their financial monopoly. It is an oversimplification merely to say that feeding its box office income back would in itself have created a foundation for a national film industry. Yet it is likely that the total absence of such a cycle has been stultifying to the development of ambitions and energy in the sphere of film production. The leading producing companies in both Sweden and Denmark have simultaneously been cinema owners, so that the box office income does get ploughed back into the industry. In Norway, the cinema monopoly has encouraged, and not hindered, the entry of Americanism via celluloid—the reverse of what was meant. It had been intended that a strict official monopoly, combined with strong state control, would "purify" the foreign films and their potential ill effects on national tastes and habits.

Phonograph Records

The next mass medium to invade the periphery of Europe was the record industry. Here the market was opened up and wholly supplied by foreign products. Recordings of the great Scandinavian artists were made right from the very beginning of the century, but the companies that pressed the plates and launched them were all foreign. Only in the 1950s was there a real upswing in Scandinavian national record production, and it did not affect Norway until as late as the 1970s. The typical record company in Norway is still the agency, the importer from foreign companies, which occasionally includes a Norwegian production in their repertoire. An independent market where national products finance themselves does not seem to exist.[3] As a record market, Scandinavia historically stands out as an underdeveloped region and has suffered the fate of other such regions. At least until the 1930s, it was a market for outdated material from the record industry. The pathephone, for instance, and various other outmoded stages of record production were marketed and sold longer there than in the bigger cultural markets, which had already gone over to the round 78-record by the turn of the century. However, since World War II, the Scandinavian market has not lagged so far behind in launching innovations, partly because of the growth of an advanced home electronics industry (Tandberg in Norway and Bang and Olufsen in Denmark).

Because historically records are not a national medium, the press has not played a prominent role in their development. The situation is different as far as the great media innovation of the 1920s, radio broadcasting, is concerned.

Broadcasting

Broadcasting came to Scandinavia from abroad. It was not only that the United States and Great Britain were the first in the field, but rather that radio programs were something one took in on one's receiver from distant parts of the earth. Well into the 1930s, the radio program was essentially an international event. The national program companies that rapidly emerged in all of the Scandinavian countries were a long way from being central national institutions, which they were later to become, or which the BBC already was in Great Britain. Quite apart from any other factor, the daily transmitting times were too sparsely scattered for that. Until World War II, radio receiving sets were marketed and advertised as instruments that could take in the whole world. Yet all the same, national program companies came into being in Scandinavia close on the heels of and often under the direct influence of the BBC. In this process, the press came to play a very considerable role, quickly emerging as the competent participant with legitimate rights in radio broadcasting, a place it retained right up to the breakthrough of television in the 1950s. The radio was simply a continuation of the newspapers. Broadcasting was therefore the editors' extended domain, and to an altogether much greater extent than in Great Britain.

Broadcasting in Scandinavia rose out of the meeting between the press and the electronics industry. In the 1920s the latter was overwhelmingly foreign and existed in the form of agencies that imported material from Marconi, Telefunken, and RCA. In Sweden there was in addition a certain amount of national electronic production, in Norway and Finland practically none at all. The industry therefore that exerted pressure in order to obtain official broadcasting, which could stimulate the sale of radio equipment, was what we today would interpret and regard as the local branch of the multinationals.

The press came into broadcasting as news vendor. The national news agency played a central role in all of the Scandinavian countries—in Denmark and Sweden by attaining a distinct role in the program companies that were set up and in Finland and Norway by going into broadcasting as a direct investor. In Sweden the press invested 66 percent of the capital behind the broadcasting company; in Finland that amount was somewhat less; and in Norway the press's share was a mere 10 percent of the industry's.[4] Even if the percentage invested was low, nevertheless it was significant for its influence in the process, which was just as important for the raising of funds as getting broadcasting acknowledged as a serious institution. In all of the northern countries, the press sanctioned broadcasting in public opinion and made a technical toy into a mediator of news, drawing it into what we would today call the general media picture.

99

The role of the press in both the innovation and the legitimation of the new medium of the 1920s can be described in detail for Norway. The institution whose archives show the first sign of interest in the establishment of broadcasting was the Norwegian News Agency (NTB), which, in June 1922, two and a half years before Norwegian broadcasting got into regular operation, entered into negotiations with the Marconi company's agent in Oslo. The first time the matter was mentioned in the national assembly in 1922, it was taken up by a press man. Even a premature concept of a media policy envisaging the forging of cinema and broadcasting into one unit under public direction was to come from a newspaper editor in a small town, who had previously directed both his own newspaper and the local cinema and who in 1924 could very well envisage a local broadcasting company under the same hat. Nothing came of his vision, but it marks an interesting stage in the opening phase of the broadcasting medium. In Norway, as in several other countries, the idea of a broadcasting program was realized in the form of a telephone newspaper. That was in Haugesund, a small coastal town, where one of the town's newspapers in 1918 gave telephone subscribers news, lectures, and music over the line at certain determined times in return for a set fee, a form of early protobroadcasting as good as any.[5]

There is also rich and detailed material covering the part played by the press in the broadcasting system, which eventually was set up in 1925. The Norwegian Broadcasting Company soon ran into problems in its relations with its biggest investor, the radio industry. Broadcasting had definitely and rapidly come to be seen as a public good, and it was not long before it was felt to be unreasonable that the radio industry should be making profits from the music, information, and news put out as a service—and a cultural service too at that, as soon came to be said—for Norway's scattered communities. Private profit from public activity has always given rise to problems in Scandinavia. When Norwegian authors went to court against the broadcasting company in 1928, it was in indignation over the fact that the profits of their own literary productions put out over the radio were going to the foreign radio industry by way of dividends from invested capital. Of course, judicially it was indisputable that shareholders should enjoy the benefits of the company's activities. But morally speaking it caused a bad taste within the sphere of public debate. From the close of the 1920s, the industry's economic advantages accruing from radio as a cultural public good came to be felt as illegitimate, and the state went in for the nationalization of broadcasting in order to prevent private interests from making a profit from it.[6]

The newspapers were, of course, private firms, as was the Norwegian News Agency, their joint investor in the broadcasting company. But unlike the radio industry, the press was not attacked; it was a legitimate partner in broadcasting. In the first place it was not foreign, and in the second place it was itself a cultural factor. On the way toward the state broadcasting company, which was set up in 1933, one of the many official plans considered the transfer of the whole of the new company's program activity to the Norwegian Press Union.

The press has played a historical role in the broadcasting media in Scandinavia. The role came to an end simply because the broadcasting system quickly developed into an independent institution managing its own affairs. The press was as unimportant with regard to the establishment of television in the northern countries in the 1950s as it had been the opposite with regard to radio in the 1920s. In the development of television, the broadcasting companies themselves took the lead, with the press merely on the periphery of decisions. It is only when a medium is introduced without its own institution, as was the case with film and radio in the early years, that the press has been able to play a decisive role in the establishment of the media structure in Scandinavia.[7]

The Videocassette

Such a new medium appeared again toward the end of the 1960s, when the videocassette was introduced as a consumer medium in Scandinavia. In the course of the winter of 1970–1971, American firms traveled around seeking out interested buyers. They were careless enough to let the publishers outbid each other, the one behind the other's back. As a countermeasure, in a sort of Scandinavian chain reaction, press, publishing, and educational capital suddenly stood together in each country and combined in the firm Nord-Video. The pattern is not exactly the same as that for film and radio. It is not the press as an institution that has accepted the videocassette, but its biggest publishers: the Schibsted group in Norway (Aftenposten, Verdens Gang), the Bonniers group in Sweden (Dagens Nyheter, Expressen), and the Berlingske House in Denmark (Berlingske Tidene and B A).[8] It can also be said that the press is a less eager participant in the video medium than the publishers are, for the videocassette is in the first place an educational medium that goes hand in hand with books rather than with newspapers. All the same, the development of the cassette follows the general media pattern, with the press as the backbone of a national media structure playing a leading role in the defense when the multinationals threaten to flood the market with a new product. Without a national press, a peripheral area such as Scandinavia would lie open as a defenseless underdeveloped country in the media imperialism prevalent in the twentieth century.

Media Policy

Some consideration should be given to the part the press plays in the formulation of public media policy. It is generally reckoned today that overall governmental policy or regulation offers a possible bulwark of defense against a foreign domination. A general media policy, which is abundantly discussed in Scandinavia at the present day, is expected to clarify such difficult problems as international satellite transmissions over television, the extent of the press subsidies, the international program exchanges, and eventually also the news structure within the media. Does the press contribute to the establishment of public institutions directed toward such goals? The answer is, not surprisingly, no. The press in Scandinavia is against state control of the international media just as the press in the West has set its face against any attempt at regulation of a general kind. The press in Scandinavia has kept official regulation away from itself entirely. Such control—and complaint—committees as have now been officially established for film and broadcasting are unknown in the press world. There exist an official film council and a broadcasting council nominated by the administration and Parliament together but no standing press council. Internal regulation has high priority with the newspapers, but they set their faces hard against any one but themselves exercising such a function. Practically the whole of the Scandinavian press was against the UNESCO declaration concerning the content and tasks of the mass media promulgated in 1978; it represented a view on state intervention that was rejected by the press organizations. The press tends to oppose official regulation to such an extent that today press organizations over the whole of Scandinavia are looked upon as conservative in media policy.

What else could one expect? The press is the backbone of the national media structure, a factor that has prevented these intermediate countries from being totally flooded by foreign products. But the press is at the same time itself a medium, guided by its own interests in the home market. It is a controller of others but also a participant, the oldest of all the media.

Notes

1. The pre–World War I Danish newspaper market consisted of some 64 publishing sites. The corresponding number for Norway (eight times the size of Denmark) was some 110. The figures are taken from the main sources of Scandinavian press history, Niels Thomsen, *Dagblad-konkurrencen 1870–1970* [The competition between Danish newspapers, 1870–1970] (Copenhagen: Gads Forlag, 1972), and Svennik Hoyer, *Norsk Presse mellom 1865 og 1965: Strukturutvikling og politiske mønstre* [The Norwegian press, 1865–1965: Structural development and political patterns] (Oslo: Institute of Mass Communication Research, 1978). The history of the Swedish press is dealt with in a large number of monographs; the one perhaps most often quoted is Lars Furhoff, *Upplagsspiralen* [The spiral of newspaper growth] (Stockholm: Norsteds, 1967). See also Stig Hadenius et al., *Partipress, socialidemokratisk press och presspolitik 1910–1920* [Party press, labor press and press policy] (Stockholm: Raben & Sjogren, 1970).

The classical structure of the Scandinavian press underwent drastic changes after World War II. In the years 1950 to 1975, the total number of daily newspapers shrunk from 112 to 50 in Denmark; from 133 to 89 in Sweden; from 191 to 156 in Norway; and from 104 to 88 in Finland. It was not so much the number of publishing sites as the number of competing papers within each local region that was reduced. Figures as quoted in Hoyer, *Norsk Presse*, p. 305.

2. The best account is Sigurd Evensmo, *Det store tivoli. Film of kino i Norge gjennom 70 ar* [The great variety: Films and cinemas in Norway, 1907–67] (Oslo: Gyldendal, 1967).

3. No record history is written for either of the Scandinavian countries, and the reliable statistics seldom go further back than the 1950s (for Norway, only the 1960s). Indeed most record company agencies seem to have thrown away their archives, an unhappy state that probably reflects the particular underdeveloped state of the market in Scandinavia.

4. See also H. F. Dahl, "The Scandinavian Broadcasting Monopoly: An Economic Interpretation," in M. Berg et al., eds., *Current Theories in Scandinavian Mass Communication Research* (Grenaa: GMT, 1977).

5. I borrow the term from Carolyn Marvin, whose unpublished paper "Proto-broadcasting" throws a very interesting light on the sources of the early radio broadcasting program.

6. More details in H. F. Dahl, *Hallo Hallo! Kringkastingen i Norge 1920–40* [The history of Norwegian broadcasting, 1920–40] (Oslo: Cappelen, 1975).

7. The introduction of television in Denmark is treated in the official broadcasting history of that country: Roar Skovmand et al., *DR 50* (Copenhagen: DR, 1975). Two interesting studies of Norway are Helge Østbye, "Om innføring av fjernsyn i Norge" [About the introduction of television in Norway] (Bergen Institute of Sociology, 1972), and Erling Kjekstad, "Da fjernsynet kom til Norge" [When television came to Norway] (Oslo Institute of History, 1974) (both are university dissertations). There are no similar studies from Sweden or Finland.

8. "Video—den lange revolusjonen" [Video: The long revolution], *Dagbladet*, December 8, 1977.

5

The Press Subsidies of Sweden: A Decade of Experiment

Karl-Erik Gustafsson

Theoretical Basis

In our view, the state has a responsibility for the mass media. Firstly, it has the responsibility to ensure that freedom of expression and freedom of the press are formally and in reality guaranteed by legislation. Journalists must be guaranteed the right to seek information and to disseminate their knowledge. However, the state's responsibility is wider than this. In the service of democracy and its citizens the state has a responsibility to create and maintain an information and press system that will accommodate many and diverse voices. In Sweden this means in concrete terms a press subsidy of more than Kr. 300 million a year.

This passage comes from an article by Bert Levin, the Liberal undersecretary for education, in the largest Conservative daily newspaper in Sweden, *Svenska Dagbladet* (circulation: 180,000), at the beginning of December 1978. He was discussing the declaration that was adopted by the UNESCO General Conference in Paris in 1978. This position does not occasion much debate in Sweden any more. It is no longer controversial to maintain that the state has a responsibility for the structure of the mass media or that the press can preserve its independence under a system of selective subsidies.

Criticism of the principle of selective subsidies at present comes solely from the Conservatives. The Conservative members of parliament (55 out of 349 in the Riksdag) and editorial writers (usually those who write in sound and profitable newspapers) want selective subsidies reduced or abolished altogether and the general subsidy increased. The Conservatives regret that their largest newspaper, *Svenska Dagbladet,* receives a subsidy. Some of them seriously maintain that it does so only because the authors and advocates of the system need a hostage in the debate on subsidies and "an alibi for the objective unimpeachability of the system." *Svenska Dagbladet* itself is the only Conservative paper that defends the system of selective subsidies, but not out of gratitude.

Naturally the greater the state's contribution to the press, the more important it becomes that the purpose of the subsidy should be formulated with precision. Before the subsidy was introduced, and even after the first subsidies were paid, the aims were very general. They gradually became more specific.

The policy of the subsidy system is based on the conviction that the press fulfills or may fulfill certain tasks that are essential for the maintenance of the democratic system. In its formulation, its authors were influenced by the social responsibility theory of the press, which was developed at the end of the 1940s by the Hutchins Commission on Freedom of the Press. This influence was seen in particular in the thorough analysis of the functions of the press made a few years ago by a state committee that discussed the role of the press on the basis of the following four functions attributed to it:

- To give information to citizens so that they can form views on social questions (and to provide elected representatives with information regarding the views of citizens and groups).
- To comment on events in society either independently or as a representative for organized social groups.
- As a representative of the public to scrutinize the activities exercised by those holding power in society.
- To promote communication within and between political groups, trade unions, and other voluntary groups in society.

The availability of daily newspapers varies throughout the country and it is difficult to make any generalizations about the role of the press in Sweden. However it is no exaggeration to say that it has a special position. Despite their great success, radio and television have not eliminated newspapers. Generally newspapers contain fuller information on many social questions than radio and television do. They are extremely important for local and regional news. With regard to comment, they are in a different position from that of radio and television. Sveriges Radio, which has a monopoly in radio and television broadcasting, must, by law, be impartial and objective. The scrutinizing or critical function of the press has developed differently in Sweden than in the Anglo-American countries. One reason is the strong political connections of the Swedish press. Most Swedish papers have political sympathies with one or two of the five parties represented in the Riksdag. A paper is either a government organ or an opposition paper. Compared with individual papers, radio and television can therefore fulfill the scrutinizing function more consistently, and the newspapers are much more important for promoting communication within and between organized groups than radio and television are.

The press is considered better equipped for its tasks if, as the traditions of the party press in Sweden ensure, many views are represented by many separate newspapers. It is regarded as a minimum requirement that the various political factions should have newspapers in which they can express their views.

The policy of the Swedish government emphasizes the press as an instrument of representative democracy. This is a deliberately restricted view of the role of the press, since it has other functions. Newspapers are also organs for news and advertising; they report family news; they report entertainment news; and they publish radio and television programs and comment on them. However the government's policy is not aimed at these general functions. It is important that advertisers should have access to effective organs and that consumers should be able to obtain comprehensive information on goods, but to create many outlets for advertising is not one of the aims of the government's policy. Even if all newspapers were monopoly newspapers, they could still serve the economic system effectively as advertising media. The government's policy is concerned with the functions of the press in the democratic system. Its aim is to preserve competition in the places (there are about twenty of them) where it still exists and to attempt to create competition in places where it has disappeared or has never existed.

This policy and the program of subsidies were formulated during the 1970s. Will they also suffice for the 1980s? The answer to this question is uncertain. Developments in this field may entail changes. There are signs of a lesser degree of political alignment in the press. Since 1973 the biggest morning daily in Sweden, *Dagens Nyheter,* with a circulation of more than 400,000 has described itself as independent of any political party. Other papers have placed the word *independent* before the political adjective in their masthead, e.g., "independent Liberal" or "independent moderate." These changes have affected only nonsocialist papers, and none of them has ceased to be a member of that group. However less dependence on a particular party may mean that a paper can perform its scrutinizing role in a different manner.

Since 1977 local radio has been added to the activities of the national radio and television board. Broadcasting has begun from twenty-four local stations. Thus radio has entered a field, local news, in which the press has a leading role. Experiments recently initiated with neighborhood radio are intended to give political, professional, voluntary, and religious organizations a new means of communicating with their members and sympathizers at the local level. This may give radio a greater opportunity to compete with the press, promoting communication within and between groups.

During the 1960s, press matters came within the Ministry of Justice. At the beginning of the 1970s, they were transferred to the Ministry of Finance. At the end of 1978, they were transferred to the Ministry of Education, which also oversees matters relating to radio and television.

These changes reflect three stages in which different aspects predominate. The first two are the legal aspect (the press subsidy and freedom of the press) and the economic aspect (financing of the subsidy). The recent change may mean that press matters will now be seen in the context of the mass media of communication as a whole, where they naturally belong.

The purpose of this chapter is to provide a basis on which the question may be considered of how effective selective press subsidies are in Sweden. A survey of the structure of the press is followed by a short summary of the program of subsidies to provide the necessary background.

Because the decision to grant a subsidy is a political one, the political basis of the subsidy system is of interest. I shall consider the questions of the source of the initiative for the system, the degree of support that it has received, and the extent of political opposition and show that considerable difficulties arose before the system was adopted.

On the other hand, the distribution of the subsidy should not be decided by political criteria. Since it is essential that the press should preserve its independence from the state, the distribution system must be determined objectively on the basis of criteria regarding economic conditions for newspaper publishing. The scientific basis of the system must therefore be described before the efficacy of the system itself can be considered.

The final section, "Structural effects," deals with the questions of whether the press can preserve its independence and whether the system has had any effect on competition.

The Structure of the Press

Newspaper coverage in Sweden is among the highest in the world. Despite the fact that many papers have disappeared and there have been few new papers started in recent times, readership has not fallen. About 80 percent of all households buy at least one morning paper. About 1.2 million single copies of evening papers are sold every day. Surveys have shown that 97% of all Swedes between the ages of fifteen and sixty-five read newspapers regularly and that the average time spent in reading papers is thirty minutes per day.

One reason for these very high figures is an efficient distribution system, covering both early delivery of morning papers to homes and the sale of single copies. The number of inhabitants per retail sales outlet for newspapers (whether exclusively or together with other goods) is about five hundred. The home delivery system covers about 2.5 million subscribers every day. In countries with a low newspaper consumption, there is, characteristically enough, no delivery service, and the number of inhabitants per sales outlet is many times greater.

There are about 150 newspapers in Sweden, only four of these evening papers (table 5.1). Papers are sold mainly on subscription, with the exception of the evening papers, which are sold in single copies. About 40 percent of Swedish newspapers do not appear more than three times a week. Only 13 papers (the 4 evening papers and 9 morning papers) appear seven days a week. These account for about 50 percent of the total sales of all papers (4.8 million), mornings and evenings each having 25 percent. The population of Sweden in 1978 was about 8.3 million.

Swedish papers, even those in the largest towns, are mostly local or regional. The only really national papers are the two Stockholm evening papers: *Aftonbladet* (Social Democratic) and *Expressen* (Liberal). Only about a third of their sales are in the Stockholm area.

The geographical distribution of newspapers sold by subscription, with well-defined local and regional markets and very little national coverage, means that newspaper publishers are relatively small. There are only five morning papers with a circulation of more than 100,000: *Dagens Nyheter,* Stockholm (405,000), *Göteborgs-Posten,* Göteborg (300,000), *Svenska Dagbladet,* Stockholm (180,000), *Sydsvenska Dagbladet,* Malmö (115,000), and *Arbetet,* Malmö (105,000). The last is a Social Democratic paper and the rest are nonsocialist papers. The next four biggest papers have circulations ranging from 50,000 to 100,000. The evening papers, *Aftonbladet* and *Expressen,* have circulations of 430,000 and 520,000, respectively. The circulation of the other two evening papers is about 100,000.

Swedish morning newspapers can be divided into three main categories: monopoly newspapers, competing newspapers, and complementary newspapers. Within the last category there are two sub-

Table 5.1 *Types of Newspapers in Sweden*

Category	Number of Newspapers
Morning newspapers (mainly subscribed)	
Monopoly newspapers	
High periodicity	43
Low periodicity	29
Competing newspapers	40
Complementary newspapers	
Editorial (mainly opinion weeklies or biweeklies)	29
Other (suburban weeklies)	7
Evening newspapers (single copy sold)	
National distribution	2
Regional distribution	2
Total	152

groups, opinion weeklies and suburban weeklies (see table 5.1). With the exception of the opinion weeklies, some immigrant newspapers, and one national religious paper, Swedish papers have a wide readership. There are no "quality" newspapers.

Newspaper circulation as a whole showed a net decrease of about 1 percent in 1978. The losses were mainly in large towns, particularly Stockholm. Almost two-thirds of the decreases were suffered by the evening papers, whose circulation has been falling gradually in recent years. One of the reasons for this is probably a slight reduction in the efficiency of the distribution system. Another is that the market segments at which the Stockholm morning and evening papers are aimed are shrinking.

Newspapers are an important medium for advertising. Together with other press media, the daily press has the biggest share of the Swedish advertising market, amounting to about 40 percent. Direct advertising is second with about 20 percent. There is no radio or television advertising in Sweden. Broadcasting is financed by licenses. One of the main reasons for this is that the government does not want to weaken the position of the daily press in the advertising market. Apart from the evening papers, advertising revenue accounts for about 65 percent of the total revenue of Swedish papers. In the case of evening papers, the figure is only 25 percent. Attempts have been made to make nonevening papers less dependent on advertising revenue (and therefore also on general economic conditions) by increasing the newspaper price, but the effect has not lasted. One reason is that publishers are concerned with increasing circulation. Despite the fact that the opportunities for greater sales are small, all publishers like to show an increase, however tiny. They are therefore reluctant to increase newspaper prices, which may cause a drop in circulation, even though this would be more than compensated for economically by the higher sales revenue.

Until the beginning of the 1970s, structural development in the newspaper sector was in line with that in the rest of the economy and followed the trends in the most closely comparable retail sectors. The most prominent feature was a reduction in the number of publishers.

During the 1940s there were more than two hundred newspapers producing one to seven issues per week. Closures began in 1950, and over a period of twenty years about one hundred newspapers disappeared, either closing down or incorporating in other papers. During the same period about fifty newspapers were started, of which about twenty still are published.

Structural reorganization hit mainly the small papers. Most of those that disappeared were small. In 85 percent of the cases, circulation was less than 10,000, but some of them had circulations that were large for Sweden. If this trend had continued, many of the bigger papers would have been in danger.

During the 1970s, closures did not stop completely, but the trend has been arrested and only one large newspaper has closed. Many attempts were made to rescue it (some of which may have hastened its demise). Also new papers have been started in recent years. Even though they are small and only appear once a week, they are an important addition to the stock of papers available. The most important factor in this new situation has been the state subsidies.

The Subsidies Program

The support provided by the state for newspapers (general newspapers appearing at least once a week) consists of both selective and general measures. Selective measures take the form of loans and subsidies in particular cases to an individual or to cooperating newspapers. An example of the general measures is tax concessions. Although the general measures have been in force for a very long time (there has been a special postal rate for newspapers since the beginning of the nineteenth century), selective aids are of recent date. The subsidy system was introduced in 1969 and has gradually been strengthened. The program of subsidies for the 1977–1978 tax year is shown in table 5.2.

The need for state subsidies for the press has been analyzed in three parliamentary reports on the press, in 1963, 1967, and 1972. The fourth state committee was appointed at the beginning of 1978. Its task is to make a general survey of the present system, but it is not expected that there will be any changes of principle. The committee's terms of reference provide that the system of subsidies should have the same object as at present: that is, that it should promote a multiplicity of

Table 5.2 *Selective Subsidies to the Press, Fiscal Year 1977–1978*

Type of Subsidy	Year of Introduction	Amount in Million Swedish Kroner
Operational subsidies to newspapers in a weak market position (yearly)	1971	156
Development aid to needy monopoly newspapers (time limited)	1976	7
Establishment aid to complementary newspapers (time limited)	1976	3
Incentives to collaboration		
Joint distribution (yearly)	1970	53
Coproduction (time limited)	1976	5
Cooperation on the advertising market (time limited)	1976	
Loans fund (time limited)	1969	109

newspapers, and that it should be selective (to ensure that weaker papers are helped in their competition against stronger ones).

The main emphasis of the program of selective subsidies is on operational subsidies for low-coverage papers, defined as those whose circulation covers less than 50 percent of the households in their place of publication. It has been shown that a circulation of less than this is not usually enough to make a paper competitive. Production subsidies were introduced in 1971 and have since been increased in 1972, 1974, 1976, and 1978. They were almost doubled in 1972, but subsequent increases have been less: about 50 percent in 1974 and 1976 and about 20 percent in 1978. In 1979 the committee proposed that the subsidy granted to low-coverage newspapers with a particularly low coverage (less than 21 percent) should be increased by 25 percent, a total increase of less than 10 percent. The proposal was accepted by the Riksdag.

In certain circumstances and after special scrutiny, an operational subsidy may also be granted to high-coverage papers, those whose circulation covers at least 50 percent of the households in their place of publication. The operational subsidy is paid solely to subscription newspapers.

For high-periodicity papers, the amount of the subsidy is calculated on the basis of the consumption of paper for editorial text. Consumption is taken as the average over three years so as to eliminate the effect of large fluctuations in particular years. The degree of coverage is also calculated in the same way. There are certain minimum and maximum limits.

For low-periodicity papers, the operational subsidy takes the form of a fixed amount; it is lower for regional papers and higher for national papers. The coverage limit for low-periodicity papers is lower than that for high-periodicity papers. Operational subsidies have been paid, either continuously or for a limited period, to about seventy papers.

Selective subsidies are also paid to two other categories of newspapers. Two forms introduced in 1976 were development subsidies, granted for a limited period mainly to small papers with a monopoly in their place of publication, and establishment subsidies, which are mainly intended for the establishment of low-periodicity papers. These subsidies are granted after scrutiny of the particular case. Since their introduction, development subsidies have been granted to eighteen papers and establishment subsidies to six papers.

Other subsidies are intended to encourage newspapers to undertake joint activities. Since 1970 a certain amount per copy has been paid to papers that use the same distribution system. This distribution system is operated by two national and two regional distribution companies and is used at present by practically all newspapers. The amount of the joint distribution subsidies has been increased three times.

Since 1976 subsidies have been granted to encourage joint production operations (typesetting and printing) and sale of advertising space. A subsidy may be granted in certain cases for large joint projects in the industry as a whole. In order to qualify, the project must be economically justifiable. So far, only seven of these subsidies have been granted, and they have been used solely for technical cooperation and projects covering the sector as a whole. There is much greater scope for a joint project than that represented by the number at present subsidized, but the party press traditions are an obstacle to cooperation. It is difficult to get the nonsocialist papers to cooperate with Social Democratic papers. Principles are sometimes more important than practical realities.

Newspaper publishers may obtain loans wtih favorable terms from the Press Loan Fund, which was introduced as an experiment in 1969 and made permanent in 1976, when qualification for a loan was made more stringent. A loan will not be granted to individual newspapers if it is considered that a cooperative arrangement could be achieved on reasonable terms. Moreover, even if that is not the case, a loan will not be granted unless the paper is in a weak competitive position. Fifty-three newspapers have received loans so far, usually for plant renewal.

One of the main principles in the formulation of the system of subsidies has been that the rules should be objective, easy to apply, and operate automatically as far as possible. It is considered that there should not be any opportunity for the state to interfere in the content of a newspaper by means of the subsidy system or any reason for anxiety that such interference could occur. The largest portion of the subsidy is distributed in accordance with that principle, although certain forms of subsidy do entail scrutiny of the particular case.

The system is administered by a committee of eight members, five of whom represent the five parties in the Riksdag. The committee has a secretariat, which processes applications and is responsible for the administrative management of the scheme. It publishes annual reports on its activities, which also provide a useful basis for continuous public debate on the subsidy system and the government's press policy. Such debate is regarded as essential for the effective development of the system.

The Political Background

The question of state subsidies for the press intended to facilitate the formation of public opinion of all shades has been one of the most debated topics in Sweden in recent years and has been the subject of several parliamentary reports. There is now a wide political majority in favor of subsidies, but fifteen years ago, the situation was completely different.

Throughout the period during which the question was examined by committees and the present system was formulated and introduced, the Social Democratic party was in power. However with the exception of

112

the period 1969–1971, it did not have an absolute majority in the Riksdag. A nonsocialist government came to power in 1976.

The Social Democratic party, most of whose papers are in a perilous state in the market, has always been the main advocate of the policy of state subsidies, and the Conservative party, whose papers are comparatively strong, has always been its main opponent. In order to obtain a stable majority in favor of subsidies, the Social Democrats have had to form an alliance with at least one of the opposition parties. The Center party, which has a weak representation among newspapers, has been prepared, upon certain conditions, to give its political support. The Liberal party was at first a confirmed opponent, but it has recently changed its views and joined the majority.

Schemes for monetary operational subsidies for newspapers in need of assistance appeared in various guises before such a policy was finally adopted. It was some time before it obtained solid political support.

Press Subsidies Paid Through the Political Parties
The first Committee on the Press (1963–1965) had the task of analyzing the economic conditions for newspaper publishing and considering whether there was any need for state subsidies. The committee found that a number of newspapers were unprofitable, hampered by economic difficulties, and waging an uneven battle with bigger competitors. The committee considered that they could not solve their problems alone. Sooner or later they would be forced to close down if they did not have outside financial assistance. The committee found that state subsidies should be given to newspapers in a weak market position.

The question was how subsidies could be channeled to newspapers in need while avoiding all danger of the state's exercising any influence in any way. It was considered that the scrutiny of applications for subsidies could not be left to a state body and that the best way would be for the decision to grant a subsidy to be taken in accordance with rules that were determined beforehand, but no satisfactory method of doing this could be found.

The committee proposed that since 80 to 90 percent of Swedish newspapers were connected with the political parties, the subsidies should be distributed through the parties represented in the Riksdag, which would receive a subsidy according to their voting strength and would then distribute it to their newspapers, without any supervision by the state. The only qualification for receipt of a subsidy would be that the paper appear at least four times a year. The subsidy could be paid to existing papers or used to establish a new paper.

The committee considered that this formula would eliminate the danger of state interference because the initial payment would be made on an automatic basis and the actual distribution would not be supervised by the state. Subsidies would also be distributed to those that most needed them, since the newspapers that were economically the weakest were associated with the parties that were politically the strongest. Most of the newspapers in question were Social Democratic, and about half of the total subsidy would go to that party. At the same time, however, a third of it would go to parties whose newspapers did not have any great financial problems: Conservative and Liberal papers.

The newspapers themselves were not prepared to accept such a system of subsidies, however. The newspaper publishers' association rejected any measures that might have structural effects. They considered that that would conflict with the provisions of the constitution concerning freedom of the press, that the system would constitute serious interference in free competition, that it would dislocate the market mechanism, that the problems of the weak newspapers could be solved by general measures, and that the fact that strong newspapers might also benefit from such measures should not matter. Other bodies consulted were also critical. The criticism blocked the proposal in this form.

Subsidies for the Political Parties' Activities in Promoting the Formation of Opinion

At the end of the 1950s, the Center party had produced a proposal for subsidies to be paid to the political parties. This proposal became the basis for an agreement between the Social Democrats and the Center party that subsidies should be paid to political parties for their activities to promote the formation of opinion. If they wished, the parties could, but would not be required to, distribute these funds to their newspapers. As before, there had to be an automatic principle for distribution, and any possibility of state control had to be excluded.

The Liberal party was resolutely opposed to selective press subsidies, but it could accept party subsidies. Like the Center party, it had greater difficulty in financing party activities than did the Social Democratic and Conservative parties. However since it was against selective press subsidies, it could not accept party subsidies that could be used in this way. It regarded the party subsidies as a concealed newspaper subsidy and therefore rejected the proposal until a committee could decide how the party subsidy could be prevented from becoming a press subsidy in practice. It also maintained that a press subsidy paid through the parties would discriminate against newspapers that were not connected with any party and that it was not in the public interest to increase the role of the newspapers as organs of propaganda. The Conservative party was vehemently against the proposal since it did not have any difficulty in financing its activities. Eventually, however, in December 1965, the proposal was adopted, thus introducing a disguised press subsidy.

Selective Operational Subsidies

The introduction of this system did not remove the danger of further newspaper closures. During the debate in the Riksdag on the party subsidies, the prime minister announced that it had been decided to

114

close down the biggest Social Democratic morning paper, *Stockholms-Tidningen,* which had a circulation of 133,000. It was closed down three months later.

A new parliamentary committee on the press was appointed in 1967, and it sat for a year. In view of the strong criticism of selective subsidies, they were not included in the committee's terms of reference. Instead the committee was asked to consider a special loan fund for the press and measures to encourage joint distribution. On the committee's recommendation, these were introduced in 1969 and 1970, respectively.

These measures were important in themselves but did not obviate the immediate dangers of further concentration. The Social Democratic government therefore took up with the opposition parties the question of production subsidies to be paid to newspapers in a weak position in the market. The same basic principles should apply as for the party subsidy. The subsidies were to be paid in accordance with rules determined beforehand to papers with a bigger competitior in their place of publication and so to operate without state control. They would be financed by an advertising tax.

The government obtained the support of the Center party upon certain conditions. Thus once again the Social Democratic and Center parties had joined forces. This time they were joined by the Liberal party, which had been converted to the idea of selective press subsidies.

The Liberals now declared that subsidies were needed to preserve a multifarious newspaper press. However they wanted certain adjustments to the rules, adjustments that conflicted with the basic principles of the system since they would mean that some Liberal papers would receive a subsidy despite the fact that they were the biggest newspapers in their place of publication. Since the Social Democratic party and the Center party wanted the widest possible support, they agreed to meet the Liberals' demands.

On the other hand, the Liberal party was decidedly against an advertising tax, which it believed would weaken the press economically. Instead it wanted the press subsidy to be financed by an increase in the tobacco tax.

The Conservative party agreed that there was a need for measures to promote the formation of opinion (it did not mention multiplicity of views) but thought that they should be general measures. It considered that the government's aim was good but that the formulation of the proposal was completely inappropriate. It could not therefore support the government.

The main question in the debate was how the subsidy was to be financed. The Center party was not completely satisfied with the original proposal that there should be an advertising tax of 10 percent for all the press, which would have generated much more revenue than was actually needed for the proposed subsidy. They were opposed to this surplus financing and considered that income and expenditure should be balanced. At their suggestion, the rate was reduced to 6 percent for newspapers, with 10 percent retained for the rest of the press. The press advertising tax was then extended to a general advertising tax, a provision demanded by the press so that it would not be in an unfavorable position compared with other advertising media.

When the Riksdag decided to introduce selective subsidies, it appointed a committee to study the effects of the system. This committee, which sat from 1972 to 1975, found that the system should be continued if multiplicity of newspapers was to be maintained. On the other hand, the majority considered that the concessions that had been made to the Liberal party, whereby three profitable high-coverage newspapers had received a subsidy every year, were not justified. This merely increased the need of smaller newspapers for subsidies. A minority of the committee, including the Liberal party's representative, favored retaining the concessions. The Social Democratic government adopted the minority view and preserved the political compromise.

The debate in the Riksdag on the committee's report in 1976 was short and calm compared with the debate on party subsidies in 1965. The Liberals considered that selective subsidies were necessary, but in addition to increasing general subsidies they wanted to abolish taxes on press advertising and general advertising. They did not, at that time, propose any other method of financing the subsidies. The Conservative party again voted against selective subsidies and wanted only general subsidies.

When the fourth press committee submitted a proposal in the autumn of 1978 to increase the selective subsidies paid to the least profitable newspapers, the Conservative party's representative on the committee dissented, although not as strongly as before. There may have been a split (perhaps only temporary) in the Conservative opposition. The party officially accepted the selective subsidy paid to the Conservative newspaper *Svenska Dagbladet,* but this line was not followed by Conservative editorialists in the provincial press.

The Conservative editorialists refer to the political decision on press subsidies as a "cow" deal (an unholy compromise), a term alluding to an agreement in the 1930s between the Social Democratic government and the Farmers' party (now the Center party) granting concessions concerning agriculture and unemployment, respectively. This term may possibly aptly describe the decision on party subsidies still being paid yearly, but not that concerning press subsidies, since only the Conservative party opposes these in principle.

116

In this debate the advocates of general subsidies sometimes seem to succeed in making them appear as impartial and having no effect on competition. This is not in fact the case. General subsidies mainly benefit newspapers in a strong position, which in Sweden are mainly Conservative and Liberal papers. Naturally, therefore, those parties, particularly the Conservatives, strongly advocate general subsidies. The same applies to the method of financing the subsidies. The Liberal and Conservative parties are opposed to the advertising tax. Regardless of any view on the effect of this tax that it may be passed on to advertisers and ultimately to consumers, it is paid mainly by Conservative and Liberal newspapers since they have the biggest advertising revenue.

The Swedish newspaper publishers' association has always been opposed to the advertising tax, and its view is supported even by publishers of Social Democratic and Center party papers. This amounts to a considerable political compromise. Those on the board of the association who are against selective press subsidies have agreed to restrain their criticism in return for an undertaking from those who are in favor of them to campaign for the abolition of the advertising tax.

The Logical Basis for Selective Press Subsidies

The government's policy is to preserve the existing competition and to create competition in places with only one newspaper. It is the business economist's difficult task to determine a method of granting subsidies that will preserve as many newspapers as possible in a market in which there is a considerable danger that competition will be restricted and to direct subsidies to publishers who are endangered or restrained by market forces.

There cannot be any disagreement regarding certain fundamental economic conditions in the newspaper industry. Newspapers operate in two markets: they sell advertising space and they sell newspapers. However the consequences of this are seen in two different ways. Some maintain that the structure of the press is determined by the buyers of newspapers, the readers, and that the newspapers they regard as the most attractive survive. Others maintain that the structure is determined by advertisers and that the newspapers they regard as the most valuable as an advertising medium survive. Those who favor the first theory point to the fact that newspapers are ultimately bought on subscription or in single copies and that readers can choose freely from among the newspapers available. Those who consider that advertisers have the greater influence on the structure of the press point to the equally obvious fact that the greater proportion of the revenue of morning newspapers comes from advertising and that although readers can choose freely, the range of newspapers available has already been determined by the advertisers.

Research in Sweden has shown that the structure of the press is determined by the mechanism of the advertising market. Since morning newspapers depend on advertising for almost two-thirds of their revenue, they must ensure that they are effective as advertising media.

The most important advertisers for a newspaper, from the point of view of both revenue and the value of the advertisement as reading matter, are local retailers who want to reach as many readers as possible in the area in which they operate. A newspaper's economic position is therefore determined mainly by the number of its readers in its area

117

and the size of that area. The more households that it covers in a given area, the more important it is for the local advertisers. This means that the value of a newspaper as an advertising medium can be measured by its coverage of the households in its area.

From studies of the press subsidies and newspaper competition made at the request of the 1972 press committee, the principle of the degree of coverage was formulated, whereby there is a positive connection between household coverage in the place of publication and a newspaper's economic position, and with a household coverage of at least 50 percent a newspaper becomes a vital medium for advertising. The term *low coverage* was used to describe coverage of less than 50 percent and *high coverage* for coverage of at least 50 percent. After the principle had been formulated, it was tested on new material, both historical and current. It has served to explain trends that had hitherto been unexplained. Statistical analyses of the correlation between the degree of coverage in a newspaper's area and its financial results for 1976 and 1977 in respect of newspapers in fifteen places with more than one newspaper have given correlation coefficients of $r = 0.94$. Further research has confirmed the principle.

Total circulation had previously been used to measure the competitive power of a newspaper. The degree of coverage (the proportion of the circulation covering the publication area related to the number of households) has proved to be of greater value as a method of analysis and forecasting. Research has provided an objective basis for directing subsidies to newspapers whose publication is threatened by market forces and for assessing the possibility of restoring competition in places where it has ceased.

A doctoral thesis in economic history regarding the importance of the effect of advertising on press concentration (Jonsson, 1977) was used as the basis for testing the principle of the degree of coverage on historical material. The study relates to newspapers in large towns during the period 1925–1954. The test showed the close correlation between the degree of coverage and the value of a newspaper as an advertising medium. Table 5.3, which is based on Jonsson's study, shows that the main criterion of advertisers is the largest possible degree of coverage. Only for three categories of advertisements is this not the case: industrial advertising requires selectivity ("quality"), official and legal advertising require equal distribution, and for family advertising the criterion is either absolute circulation or quality. For entertainment advertising both "all equal" and highest possible coverage are criteria.

118

The theory of the degree of coverage may be illustrated by various forms of mergers that have taken place. The Conservatives tried to rescue a number of low-coverage local newspapers in the 1950s by merging them into regional papers in order to obtain the highest possible circulation. The new papers did obtain higher circulations, but they remained low-coverage newspapers. The analgamations did not add even 1 percent to the degree of coverage in any of the different places of

Table 5.3 *Principles of Press Media Selection*

Advertisement Categories	Implied Selection Principles			
	Advantage for Greatest			All Equal
	Circulation	Coverage	Quality	
Industrial advertising			X	
National display advertising		X		
Local display advertising		X		
Classified advertising		X		
Official and legal advertising				X
Entertainment		X		X
Family announcements	X		X	
Real estate advertising		X		
Merchandise (for sale/want ads)		X		
Rentals		X		
Employment		X		
Miscellaneous		X		

Source: Gustafsson 1978, p. 13.

publication. However in the case of mergers of two low-coverage newspapers in the same place, the new paper has become stronger, the degree of coverage has increased.

The theory of the degree of coverage explains why newspapers with large circulations for Sweden have had to close down; among them are the two Social Democratic newspapers in large towns, *Ny Tid* (45,000) and *Stockholms-Tidningen* (135,000), and the Liberal newspaper *Göteborgs Handels - och Sjöfarts-Tidning* (45,000). Although they had large circulations, they did not have a strong position as advertising media. They were low-coverage papers, and advertisers preferred their rival high-coverage papers. A regional newspaper with a circulation of 45,000 and a coverage of 70 to 80 percent operates on an excellent economic basis. It is difficult to persuade an advertiser who uses such a paper to advertise also in a low-coverage newspaper in the same area. In other economic sectors, a company with a market share of 20 percent is in a strong position, but in the newspaper sector this is not the case.

Advertisers choose only the most successful papers.
If follows from this theory of the degree of coverage that the only
chance low-coverage newspapers have of improving their profitability
is to endeavor to increase their coverage and thus become more attractive to advertisers. However the prospects of succeeding in this are
small. The problem is that the newspaper market is saturated. Any
attempt to increase coverage constitutes a threat to some high-coverage
newspapers, which immediately retaliate with countermeasures. If
low-coverage newspapers are to survive as papers with editorial resources that allow them to compete with high-coverage newspapers,
which is the aim of the government's press policy, they must have
subsidies. In order not to prejudice their chances of survival, the subsidies must be directed solely to them. Market forces operate selectively. Countermeasures therefore must also be selective.

In 1977 the total revenue of the Swedish newspaper press from advertising and the sale of newspapers was 3,342 million kroner. A subsidy of
about 5 percent of this amount was paid by the state to newspapers in a
weak market position. Would a general subsidy of the same amount
have helped these newspapers to the same extent? Figures that may
enable this question to be answered are shown in table 5.4. They cover
thirty high-periodicity newspapers in fifteen places in which there is
more than one newspaper; in each case there is a high-coverage paper
in competition with a low-coverage paper. The actual figures for 1976
and 1977 are shown in the first two columns, profits after depreciation
and state production subsidies. The fifteen low-coverage newspapers
suffered a total loss of 3 million kroner in 1976 and 9 million kroner in
1977. The fifteen high-coverage newspapers showed a total profit of 20
million kroner in 1976 and 34 million kroner in 1977. The other two
columns show the hypothetical results had a general subsidy of the
same amount as the selective subsidy been paid to all newspapers in
relation to their turnover. No changes have been made in other respects. The figures clearly show how different the situation would have
been. The profits of the high-coverage papers would have doubled for
1976 and been about 70 percent higher for 1977. The low-coverage

Table 5.4 *Results for Thirty Competing Newspapers with a Selective
(Actual) and a General (Hypothetical) System of Subsidies*

Type of Newspaper	Number of Newspapers	Selective System (million Kr.) 1976	1977	General subsidies system (million Kr.) 1976	1977
Low-coverage newspapers	15	−3	−9	−55	−62
High-coverage newspapers	15	+20	+34	+41	+58

newspapers would not have been able to bear the huge losses that would have occurred and would have disappeared from the market. A general subsidy strengthens the market forces and hastens the concentration process. The problems of the weak newspapers cannot be solved by general subsidies.

Structural Effects

At the beginning of the 1970s when the selective system of subsidies was introduced, there was a danger of a large reduction in the number of newspapers. However it was only newspapers with a larger competitor in their area that were threatened with closure. The measures adopted obviated the immediate threat to them but did not achieve a permanent solution.

The selective nature of the system has proved to be appropriate for the purpose of preserving the structure of the newspaper sector. However the initial level of subsidies was too low, and although the total annual amount for selective operational subsidies in 1978 was more than five times greater than that paid in 1971, the first year of the system, the percentage increase has gradually fallen. The last increase was less than 10 percent and confined to newspapers facing the greatest threat of closure, those with a coverage of less than 21 percent of the households in their area. The need for a further increase was determined, as before, after an analysis of the overall economic situation of the group of low-coverage papers. Despite these increases, the total amount of the subsidies constitutes only about 5 percent of the total revenue of the newspaper sector from advertising and the sale of newspapers.

In analyzing the effects of the system, two factors may be discerned, both of which may be regarded as structural: the independence of the press in relation to the state and the question of competition between newspapers with and those without subsidies.

The Independence of the Press
The most important principle in the formulation of the system has been that of ensuring the independence of the press from the state. There must be no possibility that the system can be manipulated by the state to influence the content of newspapers or even any anxiety that such manipulation could occur. The system must also be based on objective criteria, and distribution of subsidies must be on an automatic basis.

During the 1970s both the nonsocialist and the Social Democratic press have been an opposition press. There is no evidence that subsidies have had any effect on their criticism of the exercise of power by the government. The newspapers that have received subsidies and have been dependent on them for their economic survival have not felt hampered in their scrutinizing function.

One unexpected effect that is worth noting is a sign that the dependence of newspapers on political parties is declining. There have been no dramatic changes as yet; the party press tradition still survives. However newspapers that previously depended on the financial support of certain organizations and companies have been able to assert a certain degree of independence of them when their private support has been replaced by a state subsidy.

The question of independence from the state may be illustrated by the case of the third largest morning newspaper in Sweden, *Svenska Dagbladet*. This newspaper is Conservative, but it has recently added the word *independent* to its political masthead, probably revealing the influence of the state subsidy. The paper's total circulation is about 180,000 and covers only 18 percent of the households in its place of publication, Stockholm. Almost half of its circulation is sold outside the Stockholm area. Its losses last year were about 40 million kroner. About 60 percent of this was covered by the state subsidy and about 40 percent by various industrial conpanies through a special company set up for this purpose. The difference between these two sources of funds should be noted. The commitment on the part of the industrial companies is for a limited period (at present, until 1980) and depends on the willingness of those companies (or their management) to continue to bear part of the loss. It may be renewed, but its scope is not known in advance. The state subsidy is for an unlimited period. It is supported by a stable political majority. Regardless of the party in power, *Svenska Dagbladet* can rely on obtaining the subsidy provided its market position justifies it.

Market Effects

Selective subsidies have the effect of preserving the market structure and also of freezing it. Thus preservation of the status quo becomes an aim. No closure, merger, or other structural change can be accepted, whether it has a large or small effect on multiplicity. This is an unclear point in the government's policy regarding the press. It can probably be assumed that the structure that existed at the beginning of the 1970s and has been preserved almost unchanged since then is not the most ideal one from the point of view of the government's policy.

The first press committee considered that the closure of small, local, monopoly newspapers was acceptable because this gave regional newspapers scope for expansion. Readers thus obtained papers with better resources. However this view was not maintained in the 1970s, and an attempt has been made to preserve small newspapers also. Some limited resources have been made available to small- and medium-sized monopoly newspapers to assist their own efforts. They can apply for development subsidies. This form of subsidy is now being evaluated, and it is not clear what the results will show.

The system of selective operational subsidies has preserved competition in all places with newspapers representing different political

122

views. However it was not designed to create new newspapers. An establishment subsidy was therefore added to the range of subsidies granted in 1976 to promote the establishment of newspapers appearing at least once a week. The present state press committee will be examining the possibility of fostering the development of such newspapers. Outside Sweden there is a tradition of opinion weeklies. It should be possible to create such a tradition in Sweden. Such newspapers could mitigate the effects of the present concentration, at least in some respects. The prospect of establishing new high-periodicity newspapers is regarded as extremely small, if it exists at all. The dependence of such newspapers on advertising revenue makes it even more difficult to establish them.

The selective operational subsidy is paid to newspapers that would have difficulty in surviving in the market without it. Such a system obviously affects competition, for the idea is to prevent newspapers in a weak position from continuing to lose sales and eventually disappear from the market. If that happens, the high-coverage newspapers gain the circulation of the low-coverage newspapers. In places with two newspapers, not more than 5 percent of households take both papers. Such high-coverage newspapers that have planned their activities (number of employees and investment) on the basis of the assumption that the low-coverage paper must disappear sooner or later are compelled by virtue of the subsidy to make certain adjustments. Effects of this kind are intentional.

Newspapers that receive a subsidy can use it for measures that they themselves regard as the most appropriate. In many respects they are tied by what their bigger rival does, but in principle competition is free. However they use the subsidy, it will mean that competition for readers and advertisers is intensified. Subsidized newspapers can increase the volume of their editorial text. To a certain extent they may do so because the subsidy is paid on the basis of the volume of editorial text and circulation. But since the amount of the subsidy is calculated on the basis of an average over three years and about 50 percent is paid in the form of a maximum or minimum subsidy, the rules of the subsidy system are not the main cause of the increase in the volume of editorial text. Subsidized newspapers may use more resources to obtain new subscribers (by offering discounts, for example). They can also endeavor to obtain new advertisers in the same way. All of these measures will bring countermeasures from the high-coverage papers, which will mean higher competition expenditure. If the subsidy is used to change the content of the newspaper, it will probably be to the advantage of readers. In other areas there may be undesirable disadvantages.

Subsidies may cause the general level of costs to be kept at a higher level than that which can be regarded as justified. The level would have been lower if the market forces had been permitted to compel papers to undertake structural rationalization. Since the government endeavors to keep the subsidy as low as possible, competing newspapers are en-

123

couraged to adopt joint cost-saving measures in areas other than the editorial field. Economic operation is fostered and efforts are made by the state to make the general economic conditions for the publication of newspapers as favorable as possible. Distribution is conducted almost entirely on a joint basis. Collaboration is also increasing in other areas, but the party press tradition so far has been a difficult obstacle to overcome.

Generally the subsidy system has not changed the competitive conditions in the newspaper sector, apart from preventing some papers from obtaining a monopoly for which they were striving. The figures in table 5.4 showing the total results for a number of competing newspapers prove that despite the subsidy, there is still an important difference between a high-coverage and a low-coverage newspaper.

The printing industry has criticized the loan fund but not the system of selective operational subsidies. With loans from this fund, many low-coverage newspapers have been able to introduce offset printing, which they would not have been able to do from their own resources. They have thus been able also to undertake book printing in competition with book printers. The printing industry objects to this development and has asked the government to increase its efforts to encourage joint technical operations within the newspaper sector. This criticism is justified to some extent. However, the first changes to new techniques took place long before the loan fund was introduced, and many newspapers have purchased new equipment without a state loan. In any event, the recommendation made by the printing industry coincides with the government's intentions regarding the subsidy progran.

Summary

The purpose of the Swedish system of subsidies is to encourage newspapers in the performance of their function to promote the formation of political opinion in the widest sense. The system reflects the idea that newspapers play (and should continue to do so) an important part in the democratic system and that this requires a multiplicity of newspapers. The press also has other tasks, but the system of subsidies is not concerned with them.

There is now wide support for the existing, extremely selective system. It would have had even greater support if it had not been coupled with an advertising tax. The tax has been reduced considerably since it was introduced, but even if it were abolished completely, there would not be complete support for the present subsidy system. Conservative politicians, particularly Conservative editorialists, are the main opponents. They advocate general subsidies only.

Selective subsidies are distributed automatically to individual newspapers on the basis of objective criteria. Whether a newspaper qualifies for a subsidy is determined by its market position. The amount of the

124

subsidy is not based on the newspaper's budget or profit and loss account but is calculated within certain minimum and maximum limits in relation to the scope of its editorial activity. The rules are the same for all newspapers qualifying for a subsidy. The subsidy is not dependent on any conditions. All decisions regarding the granting of a subsidy are published.

The subsidy system has stemmed the concentration process and enabled a number of new newspapers to be established. The downward trend of low-coverage newspapers has been arrested. For many of them, the subsidy has enabled them to regain positions lost, and some of them have even been able to effect improvements. The system has strengthened the economic conditions for low-coverage newspapers without affecting the capacity of high-coverage newspapers to obtain their necessary revenue from the market. The subsidy system complements the market system.

References

Furhoff, L. "Reflections on Newspaper Concentration." *The Scandinavian Economic History Review* XXI (1973):1–27.

Gustafsson, K. E. *Presstödet och tidningskonkurrensen* (State Subsidies and Newspaper Competition). Swedish Government Official Report SOU 1974:102.

Gustafsson, K. E., and Hadenius, S. *Swedish Press Policy.* Stockholm: The Swedish Institute, 1976.

Gustafsson, K. E. "The Circulation Spiral and the Principle of Household Coverage." *The Scandinavian Economic History Review* XXVI (1978):1–14.

Hadenius, S., Molin, B., and Wieslander, H. *Sverige efter 1900. En modern politisk historia* [Sweden After 1900, A Modern Political History]. Stockholm:1978.

Jonsson, S. *Annonser och tidningskonkurrens* [Advertisements and Newspaper Competition]. Göteborg:1977.

6

The Press and the State in France

Antoine de Tarlé

In France it is impossible to draw firm social lines between the worlds of big business, the civil service, finance, politics, and the press. In the course of a successful career an individual will slip easily between these worlds, benefiting from a complexity of informal links stemming from family and social ties. Despite the enormous changes that have taken place in recent years in the ownership and management of the press, this rich heritage of relationships has not altered at all. The tightly knit world of the French elite is confident and enduring.

The state's formal involvement with the press provides a further set of dependencies and connections. The state is the direct owner of Havas, the country's largest press agency (by far), which handles a high proportion of all advertising placed in newspapers. Second, the state is the owner of the majority of the larger banks, on which a good deal of the press now depends. Third, France has evolved the most costly and far-ranging set of newspaper subsidies in Europe, which means that government may bring constant pressure to bear on the press, since the latter is always negotiating for increases in the level of state remittances. No French government is in a position to ignore the newspaper industry's general state of health. No newspaper management is in a position to dismiss political realities when subsidies are under discussion.

At the beginning of the 1970s most of the large newspaper groups were in the hands of the same men who had acquired them at the end of World War II. They were now very old indeed, but it was impossible to see who their successors would be. For years the quality of their management had been slipping, and the general economic crisis, coupled with the problems posed by the new newspaper technology, served only to multiply their problems and lay the press open to further state intervention. Indeed what happened was that the government stepped into the breach, immersing itself in the internal affairs of the press on a scale never before attempted and not traditionally thought to lie within the state's direct competence. The precedents of these recent years, however, have altered the tradition, and it now seems natural for the state to intervene at many levels.

At the start of the 1970s, it was generally accepted that the great Parisian newspapers needed help. The reestablishment of the Ministry of Information in May 1972 gave the impression that the government was going to adopt a more consistent and considered policy in its relationship with the press. Also it had at its disposal an excellent consultative document, the Serisé report, produced by a commission made up of representatives from the press and the civil service (under the chairmanship of Jean Serisé, a close associate of the then minister of finance, Valéry Giscard d'Estaing), which sat for several months examining the situation concerning the different forms of subsidy to the press. Their report, however, was never officially published.[1] It is true that the commission had not reached a unanimous conclusion on all points. Although there was agreement between press and administration on the need to strengthen the joint commission's control over publishing and press agencies and to improve the conditions under which it functioned, they were unable to find common ground on the questions of postal rate concessions, taxes on turnover, and the taxation of profits. (Article 39 of the Code Général des Impôts allows newspaper companies to claim a tax rebate on proposed investments.) On each of these points, the representatives of the press went too far in their demands, particularly in insisting on the application of a zero value-added tax (VAT) rating on sales of publications and on the extension of article 39 of the CGI until 1980. The administrators did not have the authority to make any commitments on such controversial matters. Nevertheless as the conclusion of the report put it, "The members of the working party . . . believe all the same, that the explanations with which they have backed up the exposition of their differences will be sufficient to enable the government to intervene where necessary with all the facts at its disposal." The onus was therefore on the government to assume its responsibilities.

Unfortunately there was to be no follow-up to the Serisé report. In the wake of the general election of 1973, the government was reluctant to interfere in such a delicate situation. Thereafter the illness of President Pompidou blocked all decisions. Not until the election of Giscard d'Estaing to the presidency would the government once again consider the problem as a whole.

128

The State Role in Newspaper Reorganization

In the course of the next two years, the situation deteriorated steadily until the Parisian press was in a state of crisis, and the system of public subsidies at the end of its resources. The provincial daily press, meanwhile, was continuing to flourish. In 1975, the Parisian press as a whole printed only 3.3 million copies while the provincial press printed 7.39 million.[2] A process of concentration led, in almost every region, to the monopolization of information by one daily newspaper. These newspapers in many cases developed into full-fledged capitalist organizations, taking their place among the leading industrial concerns in their regions.[3] Further they were protected from competition by agreements with neighboring organizations.[4] Article 39 of the CGI enabled them to modernize their printing operations, which would often undertake commissions from outside clients, and in some cases they put printers of books and periodicals in serious difficulties. Indeed the printing plants of the *Progrès-Dauphine Libéré* and *Nice Matin* are now among the most modern in Europe. However, the large Parisian newspaper groups set up in the postwar years found themselves in trouble. Hachette, owners of *France Soir,* the largest French daily newspaper, with a circulation of around 1 million copies, was suffering the consequences of a general fall in sales of daily newspapers in the capital. Also, the most powerful figures of the national press, Jean Prouvost, owner of *Le Figaro* and the weekly *Paris Match,* Marcel Boussac, owner of the daily *L'Aurore,* and Emilien Amaury, owner of the dailies *Le Parisien Libéré* and *L'Équipe,* were all very old. There were worries in government and financial circles over who would succeed them.

Hachette and Prouvost

Hachette had been reorganized under the guidance of Simon Nora and in 1972 had supported a group of journalists who had left *L'Express* in the launching of a direct rival to it, *Le Point.* Even so, the company still continued to carry *France Soir,* though its circulation was steadily falling and its running costs rising. The death of the editor, Pierre Lazareff, in November 1973 gave rise to hopes of reform, and in February 1974, Henri Amouroux, a well-known provincial journalist who had successfully revived *Sud-Ouest,* was appointed to succeed him. Yet both the launching of *Le Point* and the appointment of Amouroux were suspected of being politically motivated. It was claimed that Simon Nora was preparing a means to back, when the time came, the candidacy of his friend Jacques Chaban Delmas for the French presidency, and Hachette consequently lost favor with the president and the prime minister. Then in January 1974, *Le Point,* in an effort to attract publicity, published an article calling for the resignation of the prime minister. He immediately summoned the chairman of Hachette and, before his very eyes, tore up a bill authorizing an increase in the government-controlled price of paperback books. This action, which cost the company several million francs (even though Hachette could hardly have prevented its newspaper from publishing the offending article), illustrates perfectly the ambiguous nature of its relationship with the state.

Not surprisingly, the defeat of Chaban Delmas in the presidential elections had swift repercussions for Hachette, since it could not afford to be on bad terms with the government. Simon Nora left his post as director general, and was replaced by Jacques Marchandise, a director of another major French enterprise, the Péchiney-Ugine-Kuhlmann group. Henri Amouroux was dismissed in May 1975. Even so, the fortunes of *France Soir* did not improve.

Following the change in leadership there was a change in the group's policy; it decided to get rid of its less profitable publications: *Connaissance des Arts, Réalités,* and *Entreprise.* The case of the last of these three weeklies is singular. Hachette began negotiations with Havas, the government-owned advertising agency, which had entered the world of the press when it gained control of Usine publications (*L'Usine Nouvelle* and *Les Informations*). The two giants organized the merger of *Entreprise* and *Les Informations,* two business journals with similar readerships. Hachette owned 50 percent of the company controlling the new journal, *Le Nouvel Economiste,* which resulted from the merger, but in reality Havas assumed all responsibility for it. Hachette appeared to have merely given *Entreprise* away.[5]

These changes gave rise to written questions in parliament. Previously, French publicly owned companies had never been connected with the press. Now Havas, with the *Nouvel Economiste* and the *Usine Nouvelle* group (which subsequently absorbed the Compagnie Française d'Edition, also known as the Ollive group), was in charge of a group of publications with a total annual turnover of around 240 million francs. On the whole, these were technical journals, but *Le Nouvel Economiste* was a very clear exception to the rule, since part of its role was to tackle questions of economic policy and therefore to deal with politics. The public could legitimately question the propriety of an advertising agency controlled by the state becoming the owner of about 40 publications with a turnover amounting in 1977 to 314 million francs and with almost 1,500 employees. The public might also ask whether this alarming process would be allowed to continue. In fact, on December 1978, Havas extended its influence in another direction by acquiring 49 percent of Interdeco, the leading agency for the management of magazine advertising.

130   To critics who suspected them of political motivation, Havas's directors replied that a group as large as theirs was obliged to diversify and that they had no intention of venturing into the political press. But this last point became less convincing with the launching of *Le Nouvel Economiste* in 1975 and the strengthening of Havas's interests in a private radio station in 1973–1974, both actions of a decidedly political character.[6] In the absence of any precise information, there are two possible explanations: either the company, whose chairman, Jean Méo,

was a senior civil servant, a former collaborator of General de Gaulle, and very close to Georges Pompidou, acted under government instructions so that the latter could indirectly gain a foothold in the press; or the Havas group, which was rich and dynamic, was obliged to intervene in a sector that was short of capital and unable to find industrialists or banks willing to invest in it. Both explanations may be true.

Hachette, meanwhile, was concerned about *France Soir*. This newspaper continued to lose readers, its deficit grew larger, its staff was considered by some to be too large, and its printing operations were old fashioned. (The Parisian papers had not followed the example of the large provincial newspapers in modernizing their equipment at the time when they were making a profit.) Yet despite being run badly and at a loss, *France Soir* was still important politically. It continued to reach half a million readers, mostly around Paris. With some imagination and capital, there was a possibility of transforming it either into a large popular daily such as the *Sun* or *Daily Mirror* in Britain or into a regional newspaper for the Ile de France. Finally, it was learned in July 1976 that *France Soir* had been sold to Paul Winkler, director of Agence Opera Mundi and the *Journal de Mickey*. This transaction appeared very odd indeed: Paul Winkler was 78 years old, and the *Journal de Mickey* was a subsidiary of Hachette. It seemed highly unlikely that this man could have set up this deal entirely on his own.

A month later, in the middle of August, it was learned that Winkler was to sell 50 percent of *France Soir* to the rapidly growing provincial group controlled by Hersant. Agreements were reached whereby Winkler would remain responsible for the editorial side of the newspaper, and the Hersant group would take care of the technical side of production. This meant that there would be a rationalization of the production of *France Soir* and *Le Figaro*. Because they were published at separate times, they could use the same presses and the same network of regional presses, which would allow them to appear in the main provincial towns at the same time as the major regional papers did, under conditions that appeared financially advantageous at the time.

These agreements were justified on economic and financial grounds, but politically they were far from innocent; they gave control of one of the largest daily newspapers in France to Robert Hersant, a member of parliament in the majority camp, who was supported by the government, and especially by the prime minister, and who had also gained possession of *Le Figaro* following the break up of the Prouvost group in 1974.[7]

131

The situation of the Prouvost group had been rather different from that of Hachette but was equally worrying to the government. In 1973 Jean Prouvost was almost ninety and was therefore obliged to think about his succession. The diverse group of publications he directed were not all equally prosperous. *Télé 7 Jours,* which he half-owned with Hachette, was making enormous profits; but the monthlies, *Parents, Cosmopolitan,* and *Marie-Claire,* were just about managing to break even; the daily, *Le Figaro,* after twenty years of prosperity, was beginning to suffer losses; and above all, the weekly, *Paris Match,* was very expensive and was losing more and more readers (its circulation dropped from 1.2 million in 1966 to 580,000 in 1976). Overall the accounts appeared to balance, but in 1973 Prouvost bought up the share held in *Le Figaro* by Béghin and the acquisition forced him to incur debts. The group did not make enough funds available to allow him to repay these debts. The banks became anxious. The only way out was to sell *Le Figaro.*

These transactions were of great concern to the government, especially to Prime Minister Jacques Chirac and his advisers. *Le Figaro* was still one of the important Parisian newspapers. In recent years, it had tried to change its image to attract new readers and to keep up its circulation, which was beginning to fall. It had thus become more liberal and more critical of the government, a development that incurred displeasure in high places, despite the fact that the political editor of the newspaper, Xavier Marchetti, had been the head of Georges Pompidou's press service. The sale of *Le Figaro* offered the opportunity of getting it back into safe hands. There were several possible buyers: Jean-Jacques Servan Schreiber; Simon Nora, who had become available after his dismissal from Hachette; and the managing director of the Möet-Hennessy group. However, the last two candidates were too closely linked to Jacques Chaban Delmas to be approved of by the prime minister, and it was clear that to be successful the operation had to enjoy his approval. In such a situation, it was therefore the government's candidate, Robert Hersant, who succeeded. Once sold, the newspaper was brought to heel; journalists critical of the government departed and the political line of the paper moved noticeably to the right. This change did not bring any increase in the number of readers, however; the circulation of *Le Figaro,* which had been 402,000 in 1974, managed to reach only 360,000 in 1976.

The fate of the Prouvost group was still to be decided. After long negotiations held under the auspices of the Banque de Paris et des Pays Bas and after consulting two experts, the former managing director of the Crédit Agricole and the managing director of Havas, it was decided to break up the group. In 1977, Hachette took on *Parents, Paris Match,* and the other half of *Télé 7 Jours;* the Filipacchi group then bought *Paris Match* from Hachette; and the granddaughters of Jean Prouvost kept the monthlies *Marie-Claire, Cent Isles,* and *Cosmopolitan,* and set up a company in which the large cosmetics group L'Oréal also had a share.

The outcome of these various operations was important for several reasons. First, the Prouvost group had ceased to exist. Second, Hachette found itself in charge of an extremely profitable group of publications, which, except for *Le Point* did not concern themselves at all with political problems. Third, two relatively new groups, Hersant and Filipacchi, had consolidated their positions. And finally the banks, especially Her-

132

vet, Vernes, Worms, and the Banque de Paris et des Pays Bas, had taken on an increasingly large role in the management of the affairs of the press.

These maneuvers are an impressive illustration of the part played in France by large capitalist finance anxious to maintain profitability and to reorganize. Seen from this point of view, the restructuring of Hachette is an example of how in two years an unprofitable and badly managed company can be transformed. It also shows how in France the interests of the state, public companies, and large financial and industrial companies are inextricably linked. Another important facet of this closeness is the ease with which men move from one sector to another, as is shown by the career of Jean Méo, who from 1958 to 1960 was a senior civil servant in the department of mines and a collaborator of General de Gaulle, a director of Elf-Erap from 1967 to 1972, director of *France Soir* from 1972 to 1974, and chairman of Havas since 1974. Moreover, the president and the prime minister follow the departures, changes, and appointments announced in the press very closely. Georges Pompidou, for example, found it quite normal to attack Jean Prouvost for the publication of an unkind article about French television service in *Télé 7 Jours*.[8] And Valéry Giscard d'Estaing did not hesitate to chastise the director of *France Soir* for the reporting of one of his official visits.[9] In a world such as this, were everyone knows everyone else and where the civil service is omnipresent, liberal, capitalist, free enterprise is as unthinkable as forced nationalization, and no important newspaper could possibly change hands without at least the tacit approval of the government. The logical outcome of this state of affairs is that companies more or less controlled by the state involve themselves in the affairs of the press, and, the banks also play a crucial role at the meeting point of business and politics. Private banks play a part, but the state, because of the power of the nationalized banks, has the means to help or discourage anyone wishing to buy a newspaper.[10]

From this point of view, the resources open to Robert Hersant were impressive. In 1973 he had been in charge of a reasonably prosperous group made up essentially of *Auto Journal* and some small provincial dailies. Then, he bought *Le Figaro* and half of *France Soir*, becoming the most important press baron in Paris. At the same time he was preparing to begin the facsimile printing of these two newspapers in several provincial centers and thus put himself in a position to dominate the French daily press. It is not known where Hersant obtained the funds for these operations, but it is certain that those who provided the capital necessary (a figure of 40 to 50 million francs has been quoted) could not have done so without receiving the approval of the government, acting through its banking institutions.[11]

For what reason, one may ask, did Hersant enjoy such favor in the eyes of the prime minister, if not of the president? Even if one passes over his activities during World War II one cannot remain unaware of the ambiguity of his political past. For a long time he was well thought of on the left. Once an opposition member of parliament under de Gaulle, elected in 1967 under the patronage of the democratic and socialist Federation of the Left, it was he who had saved the fortunes of the socialist daily in the Nord department, *Nord Matin.* Furthermore he had close links with Edgar Faure, president of the Assembly, and one of the latter's associates was on the staff of *Le Figaro.* Thus Hersant belonged to no specific political party or label; he simply understood that in order to ensure the prosperity of a large newspaper group in France, he had to be on good terms with whomever was in power. It is also worth noting that apart from *Auto Journal,* which was the origin of his group's prosperity, Hersant has never launched a new journalistic formula. This lack of originality distinguishes him from the Prouvost and Hachette groups, which have on occasions been daring in their promotion of new publications. Surrounded by lawyers and financial experts, Hersant is first and foremost a businessman anxious to make a profit through a product: the press.[12]

Hachette's *France Soir* transactions drew some unforeseen reactions. The journalists employed on the newspaper went on strike and went before the courts claiming that the order of August 26, 1944, which forbade the use of figureheads' names in deals and the ownership of more than one daily newspaper, had been violated.[13] (The issue later became moot, however; new legislation, adapted to the realities of the French press in 1978, was passed, rescinding the order.) Editorials unfavorable to Robert Hersant appeared throughout the press, from the right-wing *L'Aurore* to the left-wing *L'Humanité.* Most surprisingly, television, especially Antenne 2, joined in the criticism. This attitude tended to confirm the rumors circulating at the time that suggested that one of the factors separating the president of the Republic from Prime Minister Chirac was the latter's support for the Hersant group through one of his aides.

In early 1979, the Hersant group grew even larger. It completed negotiations for a technical linking of *L'Aurore* and *Le Figaro,* thus bringing the former into the Hersant group.

Amaury and the Syndicat du livre

The government, which had been very active in overseeing the reorganization of Hachette and the breakup of the Prouvost group, showed itself more discreet but no less attentive regarding the changing fortunes of *Le Parisien Libéré.*[14] The owner of this newspaper, Emilien Amaury, was growing old and was without a successor to take over the running of the publications under his control: *Point de Vue, Marie-France, L'Équipe,* two provincial dailies, *Le Courrier de l'Ouest* and *Le Maine Libre,* and *Le Parisien Libéré,* which in 1973 ranked with *France Soir* as the most widely read newspaper in France.

Amaury was a militant member of the Christian Democratic movement before the war, then a member of the Resistance, then a Gaullist.

He had gradually become a tough, austere, and intransigent newspaper owner with very conservative, even reactionary, views. He had never sought to ingratiate himself with the government in power. He quarreled with General de Gaulle over the granting of independence to Algeria, and his papers (*Le Parisien Libéré* and *Carrefour*, the political organ of the group) backed the supporters of a French Algeria. In the presidential elections of 1974, he had supported the ultraconservative candidate, Jean Royer, and he led a permanent crusade against falling moral standards, crime, immigration from North Africa, and youths with long hair. In all these cases he did not hold back in his criticism of the government, which in his view was guilty of weakness and excessive tolerance.

It was inevitable that one day conflict should flare up between Amaury and the Syndicat du livre, a trade union organization affiliated with the Communist trade union CGT, which commanded an extraordinary authority. Since 1944 it had obtained for itself and its members three advantages, which Amaury had opposed. First, the union controlled the hiring of labor in the printing plants in the Paris region. The system was a closed shop; workers without a Syndicat du livre card could not be hired. The role of the union went even further; each week it designated which of its members would be assigned to work on which newspaper. Second, it had successfully negotiated extremely favorable working conditions. Its members were required to work only five hours a day and could set production targets far below the capacities of modern machinery. And third, members' salaries were exceptionally high. In 1974, 42 percent of the work force of *Le Parisien Libéré* earned more than 60,000 francs per year (approximately $17,000), whereas more than two-thirds of the journalists on the staff of the same newspaper earned less than that figure.

The privileges of the Syndicat du livre had been under fire for a long time; indeed in 1946, a communist minister had called it "a closed and intransigent body." However, for two decades, newspaper owners and the authorities had been happy with an organization that allowed great flexibility in the management of personnel, since the union would supply each company with the required number of workers at any given time. Yet this situation could continue only through the maintenance of a balance of power between the various forces at play. At the end of the 1960s, this balance began to break down, to the detriment of the union. Its monopoly was first broken in the provinces when the workers of the socialist newspaper group, *Le Provençal*, affiliated themselves to the rival union, Force Ouvrière. Then in Paris, newspapers were making lower profits and balked at paying salaries that they considered too high. Finally newspapers wanted to introduce new printing techniques that would lower the cost of production. The Syndicat du livre found that it had to negotiate a series of changes that would inevitably lead to a reduction of its authority and to the replacement of traditional printing workers by technicians outside its sphere of influence.

To Amaury, the moment seemed ideal to put an end to what he called the "extraordinary abuse of power by a politicized trade union organization." In 1974, he decided to transform *Le Parisien Libéré* into a newspaper for the whole of the Ile de France region. In this way he hoped to elude the conditions governing the Parisian press and to take advantage of the much more advantageous joint convention of the regional press. Nevertheless he first entered into negotiations with the Syndicat du livre with a view to obtaining a modification of the rules governing Paris. These negotiations ended on November 20, 1974, with an agreement drawn up in very vague terms that was never applied. In fact, the union had fallen into a trap. By not agreeing to revise its rules, it had provided Amaury with an excellent excuse to open hostilities. The result was certain to be unfavorable to a profession that was isolated and on the defensive. Its weak position was underscored by the fact that the communist daily, *L'Humanité,* was very discreet in its support for the strikers. Only one of the newspaper's journalists, a veteran of the barricades of May 1968, agreed to write articles favorable to them.[15] Indeed the printing workers were earning far higher salaries than were the newspaper's journalists.

In March 1975, the management of the *Parisien Libéré,* decided to abandon the Parisian printing plant and move these operations outside the region to two modern plants at Saint-Ouen and Chartres. Management emphasized that only 170 people would now be required for this work (there were 560 in Paris) and pointed out that because of the nature of the agreements linking the press to the Syndicat du livre, the workers in Paris were not actually employed by the group since they were assigned by the union to different newspapers according to demand. Thus, Amaury concluded, there was no need to give notice of dismissal. The Syndicat du livre took these decisions as an act of provocation and demanded the reinstatement of the great majority of the employees of the Parisian plant. Thus, all the conditions converged for the start of a very wide-ranging conflict.

Clearly the government could not avoid taking an interest in this dispute. It certainly had few political affinities with Amaury, but it could not frown on an action taken against the CGT trade union, whose members were for the most part communists or anarchist inspired.[16] On June 5, 1975, the minister of labor authorized the layoff of employees in the Parisian plant. Its decision can certainly be construed as a political gesture expressing the government's thinking on the matter.

During the months that followed, the conflict deepened. The Syndicat du livre attacked distributors of the *Parisien Libéré;* occupied the Paris Stock Exchange, Notre-Dame, and the ocean liner *France;* and ordered twelve general strikes in the newspaper industry, whose paradoxical outcome was that the *Parisien Libéré* was the only newspaper to appear in Paris on strike days, since its new staff was not affiliated to the union. Its actions had little effect on public opinion. Indeed many people had been astonished to learn of the size of the salaries earned by the

Syndicat du livre workers, and, moreover, many did not understand the particularly complicated situation. The climate surrounding the affair was further clouded over by the assassination of Jacques Cabannes, the chief editor of AFO and namesake of one of the directors of the *Parisien Libéré*, who was probably the target of the killing. The killers have never been traced.

For his part, Amaury had to bear the very heavy financial burden of his antitrade union action. He was forced to subcontract the printing of part of the newspaper in Belgium, and he had to take on the distribution of the paper himself because the distributors' union refused out of solidarity to do the work. The paper's circulation fell enormously; in 1974 it was 760,000, and by 1977 it was only 300,000.

The conflict progressively weakened both contestants. The union exhausted its resources by its financial aid to the 560 striking workers who were occupying the buildings in the Parisian plant.[17] And Amaury endangered the balance of his group by helping his newspaper to survive. What is more, the general strikes meant that losses were sustained by all newspapers without providing any solution to the problem. By the end of 1976, it was quite clear that the union was ready to reach a compromise, and it made a major concession by giving up the closed shop. Its leaders were very conscious that their obligation to pay the strikers at the *Parisien Libéré* was putting them in a disadvantageous position when negotiating with the other Parisian newspaper owners, notably Robert Hersant. Indeed Hersant was well aware that the union could not afford to challenge both himself and Amaury at the same time. In fact, when he took charge of *France Soir* in August 1976, the workers belonging to the Syndicat du livre broke with the journalists' strike and agreed to negotiate with Hersant.

In contrast, the owner of the *Parisien Libéré* appeared to become more intransigent, and on December 5, 1976, the government intervened. It ordered the police to evacuate the buildings occupied by the strikers since May 6, 1975, and appointed a mediator, Jean Mottin.[18] Mottin was well acquainted with the world of the press. But over a period of two months, during which he held a series of negotiations with all parties, he was unable to reach a solution on one fundamental point: the *Parisien Libéré* refused to reinstate the striking workers, and the union considered this point essential. At a press conference in February 1977, Mottin put forward the arguments of both sides, as well as his own proposals for the redeployment of the 562 people in question, mainly with the aid of public funds and those of the national unemployment insurance system. His proposals were not accepted, and his mission ended in failure. Yet the situation had changed, though in an unforeseen way; on January 2, 1977, Amaury had died.

Amaury's death put his close associate, Claude Bellanger, in charge of the group. Bellanger was one of the most prestigious figures of the French press. After brilliant service in the Resistance, he had for thirty years been a newspaper executive, coauthor of a monumental general history of the French press, and one of the leaders of the International Federation of Newspaper Publishers.[19] He was less personally involved in the battle over the *Parisien Libéré* and was without doubt more aware than Amaury of the enormous burden that this conflict placed on the group as a whole. For its part, the Syndicat du livre was seeking an honorable way out of the problem. Discreet negotiations were therefore reopened and in July 1977, Bellanger and the union announced that they had come to an agreement, which included the reinstatement of 114 workers, the payment of an indemnity of about 60,000 francs to any worker wishing to leave the profession, the settling of overdue subscriptions, the distribution of around 230 workers in other Parisian printing plants and to the national newspaper distributors' organization, and the payment of 10,000 francs to each of the 514 workers to mark the end of the dispute.

The press and the trade union organizations rejoiced at the solution of a dispute that had endangered the future of the entire industry, but their relief was premature. The redistribution of the workers of the *Parisien Libéré* necessitated the intervention of a third party—the state, which had in effect to finance a large part of this operation; but it appeared that no firm commitments had been obtained from the authorities before the signing of the agreement. Nevertheless an agreement was finally reached at the ministry of labor on August 16, 1977. The authorities agreed to finance the cost of redistribution and social security up to a ceiling of 8.5 million francs and both sides in the dispute agreed to drop the legal proceedings they had initiated in the course of the affair, under French industrial law.

Thus a conflict was resolved that had highlighted the weakness of both the press and the anachronistic corporatism of the Syndicat du livre, which was in practice forced to give up its closed shop. It also proved that in a situation of such delicacy, nothing could be solved without the agreement and the participation of the government. The affair of the *Parisien Libéré* proved to be an affair of state.[20]

SNEP

The long dispute over the *Parisien Libéré* must be placed in the context of the continuing crisis of the printing industry in France. For years, this sector of industry has faced innumerable difficulties. Because of extremely high production costs, it has borne the brunt of competition from companies in the other common market countries, Belgium, and Italy, which attract customers not only from book publishing but also from the newspaper industry. The result was that more publications were printed abroad, reducing the amount of work carried out by the industry in France.[21]

The state has taken an interest in the survival of the printers not only as the authority supervising such an important industry, but also as the owner of the Société Nationale des Entreprises de Presse (SNEP), which directly controls most of France's printing capacity. At the be-

138

ginning of the 1970s SNEP was struggling. In a critical report published in 1973, the commission for the auditing of the accounts of publicly owned companies drew attention to the fact that

during the last three financial years, the SNEP has been forced to give added financial assistance to its subsidiaries, not only to finance new investments, but also, increasingly, to cover production losses. . . . In order to finance such help, the SNEP, which had already exhausted the funds originating from the liquidation of its holdings in the press and realized most of its share portfolio as well a part of its real-estate holdings was forced, in 1969, to sell off the most important part of its heritage, the Poissonniere printing works, and then had recourse to loans.[22]

The commission concluded by suggesting a redefinition of the aims of the company, a reform of its statutes, a reorganization of the group, and the retaining of only those subsidiaries that matched up to its aims and offered guarantees of profitability. In effect, the commission was calling for a total reorganization of the company. The state would not allow the demise of SNEP, which provided valuable services, especially overseas.

At about this time, SNEP's leadership changed. It's chairman, Jean Mottin, was made a member of the Council of State and was replaced by Guy Sabatier, a Gaullist member of parliament for the Aisne region from 1962 to 1973 and for several years the chief member responsible for the budget in the Finance Commission of the Assemblé Nationale. He had just been defeated in the elections. Sabatier immediately undertook a revision of the company's legal organization and drew up a consolidated balance sheet.

In spring 1973, SNEP began to reorganize. It sold the buildings and the plant of its Henon printing plant in Paris, thereby recovering some of the money invested, and transferred the business of another printing plant to a new company in which it retained a 20 percent share of the capital. Although the expected revival in business did not take place, these changes, as well as the anticipated payment of installments from the sale of the Poissonnière works, allowed SNEP to repay certain debts and help its two most important subsidiaries, Paul Dupont and Montlouis.[23] In 1974, the company succeeded in making a profit of 6 million francs, though in 1975 its accounts revealed a loss of 25 million francs.

Abroad SNEP continued to act as an adviser for the setting up and printing of newspapers, taking part in the activities of companies in Niger, the Ivory Coast, Senegal, and Madagascar. In France, through the Paul Dupont printing establishment, it played an important role in the restructuring of the heavy offset industry in Paris. In order to invigorate this particularly sick sector, it set up the Groupement d'Interets Economiques in which the publishing house Editions de Montsouris took a 20 percent share. In 1977, Paul Dupont succeeded in balancing its books, reducing production losses from 8 million francs to only 882,000 francs. However the Montlouis printing works still sustained losses of 5,538,000 francs.

What is most striking, however, is that over the years the role of the SNEP was transformed. In 1970, it functioned largely as the administrator of printing works inherited by the state after the Liberation. Gradually it was transformed, according to the wishes of many parliamentarians, into an instrument of the authorities, both abroad and at home where the printing industry was in severe straits. Such a role, however, was not without its problems. SNEP's activities in the West Indies provide an example. In 1963, following an agreement between the government and Robert Hersant, SNEP invested 1 million francs in the creation of a printing company, SIGA, in Martinique and Guadeloupe, which would allow the printing of a new daily newspaper, *France Antilles,* launched by the Hersant group in March 1964. The newspaper flourished and quickly became profitable. Then on October 15, 1973, the minister of information ordered SNEP to sell 90 percent of its share in SIGA to Hersant. Thus, in the transaction SNEP effectively played a supporting role for the Hersant group.[24] Nevertheless the transaction proved quite profitable, for SNEP, on an investment of 1.5 million francs, received 1.9 million francs for the transfer of materials and repayment of credits on top of the one million francs received in rents over ten years.

All in all, the fate of the SNEP remains closely tied to that of the rest of the French book printing industry, but the company cannot act effectively without the support of a supervising authority that is often rather remote.[25]

Le Parisien Libéré and L'Aurore

By 1978 the Parisian newspaper industry was less prosperous than ever. Newspapers with wide circulations such as *France Soir* and *Parisien Libéré* had seen their sales drop by a third to a half in five years. Newly created papers such as *Le Matin* and *Libération* were having a difficult time and suffering from poor circulations (90,000 and 30,000, respectively). The Parisian press now accounted for only a quarter of the total sales of daily newspapers in France. Almost all of the papers, including *Le Monde,* recorded losses for the 1977 financial year, and *Le Quotidien de Paris* had to stop publication. Nevertheless the status and prestige of the Parisian press continued to be important to the politicians. Although the newspapers of the capital were progressively losing their national audience, both government and opposition still dreamed of controlling one of these newspapers, which were believed to bring power and prestige to their owners.[26]

After the March general elections, which allowed the previous majority to stay in power, the president concerned himself with the future of two newspapers that were in danger of collapsing, *Le Parisien Libéré* and *L'Aurore.*

Claude Bellanger, the chairman and managing director of the *Parisien,* had recently sold his shares in the company to a promoter and had died shortly afterward. Despite having been considerably weakened by the dispute with the Syndicat du livre and despite a circulation of only 350,000 copies (versus 800,000 copies in 1974), the *Parisien Libéré* had a firm grounding in the Parisian suburbs and its working-class readership. Complex negotiations, of which little is known, and in which it would appear that a former minister, Pierre Henri Teitgen, played an important part, were entered into with the aim of choosing a successor to Bellanger. The board of directors chose André Fosset, a centrist senator, a former minister for the environment in the first Barre government, and a strong supporter of the president of the republic. In order to take up this new post, Fosset gave up the job he had held since December 1977—adviser to the Hersant group.

With the *Parisien Libéré* firmly fastened to the majority boat, only the case of *L'Aurore* remained to be settled. Bought by Marcel Boussac after the war, *L'Aurore* had had its years of glory and prosperity. Vigorously anti-Gaullist, pro-Israeli, and in favor of a French Algeria, by the early 1960s it had managed to assemble a readership of dissatisfied conservatives, and its circulation had passed the 400,000 mark. Unfortunately this period of prosperity was short-lived. The paper had been unable to adapt to the changing tastes of its readership and thus suffered the full force of the crisis of the Parisian press. Its remaining readers had grown considerably older, its circulation had dropped to 250,000 copies, and it had sustained heavy losses (30 million francs in 1977), which were not covered by the profits from Boussac's other daily, the racing newspaper *Paris Turf*.

For several years, the entire Boussac group had been declining. Specializing in textiles, it ran up against increasingly strong international competition and shared in the crisis that hit the textile industry all over France; its losses ran into hundreds of millions of francs. Boussac, who was over eighty, made up for these losses by gradually selling his personal property. But this solution could not carry on indefinitely, and in early 1978, it became clear to the banks and to the state that the group had to be sold and completely reorganized, even if this were to be delayed until the general election in March. The president was particularly concerned over the future of *L'Aurore*, which he could not allow to fall into the hands of financiers associated with his rival Jacques Chirac.

The newspaper was finally bought by a consortium of banks and industrialists headed by Marcel Fournier, chairman of the Carrefour supermarket chain.[27] It was announced that the political direction of the newspaper would be in the hands of Pierre Christian Taittinger, a senator for Paris belonging to Giscard d'Estaing's party. The transaction took place at the end of June. A few days later, the minister of commerce gave Fournier permission to open two hypermarkets at Limoges and Nice. Some press commentators linked the two events, suggesting that Fournier had obtained this exceptional license in exchange for his intervention in *L'Aurore*.

141

Thus, in less than three years, four of the five major Parisian daily newspapers had changed hands following negotiations in which the banks and the offices of the president and the prime minister had played a decisive role. The four newspapers have not changed their political affiliations; they were favorable to the majority before being sold and remained so despite internal wranglings among the partners. Over the years they have continued to lose readers despite their change of owners; indeed the only Parisian newspaper to see a growth in circulation in the last three years has been the small left-wing newspaper *Libération,* which is of no interest to government or the banks and whose growth now appears to have come to a halt.

Public Subsidies

While this process of restructuring the ownership of the press had been going on, the authorities and the press had been trying to reform the system of public subsidies, which had long been an issue. Since an overall reform seemed impossible to attain, the problem had been approached through the question of tax benefits. The initiative came from parliament. In October 1974, after the election of Valéry Giscard d'Estaing to the presidency, Robert André Vivien succeeded in getting the Assemblé Nationale, to which he was responsible for its information budget, to amend the finance law by calling for the establishment of a committee to study possible improvements in the fiscal status of the press.[28] The government assembled this committee on February 15, 1975. It was made up of representatives of organizations within the press, of the administration, and of parliament (the chairman of the finance committee of the two houses and those responsible for the information budget). It was chaired by André Rossi, secretary of state for information, and Christian Poncelet, secretary of state for the budget.

This procedure itself was remarkable. Rarely had the state associated a profession and parliament so closely in the preparation of a reform with as yet unspecified aims. The move may well be explained by the singular nature of the problems of the press in which the government was hesitant to take any initiative for fear of being suspected of authoritarianism and antiliberal intentions.

The government put its first proposals before the committee on October 17, 1975. The main one was to submit the totality of the press's income to a VAT rate of 7 percent, against which the daily newspapers could claim a rebate of 60 percent, so that their effective rate of tax would be 2 percent. The press reacted with hostility, since this change would increase its payments from 110 to 120 million francs. The press was not happy that the financial administration should want to increase its revenue at the expense of a sector of industry whose situation was so precarious. At this point, Vivien intervened with a compromise based on two points: the existing fiscal situation would be maintained,

142

and the government, in collaboration with the industry, would prepare a bill to be put before parliament during the spring session of 1976.

The government reluctantly accepted these proposals, which avoided a breakdown of the talks, but shortly afterward it tried to put them in question once again by introducing into the finance bill for 1976 a clause that excluded monthly publications from the terms of article 39, which allows newspaper companies to claim a tax rebate on proposed investments. But members of parliament rejected the amendment and instead adopted one proposed by the Senate that demanded that before April 2, 1976, a bill be put before parliament designed to improve the fiscal status of the press. Thus, after a year of fluctuation and confused negotiations, the issue was back to the original problem. Eventually the reaction of parliament and pressure from the professional organizations carried the day. The committee met again, reaching an agreement that was shortly afterward put before parliament in the form of a bill. The two essential provisions of this text dealt with the questions of VAT and Article 39 bis. Regarding VAT, it was decided to fix a rate of 7 percent on income from sales, but this would be subject to a rebate based on the frequency of publication. The intention was to help the dailies, for which this rebate meant an effective VAT rating of 2.1 percent on a permanent basis. For other publications, the effective rate of tax would be 3.5 percent and would be regularly increased to reach 7 percent by 1981. Article 39 bis was extended for four years, but the percentage of income that could be assigned to proposed investments was reduced to 70 percent for dailies and 50 percent for other publications.

This arrangement had considerable advantages for the press. By submitting itself to VAT on the whole of its income, the press broke the economic isolation that arose out of its peculiar fiscal status, and put an end to the other taxes resulting from it, the tax on salaries and residual VAT. An end was also put to the inequalities among publications.[29] From now on, a newspaper with a large advertising income would be treated in the same way as one that drew its main revenue from sales. It was thus the first step toward the institution of a more equitable and effective system of public aid to the press. For financial year 1977, it resulted in a reduction of 54 million francs in the tax contributions of daily newspapers and of 57 million for other publications.

The decision to extend the provisions of Article 39 bis for another four years also was favorable. Previously the article had been extended year by year only after difficult negotiations between parliament, the government, and the industry. Each autumn, at the time of the budget, the minister of finance would wait until the last moment before placing the saving amendment granting the press a respite, thus constantly putting it in the position of supplication. This situation has now been provisionally ended. The benefit to the press in 1977 has been calculated at 47 million francs.

Because the agreement and the bill discriminated between daily newspapers and other types of publications, it gave rise to dissent within the profession. Several political weeklies—*Le Point, Le Nouvel Observateur, Valeurs Actuelles, L'Humanité Dimanche, Minute,* and *Le Canard Enchainé*—opposed this discrimination. They claimed that they were much closer to the daily press than other periodicals and demanded the same fiscal status.

These demands raised a problem of principle. Trade unions within the press and the authorities had always refused to make subsidies dependent on the content of a paper. They maintained that it would endanger public liberties to base such a choice on the analysis of texts published by a newspaper preferring frequency of publication and the proportion of space devoted to advertising as more objective criteria for making judgments. A decision that one publication is political while another is devoted entirely to entertainment cannot be made without running the risk of being arbitrary. It would be simple to pick out extreme cases, but in most periodicals there is great diversity of content. Between the most serious journal and the most frivolous magazine, there is an often imperceptible dividing line. How is it possible to distinguish between a publication that still has some serious intent and a purely commercial magazine?

In theory discrimination on the basis of content would have many advantages. It would permit the concentration of subsidies only on publications that contribute to the political debate and the movement of ideas. The subsidy would thus be more effective and more useful and the resources at present available would achieve much better results. However, there is a gulf between this ideal and reality. It is difficult to imagine what independent, objective, and infallible process would distinguish between good and bad, a distinction made more difficult by the pitfalls of yielding to political pressures or to the more subtle persuasions of financial arguments for the removal of subsidies, which could well have grave consequences for a company and even lead to bankruptcy and closure.

In the debates over subsidies to the press, there has been general agreement on the advantages discrimination on the grounds of content might bring, but no one has been willing to take the responsibility for making the choices. The government and parliament have said that only the press itself could make such judgments and the press has declined that dubious honor.

The aims of the weekly newspapers of the Association of the Periodical Political Press led by Ollivier Chevrillon, editor of *Le Point,* and Claude Perdriel, editor of *Le Nouvel Observateur,* were not so ambitious. They did not want to change the subsidy system; they merely sought to be considered on a par with the daily press regarding the imposition of VAT. They believed that they fulfilled the same functions and played the same role as the dailies and therefore ought not to be the object of discrimination. Nevertheless their position went against the

144

philosophy governing the distribution of subsidies, and they failed to propose any solution to the problem of assessing content objectively.

Unable to sort out this dilemma themselves, the professional organizations called for a modification of the timetable leading to the imposition of a VAT rating of 7 percent. The government hesitated and delayed the inclusion of the bill. In the end, the centrist René Monory, who at the time was the chairman of the senate finance commission, intervened, asking for concessions to the press. The Ministry of Finance put forward some complex provisions favorable to the nondaily press. These provisions were adopted with only slight modification by the two assemblies and became law on December 29, 1976.

There was no change in the initial proposals for the daily press. It would be subject to a VAT rate of 2 percent, which would free it from residual taxes and tax on salaries. Other periodicals would be allowed to maintain the existing system of exemption for a period of five years, at the end of which they would become subject to a rate of 7 percent. However, if they preferred to opt immediately for the imposition of VAT, they could do so, and until the five years were up, they would be subject to a preferential rate of 4 percent. Since dependent industries, notably printing, would now also be subject to VAT, the state agreed to compensate for the extra expense incurred by companies that chose to maintain their exemption at a cost of around 250 million francs per year. Also, as expected, Article 39 bis was extended for four years.

It must be concluded that the press came out of the two years of fiscal negotiations as the victor. Parliament had been an effective ally. Deputies such as Robert André Vivien and senators such as René Monory did much to persuade the administration to make concessions to an industry for which it felt more hostility than sympathy. The two assemblies failed to make progress on one point, the fiscal status of political periodicals, although the government did not shut the door on them completely. The secretary of state for the budget declared in the Assemblé in December 1976 that he was prepared to examine any proposals on this question that the French National Press Federation (FNPF) might care to submit. In early 1977, the Association of the Periodical Political Press, which had become the union of the political periodical press (SPPP), set to work on the problem. It called on the legal advice of Georges Vedel and submitted a text to the FNPF. This body agreed to go back on its consistent refusal to consider any discrimination on the grounds of content, but whereas the SPPP had called for the setting up of a selection committee made up entirely of magistrates of the Council of State and Court of Cassation, the FNPF suggested a committee of five magistrates and five representatives of the profession. A request from an editor of a publication to have it treated as a daily newspaper was to be put before the committee for assessment. The administration could overrule the committee, but it could not make a decision without having first obtained its opinion. To obtain such recognition, a publication had to have produced for a weekly at least twenty-six editions, and for a monthly at least six.

On March 31, 1977, the president of the FNPF and the president of the union of the Parisian weekly press submitted these proposals to the prime minister's office. Clearly the press had fulfilled its part of the bargain, and was now up to the authorities to declare themselves. Discussions went on during the summer and autumn of 1977, ending in the submission of a bill passed by parliament in December, just before the conclusion of the business of the legislature. This law of December 27, 1977, appeared to be a compromise between the proposals of Vedel and the FNPF on the one hand, and the government's wishes on the other. It limited the category of beneficiaries to weeklies that devoted more than a third of their editorial space to political information. It set up a committee with the task of designating which publications answered this description, to be made up of three magistrates appointed for a period of three years, a member of the Council of State, a councillor of the Court of Cassation, and a councillor of the Cour des Comptes. This committee did not have any power of decision. Its role was limited to the presentation of a list of weeklies to the prime minister, who would then pass judgment.

Thus the authorities and the press took a step toward accepting that a form of public subsidy be accorded on the basis of the content of a publication, though they allowed only a very limited exception to the rule of nondiscrimination. The committee decided to apply the terms of the law to only seventeen of the thirty-one weeklies that asked for consideration.

Conclusion

Over the course of recent years, it has been possible to observe two types of state intervention in the organization and management of the French press. First, the authorities have played an active role in the reorganization of the large newspaper groups so as to replace the owners who had been in charge since 1945 with faithful and reliable supporters. Second, the system of public aid to the press has been expanded and improved in a skillful and liberal fashion so that newspapers feel indebted to a government that has been so generous to them. Thus in France today, discreet intervention and generous subsidies together have combined to tighten the links between the government and the press.

Notes

1. It was published by *Cahiers de la presse française*, no. 92 (1972).

2. François Archambault, *Quatre Milliards de Journaux* (Paris: Alain Moreau, 1977), p. 15.

3. The newspaper *Sud-Ouest* is the third largest company in the Gironde department.

4. The prototype of these agreements is that which linked *Le Progrès* and *Le Dauphiné Libéré*. These two daily newspapers set up a common press agency, the agence Aigles, and shared the readership in the region of the Rhône-Alpes.

5. The majority of the management of *Entreprise,* notably the editor in chief, left it at the time of the merger.

6. At the end of complex operations, which went on from December 1972 to May 1974, Havas and its subsidiary, Information et Publicité, took, respectively, shares of 15.2 percent and 13.3 percent in a holding company, Audiofina, which held 56.4 percent of the capital of CLT (Compagnie Luxembourgeoise de télédiffusion), the parent company of RTL (Radio Television de Luxembourg). Thus Havas held a strategic minority share in Audiofina, the principal shareholder in RTL, giving it a voice in the appointment of the chief executive of the company.

7. On this point, see the views of Jacques Sauvageot in *Le Monde,* August 15–16, 1976.

8. Quoted by Jean Diwo, director of *Télé 7 Jours* in his book, *Si vous avez manqué le début* (Paris, 1976).

9. Evidence obtained by the author.

10. In August 1976, Edmond Maire, general secretary of the trade union, CFDT, publicly accused the nationalized banks of financing the operations of Robert Hersant.

11. According to *Le Monde,* August 19, 1976, the Hersant group was comprised of eleven daily newspapers (plus *France Soir*), nine weeklies, eleven technical or specialized journals, a press agency, an advertising agency, and several printing works. The group was responsible for 16 percent of daily newspapers printed in France. See also Marie Louise Antoni, "Hersant à la une," *Le Nouvel Economiste,* November 15, 1976.

12. See also on these various points, Dominique Pons, *H comme Hersant* (Paris: Alain Moreau, 1977).

13. Some people sustained that the hurried sale of *France Soir* occurred in the middle of August owing to the imminent departure from the government of Jacques Chirac, who had been backing the operation. There is very little evidence on this question. However it is worth noting that in the elections of March 1978, Robert Hersant was backed by all of the parties of the majority, including the followers of Giscard d'Estaing.

14. There is a good account of this affair in *Regards sur l'Actualité* (March 1977). See also, Jean Legres; *l'Affaire du Parisien Libéré, Etudes* (October 1976).

15. Evidence obtained by the author.

16. The Syndicat du livre did ascertain that Jacques Dominati, a member of parliament for Paris and leader of the independent republican party, was being paid by the *Parisien Libéré,* where he had been a journalist before his election in 1968.

147

17. It is calculated that during this period, the workers belonging to the union had to contribute 10 percent of their salaries to pay their colleagues on strike and that the affair cost the union 30 million francs.

18. This action took place on the very day of the congress that set up the RPR, and since its obvious consequence was a strike of the daily press the next day, some commentators suggested that the government chose the date in order to minimize the publicity surrounding the taking in hand of the Gaullist party by Jacques Chirac who had become an opponent of the president.

19. Claude Bellanger et al., *Histoire Générale de la Presse Française* (Paris: Presses Universitaires de France, 1969–1976), 5 vols.

20. See the conclusions of Jacques Buisson, "Le Parisien libéré—le fin du conflit," *Presse Actualité* (September—October 1977): 14–21.

21. In 1974, the imports of publications amounted to 481 million francs; exports were 349 million francs. Even some publications with communist allegiances of the Miroir des Sports group were published abroad in order to benefit from lower prices.

22. Commission de vérification des comptes des entreprises publiques, *Thirteenth Report,* p. 110.

23. Commission de vérification, *Fourteenth Report* (1976) p. 105.

24. Pons, *Hersant* p. 104.

25. For a study of the overall problems of the French printing industry, see the report of the working party under Jean Philippe Lecat, Ministry of Industry, March 1975.

26. In September 1977, a group of industrialists and financiers launched the evening newspaper *J'Informe,* edited by the former centrist minister, Joseph Fontanet. It ceased publication on December 17, 1977. Its circulation had dropped to 20,000 copies and it had lost 30 million francs. See Hubert Jetrex, "J'Informe: autopsie d'un disparu," *Presse Actualité* (January 1978).

27. Marcel Fournier had been one of the financiers involved with the attempted launching of *J'Informe* in September 1977.

28. See the report by Robert André Vivien on the bill relating to the fiscal status of the press (AN 2310, 1976).

29. In 1973 and 1974, the authorities tried to remedy these inequalities by giving special financial aid to dailies with a small circulation and low advertising revenue: *La Croix, le Quotidien de Paris,* and *l'Humanité.*

III

Press and State in the Newer Democracies

There exist within the Western world examples of societies where the traditional argument concerning press freedom is still working itself out and doing so in the context of modern consumer economics. Spain and Portugal are the classic cases where the ending of a nineteenth-century style of press censorship has taken place only in the last decade with the collapse of the dictatorships of Franco and Salazar. The first impact of the new regimes on the press was a tremendous flowering reminiscent of the 1850s in other parts of Europe, when the sudden establishment of nation-states and the final abolition of feudal regimes brought about a sudden proliferation of vernacular journalism. Yet in the course of a very few years, Spain has seemingly run through the stages that other societies took several generations to traverse. The ending of a censorship that repressed social, sexual, and political journalism for forty years caused an eruption of scandalous and erotic media. As José Antonio Martinez Soler explains, the Spanish public ran through its capacity for surprise in a few years, leaving the rapidly created periodical press in a financial crisis comparable with that of Spain's democratic neighbors. A familiar pattern of social control through commercial and industrial structures has supplanted a pattern of controls through direct censorship. In the case of Portugal, the belief, and the hope, that the media would function in the twentieth century like the party propaganda of the nineteenth has been similarly shattered. So great and so ingrown were the practices of self-censorship under the old regime that virtually no journalists in the country could remember what it was like to live with a journalism of polemic and controversy.

Portugal today presents the argument about state intervention and private control in a completely different guise from elsewhere. In Portugal state control of a privately owned newspaper industry has been replaced by liberation of debate within a largely state-owned industry. As the revolutionary period has moved on, new private papers have come into existence alongside the state-owned ones (and one of the latter has ceased publication altogether). What has preserved the pluralism of the press as the revolution has moved from phase to phase is the pluralism of the journalist community itself. The reporters' committee has become the principal guarantor of the free flow of expression, a formulation that presents paradoxes for both journalists and publishers in much of Western Europe and America. Jean Seaton and Ben Pimlott show how each society today has to register for itself the conventions by which cultural and political freedom is maintained (or achieved). There is no longer a universal formula reserving the role of government to one or another level of intervention, or to none at all.

It is here that the Japanese situation is of particular interest to the nations of the Western world. William Horsley shows how new roots were planted in Japanese life of public and personal rights in the aftermath of World War II. A strong national will survived and established a new wave of prosperity in the country, not least for its media industries. Politicians founded institutions that in effect controlled the flow of information from their ministerial or opposition offices outward through the society, and the press increasingly came under the control of an oligarchy, which has reduced ideological distinctions between the vast national newspapers almost to negligible proportions. Nonetheless, the *kisha* clubs, wartime institutions for controlling information which turned themselves into modern lobbies around important public figures, did not prevent a quantity of social power passing into the hands of journalism to the point of bringing about the overthrow of corrupt politicians. Where America's Watergate and South Africa's "Muldergate" have been heralded as classic triumphs for investigative journalism in modern times, the Japanese version of a similar episode represents at least as remarkable an event and one that has exercised a considerable influence over the institutional and corporate development of the national press of Japan. The freedom of information question, crucial in the development of information flow between modern bureaucracies and modern newspapers, takes on a new salience in societies where the press maintains a formal investigative role but operates in practice normally in close relationship with the actual political sources of information. Britain's parliamentary lobby, in the period of James Callaghan's prime ministership, has attempted to overcome the public taint of being in the pocket of ministers (notably by announcing in print the sources of information that it used formerly to keep private). At a time when public bureaucracies in practice monitor (and therefore conceal) a very large proportion of the total sum of national information, new lines have to be drawn between the public's need to know and the administration's right to conduct its business without undue interference. Many societies are attempting to open up more files to public (in effect, journalistic) perusal than ever before, and this imposes a greater rather than a diminished strain upon reporters' skills and willingness to investigate.

The press of Italy, the subject of Giovanni Bechelloni's study, is in some ways in a similar position to that of Spain and Portugal in that only in the 1970s has it fought its way to an audience of the entire society. It is therefore still searching for an appropriate new journalism to suit the circumstances of the age. What makes the Italian press so fascinating an object of inquiry is the sheer variety of the ways that government has acquired for intervening. The forms of intervention, dating back to the 1930s, clearly influence the styles and modes of Italian reporting and have helped to keep newspaper circulations within the orbit of a narrow political class. The Ordine dei Giornalisti, founded by Mussolini, continues to license journalists and to this day provides them with a highly privileged position financially and socially. The Italian mass audience developed relatively late, in the decade preceding World War II, when radio and movies were already fighting for its attention, and the newspaper, swathed in governmental controls and privileges, has remained therefore somewhat stunted in its growth.

What we can observe from the four countries in this part is that where the newspaper has arrived late as a mass medium, it can still perform the repertoire of roles that belong to the older established mass newspapers: investigation of misbehavior by politicians, entertainment, and the furthering of partisan political discourse. However it is obliged to do so alongside rival electronic, largely entertainment media, and this fact obliges it to veer sharply from role to role and to feel insecure in the loyalty of its audience.

7

The Paradoxes of Press Freedom: The Spanish Case

José Antonio Martinez Soler

It is generally held that as the press in Spain has achieved greater official toleration and freedom since the death of Francisco Franco in 1975, so it has lost its credibility.[1] On January 12, 1978, *El Pais,* one of the most influential Spanish newspapers, ran a four-column back-page article, "Crisis of Confidence in the Daily Press," subtitled, "Spaniards Read Fewer and Fewer Newspapers"—this at a time of democratic euphoria when the press was enjoying the highest degree of freedom after forty years of dictatorship. According to the article, the spectacular decline in circulation and advertising in papers are two of the indicators of this crisis of confidence in the press which ultimately stems from readers. "Why?," *El Pais* asks, "this progressive withdrawal of the Spanish reader from the media?" On behalf of publishers, the president of the Daily Press Association, Pedro Crespo de Lara, wrote that "the crisis of the Spanish Press is so grave that if immediate measures are not taken, many publishers will have to close their doors."[2]

Only four years before, still under Francoist censorship, the so-called press boom had started. Publications grew by the hundreds, the number of professional journalists tripled, and circulation figures increased remarkably, approaching almost 3 million in 1975 (96 newspapers per thousand inhabitants).[3] In the year that Franco died, after forty years of dictatorship, Spanish daily newspaper circulation was back at the figure it had reached in 1934, two years before the civil war.

Official toleration during the political transition from dictatorship to democracy has now become de facto freedom of the press. In this peculiar state of transition—the Francoist censorship recently abolished and no new and more sophisticated systems of control yet taking its place—the Spanish press has as great a freedom as any other in the world. Nevertheless this greater degree of freedom has produced a turbulent, and unmanageable free market, a fierce competitiveness, and a crude, commercial, sensationalist press that has somewhat abandoned itself to the worst taste of the majority of the new readers. A symptom of this is the birth of some fifty erotic magazines; *Interviu,* the most successful weekly of this sort, has reached a circulation of one million issues. This explosion in the free market is a logical reaction to 40 years of repression. Since the death of Franco a morbid combination of blood, sex, and frivolous, barely authenticated political-financial scandal has poured weekly into a million Spanish homes. As a result, the public has been losing its capacity for surprise. One section of opinion blames this political-pornographic boom for the loss of the press's credibility and prestige, but the crisis seems to be more profound and complex.

In contrast to this pornographic wave, which has flooded news agents, the combined circulation figures of the 200 serious publications of the militant political parties do not add up to 400,000 weekly issues.[4] In general, according to a study in *Fomento de la Produccion,* the sales indices of the press are now even lower than at the end of 1975, when Franco died.[5] Why, when the press is freer, is readership declining? Perhaps the press is not freer now. Can freedom have negatively affected the quality and interest of the press? Many questions are raised by the crisis of the Spanish press in the transition from dictatorship to democracy. Rarely has a crisis of this kind—the jump from an absolutely controlled or authoritarian press at the service of the state to a free, libertarian or uncontrolled press—happened so quickly without abrupt changes in the economic, social, and political structures of the country. And rarely, also, have the contradictory effects or paradoxes of freedom been so uncamouflaged as in this rapid and surprising Spanish evolution.

The press, as Siebert and Peterson recognize, always takes the form and coloring of the social and political structures within which it acts and reflects, ultimately, the system of social control through which the relation of individuals and institutions is adjusted.[6] The press, then, cannot be detached from a reform like that which has taken place in Spanish society in the last five years.

The Spanish press, more than any other, has demonstrated a chameleon-like ability to adapt itself quickly to a changing society and reflect each aspect of change. If the social, political, and economic structures inherited from Francoism fell into crisis, the press could only collect and reflect the results. In its process of adaptation to the new rules of the democratic game, the press will come out strengthened by freedom, according to all the predictions, although for the time being, the paradoxical effects of this freedom fill with doubts many professionals of the press and many readers as well.

The apparent disillusion, the disenchantment with democracy perceived in the media—what one ex-director of newspapers has qualified as "the collective failure of our profession"—is, among other things, the interpretation of a generalized frustration.[7] The expectations of change were so great for so many years, the desire for freedom so enormous, the repression so severe, and the daily struggle of the press to win freedom so impassioned that the grounds were well laid for false illusions of a miraculous democracy. After such high expectations, the freedom now won has enormous creative and communicative potential, but it is still to be developed and exercised. The press has lost its heroic and active role of permanent promoter and initiator of the fight against dictatorship, politicians have withdrawn from the newsrooms and gone into Parliament and government, and the press under freedom becomes tremendously boring—when not sensationalist—in its new passive role reflecting society, sometimes wildly and irresponsibly.

Such high expectations and such low results have no doubt contributed to the feeling of collective frustration that reigns in the journalistic profession and of criticism or cold withdrawal by readers. All this does not mean that there is a nostalgia for censorship. Few have expressed any desire to go backward. But there does exist in all of this a desire for a time of reflection on the consequences of freedom of the press, on its worth, and on the limits—if there are to be any—on this growing freedom so that the press may fulfill responsibly its role of informing the public.

In this public discussion, something stands out clearly: freedom does not work miracles, although it offers the possibility of doing them. As the Commission on Freedom of the Press affirmed, "Freedom is experimental and implies, therefore, rehearsals, and trial and error."[8] And although freedom of the press involves risks, these are, in the end, infinitely less than those that result from no freedom.

Freedom of Propaganda

Analysis of the Spanish press under the dictatorship is simple. From Plato to Machiavelli, the basic principles are readily found of the authoritarian system where the press is an instrument at the service of those in power, where power in the hands of the dictator is the fountain of truth that all the media must defend and exalt. In this system one of the fundamental functions of the modern press—that of criticizing the government—does not exist. The authoritarian press serves only to transmit messages from the dictator to the citizens. The essential raw material for a flourishing press, individual freedom, does not exist, and without freedom, the press becomes simply an organ for propaganda. It can vary only the intensity of its applause—with more fervent or less fervent enthusiasm—for the decisions of the dictator. There is no freedom of the press but rather freedom of propaganda. These were the basic features of the press in Spain in the period that began with the provisional press law, dictated by Franco in 1938 in the midst of civil war, and ended with its repeal in 1966. The press of this period could be characterized as "war journalism." Its characteristics vary little from Hitler's or Mussolini's press.

The preamble of the 1938 law shows concern for "the masses of readers poisoned daily by a sectarian and antinational press" and declares, "The times do not allow an attempt to reach a definitive ordinance, which initially should limit the action of the government to taking the first steps that later will continue, firm and determined, towards this proposed goal of awakening in the press the idea of service to the State and returning to men who make their living in the press the material dignity that one who dedicates his efforts to such a profession deserves, becoming an apostle of the faith and the philosophy of a nation returned to its destiny."

Normally when media do not reflect the reality of the country, they lose interest for their readers. Thus the circulation of the apostolic newspapers of Francoism was extremely low in comparison with the preceding democratic period of the second republic. In the 1950s, the circulation of dailies dragged along at about 1.2 million, less than half the circulation of newspapers in the 1930s.[9]

In 1940 General Franco ordered the expropriation by the state of all newspapers opposed to the Only Party but permitted a few publications to survive that "with more or less adaptation would support the principles that today are entrenched in the Spanish state."[10] By these means, Spanish journalism was reduced to a desert of conformity, and journalists were practically converted into officials of the Only Party, motorcyclists who picked up official notes from the different government offices and reproduced them, more or less verbatim. All newspapers contained the same official news, supplied also by official news agencies and jealously watched over in each newsroom by a government official responsible for censoring all original texts before publication.

The monolithic press of the dictatorship, entrusted with holding back, falsifying, or concealing information, always at the service of the truth of the dictator, reflects a hermetic society, with no lines of communication or intermediaries among groups or individuals; it reflects a society where not only freedom of expression is banned but also freedom of association and meeting. In it, the system of press relations is very simple: the press transmits directly from the dictator to each individual.

156

Fraga's Spring

The economic isolation imposed on Spain by the international boycott of Franco after World War II ended with the recognition of the Francoist regime by the United States in 1959 and was followed by the liberalization of foreign commerce. The borders were opened to trade and through them came also new ideas of modernization with the continuing interchange of tourists and Spanish emigrant workers. The 1960s, a period of strong economic development in the Western world, brought to Spain a new state of well-being and consumerism, considerably enlarging the middle class. The absolute uniformity of the war journalism still in force did not meet the demands of this newly emergent middle class, who now wanted a certain degree of political participation. The official propaganda, overtaken by social change and with no capacity for persuasion, became indefensible in the face of the growing needs of a new industrial and urban society. The first demonstrations of protest occurred in the universities and in factories with the creation of free unions, which were illegal, and their corresponding and abundant clandestine press. With this clandestine press, a new generation of very politicized journalists more in contact with the real nonofficial Spain emerged.

In 1966, the new press law of Fraga Iribarne, minister of information, tried timidly to respond to the demands of the new situation.[11] Article 1 of this law recognized the right of freedom of expression, but article 2 practically prohibited it again by a long series of imprecise limitations within which almost any information could be included. Freedom of expression could be limited according to article 2 for various reasons: "The respect for truth and morality; adherence to the Law of the Fundamentals of the National Movement and the rest of the Fundamental Laws; the demands of national defense; security of State; maintenance of internal public order and external peace; due respect for Institutions and persons in any criticism of political and administrative action; independence of the Courts; and respect of personal and family privacy and honor."[12]

After the passage of article 2, hundreds of arbitrary sanctions were imposed. From 1966 to 1974 there were, on average, forty-eight seizures of publications by the government each year. Altogether some five hundred publications were confiscated or closed during this period.[13] Government confiscations for the publication of an article, a photograph, an insinuation, or even, publication of a single word considered to be an infraction of article 2, were followed by various penalties: police seizure and sealing off of warehouses; total destruction of the edition; destruction of the material used for printing; judicial prosecution, indictment, and trial; prison or provisional freedom on bond; exile or professional disqualification of the author of the infraction and/or the editor of the publication; fines for the publishing enterprise; suspension of the publication for several months or forever; and embargo. At other times, to avoid scandal, the publishing firm would be pressured to fire the editor or certain journalists.

The ambiguous article 2 (less rigid than the law of 1938) was a new valve by which the government regulated the limits of self-censorship. It was like a noose around the neck of each journalist, but under this

157

more capricious control the press began—timidly at first—to change and develop. The Ministry of Information (the old General Directorate of Press and Propaganda elevated to ministerial level) decided, according to the internal tensions in Spain at the time, when it ought to ban or allow certain subjects or the social or political situation to be written about. During brief and intermittent spurts of official tolerance, readership increased abruptly. When a particular article or piece of information that approximated reality got past the censor, all issues of the heroic publication were immediately sold out and acquired almost black market or collector value.

Responsibility for published material did not belong to the government official entrusted with censorship before printing. The censors were withdrawn from newspapers and reunited in the Ministry of Information. According to the new law, the media editor was now responsible for everything published. Censorship was exercised, therefore, after printing and before distribution, and so the publishing firm, which had covered the costs of paper and printing, was at the mercy of the censor who authorized (or not) distribution and circulation of the publication after its official analysis.

There now began a period of rigorous self-censorship. The responsibility of journalist to editor, of editor to publisher, and publisher to media editor, from whom he had directly received the special permit— always provisional—to publish now complicated the previously simple and monolithic situation of the period of the authoritarian war press. Only those who seemed sufficiently loyal were granted licenses to publish. There was an agreement on principles between each publisher and the regime. When the agreement was broken and the publisher weakened in his devotion to the state, he lost, temporarily or definitively, his permission to exist as a publisher, and his business and publications automatically disappeared. That was the case, for example, for the newspapers *Nivel* and *Madrid,* which ceased publication in 1969 and 1971, respectively.

In this situation, each firm had to calculate the material cost of its dissent from the regime. The adaptation of the press to this new situation was rapid, although it did not avoid all danger; several publications ceased publication in their attempts to conform. Others survived by negotiating with the administration to reprint new editions in which critical parts would be suppressed, without the public's knowledge of the censorship. These negotiations, a product of the government to avoid scandals, took place in a technocratic period when the country was striving to develop economically and trying to gain admittance to and incorporation in the European Economic Community, which necessarily was tied to a change in the foreign image of the Franco regime. Franco now had to measure his actions against international opinion. The managing editor of the banned newspaper *Madrid,* Miguel Angel Aguilar, in a semiclandestine meeting with foreign correspondents to explain why the newspaper has been ordered to close, began his communiqué with these words: "Francisco Franco, responsible, as all of you know, to God, History, and the Foreign Press. . . ." *Madrid*'s offense was the publication of an article about General de Gaulle abandoning power, entitled "Retiring in Time." Naturally the author of the article did not dare to mention any parallel with Spain. However, someone apparently felt that some reference to it had been implied.

The ways of freedom of the press are like those of water in search of a downhill course. Sometimes it moves slowly through wide channels and at other times it rushes through narrow and tortured straits with a fierce current. For those who have survived such periods it is easy to think, at times, that freedom is neither created nor destroyed by ministerial orders; it simply adapts itself as best it can to the circumstances. In Spain, a new language full of euphemisms was developed. Meanings of words were changed, and a complicated, picturesque, suggestive, and creative between-the-lines writing appeared. The influential reader, always an elite minority, possessed the precise code to understand and translate the obscure language that journalists employed to counter censorship. Through these tricks of the trade, the press began to enjoy credibility and prestige. Risky information was grouped on the same page or fold so that if it were censored, substitution would be easy without damaging the rest of the publication. Some printers even employed experts in unbinding and rebinding proscribed issues.

The Spanish situation was also written about obliquely by changing the scene of action to another place and another time. International news proliferated, and a number of pages were devoted to other countries, especially those ruled by dictatorships. Little was written directly about Spain, but almost everything referred to it indirectly. A new and unaccustomed interest in history allowed journalists to unload their anger against the absolutist King Ferdinand VII (1808–1833) and to criticize the tyrannies of the past without having to mention the present. The hypersensitivity of the government to stories being sneaked through its censorship pushed it to ridiculously extreme defensive measures.[14] Journalists always counted on the complicity of the readers (and at times the censors), who rewarded their risks and punishments by buying more copies of publications whose information most resembled reality.

During the 1970s, newspapers tried to modernize and timidly reflect the realities of society, which now pointed to a future different from that indicated by the obsolete official Spain. As the newspapers began to change and develop, the press grew in quality and to attract a greater number of new readers, many of them until then addicts of nightly broadcasts in Spanish from the BBC, Radio Paris, Radio Moscow, or Independent Radio Spain, which broadcast from the Pyrenees. With this timid development, a fragile press market was born that was attractive to a few entrepreneurs and to political or economic pressure groups who could take positions, apply for publishing permits, contract critical young journalists, and launch publications that collected sanctions from the dictator like medals of honor. Permits for the publication of dailies were granted only to truly loyal enterprises, but there was a relaxation in the granting of licenses to high-priced specialized or technical periodicals with limited distribution. The government was faithful to President Admiral Carrero Blanco's idea of selling newspapers at 50 pesetas each (five times the normal price at the time), and only in pharmacies by a prescription.

In 1971, sixteen liberal young professionals and entrepreneurs obtained from the government a permit to edit the weekly financial *Cambio 16* ("Change" or "Exchange" 16), which reached a circulation of half a million issues in four years. The technical financial information came to have more and more double meaning, and the magazine offered increasing doses of political irony about Spain. Its natural but distant tone—in a sad and embittered market—allowed the magazine to obtain a high level of toleration but it did not entirely escape sanctions. The fragile enterprise, called Impulsa, often got into trouble. The man behind it, Juan Salas, is today one of the most powerful men of the Spanish press.

The new communication effort that went into *Cambio 16* and the entry of young journalists into the old and stagnant market broke through all the official schemes of an overworked and inefficient censorship and made the state look to other defensive mechanisms. Special courts of justice, almost in disuse, intensified their action against the scantiest increase in freedom of the press. The list of banned people and subject matter grew, but each day more and more of the words that had been outlawed were printed.[15] As in all authoritarian regimes, when the mirror, which in this case is the press, reflects an ugly reality full of problems, those in power prefer to break the mirror before changing or bettering reality. And following this theory, the mirror the journalists held up was broken weekly, when not physically the journalists' own faces.

Half a dozen courts of justice and special laws that applied to journalists became the everyday gossip of the press, creating, out of solidarity, a much-read guide to sanctions imposed on some publications. In addition to the Ministry of Information with its administrative expedients, seizures, suspensions, and closures by cancellation of permits, journalists had to face the special court of public order, ordinary civil courts of justice, the special judge of press and printing, military courts, and the professional ethics jury of journalism. Charges of sedition, terrorism, subversion, libel, and illegal propaganda were common.

The growing diversity of shades of interpretation and greater richness of information, the product of publishers' changing attitudes toward the risk of dissension, was at first rewarded by an incipient but growing advertising market that added profits to the media, until then a financially ruinous business. The confrontations and conflicts were a product of a different rhythm between areas of freedom won by the press, each day dealing with new subjects and setting a precedent for all, and the greater or lesser tolerance of the state toward these advances of the enemy. These conflicts were transferred little by little to different social, political, and economic groups to the extent that Franco and his authoritarian regime were losing credibility, strength, and faithful followers.

The press, which for 30 years had not sounded an off-key note in the authoritarian concert, in the 1970s became the protagonist in a great many confrontations with the regime. The possibility of entering into conflict or not became an option, an indication of more freedom. To the extent that freedom grew, the sanctions of a state incapable of stopping the avalanche of the press or even capable of controlling sources also skyrocketed. The number of sanctions against the media in 1972, for example, under the rule of Alfredo Sanchez Bella at the Ministry of Information, was on average 2.5 a month. One year later, with Linán y Zofío in the ministry, the number of sanctions grew to an average of 3.14 a month.[16] But this spiral drastically changed direction after the assassination in December 1973 of President Carrero Blanco (Franco's right-hand man) and the appointment of Pio Cabanillas as minister of information in January 1974.

Parliament in the Press

Between the so-called "opening of the hand" by Minister Pio Cabanillas in 1974 and his dismissal in November of the same year (when the number of sanctions against the press sank to an average of 1.49 a month), the open offensive of the press against Franco's regime began. In this period, the majority of Spaniards who supported a democratic system came out into the open and began to organize. Private clubs and neighborhood associations multiplied; professional associations, remnants of the unions and trade guilds of Francoism and of the very administration, were infiltrated by the democratic opposition. There was no democratic parliament, but politics was practiced all over the country. Newspapers and magazines especially became centers of politics, a true press parliament for the voices of opposition, each day more numerous, more dissident, and stronger.[17] Newsrooms were filled with politicians from the opposition, and journalists affiliated with clandestine political parties began to take positions in each newsroom council. Almost all of the politicians who today have seats in Parliament or in government became known during this period through their declarations in the press. It was the most brilliant financial and political period of the press. It was also the period in which journalists were most valued in the market, achieving rather high salaries in relation to other liberal professions. There was great professional mobility and strong demand for the few young journalists with experience but with-

161

out a Francoist background. It was in this period that the schools of journalism were flooded with thousands of students, today unemployed.

The press became not only a political and economic business; it also bestowed prestige and merit to those who worked in it. During the eleven months of Pio Cabanillas in the Ministry of Information, 427 new registrations of publications were applied for and 385 licenses were granted to publish magazines, an increase of 8 percent over the 4,869 publications already in existence. The biggest increase in registrations took place in March with the record figure of 71, and coincided with the euphoria that followed the speech of President Arias on February 12, 1974. The moves toward a liberalization of the regime would later be known as "the spirit of February 12."[18] More magazines were born than died; the market grew rapidly and became diversified in an uncontrolled manner. In this race, the traditional papers, which had modernized a bit, had the advantage. In particular, the traditional newspapers with no competitors were dragged along by weeklies that offered exclusive information that they would never have dared to offer previously. Weekly magazines grew at a faster rate than daily papers, but only two years later the authorization by the government of King Juan Carlos I of the publication of the daily paper *El Pais* began their downfall.

In that "parliament of the press," who elected whom? The only candidates were those authorized by the regime. Readers could choose only between the existing options. In the new, almost free market of ideas, those who decided were mainly the publishers, although the first skirmishes were already taking place with professional journalists who demanded a voice and asked for societies of writers, conscience clauses, and so forth. Between dictator and citizen an intermediate power, the publisher, was now interposed. This situation reminds one of the discussions in the New England Conference on Conflicts between the Media and the Law; when a publisher in a slicing intervention affirmed, "We are the definitive judge," a judge answered reproachingly, "No one elected you."[19]

Freedom and Degradation of the Press

When Francisco Franco died in November 1975, the press entered into a race, almost without obstacles, toward the final goal of conquering the market. Press relations became infinitely more complex than in the past, and each interest claimed for itself a parcel of freedom. But although the dictator was dead, many dictatorial structures still remained and went on working out of inertia. The dictator had been gradually partly superseded by the publisher, in whom the dictator had placed his confidence and who therefore started off the race with advantages. Now only the reader and/or the advertising market could withdraw his license to publish by financially ruining his enterprises. Both reader and advertiser also reclaimed their parcel of influence. Last were the journalists, with their intermediary role between publisher and reader and also between publisher and advertiser. The state, publisher, reader, journalist, and advertiser were now engaged in an uncontrolled battle to divide, parcel out, and/or consolidate the freedom of the press that had so recently been exercised for the first time. The result of this struggle for the fourth power among unequals is now being felt. A symptom of it is the profound crisis and degradation that the press currently suffers in Spain.

As society has democratized, the state has relinquished almost entirely its role in the battle—perhaps because of the weight on its conscience of its repressive past—and it also forgets its responsibilities. Between the remaining groups interested in this market of freedoms, the scales are noticeably tilted toward the side of the publisher and advertiser. This is due to the property and cost structure of the Spanish press, in which advertising income decides the profitability of a journalistic enterprise more than does the income from the sale of the product, although both figures are necessarily related.[20]

In such a dynamic market, the figures and statistics for newspapers, magazines, and publishing firms change from month to month. Some are absorbed or concentrated under one ownership; others are born and, after an ephemeral life, die.[21] Of the 120 daily papers more or less firmly established, one-third are still in the hands of the state, and the rest are privately owned. Together they have a circulation of around 3 million issues. With 30 percent of the existing titles, the press of the movement reaches only 12 percent of the market.[22] The remaining 88 percent is in the hands of 73 private enterprises with 83 titles. As to the future of the official press, "We could broadly say," as the *Anuario Economico y Social de España 1977* points out, "that its profitability and audience are not even half the average of the other dailies. Only two or three newspapers of the chain are profitable. In these conditions everything indicates that, in view of the effort needed to reform the chain, the final decision will be to eliminate it."[23]

On the other hand, the private press is in the hands of a few in circles close to economic and political power. Manuel Vasquez Montalbán states that six great banks (Hispano Americano, Vizcaya, Bilbao, Banesto, Urquijo, and Central) control approximately 56.4 percent of the capital of the Spanish press.[24] The structure of the shareholdings in these enterprises shows in addition an extraordinary degree of concentration of power in the hands of a few people. Alfonso Nieto in his book *La empresa periodística en España* shows that 30 individual persons are the major shareholders in most of the private journalistic enterprises, controlling a circulation of around 50 percent of the total daily press. One must keep in mind that only 21 papers have 45 percent of total distribution.[25]

When a free press delves into a society as habitually closed and hypersensitive to the press as Spanish society is, sparks fly in every direction. The business world is concerned about its image, and the social classes that enjoyed privileges and/or were the center of corruption during Francoism are especially sensitive. The advertising boom that accompanied the liberalization of the press, although no doubt obeying a drive to sell products and public images, had also the effect of pacifying or silencing to some extent any criticism of the past. Up to a point, it can be said that during the transition from dictatorship to democracy, business corporations, among other pressure groups, have dictated in great measure the patterns and forms of the new Spanish press, above all through advertising and public relations. The impact of advertising and its influence have increased as the media have gained credibility and increased readership. Such penetration has permanently made clear the weaknesses of publishers in economic difficulties and their strengths, clearly emphasizing the existing conflict between the private and commercial nature of the press and its public function.

During this transition, pressure from economic groups on publishers and journalists occurred openly, directly filling the place of the old role of censor that the state had formerly exercised. Censorship was enforced by threats; the withdrawal of an advertisement or bribery were traditionally the most persuasive to transgressions of the unwritten law of journalistic ethics.

Sometimes corruption, but basically confusion over information, news, advertising, and public relations, has reached such an extreme in this open war to seize control of the media that hardly anyone is scandalized by public and obvious anomalies within the journalistic profession. Some active journalists on newspapers or magazines also receive a salary, at the same time, from a multinational firm, a Spanish bank, or an advertising and/or public relations firm, or are also employed in the press department of some government office. There is as well the booming sensationalist yellow press that is best represented by *Interviu,* a "combustible mix of sex photos and acid political commentary that has become a vanguard of the press in post-Franco Spain."[26] "If political saturation makes trash saleable," *Diario 16* points out in an editorial, "this is certainly the Spanish hour of *dirty* publications. But they should know that their existence is a mortal offense against freedom of expression, for which the entire press is paying." The same editorial refers to "ethical and professional disarray" while looking for the causes of the "mortal phenomena" in the press of the loss of faith "in a dismembered journalistic profession, that has passed from docility to freedom without finding itself as a professional body, without finding its bearings at the moment of organizing itself, defending itself and clarifying its specific function which inevitably gives rise to symptoms of inner sickness that, in the long run are detected by the reader."[27] This discussion about the role of the press in a free society manifests public concern for seeking reasonable limits to freedom of expression: difficult and delicate limits that guarantee this full freedom by giving the press a greater sense of social responsibility.

164

The calls to responsibility are more and more frequent. In a report before the Spanish Bishops' Assembly about "the situation of moral anomaly in which the journalistic profession finds itself," the chairman of the School of Journalism of Madrid, José Maria Desantes, arrived at the conclusion that "with a few exemplary exceptions the Spanish reporter is today amoral."[28]

Other observers, like veteran journalist Andrés Berlanga, call attention to the lack of professionalism in the Spanish press caused by swinging from one side to the other after political change: "Before, credibility was lacking," Berlanga points out, "because one knew that all newspapers printed or silenced what the censor decreed, but now some journalists forget to report both sides of a story further than is convenient, they write on hearsay, are not neutral politically at the time of narrating an event (which doesn't mean, of course, that they ought to discard personal vision, interpretation, suggestion, irony or judgment but that they too often try to twist the news to serve the particular interests of the reporter or the media) and on occasion elevate to the category of 'front page news' what for almost everyone would not rank as such or they distort the balance of an issue."[29]

As well as this general lack of rigor is a residue of authoritarian attitudes, an overpoliticization of journalists, a habit of censoriousness from the past (juxtaposing different news so that it acquires a slant of salable scandal), the general economic crisis, and something that Spaniards could not have guessed without experiencing it that: "Democracy is boring, since it requires you to listen to the mediocre as well as the brilliant."[30]

The rules of the democratic game, probably because of a forty-year lack of experience, were mostly being established on the feeble and inconsistent lines of the old libertarian theory of the press. The law under the dictatorship had lost, by disuse and anachronism, almost all respect, and few officials felt they had the strength to apply it.[31] From the monarchy of transition to the constitutional monarchy, a wave of official bad conscience, partly due to the repressive tradition, created a vacuum of official power; the state seemed temporarily to forfeit its responsibility for the press. But the miracle of a happy free market of ideas where man is capable of discerning between truth and falsehood, choosing good over evil, did not happen. The invisible hand of Adam Smith did not correct the disequilibriums of freedom, and John Milton's process of self-justice did not work. The result has been the unequal parceling out of influence, the loss of readers, the loss of quality and credibility of the press, and economic crisis. In the free encounter of ideas in an open market, the truth favored by Milton has not triumphed, nor has the sum of egoisms and private interests produced general harmony of the press.

From the death of Franco in 1975 until the present, 1,112 publications were born in Spain, but many perished before reaching their fifth issue.[32] It is very difficult for new publishers to get access to the market, and even some veterans have failed. After the initial euphoria of the press opening when all citizens had been noticeably worried about their future after Franco's death, and with political and erotic curiosity satisfied, the tired and bored Spaniard returned to his lifelong habits of not reading. It is partly the loss of interest in the press that has dragged it into commercial sensationalism and muckraking in order to sell more, or, at least to survive. Perhaps the new Spanish press has realized the thesis attributed to William Peter Hamilton of the *Wall Street Journal*: "A newspaper is a private enterprise that owes nothing to the public, that does not grant it any exemption. Therefore, it doesn't affect any public interest. It ends up as emphatically the property of its owner, who sells a manufactured product at his own risk."[33]

Public debate has now begun on the social function of the press and the necessity of a certain degree of protection or official subsidy to guarantee freedom of expression and to avoid the disappearance of newspapers or the too easy concentration of titles in a few hands. Crespo de Lara, president of the Association of Daily Press and general secretary of the newspaper *Informaciones,* has affirmed recently that "the means of social communication are too important to be abandoned to the forces of the market alone."[34] At the same time, Manuel Martin Ferrand, from the *Interviu* group, writes that "Privileges are not what our daily press needs. Those that can't withstand the buffeting of the free market should die."[35]

Between the two sides, the government opted finally for intervention and granted in September 1978 350 million pesetas (roughly some $4.3 million) as subsidies to private enterprises. The preamble of the royal decree specifies, "The importance of press reporting carried out by journalistic enterprises and their close connection with the democratic process, determines that the State ought to extend to them some degree of economic protection: especially in situations like the present, in which the increase in costs due to expanding activity, the consequence of a greater spread of newspapers in all areas of society, makes this protection indispensible."[36] The first democratic government of the king took the initiative, indicating its future attitude to the profound crisis of the press.

Conclusion

166

In Spain today, contradictions difficult to clarify abound. Both on a theoretical and a practical level, there is great general confusion about freedom of the press. In this leap from an authoritarian to a libertarian press, the principal paradox of press freedom becomes clear: in order to guarantee and preserve freedom of the press, it must be limited. It is a freedom that contains within itself the seeds of its own destruction and, therefore it must be limited, be destroyed a little, so as not to be lost completely.

If by paradox we understand an expression or phrase that contains a contradiction, the very words *freedom of the press* are a paradox. Freedom can be understood as a dynamic capacity for choice, not an absolute human value. It is a relative potential of possibilities, a growing or diminishing tendency toward an increase or a decrease of options. Absolute freedom in the maximum utopian degree can exist only when there are infinite options to choose from. The press offers only limited options. Technological progress could have increased quantitatively and qualitatively the possibilities of choice, in which case freedom would also have been increased. However, experience has shown that although circulation figures have gone up, the number of publications has been dangerously reduced, diminishing competition and pluralism and facilitating monopoly.[37] The high cost of publishing is more and more the barrier that denies citizens access to the press to exercise their right to communicate or receive different opinions. Given modern technological and industrial costs, freedom of the press can only be interpreted as freedom of already existing organs of press. Since these, for the most part, are at the service of particular interests, they do not add up to the harmonic representation of the general interest preached by Adam Smith.

But freedom of the press, relative and small as it may be, is still infinitely better for the harmony of a community than the total absence of it. The risks of such freedom are clearly less than the well-known risks of the lack of freedom. The freedon of the press of the democratic Western countries is, with all its defects, the lesser evil. It is fundamentally valuable because it removes social conflict, as the Commission on Freedom of the Press says, "from the field of violence to the field of discussion."[38] For many Spanish journalists, the choice has been as simple as for Thomas Jefferson: we preferred, in full dictatorship, newspapers without government before government without newspapers. Perhaps the present disenchantment with freedom of the press in Spain is partly a psychological effect of the authoritarian past from which we have just emerged, which has distorted the concept of freedom of the press into an emotional belief only in the total absence of intervention by the omnipresent and omnipotent totalitarian state. According to the Commission on Freedom of the Press, "Protection against government is not sufficient now to guarantee that a man who has something to say, will have the opportunity to say it. The owners and business managers of the press determine what persons, what deeds, what versions of said deeds will reach the public."[39]

With the dictator dead, we have seen that the result of the passionate battle for control of information and the media was financial crisis and degradation of the press, controlled now by established publishers, with interests in the market, instead of being controlled by the state. The problem is not a matter of supplanting one power by another but of finding a balance of several powers that would make possible the exer-

cise of freedom, that would mitigate the excesses of the press and limit
its influence and freedom to the point where freedom of others begins.

In this model, if one of the powers does not itself set responsible limits
to its freedom, another will step in to limit it and correct the balance.
The objective of this dynamic equilibrium will be to obtain the greatest
degree of freedom of the press for the community and for each individual. With the disappointment of the anachronistic concept of freedom of the press as a purely individual right and with the present
compromise in all developed societies between the old individualist and
new collectivistic theories, freedom of the press as a measure of democracy ought to be gauged by the greater or lesser capacity of the last
marginal member of society to express his ideas and receive others. A
guarantee of a minimum degree of choice to the least member of society
assures this minimum for the rest of the community. Only in this way
can progressive freedom of the press be understood. It is not only the
right of the individual but also, and very especially, a collective right.

It is an old argument that freedom in a society of unequal members
favors and increases inequality and diminishes areas of choice, including, in the long run, freedom itself. Nevertheless it seems obvious that
even starting from an imaginary and utopian equality, freedom without limits would make people unequal. Within this vicious circle of
political philosophy and human nature, a permanent correction of freedom is needed so that it may be progressively redistributed to redress
inequality as far as possible, conferring greater opportunity of choice to
those who have the least.

In contrast to the conclusions of Samuel P. Huntington in his report
for the Trilateral Commission on The Crisis of Democracy that the crisis
is caused by the 'excesses of democracy', the generally held opinion in
post-Franco Spain coincides more with that of Al Smith when he said,
"The only cure for the evils of democracy is more democracy."[40] It is
along these lines that solutions are sought today in Spain in numerous
public debates to the problems of making the press more democratic.

Juan Luis Cebrian, editor of the newspaper El Pais, possibly the
paper of greatest credibility and influence at this time, describes the
press in democracy as an autonomous power: "The role of the press is to
challenge Power. The press itself is a power and its basic function,
along with that of informing, is to criticize others. The limits of freedom
of the press, lie in the limits of the other freedoms."[41]

The theory of social responsibility of the press, now widely held,
proposes that the press should regulate and discipline itself in order not
to fall completely into the hands of the executive, legislative, and judicial powers of the modern democratic state—or of the three together in
the hands of a dictator. Still to be solved is the problem of determining
suitable mechanisms of self-regulation by which each power (state,
publisher, journalist, and reader) can exercise its rights and fulfill its
responsibilities.

The state should not always take the neutral role of arbitrator in the

168

press market. It is above the private interests of different groups and should be the watchguard of the general interest of the community and of the individuals who compose it. As the press affects social groups not represented in it, and even future generations, the state ought to be involved in its regulation to protect and facilitate the greatest pluralism possible by means of such things as special loans and subsidies. The role of the state is, in this sense, to redistribute freedom, preventing monopoly and/or concentration of ownership or the disappearance of newspapers.

The publisher is equally responsible to society to present diverging opinions impartially and facts with maximum objectivity, maintaining his independence against the pressure of economic and political power and keeping vigil over the informative, educational, and orientating function of his publication.

As for the journalist, Cebrian points out, "The problem lies in how to guarantee that the journalist can defend himself from economic, political, business, and union pressures and uphold his own decisions."[42] One of these guarantees that is now suggested as a possibility in the short term in Spain is the establishment in each newspaper of societies of writers that can defend the so-called conscience clause and the interests of the journalist, as well as share with the publisher decisions on news content and evaluation. The journalist, as the guardian of democracy, should also have the right of access to sources of information within the government in order to exercise his critical function.

As the fourth power within the press, the role of reader will not be limited in the future to that of a passive receiver of information. If consumers are king in present society, they will be able to organize directly, or through representatives, to demand guarantees against any irresponsibility of the state, publisher, or journalist in press material or for the maintenance of freedom of the press. "In democratic states, where there is no censorship of the media," points out Jean Marin, ex-president of the agency France-Presse, "certain organisms or groups of representatives of the popular will are necessary to establish needed guarantees so that an authentically pluralist freedom of expression is achieved."[43]

In the end, organized and well-informed readers have the innate right not to buy a newspaper, not to listen to the radio, to turn off the television, and above all the inalienable right of not believing what they are told. The reader, first and last power in the press, is not the irrational or lethargic man, "easy prey to demagogues and advertising," that advertisers and sociologists of mass communications so often imply. In spite of the period of propaganda that we have lived through, little is known about the production of persuasive information and even less of the attitude of the readers or spectators who are its object. On this it may be interesting to end with an observation of Professor George Hills of the BBC while chairing a seminar on the limits of television as press media: "Television is a means of persuasion. Is this correct? For some twenty odd years Spanish television was at the service of a determined regime. If television had as much importance as it is given, if it had this influence that it is said to have over the spectator, would the results of the last elections [of June 1977] have been what they were?" Hills concludes, "We must investigate much more the influence of television."[44]

This could be our hope in the face of the contradictions that the press presents: freedom as a permanent and indestructible potential of human nature. People tend always to be free and to search out alternative means of obtaining information that they need. The impressive and valuable treasure of Spanish oral tradition exists, a result of the Holy Inquisition.

Notes

1. By *press,* I generally include all means of mass communication.

2. José F. Beaumont, "Crisis de confianza en la prensa diaria," *El Pais,* January 12, 1978.

3. According to UNESCO statistics of 1975, Spain has a circulation of 96 newspapers per 1,000 inhabitants, France has a circulation of 230, England 442, and Sweden 536.

4. "Prensa y Democracia," *El Pais,* April 9, 1978.

5. Beaumont, "Crisis de confianza."

6. Fred S. Siebert and Theodore Peterson, *Tres teorias sobre la libertad de prensa* (Buenos Aires, Argentina: Editorial La Flor, 1967), p. 9.

7. Manuel Martin Ferrand, "El suicidio de la prensa," *Hoja del Lunes de Madrid* (July 1978).

8. Cited by Siebert and Peterson, *Tresteorias.*

9. J. Ugalde Apalategui, "La crisis de la prensa espanola," *Comunicacion* 1, (1977):67.

10. Cited by Daniel Gavela in "Prensa estatal," *Las reformas urgentes* (Madrid: Taller de Ediciones JB, 1976), p. 406, from the *Boletin Oficial del Estado,* July 13, 1940.

11. "Between 1956 and 1962 the consumption of paper in Spain rose to eighty five thousand tons, an increase of 15%, a consequence of the press 'opening' of 1962, reaching a maximum in 1967 (150,000 tons) after the new Law." Juan Beneyto, *Conocimiento de la Informacion* (Madrid: Alianza Editorial, 1973), p. 118, according to data in the Boletin de la Federacion Internacional de Empresas periodisticas, *Fiej-Bulletin* (April 1973).

12. "Ley de Prensa e Imprenta," *Boletin Oficial del Estado,* March 19, 1966.

13. Juby Bustamante, "La euforia aperturista," *Comunicacion* no. 19 (1977):22.

14. One of the judicial prosecutions of which I was the object, in November of 1975—coinciding incidentally with the long death agony of Franco—was when I was editor of the monthly magazine *Historia Internacional,* a title which ensured that permission to publish was easily obtained. The magazine published a sentence of Pablo Iglesias, founder of the Spanish Socialist Workers party (PSOE) in the last century, declaring that "the tyrant deserved death," referring to the assassination in 1904 of the prime minister of the czar of Russia, Plehve. The magazine was confiscated by police and threatened with closure by the Ministry of Information. In my evidence before the special judge of public order, I could demonstrate that the phrase could be read in history books on sale in any bookstore and that even in the Council of Trent the theme of death to a tyrant was treated. In any case, I held, it was not our intention, as the ministry accused, to allude to the head of the Spanish state. The judge ordered the lifting of the confiscation and left me in complete liberty. Another similar prosecution against me when I was editor of the weekly *Doblon* was due to a cover story in April 1975 about torture in Chile. Less lucky than *Historia Internacional,* this entire edition was destroyed by the police.

15. As managing editor of *Cambio 16* during its first three years, I recall the negotiations with the government to get banned words back in use. In spite of these negotiations, we had to substitute *technical work stoppage* for *strike.* Years later, the new minister of official unions, Alejandro Fernandez Sordo, former

general director of the press, made a famous public declaration when he announced, "From now on we will call a strike a strike."

16. 'Sanciones de tres anos y tres ministros en la prensa espanola,' *En Punta* (October 1974):28.

17. "The official source ceased to be an article of faith. Notes from the General Directorate of Security as well as ministerial pronouncements could be commented upon. Only a short time before, it had been mandatory to print them, word for word in their entirety. The interests of the Administration were not now presented as coinciding with those of the citizen, and the stereotyped press references in which the only thing demanded of the journalist had been to report the Ministers present in correct order of protocol now contained news selected on the criteria of its possible interest of the reader." Andres Berlanda, *El ano literario espanol* (Barcelona: Editorial Castalia, 1976), p. 98.

18. Authorized publications inscribed in the official registrar during the opening of Pio Cabanillas: "January, 18; February, 32; March, 71; April, 25; May 35; June, 42; July, 69; August, 35; September, 41; October, 17." Bustamante, "La euforia aperturista," p. 22.

19. Cited by James C. Thomson, Jr., "Journalistic Ethics: Some Probings by a Media Keeper," *Nieman Report* (Spring 1978).

20. "The average production cost of a newspaper is almost 40 pesetas, an impossible situation for the press were it not for the income received from advertising. The solution to this disparity between the cost of production (40 pesetas) and the selling price (18 pesetas) does not lie in increasing the sales price; if this rises above the level of dissuasion the reader will not buy the newspaper." Pedro Crespo de Lara, president of the Agrupacion de Prensa Diaria, *Informaciones* (Madrid), July 5, 1978.

21. According to the data of the National Institute of Statistics as cited by *Arriba, dominical* (Madrid), July 16, 1978, there are in Spain 170 newspapers of general interest dailies and nondailies with an overall circulation of 3.3 million issues; 515 weekly magazines, with a circulation of 8,294,000 issues; 194 semimonthlies, with a circulation of 3.9 million issues; 1,524 monthlies, with a circulation of 13,918 issues; and 1,633 publications of different periodicity, with a circulation of 7,187,000 issues.

22. This name is commonly given to the press chain composed of the newspapers expropriated by the new state from anti-Franco enterprises at the end of the civil war. As an official organ, the chain belonged initially to the National Delegation of Press and Propaganda of the Traditionalist Spanish Falange and of the National Syndicalist Offensive Juntas. The name was changed later to that of the one-party National Syndicalist Movement, later just the National Movement. After Franco's death, it depended upon the secretariat of the movement (no adjectives) and was known as the press of the movement. Under the democratic monarchy, it has just received the denomination, Means of Social Communication of the State.

172

23. Carlos Elordi, "Los medios de informacion," in *Anuario Economico y Social de Espana, 1977* (Barcelona: Editorial Planeta, 1977), p. 143.

24. Cited by Apalategui, "La crisis," p. 66.

25. Ibid.

26. James M. Markham, "Nudity and Insults: Spanish Magazines Mix Sex, Politics," *International Herald Tribune,* May 16, 1978.

27. "La prensa carronera," *Diario 16* (Madrid), June 1978.

28. "El informador espanol es amoral," *Diario 16*, June 22, 1978.

29. Andrés Berlanga, "El Periodismo," *El ano literario espanol, 1977* (Barcelona: Editorial Castalia, 1977).

30. Gabriel Jackson, "Perspectivas para Espana, hoy," *El Pais* (Madrid), June 1, 1978.

31. Pedrol Rius, "Todos estamos fuera de la ley," *Doblon* (Madrid), 1976.

32. Jesus Infiesta, "La prensa," *Arriba dominical* (Madrid), June 16, 1978.

33. Cited by Siebert and Peterson, *Tresteorias*, p. 89.

34. Pedro Crespo de Lara, "Contacto de los obispos con la prensa," *Informaciones* (Madrid), June 21, 1978.

35. Ferrand, "El suicido."

36. *Boletin Oficial del Estado* (Madrid), September 8, 1978.

37. "In the United States, between 1914 and 1967 the number of titled dailies dropped from 2,580 to 1,710, while during the same period the entire circulation of the dailies increased from 22,700,000 to more than 60,000,000. From 1909 to 1960, the number of cities where a *de facto* monopoly existed, was 150 in 1880, and 11,400 in 1960. The number of dailies in New York, 25 at the turn of the century, dropped to 4 in 1967." Fernand Terrou, "Que sais-je?" in *La Informacion* (Paris: Presses Universitaires de France, 1968).

38. Cited by Siebert and Peterson, *Tresteorias*, p. 12.

39. Ibid.

40. Samuel P. Huntington, *The Crisis of Democracy: Report on the Governability of Democracies to the Trilateral Commission* (New York: New York University Press, 1975), p. 113.

41. Juan Luis Cebrian, "La libertad de prensa, base de una sociedad democratica," *Diario 16*, July 21, 1978.

42. Ibid.

43. Jean Marin, Inaugural Conference of the Symposium on Freedom of Expression), organized by *Cambio 16* and *El Pais*, January 25, 1977.

44. George Hill, "Los limites de la TV como medio informativo," *Mensaje y Medios* (Madrid: Instituto Oficial de Radiodifusion y Television, April 1978), p. 48.

8

The Role of the Media in the Portuguese Revolution

Jean Seaton and Ben Pimlott

During the Portuguese upheaval of 1974–1975, newspapers, radio, and television provided key, even decisive, battlegrounds. The media were seen not merely as disseminators of news and opinion but as potential instruments of manipulation. It was widely believed that power over mass communications would lead to power over the people.

Was this belief that the media could change and shape opinion correct? Portugal provides an opportunity to test assumptions about the media that have been based on the experience of comparatively stable liberal democracies in contrasting conditions of unrest and rapid change. It is arguable that during the revolutionary period in Portugal the role of the media was more symbolic than persuasive, and that the rapid evolution that began under the old regime was an integral part of the political and social transformation— as much a manifestation as a cause.

Evolution and Revolution

Press "pluralism" is not normal in Portugal.[1] At the time of the coup d'état on April 25, 1974, there were scarcely any journalists who could remember what it was like to work without exercising an internalized literary self-restraint that took account of prevailing official attitudes. Before the beginning of the

We wish to thank Professor Kenneth Maxwell for permission to publish this essay, which is based on a paper delivered in October 1978 to a conference, "The Iberian Peninsular in Transition: Political Culture in Spain and Portugal" at Columbia University. We are also grateful to the British Academy for the award of European Exchange Grants, which made the research possible.

dictatorship there had been a long period of comparative freedom, during which the newspapers, magazines, and books displayed "amazingly good style and a general tendency towards rational and clear thinking."[2] But the military intervention of 1926 put an end to this golden age in Portuguese culture. Since the 1860s, the press had grown and flourished; now the quality rapidly fell. The best authors ceased to serialize their work in daily newspapers. The number of papers and magazines continued to increase for a time, and Portuguese literary output rivaled in sheer scale that of the most advanced nations.[3] But by the early 1930s, an official censorship and regulation that demoralized and diminished Portuguese journalism had become an accepted and unavoidable way of life.

Yet Salazarist policy toward the press was authoritarian rather than totalitarian. The press was seen not as part of the regime's ideological apparatus but as a potential vehicle for the opposition. Distrusted and circumscribed, it was never given a positive role; there was little attempt to use newspapers as the instrument of a persuasive propaganda. Indeed the censorship reflected the unusual nature of Portuguese fascism, which was not dynamic, failed to develop a mass movement, and whose main domestic objectives were to maintain stability and order.

Hence, though controlled, the press always provided a chink in the armor of the regime, especially after 1945. Except during brief election periods, when some restrictions were partially removed, newspapers provided the only legal forum for political discussion, however muted. Overt criticism was not permitted, but hints and innuendo were possible and were used more and more in the 1960s as support for the regime eroded rapidly.[4] The liberal, radical, progressive Catholic, socialist, and clandestine communist tendencies that characterized the opposition, "a sort of permanent ghost haunting the regime's victories and achievements,"[5] pushed and pressed the official censor in a highly ritualized battle of wills from which actual terror—the fear of arrest and physical sanctions—was increasingly absent. This battle, perhaps more than any other in civilian life, paved the way to April 25.

It was a struggle that involved the elite but did not directly affect the masses. There was an important working-class opposition to the regime—especially within the Lisbon-Setubal industrial region and among the agricultural laborers in the south—but in this the press (as distinct from clandestine newssheets) played little part. There were (and there are now) no mass-circulation papers. The Salazarist principle that educating the poor carried dangers for a well-ordered society and that peasant culture would be better preserved if it was not infused with new ideas helped to maintain the highest illiteracy rate in Western Europe (37 percent in 1971).[6] Poor distribution also helped to ensure that only a very small proportion of the population would have regular access even to papers which were loyal to the regime, let alone those (like *Diário de Lisboa* and the socialist *República,* and later the weekly *Expresso*) that occasionally were not. Many small communities seldom even saw a local newspaper. Records of the Salazarist *Grémio da*

Imprensa Regional show a steady decline in the provincial press: from 210 papers in 1926, 170 in 1933, 80 in 1944, to a mere 17 by 1963.[7] This erosion was particularly severe in Alentejo, where the potential for mass revolt was always greatest and where some papers were forced to close after campaigning on agrarian issues. José Cutileiro records that in "Vila Nova" in the district of Évora five periodicals were published under the Republic, three of them concurrently. By the 1960s, there were none.[8]

As far as the city press was concerned, the censor ensured that there was little enough to interest the working people. Uneducated readers were not drawn by "a hybrid style, tailored to official taste with clichés inspired by the speeches of Government figures ("structures of the nation," "the Portuguese way of life," "historical compromise," etc.)."[9] The main function of the press under the dictatorship was not to inspire, enlighten, or convince but to communicate official attitudes. Opportunities to circumvent this role and use the press as a vehicle for criticism existed, but they were intermittent and covert and could only be aimed at the sophisticated. One result was the lowest consumption of newsprint per head of population in Western Europe.[10] Another was a press industry and profession almost entirely catering to a small, inward-looking, urban middle class. More than with the press of any other European country, the bulk of the population was left out of account.

Ownership and Evolution

The stagnation of the Portuguese press was not just a result of censorship. It was also a product of ownership. Changes in the control of the newspaper industry have been crucially important for its development and have a symmetry of their own. In the last years of Caetano, the press slipped into the hands of the great monopolies, apparently solidifying corporate support behind the regime. But the loyalty of newspapers was guaranteed only as long as the monopolists could control them. When the regime fell, the papers became subject to a variety of new pressures, internal, political, and governmental.

When the press is not directly managed by the state, market forces, more than the attitudes of journalists or the political culture in which they operate, may determine the orientation and interests of the press. For example, the concerns of an indigent majority may often be neglected in order to capture the attention of an affluent and high-consuming minority whose spending power will attract revenue from advertisers. The market may therefore have the political effect of creating a middle-class-oriented, and hence conservative, press. But under some conditions, the effect of the market may be very different. Elaine Potter has shown how the previously conservative English press in South Africa expanded its sales and profits by appealing to English-

176

speaking black Africans and was encouraged by the market pressure that this caused to become an important source of liberal opposition.[11]

In Portugal, the main pressures were "bourgeois" under Salazar, but with some signs of the "Potter effect" under Caetano. Until the late 1960s, an urban, middle-class readership in Lisbon and Oporto provided few incentives for newspaper owners or editors to be outspoken in their criticisms of the regime. Advertising was scarcely a pressure that was likely to stimulate journalistic opposition, encourage a wider circulation, or initiate innovation. In 1960, 25 percent of advertising revenue came from personal and classified advertisement and no less than 21 percent from state agencies.[12] The circulation of *República,* for long the most effectively critical paper, seldom rose above 20,000. From the late 1960s, however, a rapid growth in the white-collar and technical middle class in Lisbon and Oporto and the steady erosion of the loyalty to the regime of large sections of the urban bourgeoisie encouraged opposition in the press. Both the foundation and the success of *Expresso,* a commercially as well as politically ambitious weekly, can be directly related to the increasing "liberalization" of the Portuguese middle class largely as a result of economic expansion.[13] Nevertheless, it is only at the very end of the Salazar-Caetano regime that this kind of market pressure can be discerned.

Even if liberalizing economic pressures had existed at an earlier stage, a lack of imaginative or ambitious management would probably have reduced their effect. Both the resources for development and the will were lacking. Without the stimulus of a mass market and in the stagnant conditions of the New State, "press barons" failed to establish themselves. As late as 1937, eight out of ten Lisbon papers and three in Oporto were in family ownership—mainly small, traditional, conservative, single enterprises, unconnected with outside interests. This structure of ownership did not encourage risk taking in either a commercial or a political sense. Only in the 1960s did the situation begin to change. The Rocha family (with interests in food canning) bought *Diário de Lisboa,* which soon became the most important voice of the liberal opposition in Portugal, with strong clandestine Communist infiltration on its staff; and the Balsemão family (with a background in textiles) acquired *Diário Popular,* which later gave birth (through Francisco Balsemão) to the oppositional *Expresso.* In both cases, a cushion of industrial ownership and wealth provided the necessary security for a degree of political and commercial innovation that rivals could not so easily contemplate.

177

But the major change in ownership, occurring when the old regime was already moving into the shadows, was not brought about with any intention of transforming the press. At first sight, the purchase of six Lisbon and two Oporto papers by the giant conglomerates Champalimaud, Quina, and Espírito Santo, with their wide-ranging industrial, commercial, and banking interests, paralleled a pattern of press ownership in developed countries. In Portugal, as elsewhere, early

nineteenth-century political newssheets had become family businesses
and were now, at last, acquired by large corporations. But one important difference was that the Portuguese consortia did not buy newspapers in order to make money out of them—at least not directly. By the
late 1960s all but one of the Lisbon daily papers were running at a loss,
and they continued to do so after they had changed hands. *Diário Popular,* the exception, was sold to the Quina group at a price that a former
shareholder, Francisco Balsemão, regarded as absurdly high.[14] Other,
insolvent papers were also sold above their market value in strict accounting terms. It might have been expected that a change of ownership would be accompanied by streamlining and modernization. This
did not happen. At the time of the 1974 coup, most papers had an-
tiquated production methods and grossly inflated staffs.

It is clear that the real motive for the acquisitions was only indirectly
economic. In an increasingly uncertain world characterized by a regime
more and more open to pressure, a newspaper was a political asset for
any monopoly dependent on its privileged relationship with the government. Thus Champalimaud started a paper in Angola in 1971—and
closed it two years later, after valuable mineral rights had been
acquired. In Portugal, the consortia—still the main backers of the regime—were actively encouraged to take over newspapers; early in
1972 a law made losses on "organs of information and culture" tax
deductible.[15] This accompanied bitter battles in the National Assembly on the question of an eventually emasculated press law, which
resulted in the resignation of members of the liberal opposition within
the state-approved party. Although the government won this battle,
press freedom was an increasingly sensitive area. The control of the
press by the consortia in the dying years of the old regime may thus be
seen on the one hand as a symptom of the growing corporate power of
the giant conglomerates, benefiting from their protected economic position and Portugal's past economic expansion, and on the other hand as
part of a final effort by the Caetanists and their sympathizers to close
ranks.

The change of control of the press probably had a temporary effect as
an inhibitor. In the short run, it meant that most of the press, though
not directly controlled by the regime and employing many individuals
who were privately opposed to it, was managed by people with little
commercial or political incentive either to encourage oppositional tendencies or to expand circulation in order to reach a wider public. Nevertheless, other pressures were gathering momentum, and toward the
end even the consortia themselves were beginning to favor a political
liberalization. Corporate control may actually have had a slight effect
in permitting an editorial boldness that would have been imprudent in
earlier, more vulnerable days. But the most ironic effect of the acquisitions occurred after the coup, when the banking consortia passed into
new hands.

Journalists and Journalism

An additional reason for the failure of Portuguese newspapers to exploit market opportunities and reach a wider public was the poor quality of those employed by them—itself a consequence of enervating official policy. Under Salazar and Caetano, journalism was a low-status, essentially clerical, subprofession, providing few opportunities for an interesting career; hence few talented or imaginative people entered it. The lack of profitability ensured that salaries would be kept low; the lack of freedom of expression meant that there was no scope for developing literary or intellectual skills. The image of journalists also suffered from a feeling that it was becoming a gerontocracy. In 1973 no fewer than two-thirds of the six hundred or so registering with the journalists' *sindicato* were over fifty.[16]

To supplement low pay (far below the salary level of, for example, low-ranking civil servants), many journalists added to their incomes by taking part-time jobs.[17] There were no formal entrance qualifications. Eighty of 112 new members of the *sindicato* between 1954 and 1964 described their father's occupation as *empregado* (employee). Very few came from an upper-middle-class professional background. Journalism was not socially prestigious and provided no access to the governing elite. Journalists (unlike other professionals, such as lawyers) did not move in and out of state and business employment, and they seldom became members of the Corporative Chamber.[18] News gathering and investigative journalism in the Western European and North American sense did not exist. There was no press lobby system and there were no privileged leaks. On the political side, the role of a journalist was to transcribe or summarize statements issued by government departments and ministerial offices.

Thus the Lisbon and Oporto daily press resembled the provincial press in other countries: the passive recipient of official or semiofficial information, not the active initiator of stories intended to sell papers or build reputations. Journalism was, in fact, an occupation with little professional pride, producing a dull and mediocre product. Only at the very end of the Caetano regime did things begin to change, though habits and behavior that had developed over generations were so ingrained that sacking the censor could not alone bring about an instant transformation.

179

Semicensorship

Yet the low general quality of journalism did not prevent the existence of oases of initiative and resistance. The Salazarist censorship had been severe. Official policy reflected Salazar's personal view of newspapers not only as a political danger but as an expression of the urban sophistication that had corrupted the Portuguese way of life. The press, advocate of "change, novelty and the commercial exploitation of human failings," was the enemy of "the people" and traditional values and represented "shiftless urban man" as opposed to "shrewd country men" in whom Salazar placed his hopes for Portugal's future.[19] Any material dealing with "politics, insubordination and immorality" was to be excised.[20]

Although explicitness was forbidden, it became increasingly possible from the 1960s to convey hidden meanings, which the censor failed to notice or allowed to slip by. The result was a journalistic language of concealed comment lurking beneath the heavy orthodox prose in the more adventurous papers. There were many tricks. An editor could indicate criticism by relegating an official pronouncement to an inside page or make a point by arranging photographs and headlines in particular ways. When *Expresso* deliberately defied the censor in May 1973, the editor was required to submit not only his page proofs but also his layout for official scrutiny.[21] But the skillful use of words was the most common means of evasion. The importance of this method—which was probably understood only by an elite within the elite of newspaper readers—is hard to exaggerate, cultivating an alternative culture and set of values, widely shared, under the surface of daily life. Those who were in touch with this culture had a sense of the world never being as it seemed. Among a highly literature-conscious intelligentsia, a new language arose quite early on, permanently affecting all Portuguese literature and art. Indeed the underground had won its cultural victory long before the political revolution. "It could be said that there is a 'clandestine' style with its own key metaphors (e.g., 'dawn' or 'day-break' for socialism; 'spring' for revolution; 'comrade' for prisoner; 'vampire' for policeman; 'poppy' for popular victory)," José Cardoso Pires wrote in 1972. "These metaphors have been widely adopted and give a marked abstract and poetical flavour to Portuguese prose."[22] This process, notable from the 1940s, was fully established by the 1970s. The choice of the song *Grandola,* broadcast on Radio Clube Português as the signal for the coup d'état, was thus not accidental. The traditional lyrics contain significant words and phrases and belong to the alternative culture. The subsequent adoption of the song as a kind of revolutionary hymn referred not only to its use on April 25 but also to this tradition of resistance in which language played a crucial part.

A function of the alternative culture was to pry open literary and journalistic doors. *Diário de Lisboa* and the long-established *República* led the way, with others following more or less boldly. The founding in January 1973 of the weekly *Expresso,* modeled on British and French examples, was undoubtedly a major landmark, comparable in importance with the other great literary event of the last months of Caetanism, the publication of General Spínola's *Portugal e o Futuro* a year later. *Expresso* was less radical than *Diário de Lisboa,* but its methods and approach were more modern. It was also run by people with close personal and political links with the regime yet who were deeply critical of it and who reflected the mounting frustrations and disaffection of the bourgeoisie. *Expresso* deliberately and repeatedly challenged the censor, and the failure of the authorities to close it was a sign of the regime's uncertainties about its own support. The more the paper got away with, the bolder it became, and the less it feared retaliatory sanctions. After a failed putsch in March 1974 (six weeks before the successful coup), *Expresso* published an editorial that was virtually an invitation to moderate military officers to intervene. By April 25, the censor was still in office, but the battle against him—by other papers, editors, and publishers in addition to *Expresso*—was already half won. A sense of the authorities in retreat and of a middle-class intelligentsia on the offensive was widely felt. In a frequently quoted passage from his memoirs, Caetano commented that after finishing Spínola's book early on the morning of February 21, 1974, "I had understood that the military coup, which I could sense had been coming, was now inevitable."[23] What clearer statement could there be of the direct political power of literary expression? It was Spínola's act of defiance, as much as what he said, that mattered. Yet the publication of his book would not have occurred without the steady pressure on the censorship that preceded it.

The Media and the Revolution

The roots of the April 25 coup were social, economic, and military. But the first demand that the Armed Forces Movement (MFA) met, the demand it was most able to exploit and finally the one that destroyed it, was the demand for political freedom. Indeed the crude Marxist interpretation of the opening phase after April 25 as a "bourgeois revolution" seems remarkably apt. The MFA, although initially concerned with the privileges of the officer corps, found itself swept along both before and after the coup by a wide range of essentially middle-class, liberal grievances, which the original MFA program clearly reflects. The early decisions after the consolidation of the coup, aimed at ensuring institutional and popular support for it, were essentially liberal. They reflected almost universal desires within the urban middle class and offended virtually nobody: the release of political prisoners, the arrest of the political police, the permitting of freedom of association and assembly, the promise of free elections, and above all the abolition of censorship and the guarantee of freedom of speech and of the press. What was the revolution of April 25 about? In a word, *Liberdade*. If the MFA and the Junta of National Salvation had any doubts, the mood of the Lisbon crowds of April 25 and May 1 dispelled them.

In any scoring of severity, brutality, or arbitrariness, the generally legalistic and greatly enfeebled Caetano regime would rank low among the world's dictatorships and oligarchies. By 1974 the idea of oppression had become greater than the reality. Yet the idea was powerful, and the coup was immediately and generally assumed to be a liberating event. This early association of the 1974 revolution with ideas of freedom from repression, restraint, and control is important because it helps to explain the (otherwise inexplicable) failure of the Gonçalvists within the MFA a year later to capitalize on their success and impose a new censorship. By the spring of 1975, a paper like *Expresso* found itself in a situation that inverted its position a year earlier. In 1974 it had been a "radical" opponent of Caetano, and a year later it was a "reactionary" opponent of Gonçalves and subject to similar threats and pressure. Yet the Gonçalves regime did not impose formal or informal censorship, nor did it close *Expresso,* presumably because to have done so would have lost the support of sympathizers inside and outside the government who regarded freedom of expression as a value worth maintaining. The Socialist Party slogan "Socialism, Yes! Dictatorship, No!" was not lightly chosen.

After the coup, the Portuguese press entered a period of rapid and heady growth. A profusion of new publications appeared. Within a year eight new weeklies, two dailies, nine party papers (including three that were daily for a time), and 115 miscellaneous periodicals were started, mainly in Lisbon and Oporto. In May 1974, the ending of censorship, which in practice had been immediate, was given moral reinforcement by a judge who dismissed the case against the "three Marias" (Portuguese feminist writers whose celebrated books had been indicted for pornography); in June a new press regulation promised to "guarantee freedom to express ideas." Just as a mild liberalization in the press had preceded the April 1974 coup, so a radicalization heralded the events of September 28 and March 11.

Did the press lead, or did it follow? The leftward drift of the Lisbon press in the summer and autumn of 1974 was rapid, but it seems to have reflected, more than it fomented, developments in universities, offices, factories, and barracks. Newspapers were certainly swept up by the atmosphere of the time. In particular there was an experimenting with what had been taboo: a permissive revolution with a political as well as sexual dimension. "After fifty years of imposed thought, the public taste turned to what had been most denied—Marxist doctrine and pornography," one writer has commented. "During the first months after Spínola's resignation, the works most read in Portugal, according to the best-seller lists, were written by Marx, Lenin and the Marquis de Sade."[24] Writers and journalists returning from exile encouraged the use of Marxist interpretations and terminology, writing words and expressing thoughts that could still cause a *frisson* because of their novelty. In an increasingly crowded newspaper marketplace where editors suddenly found a need to compete for sales (though all circulations rose), the economic pressure was strongly in the direction of radicalism. Radio and television followed the same fashion, and many writers and broadcasters developed an enthusiasm for political ideas that had barely interested them before April 25. It has been suggested that after the coup, Communists moved rapidly to secure positions of power for themselves in the media, filling vacancies created by officials identified with the old regime. This was partly true. But how many Communist journalists had there been before April 25? The total number and proportion was certainly small. The "Marxism" of the press before and after September 28, and particularly after March 11, was a matter not of clandestine believers emerging from the shadows but of new conversions, convenient or real.

By the beginning of 1975, the dominant tone of the Lisbon press was in favor of the extreme left. With political authority during this twilight period disintegrating fast, it would have been impossible for the capitalist owners to restrain their journalistic employees even if they had seriously tried to do so. But what brought about the final state in the transformation of the conservative press of April 1974 into the pro-Communist press of April 1975 was not freedom or journalistic faith but the nationalization of the banking consortia. When the MFA Assembly authorized this step immediately after the March 11 fiasco, the issue of the press was scarcely a factor. Indeed the bank nationalizations were less a premeditated act of policy by a left-pushing regime than the ratification of a workers' control takeover by staff that had already happened; it was an immediate response to a crisis. The effect on the press, nevertheless, was fundamental. It gave to the state the power over the press, which, in theory, had been wielded by the conglomerates, subject only to the agreement or acceptance of workers' and journalists' committees, which (as in other enterprises) had acquired a substantial influence. The power of ownership had come full circle. From March to November 1975, of seven state-owned daily papers, six (*A Capital, Diário de Lisboa, Diário de Notícias, Diário Popular, Jornal de Notícias* and *O Século*) were broadly sympathetic to Communist positions; only one, *Comércio do Porto,* was consistently opposed to them.

The most dramatic (but, in a way, the most predictable) transformation affected *Diário de Notícias,* Lisbon's largest circulation morning paper, which had always closely followed and supported, opinions of the old regime. In early 1974 *Notícias* was still faithfully transcribing the proceedings of the congresses of Portuguese National Action (the state political party). In April 1975 it was reporting, in the same flat, deferential tone, meetings of the Communist-controlled union federation, Intersindical. The same journalists were writing in the same way, with the same acceptance of prevailing political authority.[25] After November 25, when the sixth provisional government acquired enough power to reverse some of the decisions of its predecessors and *Diário de Notícias* was put in the charge of a pro-Socialist director, the staff followed the new line with remarkably little protest.

Broadcasting and the Revolution

What happened in the press after April 25, 1974, was closely paralleled by developments in radio and television.[26] Because broadcasting reached a far wider audience and could react more quickly to events, the political anxieties it aroused were comparatively greater.

Radiotelevisão Portuguesa (RTP) was already a state-controlled monopoly and had shown few of the oppositional inclinations of a section of the press, partly because innuendo and double entendre were harder to put across and more immediately obvious (and dangerous). Although the state held only a third of the shares, it could intervene directly in appointments, editorial policy, and scheduling. After the coup, this made changes of control easier, and a series of military directors followed one another, generally reflecting the shifting complexion of the regime. A workers' committee was set up to work in cooperation or conflict with successive ministers of social communications.

A move to the left occurred with few changes of personnel. Between the coup and the elections a year later, only about forty employees left or were dismissed, and there were only sixteen new journalistic appointments. Nevertheless the left-wing leanings of the workers' committee put new faces on the screen, and some highly politicized journalists whose ideas had been shaped in Paris and London brought fresh approaches and a spirit of experimentation to Portuguese television.

Television was also used for one of the most interesting (and also, perhaps, naive and utopian) initiatives of the Gonçalvismo period: the Armed Forces Movement's cultural dynamization program. This was short-lived. Nevertheless for a time the MFA took it seriously, using television as a key instrument in a campaign aimed at bringing social and political education to the rural population. This campaign, the subject of much ribaldry both at home and in the foreign press, lacked the organization or the continuity to do much more than entertain, bewilder, and (especially in the Catholic north) occasionally annoy.

Nevertheless it is interesting because it displayed the MFA at its most ideological, with a mystical fusion of a romantic, nationalist view of "the people" and unsophisticated Marxism, producing a political approach that had (in a dynamic, rather than a Portuguese, sense) some of the elements associated with fascism. It also illustrates the firm belief of the extreme left in the power of the media as an educator. Cultural dynamization made use of television as the best means of making contact with the largest number of people, especially in the countryside. Ironically, the main effect of the MFA television programs was probably to increase urban distrust of the MFA.

After the programs had been ended following November 25, Minister of Social Communications Almeida Santos pointed to a problem that was fundamental in a country with Portugal's uneven development: how to serve not only the very different publics of north and south but also the literate and comparatively well-informed urban audience on the one hand and the semifeudal world of the rural hinterland on the other. Santos argued that educational programs should be concentrated in a special channel and was dismissive of those in television "who prefer massive doses of artistic and political vanguardism to the culture which the people like."[27] Before November 25, vanguardism had certainly been a dominant feature, and much of the ideological content of television, reared to the theoretical and factional disputes of political militants, was irrelevant, incomprehensible, and hence ineffective among the population (especially the rural population) at large.

Radio also moved sharply to the left. There had been three main stations: the state radio, Emissora Nacional de Radiodiffusão (ENR), a private "cooperative" enterprise called Rádio Clube Português (RCP), and a station owned by the Church, Rádio Renascença. There were also smaller local or regional stations in private hands. Unlike newspapers, the private radio stations were not owned by the great consortia and so were not affected by the major nationalizations. Nevertheless they were subject to general pressures experienced throughout the media, and power passed in 1975 into the hands of workers' committees whose sympathies were with the (not always pro-Communist) extreme left.

Radio was a particular source of difficulty to the moderate sixth government of Pinheiro de Azevedo, after the Gonçalvismo period had ended. On September 29, 1975, the prime minister appointed Major João de Figueiredo as director of ENR, at a time when the station was occupied by disabled army veterans, and by troops sent in to control them. It was two weeks before the veterans were persuaded to leave, and even then Figueiredo continued to have difficulties. One typical battle was over broadcasts by Angolan liberation movements on independence day (November 11). Figueiredo had to overcome strong opposition to the view that only the left-wing MPLA (Popular Movement for the Liberation of Angola), rather than all these organizations, should be put on the air.[28] After November 25, "We gained in equilibrium," as the director put it drily, "what we lost in spontaneity."[29]

Rádio Rénascença was at the center of even more dramatic battles. Taken over by workers within the station who supported the ultraleft (mainly the pro-Albanian Popular Democratic Union) and increasingly the vehicle for a stridently revolutionary propaganda, Rénascença was put off the air by a despairing decision of the Revolutionary Council to blow up its transmitter, a panic action that was one of the immediate causes of the final collapse of authority that led to the confrontation of November 25.

185

Although all accepted the importance of these battles, pro-Communist (and ultraleft) advances early in 1975 can now be seen as pyrrhic victories. Without full control either of political institutions or the armed forces, the extreme left had created an impression of power through the media that belied the reality. Hence the Communists were blamed for failing to check a deteriorating situation, which they were unable to prevent. Control of the media appeared as the most striking, and alarming, evidence—especially to the influential middle class—of Communist "triumphalism," and it invited a reaction. Thus, in the summer of 1975, when pro-Communists seemed strongest in the press, massive public support for Mário Soares in the *República* dispute marked the beginning of the end of the power of the extreme left. Continuing left-wing control of most of the media did not prevent power slipping out of the hands of the extremist factions in the armed forces, and the declaration by the Group of Nine (moderate officers on the Revolutionary Council) in August was strengthened by what was felt to be a dangerous and unfair domination of the press by the extreme left.

In fact, during the most revolutionary period—March to November—both radio and television were agents provocateurs much more than they were ever persuaders. Their effect was to outrage, scandalize, unsettle, and excite. Until the end of August, extreme left influence in the media reflected—or paralleled—the power of left-wing factions in the army and in government. But this power was never secure, and broadcasting never became the instrument of an official propaganda. With the establishment of the beleaguered sixth government in September, broadcasting reverted to an oppositional role, becoming a symbol of disorder and defiance. The government was weakened not by the influence of what broadcasters said but by their disregard of authority in saying it. Broadcasting became a means of attracting attention, and its use was often a form of political action. An extreme example—and one that brought a sharp official reaction—was the broadcast appeal in September to join the Lisbon riot that eventually burned the Spanish embassy. Day-to-day assaults on the government in news and comment were a less dramatic but more effective proof of the impotence of the authorities. Battles over control of both newspapers and broadcasting were symbolic in the sense that what was really at stake was not the ability of the media to control opinion but a demonstration of superior physical power. And for much of 1975, power was the only real source of legitimacy.

Media and Voters

The view that, as persuasive instruments, the media were at most a small factor during the revolutionary period is reinforced by the results of the assembly elections of April 1975 and April 1976. Politicians in all countries, even where parties are long established and have a reliable basis of support, are sensitive at election time to media attitudes. Concern is expressed over allegedly biased reporting. It is assumed that if the press or broadcasting lean one way or the other, the public is likely to be influenced in the same direction. Since, however, it is generally impossible to know how the electorate would have behaved if the media had presented a different view, the assumption is essentially a common-sense one. Recent Portuguese electoral experience appears to provide a unique opportunity to assess the electoral influence of the media in a less intuitive way.

In the weeks preceding the 1975 election, most of the Portuguese press, radio, and television were more sympathetic to the Communists than to any other political party. By April, five of the seven recently nationalized daily papers had newly appointed pro-Communist editors. Printing plant workers, with a long history of clandestine organization behind them, were refusing to print material that was "opposed to the revolutionary process," and a high proportion of foreign news was acquired from Soviet bloc agencies.[30] Among Lisbon dailies, only *República* and the newly created *Jornal Novo* were not sympathetic to the Portuguese Communist Party (PCP). Typical headlines during the run up to the election were "Jesuino Says Socialism Not Votes Is Important"[31] and "Vote for the People's Party with the Revolution."[32] Television scrupulously allotted equal time and newspapers gave equal space to all twelve parties in the contest, but no distinction was made between major and minor parties, so the effect was to reduce the coverage of the serious, non-Communist contenders.

The election itself was freely conducted. There was some intimidation of Centre Social Democrats (CDS) and even Popular Democrats (PPD) in Alentejo, and Communists found campaigning hard in parts of the Catholic north. But the ballot was secret, and there was no manipulation of the voting or the result. Hence the election of April 25, 1975 was the first national expression of political opinion, based on universal suffrage, in the history of Portugal. The results surprised many people. On a massive 91.7 percent turnout, the MFA "blank vote" appeal had been answered by only 6.9 percent of the electorate, a figure that included all incorrectly marked ballots, and was scarcely higher than might have been expected of an inexperienced and ill-educated population under normal conditions.[33] More important, the Communists received only 12.5 percent despite their apparently advantageous position in the media during the campaign.

A year later, much had occurred to change political attitudes without any help from the press and broadcasting: the revolutionary upheavals of the summer and autumn, the popular power phenomenon, the arrival of hundreds of thousands of *retornados* (returned settlers) from Africa, the impact of the agrarian reform, the confrontation of November 25, and the restoration of stable government and a disciplined army. But in addition, the politics of the media had been transformed. With Renascença returned to Church ownership and the other private radio stations nationalized and combined, broadcasting was now given an "independent" or "pluralist" color, which meant a sympathy for the sixth government. With its power restored, the Azevedo administration was also able to use state ownership of most daily papers, achieved in left-wing days, to change a predominantly pro-Communist Lisbon press into a liberal democratic one by appointing new directors. Of the state-

187

owned papers, *A Capital, Diário de Notícias, Diário Popular, and Jornal de Comércio* (an Oporto paper), firmly in the extreme left camp before November 25, were all broadly aligned with the Socialist party by the time of the April 1976 election. *O Século* was closer to PPD. Only *Diário de Lisboa* was permitted to retain a pro-Communist editorial control.[34] Precise figures are not available. But if at the time of the April 1975 election about three-quarters of daily papers sold in Lisbon were backing the extreme left, a year later the proportion was probably no higher than an eighth.

As might have been expected, there was a big swing to the right. CDS made big gains, at the expense of both Socialists and Popular Democrats. But the extreme left vote stayed firm, and the main contours of the electoral map remained the same. Indeed unless there were powerful unknown factors working the other way, the media seem to have had little effect. Between 1975 and 1976, the vote of the Marxist parties (including the ultraleft but excluding the Socialists) fell from 20.6 percent of the electorate to 19.2 percent; the "soft left" (PS) dropped from 37.9 percent to 34.9 percent; and the "Catholic" parties (PPD, CDS, and PPM) rose from 34.6 percent to 41.3 percent. It was hardly an electoral revolution; and the main losers were not the extreme left but the Socialists who stood to gain most in media terms from the aftermath of November 25. Most striking of all, the greatest changes were in areas where the influence of the media was weakest. CDS made its largest proportionate gains in the vote in some of the remoter districts of the north where newspaper reading was exceptional and the penetration of television far from complete. Thus at first sight, the Portuguese elections provide a sharply drawn illustration of the limited immediate effect of the media on mass opinion and one of the clearest examples of electoral resistance to the influence of press and broadcasting in postwar European politics.

The Media and Public Opinion

However, Portugal presents features that are unusual in Western Europe, and there are special reasons why the media should influence mass opinion less in Portugal than elsewhere. First, in a country with a long history of censorship, even the least sophisticated had acquired a deep suspicion of the media. The reading public had no reason to trust journalists who switched from fascist to communist copy within a few months. "What a metamorphosis our journalists have gone through," one secretary of state for information put it; "the same people who were writing our papers before 25th April, continued to write them after it, and then after 28th September, since 11th March, and finally are still writing them after 25th November.[35] Throughout the upheaval, much of the press in practice retained its traditional sycophancy, with an approach that the public found familiar. Even at times when papers were apparently defying the government in office, they often reflected the attitudes of groups and factions with most real power. Hence the Portuguese habit of not taking the press at its face value was not discarded, and people relied on alternative sources of information. Foreign broadcasts acquired an even greater importance than under the old regime. The audience of the Portuguese section of the BBC rose to more than a million in the summer of 1975, before falling back to 250,000 when the need for reliable news from outside diminished.

Yet there is another reason why the Portuguese press (as distinct from broadcasting) was a surprisingly small influence on public opinion; and this needs closer examination than we have given it so far: there are no mass papers in Portugal, and there is no mass reading public.[36] A readership survey conducted by the social and economic research body NORMA in November and December 1976, on the basis of a national sample of 5,805 adults over fifteen years in age, shows how restricted is the extent of Portuguese newspaper readership and how similar most papers are to one another in the characteristics of their readers.

In reply to the question, "Which daily papers (morning or afternoon) have you read or skimmed in the last thirty days?" only 29.6 percent gave an answer, and this small proportion was concentrated in greater Lisbon and greater Porto. Elsewhere in the country only one person in five was able to name a paper that he or she had seen in the previous month. Table 8.1 gives data from the survey. Readership is lowest of all in the smallest communities (below 2,000), which account for nearly two-thirds of the population, reflecting the high level of rural illiteracy and semiliteracy and the poor distribution of papers. In response to the question, "What papers did you see yesterday?" only 13.8 percent of the sample gave an answer. Outside Lisbon (26.2 percent) and Porto (37.2 percent), the proportion was about one in twelve, and in communities below 2,000 a mere 5.7 percent. Regular newspaper reading in the countryside is thus a quite exceptional activity.

There is no national press at all. The main Lisbon daily papers (*Diário de Notícias, Diário Popular, O Diário, Diário de Lisboa*, and *A Capital*) have no significant readership outside the south. Readership of Oporto papers (*Jornal de Notícias, Comércio do Porto*, and *Primeiro de Janeiro*) is even more exclusively northern. Readership is twice as common among those under thirty-four as in older age groups, a variation that reflects improving education and the migration of young people to towns and suggests the likelihood of an expanding newspaper public over the next decade.

189

But it is class variation that is particularly striking (see table 8.2). Among poorer, unskilled workers in the lowest economic group (39.5 percent of the sample) fewer than one person in eleven had seen a paper in the preceding month; among the top 24.8 percent, a clear majority had done so. No individual paper was mentioned by more than one person in twenty-seven in the lowest social class, nor is any paper

Table 8.1 Results of Readership Survey, November–December 1976: Monthly Readership by Region and Size of Community

Response to "What daily papers have you read or skimmed in the last 30 days?"	Total (%)	By Region (%)					By Population (%)				
		Greater Lisbon	Greater Porto	Coast	Interior North	Interior South	<2,000	2,000–10,000	10,000–100,000	100,000–500,000	>500,000
O Dia	1.4	5.7	0.4	0.1	0.2	2.7	0.4	1.6	1.6	0.9	7.3
O Diário	3.6	7.0	2.9	2.1	1.6	8.3	2.4	6.4	6.1	3.0	6.2
Diário de Notícias	7.2	30.7	0.7	3.7	1.1	6.7	3.2	4.9	11.1	1.6	33.4
Pagina Um	0.3	2.0	—	—	—	0.4	—	—	0.9	—	2.6
O Século	1.9	2.3	—	1.8	0.1	6.3	1.6	2.2	4.0	—	2.3
Comércio do Porto	3.7	0.6	17.3	2.8	2.3	1.5	2.1	4.7	5.0	27.3	0.7
Jornal de Notícias	9.1	0.8	42.4	7.7	6.9	0.2	7.3	12.9	11.8	37.2	1.0
Primeiro de Janeiro	3.6	0.1	12.3	2.6	4.9	1.1	1.9	7.1	5.9	21.5	—
A Capital	2.1	7.6	0.7	1.7	—	1.6	0.7	1.6	4.0	1.6	8.9
Diário de Lisboa	2.2	8.4	1.2	1.0	0.2	2.6	0.3	3.2	5.0	2.7	9.4
Diário Popular	4.2	21.2	0.8	1.3	—	3.0	0.9	2.5	9.5	2.0	21.7

Jornal Novo	1.2	4.4	0.1	0.4	1.0	1.4	0.4	1.7	1.5	0.1	6.0
A Luta	1.3	5.4	0.1	0.2	0.1	3.0	0.1	2.6	2.3	0.3	6.8
Others	—	—	—	0.1	—	—	—	0.2	—	—	—
Total % responding	29.6	52.9	63.3	20.4	16.4	26.3	17.7	39.6	47.3	73.8	55.1

Source: Portuguese Ministry of Social Communications (SECS)

Table 8.2 *Results of Readership Survey (see table 8.1), by Socioeconomic Group*

Response to "What daily papers have you read or skimmed in the last 30 days?"	Socioeconomic Group			
	Class I (Upper) (7.0% of sample)	Class II (17.8% of sample)	Class III (35.7% of sample)	Class IV (Lower) (39.5% of sample)
O Dia	8.2	2.1	0.7	0.4
O Diário	8.3	6.3	4.8	0.5
Diário de Notícias	22.1	15.1	6.7	1.5
Pagina Um	1.5	0.6	0.3	—
O Século	2.0	3.5	1.5	1.6
Comércio do Porto	13.0	7.0	3.3	1.0
Jornal de Notícias	12.5	15.5	11.2	3.7
Primeiro de Janeiro	15.3	3.7	4.0	1.1
A Capital	13.5	4.8	0.6	0.1
Diário de Lisboa	11.9	3.3	2.0	0.1
Diário Popular	11.8	8.4	4.5	0.6
Jornal Novo	8.1	2.5	0.6	0.1
A Luta	10.0	1.6	0.8	0.1
Others	—	—	0.1	—
Total % responding	76.8	57.1	29.7	8.8

mainly dependent on sales to the poorest people. Only the now-defunct *O Século* had its highest readership (33.1 percent of the total) in Class IV; but even in this case, nearly as many (32.4 percent) were seen in Class II. Only four papers (including *O Século*) could claim that the majority of their readers were not among the most prosperous quarter of the population. The profiles of weekly papers are even more exclusive. No weekly (apart from the sporting *Bola*) with a readership large enough to produce a significant sample had a majority of its readers outside the top two classes, according to the survey.[37]

Thus overall the Portuguese press probably remains the most elitist in Europe. Its readers most commonly urban, young, and skilled working or middle class. It is not surprising, therefore, that a change in the political control of the press barely ruffled the electoral map of Portugal as a whole.

The Media and the Second Republic

How secure is the press now from the possibility of interference and control? Guarantees in the constitution and institutional checks such as the press council and the information councils set up for each medium are important, but there is little that the media can do directly if a change of regime brings strong physical pressure to bear. On the other hand, events since 1974 have produced enough political commitment for any serious repression of the media to involve very widespread arrests. In a country with little recent history of domestic violence, this may be a powerful disincentive.

At a less dramatic level, the Portuguese press is probably much less susceptible to milder forms of influence or intimidation than it was in April 1974 or April 1975. Its quality has improved. Many new publications have had a brief life, but others have survived, including the weeklies *O Jornal* and *Opção* (on the left) and *O Tempo* (on the right). Table 8.3 summarizes changes in political tendency and circulation of newspapers between 1975 and 1978. The Portuguese official news syndicating service, ANOP (Agência Noticiosa Portuguesa), now employs eighty journalists and provides through an expanding network of correspondents at home and abroad a news gathering service that is entirely new, and vastly superior to its predecessor, the tiny Agência Nacional da Informacão. Plans are already advanced for a state-run school of journalism, the first of its kind. A national distribution agency, in joint state and private ownership, is also promised, crucial for any expansion of circulation or the development of a genuinely national press. Does the state ownership of the press make it particularly vulnerable? There is little reason to believe so. It is true that the opportunity exists for a future regime to change editorial control with slightly less formal restraint than existed before and that state ownership was a significant factor in the relationship between governing groups and the media in

Table 8.3 *The Portuguese Press in Transition: Ownership, Circulation, and Political Tendency of Daily Papers, 1975 and 1978*

Paper		Ownership*	Approximate Political Tendency October 1975†	Approximate Political Tendency, May 1978†	Circulation Claimed, October 1975‡	Circulation Claimed, May 1978‡
O Dia	morning	private	—	Social Democrat/Center Social Democrat	(started Dec. 1975)	41,000 (March)
O Diário	morning	private	—	Communist	(started Nov. 1975)	48,000 (Feb.)
Diário de Notícias	morning	state	Communist	Socialist	106,000	81,000
O Século		state	Communist	—	40,000	(closed down Feb. 1977)
Comércio do Porto (Oporto)	morning	state	Popular Democrat	Social Democrat/Center Social Democrat	95,000	55,000
Jornal de Notícias (Oporto)	morning	state	Communist	Socialist	70,000	80,000
Primeiro de Janeiro (Oporto)	morning	private	Center/Social Democrat	Social Democrat/Center Social Democrat	70,000	46,000 (Feb.)
Jornal do Comércio		private	Socialist/Popular Democrat	—	100,000	(closed down Nov. 1975)
A Capital	afternoon	state	Communist	Right wing of Socialists	60,000	ca. 25,000–30,000

				Communist influence		
Diário de Lisboa	afternoon	state	Communist		38,000	41,000 (March)
Diário Popular	afternoon	state	Communist	Left wing of Socialists	73,000	66,000
Jornal Novo	afternoon	private	Right wing of Socialists	Social Democrat	100,000	37,000 (March)
A Luta	afternoon	private	Socialist	Socialist	80,000	40,000
República		private	Communist/extreme left	—	20,000	(closed down)

*"State" includes cases where a majority of shares are held by the state.

†Descriptions are extremely rough, and represent an assessement of the closest party or tendency, not any consistent loyalty.

‡Number of copies actually sold is much lower. Proportion of rejects is generally 10%–20%, but can be much higher.

1975. However in many countries (Great Britain is the most notable example) broadcasting has been or remains a state monopoly or near monopoly and yet maintains its autonomy. In Portugal, the old regime succeeded in controlling the press for a long time while it remained in private hands. Moreover there has been some tendency to diversify in Portugal. What looked like general state ownership in the spring of 1975 now looks more like a mixed economy, with the emergence of new independent papers (*Jornal Novo, O Diário,* and *A Rua,* as well as the weeklies) and the demise of the state-owned *O Século.* The best defense of press freedom from direct intervention—whether in state or privately owned papers—is the same as in radio and television: the journalists and their committees, which have a power to block unwelcome editorial policy barely imaginable in 1974.

Now that the euphoria, and the anxieties, of the revolution are over, a more considered experimentation and development is possible. With no recent background of press freedom, new conventions in political journalism are only beginning to be established. Thus official press conferences are becoming institutionalized, and a "journalists' interlude" in cabinet meetings has been adopted. Political discussion in the press, as opposed to exhortation or denunciation, is still a novelty, and its use remains uneasy. The content of reporting has changed, with far more interest shown in news than before 1974.[38] But despite a wider range of subject matter, the general tone—official, verbose, circumlocutory, passive—remains the most unshakable legacy of the old regime.

Conclusion

The Portuguese media have changed more since April 25, 1974 than in the preceding generation. But the events of 1974–1975 did not wipe the slate clean, or create a new press, radio, or television. Many, if not most, of the same people remain, with the same habits and professional attitudes. The Portuguese press is not a fascist press suddenly turned liberal democratic; a steady literary pressure within the media helped to bring about an evolution in attitudes long before April 25. What happened in the media is part of what has happened to Portuguese social and political life in general. A period of increasingly rapid change before 1974 culminated in an explosive acceleration and was followed by a period of recovery and consolidation.

A great deal of attention was paid to the media during the upheaval, but partly for the wrong reasons. The widely held view (both at home and abroad) that control of press and broadcasting and control of mass opinion were almost one and the same was wide of the mark. Sometimes the opposite was true. In the summer of 1975, pro-Communist control in the media was very extensive, but as the *República* affair showed, this had the effect, not of converting people, but of arousing widespread resentment. The actual persuasive power of the media was very limited. In many rural areas, the penetration of television was far from complete, and newspaper readership was exceptional among poorer people, especially outside the towns. More important, people were not accustomed to believing the media and hence were less susceptible to media influence than might be expected elsewhere. As the small shift in electoral attitudes between April 1975 and April 1976 indicates, people derived their political views and loyalties from other sources.

Yet the media were important during the revolution because they could agitate among a small activist section and because control of the media gave an impression of power, when the actual bases of power were sometimes unclear. In the jockeying for position and influence, control of mass communications was seen as a way of demonstrating, especially to powerful military groups, a kind of importance. The idea that power over the media would lead to legitimacy was destroyed by the April 1975 election, which provided a basis for legitimacy wholly new in Portuguese history and by the mass demonstrations of support for Soares against the extreme left media stranglehold. Yet while the future character of the political system remained in doubt, the media retained an attraction for groups whose support among the masses was uncertain. Indeed, in a period of political disintegration, press and broadcasting seemed to provide a kind of scepter to which competing factions aspired but that conferred little actual authority.

Notes

1. Before the revolution there had been censorship for all but eighty years in five centuries of publishing history. José Cardoso Pires, "Changing a Nation's Way of Thinking." *Index on Censorship* 1 (Spring 1972):47–63.

2. A. H. de Oliveira Marques, *History of Portugal,* vol. 2: *From Empire to Corporate State* (New York: Columbia University Press, 1972), p. 36.

3. Ibid., p. 207. In the mid-1960s, Portugal ranked seventeenth in the world for the number of books published annually.

4. At the same time, the increased availability of transistor radios, with access to outside broadcasts, made controls less effective than in the past. H. Martins, "Portugal," in S. J. Woolf, ed., *European Fascism* (London: Weidenfeld, 1968), p. 325.

5. Ibid., p. 192.

6. UNESCO, *World Literacy* (New York: UNESCO, 1971).

7. A large number of very small papers, often little more than parish magazines, survived. Most of these were controlled by the Church. There were some 800 of these in 1976, 730 run by the parish priest. The majority were in the north, and their political importance was minimal. Even so, they were subject to censorship on the same basis of other journals. Martins, "Portugal," pp. 325–326.

8. J. Cutileiro, *A Portuguese Rural Society* (Oxford: Oxford University Press, 1971), p. 220n.

9. Pires, "Changing a Nation's Way of Thinking."

10. UNESCO, *World Literacy.*

11. E. Potter, *The Press as Opposition* (London: Chatto and Windus, 1975).

12. NORMA Survey of Press Revenue, 1963 (data supplied by Ministry of Social Communications).

13. On the effects of the internationalization of the Portuguese economy and the growth of a 'comprador bourgeoisie', see the argument in N. Poulantzas, *La Crise des Dictadures* (Paris: Maspero, 1975).

14. Interview, Francisco Balsemão, August 1976.

15. Decreto-Lei No. 150/72, art. 60.

16. Individual membership records from Sindicato dos Jornalistas.

17. *Jornalismo,* no. 5 (1971).

18. P. C. Schmitter, *Corporatism and Public Policy in Authoritarian Portugal* (Beverly Hills, Calif.: Sage, 1975).

19. A. Arons de Carvalho, *A Censura e as Leis de Imprensa* (Lisbon: Editora Meridiano, 1975), p. 114.

20. Norberto Lopes, *Visado pela Censura* (Lisbon: Editora Aster, 1975).

21. Marcello Rebello de Sousa, interview, July 1978.

22. Pires, "Changing a Nation's Way of Thinking." Early pioneers of the "clandestine" style were intellectual periodicals such as *Seara Nova* and *Tempo e Modo,* tolerated by Salazar because of their restricted appeal and tiny circulation. Survivors from Republican days, these provided a forum.

23. *Depoimento* (Record, Rio de Janeiro, 1975), cited by A. de Figueiredo, *Portugal: Fifty Years of Dictatorship* (London: Penguin, 1975), p. 232.

24. Alexandrino Severino, "Literary Trends and the Revolution" (unpublished paper, 1976).

25. In 1975 a group of journalists did, however, leave *Diário de Notícias* and set up a right-wing paper, *A Dia*.

26. See J. Seaton and B. Pimlott, "Sacking the Censor: Developments in Portuguese Broadcasting, 1974–6," *Index on Censorship* (1976).

27. *Expresso* (January 1976).

28. Interview, Major João de Figuereido, July 1978.

29. *O Tempo,* March 4, 1976.

30. Agência Noticiosa Portuguêsa (ANOP) records, May–July 1975.

31. *A Capital,* May 19, 1975.

32. *Diário de Lisboa,* May 21, 1975.

33. For analysis of the elections of 1975 and 1976, see J. Gaspar and N. Vitorino, *As Eleiçoes de 25 de Abril Geografia e Imagem dos Partidos* (Lisbon: Livrus Horizonte, 1975) and B. Pimlott, "Parties and Voters in the Portuguese Revolution," *Parliamentary Affairs* (Winter 1977).

34. Communists had started a new independent daily, *O Diário,* and extreme rightists had set up *O Dia.*

35. *O Tempo,* February 5, 1976.

36. A major reason for this, of course, is the high level of illiteracy.

37. It is an indication of the low level of politicization of the Portuguese reading public (and also of the possible scope for a mass circulation tabloid) that the newspaper with the widest circulation contains no political matter at all.

38. Thus, in one week in February 1973, of 132 news stories in *Diário de Notícias,* 79 percent were of home affairs and only 5 percent of foreign affairs unrelated to Portugal; in one week in March 1976, of 140 stories, the proportions were 61 percent and 23 percent, respectively.

9

The Press as Loyal Opposition in Japan

William Horsley

The Political Process and the Context of Public Debate

At both formative periods in Japan's modern history, after the Meiji restoration of 1868 and after the country's defeat in World War II, the major reforms that occurred were not the result of a popular revolution or of ideological or class conflict within the country. They were in both cases handed down from above: in the case of the Meiji constitution of 1889, as a "gracious gift from the Emperor to his subjects"; in the case of the 1946 constitution, at the direction of a victorious power at a time of national despair and utter weakness. And in spite of the broad reforms of government and society that were effected after World War II, a strong element of continuity is apparent in the exercise of state power and the conduct of public debate from Japan's beginning as a modern country to the present day. Except for a convulsive period of conflict between traditional and newly unleashed social forces in the years immediately following 1945, postwar Japan has been characterized by a concordance of views on the formulation and conduct of national policies among government, industry, press, and general public that is unique in an industrialized country outside the Communist world.

All of the modern and democratic elements on which the postwar Japanese state is founded—popular sovereignty, the supremacy of the law, the parliamentary system and party politics, and the whole range of guarantees of civil liberties—were imposed at a stroke from outside under extraordinary circumstances after the country's devastating defeat in war, and they were a radical departure from its own political traditions. True, the concept of popular or civil rights (*minken*) was one of the basic ingredients that the Meiji leadership found among the constitutions of the foreign countries its envoys toured to study and compare the political and industrial systems of the West, and it had a strong appeal among leading figures in the party movement and the press, which embodied the voice of challenge and opposition to the Meiji oligarchy. But despite the vigorous liberalism of some statesmen and intellectuals and the left-wing movement that flourished briefly, the impetus for establishing *minken,* had first faded under the urgent imperatives of achieving industrialization and victory in successive military conflicts beyond the country's shores, and later been directly suppressed by an intolerant nationalist and militarist government using censorship, intimidation, and direct police action. Before World War II, Japan never had a period of stable representative government.

There were many contradictions in the postwar establishment of a new framework of public life. In the attempt to instill new principles of integrity and independent judgment into the postwar press, the occupation authorities themselves employed press censorship, banned criticism of occupation policies, and instructed editors and journalists on what subjects in particular should be discussed (these included war criminals and the imperial household). The policy of encouraging the labor union movement (which had been harshly suppressed since the 1920s) was reversed when it led to an immediate revival of Marxist ideas and the growth of union militancy. Suspected war criminals and former leaders in many spheres with known nationalist views were released, and many of them quickly assumed commanding positions again in government and business. Similarly the plan to break up the giant industrial concerns of the prewar era was not carried through because of the urgent need to give Japan some industrial and organizational basis to reconstruct its shattered economy. Also there still existed, quite separate from the legal and institutional changes that were imposed, a more fundamental set of instincts and relationships that determined the course that the nation has followed since the occupation period. As one Western author and journalist wrote in a discussion of the strictures on the postwar Japanese press to be critical and objective toward the government and other forms of authority, "There was a basic fallacy in the presumption that the Japanese press could acquire a sense of independence and responsibility imposed from the outside. Telling a newsman that he must report the news the way he honestly and objectively sees it, when he has little in his own experience to know what that means, is a contradiction in terms."[1]

It is a conspicuous feature of present-day Japan that there is very little public mention of the country's wartime record and policies. A clear break has undoubtedly been made with the past. Yet in the political sphere, many of the wartime leaders have played a prominent role since then in public affairs. Many of the old customs of mutual obligation and dependency exert a formative hold over the conduct of party

201

politics, business enterprises, and the civil administration. Despite the formal democratization of education, traditional patterns of obedience and loyalty are still widely inculcated into the young. And because of the peculiar position of Japan in the world and the close and covert relations among all power groups within the country, the sense of news values in the press is fundamentally different from that of the West.

In Japan's history there has been no outright conflict—and so no attempt at a clear delineation of roles—between religious and governmental authority, and there had been little scope for the evolution of independent spheres of authority accorded to other social groups or institutions such as the law, the academic or intellectual world, professional and trade guilds, or the press. Even since the war, Japanese society has lacked the opposition of different ethnic, class, or occupational groups, which has been responsible for internal tensions within other societies with ostensibly similar political systems. A deeply felt sense of common purpose and obligation accounts for a variety of features of social organization and behavior in Japan that would be inconceivable elsewhere: the organization of most labor unions along enterprise rather than industrial or trade lines, so linking management and labor organically within a single enterprise; the structural integration of government, banks, and large enterprises, which makes the formal nationalization of crucial sectors of industry unnecessary because a high degree of central economic planning is possible within this unique form of capitalist system; the custom of lifelong employment without reference to any legal contract; the adoption of a system without legal compulsion for the collection of a television license fee to finance the public broadcasting corporation, Nippon Hoso Kyokai (NHK); the lack of concern for the libel laws, which enables the press, especially the popular weekly magazines, to publish scurrilous articles or make serious allegations without real fear of prosecution, while selectively observing unwritten taboos on certain figures and issues.

Nowhere is the peculiar Japanese genius for consensus based on hierarchical values more clearly apparent than in the practice of party politics. The principle of adversary politics, with its assumption of the periodic alternation of parties in office, has never taken root in Japan. Apart from a single period from 1947 to 1948 when a socialist prime minister, Tetsu Katayama, headed a coalition center-left government, conservative political forces have dominated postwar Japanese politics. The present ruling party, the Liberal Democratic party, is in effect a coalition of a broad range of political, business, and other traditionally powerful interests, which came together in 1955 from the two main conservative political groupings and has had exclusive membership of every administration since.

The opposition consists essentially of four parties: the Japan Socialist party (the largest in terms of both Diet seats and popular support), the *Komei* or Clean Government party (linked with the Soka Gakkai Buddhist sect), the Japan Communist party, and the Democratic Socialist party (a breakaway section of the JSP formed in 1960). There are, in addition, a handful of Diet members in minor splinter groups from the main parties and a number of independents. But although the opposition has on numerous occasions succeeded in delaying Diet business or extracting compromises from the ruling party by the tactic of boycotting proceedings altogether, the continuous domination of the LDP has removed any real meaning from the principle of a majority verdict in the Diet.

Power has changed hands only among the several well-defined groups or factions within the Liberal Democratic party. These factions differ from one another not primarily in their varying approaches to the main policy issues (though differences of emphasis do exist and play a part) but rather quite simply in their allegiance to a particular figure who is the leader of the faction. The political influence of the leader is precisely measured in terms of the number of members of the Diet who support him in return for the security and chance of promotion to office that they derive from membership of the group.

In all but name, these factions have been the major "parties" on the postwar political scene. The LDP monopoly of power met its first strong challenge during the premierships of Kakuei Tanaka (1972–1974) and Takeo Miki (1974–1976), and there has been a gradual dismantling of its monopoly control during the 1970s. This has coincided with a fall in the rate of economic growth and a shift in the nation's priorities from industrial expansion to the creation of a stable, long-term economic base, with a higher priority for welfare and education.

The scandal surrounding Tanaka's financial affairs was by no means unique in the record of postwar politics. Nevertheless his resignation as premier presaged a period of unprecedented public inquiry into the mechanisms of ruling party politics and the extent of corruption in the leading ranks of politics and business. The combination of circumstances that brought this about included the evidence of political abuses in Tanaka's term of office; the choice, by the common consent (initially but not later on) of LDP faction leaders, of Takeo Miki, a minor faction leader from the reformist wing of the party, to present a new and cleaner image of the party at a time of public criticism; and the unforeseen revelations, made first in a U.S. congressional subcommittee hearing, about the flow of bribes from executives of the Lockheed Aircraft Corporation to various corners of the Japanese political world to assist the sale of its planes. The series of indictments and trials over the Lockheed affair represents the most sustained activity of the judiciary in Japan since the war, and it was applied to what have traditionally been the most inaccessible parts of the body politic.

203

The legacy of the Miki regime was an incalculable new degree of skepticism among the press and the public toward the politics of the LDP. For the first time, new laws had been formulated to set limits on the permitted levels of political contributions and campaign spending, and Miki had made his own resignation conditional on the party's adopting a new set of rules governing the election of the party president. The public exposure of the behavior and motives of those in places of authority that was revealed and eagerly publicized during the terms of office of Tanaka and Miki has clearly altered and expanded the framework of discussion of public issues.

The challenge to long-established areas of arbitrary authority and the growth of the multifarious voices of an affluent and more diverse society than Japan has ever been before are both vividly reflected in the nation's press.

The Relationship between Government and Press

At the end of World War II, the standard of literacy in Japan was already very high, and the authority that newspapers possessed (especially the *Asahi Shimbun,* whose part in the spreading of official information during the war had been paramount) was further strengthened by legal privileges and various forms of encouragement given them by the occupation authorities.[2] The so-called big three papers—the *Asahi, Mainichi,* and *Yomiuri*—quickly consolidated their domination of the national daily press, each reaching circulations of several million.[3] Common agreements on editorial and business matters, come to through the Japan Newspaper Publishers' and Editors' Association, and the high priority given to the accurate relaying of detailed information have resulted in an extraordinary similarity among the three in both content and layout.[4] They differ only marginally on matters of editorial policy. All are independent of political parties, and all attempt to combine the characters of quality and popular press to appeal to the largest possible number of readers. Their huge circulations testify to the erosion of important variations of outlook by class and by region. The *Asahi,* always the most authoritative and establishment of the big three, has adopted a more positively critical tone on some issues than the others and has sometimes been regarded as slightly left of center. The *Yomiuri,* by contrast, has sometimes shown itself more sympathetic to traditional and nationalistic opinion, and many still regard it as just to the right of center. The flavor of the *Mainichi* is thought to be more literary and discursive than its rivals; the paper is proud of its feature coverage of historical and international themes. But these judgments are not always borne out by a close examination of coverage on specific issues, and their positions have altered from time to time over the years as the three have competed for the center ground of the mass reading public.

204

The radical transformation in status of the press after World War II was expressed by the late Shintaro Ryu, a leading writer of editorials in the *Asahi Shimbun,* in 1961:

Before the war there was no harm at all in the newspapers advancing a "spirit of opposition" with all their strength. . . . The system of government was semi-totalitarian in character. However forcefully some newspapers might voice their criticisms, the government would certainly not be brought down as a result. . . . In fact, it was more likely that those newspapers themselves would be destroyed. . . . But since the war that situation has altered fundamentally. The government is not the product of forces beyond our control. We ourselves vote it into office, and we support the party we think fit. If the *Asahi* newspaper were to decide that the way the Liberal Democratic Party is doing things is all wrong, and to throw its full support behind the Socialist Party, that on its own could result in the L.D.P. losing its majority in the Diet.[5]

Written in 1961, the year after the violent upheaval over the renewal of the U.S.-Japan Security Treaty, this comment reflects both the enormous influence wielded by the *Asahi* and other leading national papers and their extreme sense of responsibility in the exercise of that influence.[6]

Collective news gathering through a comprehensive network of journalists' clubs has replaced the individual and sometimes aggressively independent journalism of the prewar period. Today a bland political neutrality is normal in the national press, in contrast with the heady polemics of the early newspapers, which were often allied to dissident or antigovernment groups.

Historically the Japanese press had exhibited considerable diversity of ownership and outlook, in spite of harsh laws restricting comment. Many of those who founded and wrote for newspapers during the Meiji period were samurai who had belonged to the Tokugawa shogunate military government (1600–1868) and who, with that experience of authority, formed a naturally articulate opposition to the new clan government in Tokyo made up of young samurai from the outlying regions. Osaka, the commercial center in the west near the former imperial capital of Kyoto, was the site of most of the leading newspapers in the early part of the Keiji period, notably the *Asahi* and *Mainichi*. The serious newspapers were of two distinct kinds: those affiliated and those that eschewed party, embracing the principle of supplying a service of news from which the readers could draw their own conclusions.[7]

While yellow journalism, based on popular gossip, scandal, muckraking, and erotica, flourished in the Meiji era, extending the tradition that had been allowed to grow up in the *kawaraban* or broadsheets of the eighteenth and early nineteenth centuries, one paper more than any other succeeded in developing the art of critical satire for serious purpose in post-Meiji restoration Japan. It was the *Yorozu Choho,* formed in 1892 by Ruiko Kuroiwa. His declared aim was to disclose public vice wherever possible, and he earned the name "the adder" for his perseverance and acerbity. His style personified the crusading, individualistic kind of journalism that flourished into the 1930s in spite of oppression from the government and sporadic outbursts of right-wing activism. But during that decade, it became increasingly difficult to express criticism of the country's military adventures and its drift away

205

from international law (as some newspapers had done earlier over, for
instance, the Sino-Japanese war of 1895, and the Siberian expedition of
1919); and the press was too much wedded to official authority and
patriotic ideals to resist when uniformity and outright censorship was
imposed. This came with the restriction of the total number of newspapers to fifty-five, including one in each of the forty-seven prefectures,
in 1939 and the setting up of the *Shimbun-kai* (newspaper association)
in 1942, strictly limiting press reporting to authorized sources. These
moves instilled the principles of collective news gathering and widespread self-regulation that have survived and become marked features
of the press in the postwar period.

The basic character and organization of the postwar press, which
remains substantially intact today, was determined by 1952 when the
American occupation ended. First, the left-wing labor union movement
had been prevented by the combined action of the occupation authorities and the newspapers managements from taking over editorial
and managerial control. One of the focal points in this struggle was the
strike of *Yomiuri Shimbun* employees in 1945 and 1946, which crum-
bled under the threat of direct action by the occupation headquarters
and resulted in the management's successfully bringing about the birth
of a company union to negotiate labor issues rather than dealing principally with a larger and more militant industrial union of press and
radio workers. A similar pattern was afterward set in the *Asahi* and
Mainichi.

Second, partly in response to the militancy of organized labor, the
occupation authorities had backed the formation of the Japanese newspaper publishers' and editors' association, the *Nihon Shimbun Kyokai*.
This body assumed responsibility for coordinating policies and practices
over a wide range of activities, including editorial issues, newspaper
ethics, circulation and sales policies, the introduction of new printing
techniques, and, above all, the network of *kisha* (journalists') clubs. In
1949 the Shimbun Kyokai announced that the purpose of the clubs was
social and that they were not to be professional organs for the dissemination of news. Specifically they were not to restrict freedom of reporting or to monopolize sources of news.[8] Ironically it was stated that
behind this arrangement was the realization that the *kisha* clubs that
existed during the war had functioned as no more than carriers of
government propaganda. Yet later the Shimbun Kyokai would acknowledge that "with the passage of time the character of the *kisha*
clubs as organs of news coverage has gradually become apparent, and
the gap between the theory and practice of the system has become very
wide."[9]

206

In practice, the Shimbun Kyokai itself regulates membership of the
close to a thousand separate *kisha* clubs that exist today on or near the
premises of government ministries and agencies, political party headquarters, local government offices, main police stations, public corporations, and the like. The Diet *kisha* club, for example, has a membership

of five thousand, drawn from all the companies belonging to the Shimbun Kyokai. The Nagata club, covering the cabinet, has some three hundred journalists from seventy companies; the LDP *kisha* club has about 150 members; and each of the ministries has between one hundred and two hundred. The clubs are not open to freelance journalists or to party organs such as the communist newspaper *Akahata* ("Red Flag"), although the Japan Communist party has housed a *kisha* club at its party headquarters since 1968. The system also means that every large paper prefers to have its own representative in every club, so the role of the domestic news agencies—*Kyodo* and *Jiji*—is correspondingly limited.

The Shimbun Kyokai has made periodic general reviews of the *kisha* club system. The main issues have related to the making of improper agreements among member journalists as to the handling of news material provided through the clubs. In a statement in 1966 the Shimbun Kyokai reaffirmed the original purpose of the clubs as social but recognized, for the first time, agreements on coverage made among the editors in chief of each company, though not private agreements made unilaterally among the journalists themselves. In 1970 new ground rules were published, recognizing the function of the *kisha* clubs in harmonizing both the social and the reporting activities of members. Joint agreements on news embargoes or other restrictions were made subject to the consent of rather wider categories of senior editorial staff of each newspaper or agency concerned, and provision was made for the establishment of special joint committees of senior editorial staff to look into infringements of these rules and disputes occurring between clubs.

Foreign journalists were entirely excluded from the *kisha* club system until 1972, when the cabinet club became the first to allow them to take part. Thereafter the clubs attached to other important ministries and organizations, including the Ministry of International Trade and Industry, the Finance Ministry, and the Federation of Economic Organizations, allowed them to attend formal press conferences and briefings on certain conditions. These included obtaining prior permission from the board of the club concerned and, in the case of a ministerial press conference, submitting in advance in writing any questions not directly relating to the announced subject. All questions were expected to be in Japanese.

In spite of the supposedly social function of the *kisha* clubs, they ensure in effect that coverage of every official news source is practiced within a closed shop of companies, matching the closed shop of journalists that operates within each newspaper, news agency, and broadcasting company. This represents, in effect, a comprehensive lobby system not merely in the political field but in every other sphere of activity, ensuring that information of public concern is transmitted quickly (and usually discreetly) from its source to the readers. The newsgathering activities with which the Shimbun Kyokai has concerned itself include the more informal custom of posting reporters to take care of around-the-clock coverage of leading ministers and other politicians.

207

These *ban-kisha* ("watching reporters") have frequently been on close personal terms with the figure whom they were assigned to watch. Often they would come and go freely to the politician's house like members of the family and drink with him at his home later in the evenings, when the mood was relaxed and the most valuable hints about the inner movements of the political world could be obtained.

The value of the *ban-kisha* to his newspaper has depended on the degree to which he was able to read the undercurrents of politics because of this association. This confidence had, of course, to be mutual, and *ban-kisha* were often considered as much a part of the individual politician's entourage as they were members of their own newspaper. They would often stake their careers, in effect, on cultivating that relationship. They would not be required, as were other reporters working through the *kisha* club system, to break off from one reporting assignment and move to another club regularly every two years or so. Since the war, at least thirty journalists from the political sections of leading newspapers or other news organizations have become prominent members of the Diet themselves, generally through the patronage of a single powerful politician.

The practice of assigning reporters to be *ban-kisha* has grown steadily less common. But the Shimbun Kyokai recognized the prevalence of the system in 1965 when it declared the common intention of its members to restrict late-night visits to the homes of politicians. The editorial committee noted that since 1960 it was becoming usual for journalists to attend a late evening briefing by the spokesmen of prominent politicians, rather than for each reporter to seek access for long periods to the politician's home: "In practice politics does go on after dark; but regular late-night coverage results in both a heavy burden on the reporters who carry it out, and in inconvenience for the households of the politicians who are its object, so . . . we have determined to exercise reasonable self-restraint in this regard."

The centralizing role of the Shimbun Kyokai has ensured that instances of government action or private litigation against particular companies have been rare. The regulation of sales competition provides a clear example. Throughout the postwar period, sales competition has been intense, and newspapers have sought to increase their circulations by offering prospective subscribers discounts, free subscriptions for certain periods, or valuable gifts. In 1955 the Shimbun Kyokai, at the instigation of the government's Fair Trade Commission, set up its own body to work with the commission and investigate suspected infringements. Since then there have been only two cases of injunctions issued on newspapers to conform to the fair trading and antimonopoly laws in spite of periodic and sometimes blatant infringements.

This is one illustration of the way in which the activities of the press are governed by the force of convention and collective decision making rather than by strict reference to the law. The postwar constitution itself, while providing a formal guarantee of freedom of speech and of the press, also includes a proviso in keeping with the ambiguous tradition of Japanese law. It says the people "shall refrain from any abuse of these freedoms and rights and shall always be responsible for using them for the public welfare." Similarly the canons of journalism drawn up by the Shimbun Kyokai when it was first formed in 1946 states in its first article on freedom of the press, "The press should enjoy complete freedom in reporting news and in making editorial comments, unless such activities interfere with public interests or are explicitly forbidden by law, including the freedom to comment on the wisdom of any restrictive statute."

Under the heading of restrictive statutes are the libel and defamation laws, which have never been strictly observed, and the government officials' law (*kokka komuin-ho*) of 1947, which relates to the unauthorized disclosure of secret, official information. The only serious case involving this law occurred in 1972. It concerned a reporter of the *Mainichi Shimbun,* Takichi Nishiyama, who obtained copies of secret Foreign Office cables relating to a secret agreement between the Japanese and U.S. governments over Okinawa. Japan, the cables showed, had undertaken to repay the U.S. government for compensation payments it was making to Okinawan landowners for damage done at the U.S. bases there, once Okinawa was returned to Japan. Nishiyama obtained the cables in June 1971, about the time the terms of the treaty were agreed between the Japanese and American governments but before it had been discussed and ratified in the Diet. They were not made public until nine months later, when a Socialist member of the House of Representatives announced their contents during a Budget Committee session after receiving them from Nishiyama. By this time the treaty over Okinawa had been ratified by the Diet (in December 1971), but the reversion itself was not due to take place until June 15 of that year, and the disclosure—even at this late date—still added to the controversy. The editorials of the major national newspapers severely criticized the government for keeping secret a matter of deep public interest, but most also had reservations about the behavior of Nishiyama himself. Subsequently both the reporter and the Foreign Ministry official who had passed him the information were charged under the government officials' law. The official, Mrs. Hasumi, was convicted of releasing official secrets without authorization and was given a suspended prison sentence. Nishiyama, though, could only be charged with soliciting an official to pass on secrets. He was first acquitted in a lower court, but the verdict was overturned by the Tokyo High Court. He was eventually given a four-year prison sentence, suspended for one year. The Supreme Court upheld that verdict on appeal.

The Nishiyama case stands out for its rarity. It has been the only major case since World War II of a journalist's being prosecuted under a law relating to official secrets, and the circumstances of the decision to make public the information belied his paper's insistence that it had acted primarily out of respect of the public's right to know. At the same time it argued that it had been swayed by the knowledge that the immediate disclosure of the contents of the secret cables would have been against the public interest by adding to the protests of those forces opposed in principle to the treaty arrangements between Japan and the United States. The vacillation of the journalist himself and of the chief editor, who was party to the events, illustrates the absence of any clear-cut separation of roles between the *kisha*-club reporter (in this case, a member of the Kasumi club, attached to the foreign ministry) and the official sources that supply the bulk of his needed information. In the tightly knit society of these clubs—especially in the privileged circle of those attached to the senior ministries—it is powerfully in the interest of both sides, givers and receivers of information, to betray no confidences and to act according to the force of convention rather than the letter of the law.

It generally takes a joint decision by more than one national newspaper to expose duplicity or negligence on the part of a large company or government department. The growing volume of reporting on problems of environmental pollution during the 1960s increased this tendency. First, because these issues involved reports of events across the country, the number of different sources of information tended to be much greater than in the case of political coverage; and second, this type of story would in general be covered by reporters from the social department of each paper (rather than the political department), the *shakai-bu,* who had the reputation of being relatively fearless and inquisitive, or (to quote a public relations document of the Ministry of International Trade and Industry) being "provocative and determined." It had, in fact, been the social reporters who had written the bulk of the articles during the 1960s on subjects with an obvious popular appeal such as the rate of inflation, the consumer movement, and industrial pollution.[10]

Fearful of large companies and government departments, the Japanese press has also shown itself vulnerable to pressure from individual advertisers and the main advertising companies. In one instance the giant milk and food concern Morinaga succeeded over a period of some fourteen years in preventing the national newspapers from printing details of the poisoning and deaths of a large number of infants who were fed Morinaga powdered milk. The allegation of Morinaga's responsibility, made in a weekly magazine in 1955, was not actively taken up in the national press until 1969, when the *Asahi Shimbun* printed an interview with a professor of Osaka University who had announced new and independent evidence of his own. In the intervening years the Morinaga company had withdrawn its substantial advertising in the magazine concerned and, through the giant advertising company, Dentsu, had ensured that the press did not carry further reports on the claims of the parents. It was not until 1972 that Morinaga finally admitted its responsibility and later set up a fund to give substantial compensation to the affected families.

210

The large general trading firms and banks have thus been able in important cases to use the weapon of advertising policy to direct the tone of press reporting in the same way that government ministries have been consistently able to manage the main lines of press coverage through the *kisha* club network.[11] However, the revelation of corporate deceit in several successive pollution scandals—notably the case of the New Chisso Corporation, whose chemical plant at Minamata in Kyushu was responsible for more than a thousand cases of mental and physical deformity from mercury compound in the industrial waste—has made Japanese journalists more inclined to take the side of pollution victims and to publicize such cases.

One of the most blatant and controversial cases of restrictive pressure on reporting in postwar Japan involved neither a department of government nor a powerful commercial interest but the neo-Buddhist organization Soka Gakkai, one of the so-called new religions that appeared after the war and quickly gained adherents, especially among nonunionized, unskilled working people. Strongly nationalistic, anticommunist, and puritanical in its creed, the Soka Gakkai leadership became fiercely defensive about its own activities and internal organization. In 1964 the Clean Government party was formed as its political arm and became the sworn enemy of the Japan Communist party. In 1969 a leading author wrote a book exposing the authoritarian and arbitrary behavior of the Soka Gakkai leadership.[12] He was physically threatened, and Komei Party representatives visited various newspaper offices to advise the papers that any publicity for the book in their pages would result in a large-scale boycott by Soka Gakkai followers. All newspapers complied, but the other main opposition parties, the socialist and communist parties, insisted on debating the matter in the Diet. Eventually, at the Soka Gakkai's annual convention on May 3, 1970, the Soka Gakkai leader, Taisaku Ikeda, declared his regret for the attempt to interfere with the book's publication. Strikingly, an opinion poll conducted by the *Tokyo Shimbun* at that time found that the issue of freedom of speech was regarded as the most important issue discussed in the Diet, surpassing even the U.S.-Japan security treaty, which was renewed in June of that year. Also in June, it was announced that the formal link between the Soka Gakkai and the Komei Party was at an end.

The *kisha* club system is not the only way the broad alignment of newspaper editorial attitudes with the actions of government and business is brought about. At times of important shifts in government policy or of crucial decision making in response to international events, the representatives of the press and the other media have consistently been made a party to the process. In advance of the signing of the U.S.-Japan security treaty in 1960, Prime Minister Kishi had secured the general agreement of the press not to oppose it. And despite press support for the antitreaty demonstrators implicit in the subsequent coverage and open criticism of Kishi's management of the affair, none of the national dailies actually opposed the treaty itself. During the period of office of Hayato Ikeda (1960–1964), whose motto for his policy of fast economic growth was "double your income," an economic deliberative council was set up, including leading press figures, to advise the government on its economic policies. Similar committees with press representation were set up to consider issues such as subsidies for rice farmers, the reform of electoral constituencies, and tax reform. When Kakuei Tanaka came to power in 1972, he advanced his major domestic policy initiative, the "plan to remodel the Japanese archipelago," with the help of a committee of ninety figures from the ruling party and the business world and five representatives of the media, including one each from the *Nihon Keizai Shimbun,* the *Asahi* group, Dentsu, NHK, and NTV, the commercial television network allied with the *Yomiuri Shimbun.*

In Japan's foreign relations, the press plays a still more obvious role as the standard-bearer of the government's policies and the molder of domestic opinion. In the case of Japan's relations with its powerful neighbor, China, the press played a central role in preparing the way for the dramatic improvements that have happened in the 1970s: the normalization of diplomatic relations in 1972, the signing of successive trade agreements, and most recently the conclusion of a treaty of peace and friendship in 1978. From 1966, during the Cultural Revolution, Japanese newspaper correspondents in Peking quickly learned (after some cases of Chinese protests and expulsions of Japanese as well as other foreign journalists) to send only reports that would be inoffensive to the Chinese government. Critical comment of the excesses of the cultural revolution was printed only when it could be attributed to Western news agency sources in Peking or to sources in Hong Kong.

By the end of 1970, Japan's China reporting had taken on the tone of a crusade. In editions New Year's Day, 1971, for instance, the *Asahi* printed an editorial entitled, "Working Towards Relations with China," and the *Mainichi* began a major new series under the title "The Pulse of China." After U.S. President Nixon's official visit to China in February 1972, it was only natural that Kakuei Tanaka, who became prime minister of Japan in the same year, should follow suit, as he did in September.[13]

The result of this close coordination between government thinking and the enormously persuasive opinion of the press is that the newspapers habitually play the role of the constructive critic of the government. They are not opposed to the main lines of policy and are not prepared to do anything to rock the boat; they are always ready and equipped to offer expert analysis and to pull up those in authority when they fail to realize the nation's expectations.

In 1972 a group of twenty-two Japanese scholars wrote *Characteristics of Japanese Journalism.*[14] It identified six persistent defects in the editorial outlook of the press, which are in contrast to its achievements in the matters of speed, seriousness, and service to readers:

212

1. In spite of their claim of strict neutrality, Japanese newspapers often adopt an antigovernment stand.

2. Out of the same tradition, newspapers overdo their criticism of Japan's postwar policy of staying broadly within the camp of the West. In covering overseas governments, by contrast, they bow too easily before a show of strength and fail to present a truly balanced picture.

3. Japanese papers often "bend with the wind" when a powerful new force emerges and to prevent full debate on a subject. Given the characteristic Japanese tendency to conformity and collective thinking, this can lead to the loss of any real distinction between what is news and what is comment or opinion.

4. Japanese newspapers too easily tend to support fully any cause that appears to be progressive.

5. While the press fulfills its role of criticizing government, there is no force to keep the press itself in check. As a result, unless the press itself advances certain notions and certain news, they do not become current, preventing any real competition between different arguments and viewpoints. More regular use of individual names in reporting and more self-criticism within the press and other media would help in this regard.

6. Unlike most foreign newspapers, which each have their own particular character, Japanese papers are much the same in outlook. This is a result of the system of lifelong employment in a single firm, which prevents likeminded people from working out their own distinctive editorial line in newspapers. It also tends to make journalists become just like other office workers, concerned less with what the paper stands for than with the next wage increase or whatever other goal the labor union happens to have set.

The Lockheed Affair

While the moves to oust Miki as Prime Minister were dominating the political pages, the overwhelming majority of views we were getting on "Action Line"—the telephone link between the *Mainichi* newspaper and its readers—were in support of Miki: in the ratio of nine to one, in fact. How did such a curious phenomenon occur? That was something we discussed a great deal inside the political department at the time. I should like to re-consider the manner of our political reporting.[15]

This statement by Tadao Koike, deputy head of the political department of the *Mainichi Shimbun,* illustrates the widespread feeling among journalists working for the national newspapers that in an important way they failed the nation by the way they reported domestic political developments during the period when Takeo Miki was prime minister (December 1974 through December 1976), as well as during the premiership of Kakuei Tanaka (July 1972 through December 1974).

In the case of the Tanaka regime, the driving and relatively young new prime minister was given a rapturous welcome everywhere in the

213

established press in spite of his known criminal record, his lack of formal education, and his extravagant use of money to buy the support he needed inside the ruling Liberal Democratic party to become its leader and thus prime minister. His early popularity was sustained by two separate initiatives: his trip to China in September 1972 to effect the normalization of diplomatic relations and his ambitious plan to spread industrial output and its benefits more evenly across the whole country.

In the chastened economic mood of 1974, after the Arab oil embargo, regular elections were held for half the seats in the upper house of the Diet, the House of Councillors. Once again the Tanaka faction mobilized the vast wealth of its business connections during the election campaign, but even so only narrowly held on to the majority of the LDP seats in the Upper House. The enormous sums of money that circulated as political contributions and campaign funds now became a leading object of adverse publicity and press comment. The phrase *kin-ken seiji* ("the politics of money") was coined in that year, and press reporting and comment referred back critically to the LDP presidential election of 1972 when Tanaka had defeated his closest rival, the veteran politician Takeo Fukuda, by a margin of only two votes in a caucus election among LDP members of the two chambers of the Diet. By the autumn of 1974, public support for Tanaka had fallen to a historical low of about 10 percent. Yet still the large-circulation national dailies held back from any systematic investigation into Tanaka's own use of his money power. It was not until two freelance journalists, Takashi Tachibana and Takaya Kodama, wrote a detailed account (published in early October 1974) in a monthly magazine, *Bungei Shunju*, of Tanaka's financial past—including his association with ghost companies, his collection and distribution of political campaign funds, and nonpayment of taxes—that these facts were assembled in print.

Even at this point the national daily papers contained only the briefest references to the *Bungei Shunju* article. Its main tenor was conveyed in the daily press not by direct quotation but through reports of articles on the subject in *Newsweek* magazine and the *Washington Post*. At length, on October 22, Tanaka appeared as the guest at a press luncheon at the Foreign Correspondents' Club in Tokyo, where he was asked several times if he would reply to questions about his personal assets raised by the *Bungei Shunju* article. His answer was that in Japan, "high government officials and in particular the Prime Minister are not subject to any particular public scrutiny as in America"; but he said, "If an article like that impairs in any way whatsoever the people's confidence in political administration, I am sorry." When the questions on this theme continued, he broke off the session early. Thereafter the details of what occurred at the Foreign Correspondents' Club were meticulously reported in every major Japanese news organ. On November 26, after trying unsuccessfully to shore up his position through a reshuffle of cabinet posts, Tanaka resigned.

214

At every stage of the reporting of these events, the national press had failed to initiate any serious probe into what eventually was taken to be the largest instance of political corruption ever exposed in Japan. This was clearly because of the system that has been dubbed by some commentators "results journalism," meaning that the daily press is free to report any issue only once the allegations or facts of the case have been made public by some other means. In the case of Tanaka's resignation, the facts leading to it had been publicized initially from two sources outside the system, a monthly magazine and the foreign press corps in Tokyo. The established press, with its constant access to the inside of the political machine through the *kisha* club system, had not made use of its vast store of knowledge about the Tanaka case until the lead had been taken by these outsiders.

Tanaka's unorthodox background in politics and his personal qualities had at first made him the darling of the established press. On the evening of July 5, 1972, the headlines of the *Yomiuri Shimbun* reporting Tanaka's election to the LDP presidency referred to him by the endearing diminutive "Kaku-san." It spoke in welcome of the "wild president" (a reference to his origins as a farmer's son) who had appeared with "his old-fashioned popular songs and his electric bulldozers!" and urged him to "blow away secret politics!" The following morning, the *Asahi Shimbun* headlines also spoke sympathetically of his mannerisms—"frowning, weeping and rambling on"—and his habit of "mixing statistics with easy colloquialisms."

By stark contrast, after his two consecutive disgraces—when he resigned under pressure in 1974 and was arrested and charged with receiving bribes in 1976—the national dailies would write of the same man: "Why did we ever allow such a man to climb to the top of the ladder and represent this country? Who was dazzled by the extravagant dreams of "high economic growth" which he stood for? It was we ourselves, who cheered him on madly, taking his cheek for true boldness, and his recklessness for strong leadership."[16]

Tanaka, the self-made man, also differed from his predecessors in his undisguised attempts to manipulate the press for his own purposes. These attempts were initially successful and even today may have some residual effect because he remains a powerful influence in politics (particularly since his support was crucial in the elevation of Masayoshi Ohira to the premiership in December 1978). Almost as soon as Tanaka became prime minister, he made clear to the press what he construed its role to be. During a visit to the highland resort of Karuizawa in August 1972, the month after his election to office, he advised the reporters with him that if any of them wrote anything that displeased him, he could see to it that they lost their jobs, because he "knew everybody in the newspaper companies from the presidents down to the heads of department."[17] This threat was a serious one since few people in Japan move successfully from one company to another in the same industry; to be fired from a good job would probably mean being unemployable in any responsible position again. In particular, Tanaka told them they were not to try writing anything "flippant or clever" in the "personal view" columns, which were in vogue about that time.

This domination of the Japanese press survived the reversal in his fortunes. After the *Bungei Shunju* article and his disastrous meeting with the foreign correspondents, each of the big three papers printed their own perfunctory accounts of Tanaka's background, but they added little to the original catalog of facts assembled by the *Bungei Shunju* journalists.[18] Tanaka, although he had resigned the premiership, remained inside the Diet with the largest single following of Diet men. Not until 1976 would the Japanese press further scrutinize Tanaka's conduct in office and the roots of money-power politics. Again the impetus for the inquiry came from outside the discreet world of Japan's government and press. On February 4 and 6 1976, the U.S. Senate subcommittee investigating multinational corporations heard evidence from two officials of Lockheed Aircraft Corporation that some 3,000 million yen had been paid to secure the sale of Lockheed aircraft in Japan. These payments had been made initially to Yoshio Kodama, a known right-wing activist and former war criminal who acted as the secret agent on Lockheed's behalf in Japan, and the giant trading firm of Marubeni, which was Lockheed's official agent.

The prime minister at the time was Takeo Miki, a veteran LDP politician from the reformist wing of the party who had served in the short-lived, socialist-led coalition government shortly after the war. He had been chosen as leader of the LDP in private talks among senior party members and on the recommendation of the then party vice-president, Etsusaburo Shiina, at the time of Tanaka's resignation. But his main policy concerns had turned out to be ones that the mainstream of the party would not willingly embrace.

Miki had been given a good press in his first year of office, acquiring the nickname "Mr. Clean." But he was the leader of only a minor political faction within the ruling party. His term of office, already anomalous in the tradition of LDP politics, became increasingly injurious to the long-established interests of the party after he became personally identified with the pursuit of the Lockheed affair "at whatever cost to the reputation of Japanese politics."[19] The period from February 1976 to Miki's resignation in December of the same year—and more particularly, from the day of the arrest of his predecessor, Kakuei Tanaka, on July 27—was a time when the judiciary as well as the press in Japan enjoyed an unprecedented authority of their own in relation to the powerful vested interests of the country.

For the first time in Japanese history, a formal joint investigation was launched in February 1976 involving the Tokyo District Prosecutor's Office, the Police Agency, and the Tax Office. Arrangements were made to permit the transfer of secret depositions made before the congressional subcommittee to the Japanese judicial authorities. Also in June the Diet's own special committee on Lockheed held televised

216

hearings in which executives of Marubeni and All Nippon Airways answered questions put by Diet members of all the political parties. Much of the questioning centered around receipts signed by Yoshio Kodama, two executives of Marubeni, and another middleman, Shig Katayama, for various "units," "pieces," and "peanuts" whose true monetary value the signatories denied knowing. This extraordinary publicity gave rise to the birth in March of a four-page weekly tabloid newspaper, *Shukan Peanuts,* devoted solely to spreading news and speculation about the Lockheed inquiry, as well as the timing of popular demonstrations against the political corruption now brought to light.

The first arrests arising from the Lockheed investigation—those of several executives of Marubeni and All Nippon Airways, on charges of perjury and violation of the foreign exchange laws—were made on June 22. The inhibitions affecting the established press at this period were not primarily, if at all, the result of fear of prosecution under the libel laws. It was a more subtle kind of inhibition, as described in retrospect by the editor of the serious political weekly, the *Asahi Journal:*

To investigate both the details of the Lockheed bribery case, and the subsequent response of Japanese politics and law was frankly a very difficult task. The corruption involved the most powerful, and the most violent forces within Japan. That is precisely why, before the matter came up in the American Congress, it had been shrouded in complete secrecy and the nation knew nothing whatever about it.[20]

After the main disclosures from abroad, it was all too obvious who were the guilty parties. The Japanese press, though, was still constrained because the Lockheed affair cast such a wide net:

It was as though a detective, acting in front of an audience that already knew the main lines of the plot and the culprits, were to go around casually obliterating the clues one by one. In the early stages of the inquiry, we insisted on imposing editorial limits to the detective's freedom of action . . . and we still mouthed the idea that this represented a "healthy spirit of criticism."[21]

At each press conference and television interview that he gave, Prime Minister Miki stressed his commitment to seeing the Lockheed investigation through to the end. The determination of the other faction leaders and party elders within the LDP to remove Miki from power first became clear in early May with a series of private meetings between the party vice-president, Etsusaburo Shiina, and Kakuei Tanaka, Takeo Fukuda, and Masayoshi Ohira, the leaders of the three main party factions. The first report of these meetings appeared in the *Yomiuri Shimbun* on May 13. Thereafter each of the main national newspapers carried almost daily accounts of the intraparty maneuvers in what quickly came to be called the oust-Miki campaign.

In the statements of the prime minister's rivals, as reported on the political pages of the national press, little attempt was made to conceal the fact that the opposition stemmed from a dislike of Miki's firmness in

217

allowing the full-scale judicial inquiry to proceed. The internal protests from other LDP leaders centered on the theme that Miki was dividing the party by his stand and that his was a weak leadership. This was true, but only in the sense that legislation carried forward under the Miki cabinet—including the new election laws and the antimonopoly law reform—was far from wholeheartedly supported within the LDP, so their passage had been slow. Also the formulation of the 1976 fiscal budget had been delayed by several weeks, largely as a result of opposition party obstructions and attempts to link the budget's passage with further government promises over the Lockheed inquiry.

The open disunity of the party clearly showed up its character as an arbitrary alliance of powerful groups acting together for their mutual advantage rather than out of any concordance of policies. And the press reporting of this rift illustrates, equally, the character of the newspapers as more or less faithful relayers of that balance of power. The tight network of *kisha* clubs—especially those serving the political pages— was crucial in carrying out this brand of results journalism. As Tadao Koike describes it:

The coverage of politics is normally the responsibility of the political department in general, but in the actual writing of articles the Hirakawa club [the LDP *kisha* club] plays the central part. The articles reflect the activities and statements of the various faction leaders and officials. Under this system the three big factions—those of Tanaka, Ohira and Fukuda—make up two-thirds of the whole party; and they, combined with the "middle ground" factions of Shiina and Funada, were bound to have the largest voice; while the so-called leadership factions—comprising those of Miki and Nakasone—only account for one third of the party membership, so their voice was correspondingly small. That balance of power was directly reflected in the space each side took up in the press coverage.[22]

Unlike the political pages, the editorial columns of the national press at this period took full account of the popular mood supporting Miki's domestic policies.

On July 27, 1976, Kakuei Tanaka was arrested on charges of breaking the foreign exchange control law. Later bribery charges were added. The press now produced a torrent of scathing criticism of the man and what he had stood for. His guilt was assumed in a great many articles, even before all the charges had been brought or he had made his first appearance in court (which was not until January 1977). Many articles betrayed a tone of exultation at Tanaka's downfall, as well as self-congratulation on the unexpected testament to a free press and a strong judiciary.

After Tanaka's arrest, the momentum of the Lockheed inquiry slackened sharply. No further arrests were made. Large play was made in the press of an incident calculated to show that the arrest of Tanaka had been politically motivated. A former high court assistant judge, Shiro Kito, was alleged to have telephoned Miki on August 4 and, impersonating the director of public prosecutions, to have asked the prime minister to intervene to order the withdrawal of charges against Tanaka. Miki had indicated that it was important that justice be done, wherever it led. A tape recording of the conversation was later sent to the *Yomiuri Shimbun*. Although Kito was a member of a right-wing organization and was known to have been behind another stratagem to discredit the Communist party leader, Kenji Miyamoto, only one year before, the focus of the reports was less on the suspicious motives for the trick phone call than on the precise response of Miki; and the case undoubtedly served to damage the public's view of the prime minister.

In August 1976, Miki's rivals formed the United Party Council, comprising the Fukuda, Ohira, and former Tanaka factions, whose declared aim was to fight the forthcoming general election in December on a separate platform from Miki, to remove him from the leadership as early as possible, and to achieve internal party reforms less radical than those he was proposing. The press continued to criticize Miki's rivals strongly in the editorial columns, while devoting most space on the political pages to their policy statements and campaign activities.

When Tanaka announced his intention to stand for reelection in his own constituency, the press denounced it as a "challenge to the law and to common sense" (*Mainichi Shimbun*), and a dereliction of "moral and political responsibility" (*Yomiuri* and *Asahi*). Even the regional newspaper serving that area, *Niigata Nippo,* questioned if it was right to choose a politician who openly diverted large funds from the central government to his own constituency to ensure his continued popularity there.

In the election on December 6, Tanaka was returned with an overwhelming vote. The Liberal Democratic party, while hanging on, in effect, to a tiny majority in the lower house, had lost a lot of ground. Miki resigned as prime minister and was succeeded by Fukuda. The resignation was a natural step, as Miki had himself declared the target of 271 seats for the ruling party to win in the general election, and in the event the number fell well short. But the outgoing leader set a number of specific conditions for his departure. These hinged on the adoption by the party of a new set of rules governing elections to the party presidency. They were to involve party members and supporters around the country in a preliminary, or primary, election, followed by a runoff between the two candidates placed at the top of that poll in a second vote involving the caucus of the parliamentary party and regional representatives. This proposal was subsequently adopted. The year-end reviews and editorials in the national press reflected considerable skepticism as to the sincerity of Fukuda's commitment to reform on the political side. Fukuda opened his premiership with a round of conciliatory talks with leaders of the opposition parties, but as the *Asahi Shimbun* commented on December 30, 1976: "Prime Minister Fukuda . . . is tarnished by the fact that he brought down the former prime minister, Mr. Miki, who had held firm over the Lockheed investigation, and came to power through the strength of the 'United Party

Council' as the leader of the mainstream conservative forces in the party. We feel that he is merely trying to wash away that image through his talks now with the other party leaders." And on December 31, it wrote:

The spectacular Lockheed inquiry, which led to the arrest of the former prime minister Tanaka, has become bogged down over the investigation of the "Kodama and Osano routes" in the affair. We are still not able to say that the facts about the right-wing "fixers" who are like a cancer in Japan, or the murky side of politics, have been brought out into the light. Many of the "black" and "grey" officials involved in the Lockheed affair have managed to cling on to their membership of the Diet.

And yet when Fukuda announced his slogan for the coming year, 1977, as "the year of the economy," the effect was dramatically to shift the emphasis of subsequent report and comment in the national press away from questions of political reform and Lockheed and toward the country's economic performance. Recovery from the recession and the upturn of the economy became the new catchwords in the press, replacing "oust-Miki" and "thorough investigation of the Lockheed affair."

As early as January 5, 1977, Prime Minister Takeo Fukuda conferred with the minister of justice in his new cabinet, Hajime Fukuda, and decided to end further prosecution of the affair. The new government effectively closed the accounts of the inquiry with the second Justice Ministry report on Lockheed, which was read to the lower house's Lockheed Investigation Committee on February 24. And yet an *Asahi Shimbun* opinion survey at the end of February showed that 70 percent of the nation still hoped for further positive action in the Diet and through the law.

Thereafter appeals in the press for an end to political pressure on the judiciary, and for individual politicians named as "black" or "grey" officials to withdraw from politics, were heard from time to time but at increasingly long intervals. On October 27, near the end of Fukuda's period of leadership, the *Yomiuri Shimbun* wrote: "The 'fresh start' of the Liberal Democratic Party proposed by Prime Minister Fukuda was supposed to have been motivated by the party's remorse following the Lockheed payoff scandal. Now, the Lockheed affair has been forgotten, and there has been no progress in the reform of the party."

While in office, Miki had spoken publicly of the faction system inside the ruling party as "the root of all evil." Such was the pressure of the demand for internal reform of the LDP that each of the major factions had announced its dissolution. But most of them promptly formed, instead, their own "study groups" with similar memberships, suggesting a continuing disregard approaching contempt within the ruling party for its critics, even when these critics were clearly backed by public opinion. By the beginning of 1978—the year in which a new party presidential election was due—very little remained of the pretense that the factions had gone. As the *Asahi Shimbun* wrote in an editorial on February 12, 1978:

220

What needs to be pointed out is that the revival of LDP factional activity may undermine the new election procedure . . . designed to open the party more to the public. The LDP factions and their leaders are putting all their efforts into increasing the number of their respective followers around the country, in order to win nomination for themselves in the poll. . . . Many speculate that the election may be manipulated from behind the scenes through prior deals struck between the major factions—of Ohira and former Prime Minister Tanaka.

That is precisely what happened in the LDP primary election of November 27, 1978. After Ohira's victory—the result of a public alliance with the forces of the disgraced former premier—the *Asahi Shimbun* wrote on November 28:

The primary campaign was fiercely fought by the four contestants, but there were no clear political issues at stake. . . . What was conspicuous was the regrettable expansion of the following of each of the factions within the LDP. . . . Another point that deserves attention is the fact that the forces led by former Prime Minister Tanaka, a defendant in the Lockheed pay-off trial, continued to cast a dark shadow over the primary campaign, and indeed had a decisive effect on the outcome.

As these examples show, the legacy of the Miki era of 1974–1976 has been a limited but significant expansion of the areas of Japanese public life that are taken to be the proper subject of public scrutiny and judicial action. In the political sphere, the advent of a reformist and effectively minority government under Miki demonstrated more clearly than ever before the secretive and self-seeking way in which power is exercised within the LDP and the bureaucracy. The Lockheed revelations served to accelerate the process of exposing this "structural corruption," as it was often described in the press. The period of upheaval and uncertainty also served to demonstrate the effects of collusion—of a more or less conscious nature—between the powerful national press and government authority. It is perhaps no coincidence that half-hearted reform of the factional system in the ruling party after Miki's resignation should have been matched by a period of critical self-analysis inside the established press and changes (announced in November 1978) in the policies of the Nihon Shimbun Kyokai on the question of enlarging its membership and relaxing the *kisha* club system. The clubs, in fact, restrain the work of the press within agreed boundaries just as the faction system keeps political power within the grasp of a few party elders. On a wider scale, the fragmentation of political power during the 1970s, with the gradual decline of the ruling party and the appearance of new middle-of-the-road groupings, has been matched by a marked growth in the diversity of opinion offered in the fields of journalism and information. This has been true both of the national daily press and of other forms of journalism. Television has grown in importance not just as a supplier of entertainment and official information of various kinds (though both are plentiful) but also as a leading medium of political or current affairs coverage rivaling the national press.

221

Similarly the profusion of weekly and monthly magazines provides more analytical and background articles than the daily press has the resources for. The weekly press, in particular, attracted readers with its more adventurous and iconoclastic treatment of the Tanaka and Lockheed episodes. In addition, two tabloid dailies have appeared to compete with the evening editions of the national papers in the capital area. The *Yukan Fuji*, launched by *Sankei Shimbun* in 1969, is directed at young business executives; its appeal is in a more informal treatment of news and opinion than that offered in the *Sankei* itself. The *Nikkan Gendai*, launched by the Kodansha publishing company in 1975, offers a deliberate alternative reading of public life. It caters to the generation of radical students from the 1960s and the disaffected, interpreting all of the works of the government, especially of the leaders of the ruling party, as uniformly contrary to the popular interest and motivated by duplicity and greed. It also contains features on the personal lives (and, frequently, the indiscretions) of company presidents and other public figures, as well as entertainment guides, erotica, and heavy sports coverage. These newcomers have gained a regular readership in the Tokyo area of several hundred thousand, though they are sold exclusively on newstands, and not delivered to the home as other papers are.

The national papers, too, have responded to their more demanding and critical readership by providing a wider range of views in new opinion pages. This has meant more individually signed articles not only by correspondents overseas but by domestic reporters and editorial writers offering their own views, sometimes on contentious subjects. The *Mainichi Shimbun*'s column, "A Reporter's Eye," for instance, caused a considerable stir with one signed article arguing in favor of the legalization of marijuana. Another, during a period of tense relations with the Soviet Union in 1977, advanced the idea that much Japanese press comment on issues in Soviet-Japanese relations was excessively nationalistic and emotional. Such unorthodox views would scarcely have reached the public at all some years ago. Another related development has been the decision by some newspapers to credit not only the authors of articles but also the reports taken from the domestic news agencies, Jiji and Kyodo.

In November 1978, the *Nihon Shimbun Kyokai* announced a new set of guidelines. Foreign correspondents have for the first time been granted observer status at all government ministries. The present restrictions on membership are to be reconsidered. And in a gesture of economic independence from the ministries, agencies, and other official sources of news, a distinction was drawn for the first time between the work of the reporters' clubs themselves, which "assist in the coverage of news," and the extra facilities, which traditionally have also been provided free of charge for the comfort and entertainment of those using the reporters' rooms.

Meanwhile the Shimbun Kyokai has protested against several pro-posals in the overall revision of the penal code, which appeared in draft form from the Justice Ministry in 1976. They concern the possible introduction of new restrictions on the press relating to the laws of libel, the leaking of industrial secrets, and the passing of secret information by government officials. Since then the government has declared it would move only with great caution on the last two areas. Indeed any attempt to introduce such new restrictions would run counter to the trend of recent years toward more openness and pluralism. But this conclusion must be qualified by observing that the frontiers of Japanese press reporting have come to be determined less by the letter of the law than by organized discretion and patronage, which still remain deeply entrenched.

Notes

1. Richard Halloran, *Japan: Images and Realities* (Tokyo: Tuttle, 1970), p. 164.

2. Foremost among these privileges is the exemption (since 1951) from the ordinary requirement of companies to make their shares available to the general public. Most newspapers in Japan rely for their capital on money invested by their own staff and management.

3. Since the war, two other national papers have also grown to have a circulation of over a million: the *Sankei Shimbun,* which takes an editorial stand loosely linked to the Liberal Democratic party, and the *Nihon Keizai Shimbun,* with close links to the big business houses. The *Asahi* has recently lost its long-standing circulation lead to the *Yomiuri,* and the *Mainichi* lagged badly behind during the 1970s and was forced to declare itself bankrupt and form a new company in 1977 to remove the debts of the old *Mainichi Shimbun* proper and attract new investment.

4. On an ordinary day the *Asahi, Mainichi,* and *Yomiuri* each have a morning edition of twenty-four pages. The front page of each is made up of twelve columns of print, arranged horizontally, with the bottom ten centimeters given over to printed book advertisements. The twelfth column of print in each case is given over to the editorial notes column, which is unsigned but which is one of the most popular regular features of each paper. The names of these columns are respectively, "Vox Populi, Vox Dei" in the *Asahi,* "Editor's Notes" in the *Mainichi,* and "Side Record" in the *Yomiuri.* The front page carries the main news, both domestic and foreign; the second page is for domestic political news; the third some combination of domestic news and feature articles; the fourth page is the main foreign page; the fifth has the editorial column and related material, such as readers' letters. The following pages are given over to a mixture of business, women's literature, sports, and local subjects, and finally, the penultimate and back pages of each paper contain, respectively, the crime page and the broadcasting program listings. The space given over to advertising—including classified ads—is between about 15 and 30 percent of the total, including the bottom two or three column spaces on almost every page of editorial matter.

5. "Modern Journalism" (*Gendai Journalism*) (Tokyo: Jiji Tsushin-sha, 1973, vol. II, pp. 62–63.

6. In reality, the *Asahi* in 1960 had been in the forefront of a showdown between the government of the day, headed by Prime Minister Mobusuke Kishi, and the opposition parties, students, artists, and others who had tried to prevent the treaty's renewal. The government had gone to considerable lengths to ensure that acceptance of the treaty would go smoothly. Prime Minister Kishi himself had, as was customary, invited leading figures from the press world to seek their cooperation.

After Kishi signed the treaty in January 1960, it was submitted to the Diet for approval. The opposition parties refused to take part in the Diet proceedings in protest against the treaty, but in May the LDP majority went ahead and passed the ratification bill. This produced a storm of protest, including a 100,000 strong demonstration outside the Diet building. In the reporting of this and other protests against the government's action, the national press, especially the *Asahi,* often betrayed sympathies with the demonstrators and made much of the injuries they suffered in clashes with the riot police. When the rioting grew to dangerous proportions, the prime minister made a new appeal to the press for restraint and to join in welcoming President Eisenhower, who was shortly due to visit Japan. The visit was cancelled because of the violence of the demonstrations, but the seven newspapers based in Tokyo published a joint appeal (which was also printed in provincial papers) for the maintenance of order and "the survival of parliamentary democracy." However the same papers unanimously called for the resignation of Kishi and his cabinet because of their highhanded treatment of the political opposition and the crowds of demonstrators. In the middle of July 1960, Kishi did resign.

7. Foremost in the first category was the *Tokyo Nichi Nichi Shimbun,* founded in 1870. Its dominant figure was Ochi Fukuchi, a former shogunate official closely allied with Prince Hirobumi Ito, the Meiji oligarch mostly responsible for the wording of the Meiji constitution of 1880. The paper began under the inspiration of newspapers in England and elsewhere abroad, which were unafraid to criticize their governments; and Fukuchi made much capital at first out of his ready access to information from government sources. Later, though, when the newspaper became closely identified with the voice of the government, its readership fell off quickly, and in 1911 it was saved only by being merged with the *Mainichi Shimbun.*

The outstanding example of a newspaper founded on nonpartisan principles was *Jiji Shimpo,* founded in 1882 by Yukichi Fukuzawa, the son of a samurai who became known as the Father of Japanese Education. He, too, had been deeply impressed when on a trip to Europe as an official interpreter by the respect accorded there to the opinions of the press and the fact that newspaper editorials had sometimes "enough influence to alter the action of the government." The *Jiji Shimpo* was based on two sets of principles: the first was that of freedom and independence in accordance with the spirit of integrity which Fukuzawa so admired in Western countries. The second was that of expansion of the national interest, in accordance with the obvious urgency for Japan to catch up with the Western imperial powers.

The *Asahi Shimbun,* which has remained the colossus of the newspaper world from the war until the mid-1970s, began in Osaka in 1879 when the question of the forthcoming constitution was the paramount issue. Initially the paper had strong links with the party of opposition, the Freedom party, but in 1882 it announced new guiding editorial principles, which were to be nonpartisan, presenting the movements within the society as they occurred. Unlike *Jiji Shimpo,* its aim was not to set itself up in judgment but to report facts plainly, leaving readers to make their own judgments.

The *Mainichi Shimbun* mirrored the progress of the *Asahi* in its early development. The paper began as the *Osaka Nippo* in 1876 as one of several papers opposed to the new clan leaders in Tokyo. It was taken over briefly by a minor political party dedicated to constitutional politics, and then restarted as a business paper with a literary bias. Only in 1888 did the *Osaka Mainichi* adopt the policy of nonpartisanship already exploited with success by the *Asahi;* thereafter it became the chief rival of the *Asahi* as an independent and authoritative voice.

The *Yomiuri Shimbun,* the third of the big three papers of modern Japan, became a rival to the other two in the 1920s. It began as a popular paper, whose strength was not in political seriousness but in the areas of photography, crime reporting, and business enterprise. The paper sponsored *go* tournaments and launched the first column listing radio programs at the time of the Manchuria

225

incident (in 1931); it despatched many reporters to the war front throughout the 1930s; and in 1934 set up its own baseball team, the Yomiuri Giants, which is still immensely popular and successful today.

Circulation figures for the five national newspapers are as follows (the first figure is for the morning edition and the second for the afternoon): *Yomiuri Shimbun,* 7,541,000 and 4,473,000; *Asahi Shimbun,* 7,311,000 and 4,593,000; *Mainichi Shimbun,* 4,433,000 and 2,506,000; *Sankei Shimbun,* 1,776,000 and 952,000; and *Nihon Keizai Shimbun,* 1,740,000 and 1,133,000. *Yomiuri Nenkan* [Yomiuri Yearbook](1979). The figures are as of March 20, 1978.

8. Nihon Shimbun Kyokai, statement of policy on *kisha* clubs, 1949.

9. Nihon Shimbun Kyokai, thirty-year history (1975), pp. 162–163.

10. The reputation of these reporters for being relatively fearless and inquisitive was reflected in a document published in December 1970 by the public relations department of the Ministry of International Trade and Industry. It was a forty-seven-page document, entitled "Public Relations Notebook," intended for the guidance of ministry officials in their dealings with the press. It contained advice as to what sort of information should be given out to ensure that the resulting articles would contain a favorable interpretation. It also contained a special warning about these reporters, whom it describes as "emotional," as having "their own special outlook," and as being "provocative and determined."

11. Advertising revenue accounted for 60 percent of the revenue of the national press in 1973. But partly because of the rapid growth in television advertising, it has been falling until, in 1975, it became a smaller source of revenue annually than that from sales.

12. Hirotatsu Injiwara, *Soka Gakkai o Kiru* [Profile of the Soka Gakkai] (Tokyo: Nisshin Hodo, 1969).

13. As in the case of China reporting, the Japanese press has often bowed to pressure from other foreign governments when the occasion has required it. Following the imposition of the state of emergency in India under Indira Gandhi, Japanese correspondents conformed with the censorship laws and reported nothing overtly critical of her policies. Similarly after the Arab oil embargo of 1973, which included Japan among the list of "unfriendly nations," the tone of comment in Japanese newspapers became markedly pro-Arab. The combination of hasty diplomacy and the shift in Japan's press coverage of Middle Eastern affairs resulted in the lifting of the OPEC embargo on Japan.

14. Nihon Shimbun Kyokai, thirty-year history, pp. 100–102.

15. Tadao Koike, "Continuing the Probe into Lockheed and "Miki-oroshi," *Shimbun Kenkyu* (December 1976).

16. *Asahi Shimbun,* July 28, 1976.

17. This occasion was first described in the weekly magazine *Shukan Gendai* and the monthly *Bugei Shunju* (November 1972). A full account is given in *Gendai Journalism,* vol. II, pp. 144–146.

18. A special article in the *Asahi Shimbun* of November 23, "Report on the Suspicious Money Sources Forcing the Prime Minister into Resigning," was prefaced, characteristically, with the remark: "The reason we have investigated this matter is not simply to whip up interest for the sake of it, but because it is a matter which ought to be of fundamental concern to the people of Japan."

19. Prime Minister Takeo Miki, Lower House Budget Committee Session, February 6, 1976.

20. Y. Shioguchi, "The Lockheed Scandal Enquiry Is Not Over," *Shimbun Kenkyu* (February 1977).

21. Ibid.

22. *Shimbun Kenkyu* (December 1976).

10

The Journalist as Political Client in Italy

Giovanni Bechelloni

Italian journalism draws its inspiration from Anglo-Saxon liberal traditions, but the special nature of Italy's political and cultural development has led to a hybrid form of journalism in which one can see some features (more accentuated in recent years) that are typical of European and North American countries and others that are typical of Mediterranean and Latin American countries. There is even some comparison to be made with journalism in Eastern Europe.[1] By journalism here is meant the entire range of activities in the sphere of information, from the traditional framework of news agencies, daily newspapers, and periodicals to radio and television.

In Italy there is a complex relationship between public and private sectors of the mass communication industry. The political system has greater influence than in other industrialized capitalist countries, and the market plays a much greater role than in Latin America or Eastern Europe. Unlike any of these countries, but like Spain and, to a lesser degree, Portugal, the mass media and journalism have become the scene of intense social and political conflict in recent years.

This essay attempts to describe Italian journalism in the context of the political and mass communication system and to draw attention to the points at which it differs from that in other countries, starting with the present situation and going on to outline the factors that have influenced its evolution.

Journalism, Mass Communications, and Political Parties

The state-owned companies directly control the largest broadcasting company (RAI-TV, which exercised a monopoly until 1976), as well as the largest news agency (ANSA), and a number of daily newspapers, periodicals, printing plants, and papermills. Moreover the state fixes the price of all daily newspapers and the cost of subscriptions to the RAI-TV; controls the paper trade through a public body, the Cellulose and Paper Authority; and provides daily newspapers and periodicals with various kinds of subsidies, covering paper, postal, and telegraphic costs, plus contributions toward the renewal of equipment. Most periodicals and daily newspapers, however, are privately owned, and so are an unspecified number of local television and radio stations (about five hundred and two thousand, respectively), which have been mushrooming all over Italy since 1976. In addition, the political parties, on which the whole system hinges, each control their share of daily newspapers (almost one per party), press agencies of limited range, periodicals, and an unknown and variable number of local radio and television stations. Let us examine the present situation in each sector.

The daily newspapers have almost all been running at a considerable loss in recent years because of the enormous rise in the cost of paper and wages and the impossibility of introducing technical innovations, which are strongly opposed by printers and journalists, who are organized in strong and militant unions. Every so often, a newspaper closes down or threatens to do so, and at the same time amalgamation proposals of a more or less realistic nature are put forward by captains of industry such as Monti, Agnelli, or Cefis or by publishing houses such as Mondadori or Rizzoli. Every attempt at closure sees the mobilization of opposition from journalists and printers, and following lengthy negotiations between publishers, government and unions, compromise solutions are found to allow journalistic activity to continue on some new basis. On the other hand, while established papers close down or threaten closure, new papers with varied political leanings are being founded or revived.[2]

Periodicals, which until a few years ago enjoyed a very large circulation that counterbalanced the small circulation of the dailies, are also in decline. They are going through a period of intense and profound change as they adapt themselves to European patterns, with more specialized magazines catering for particular interests and tastes, and fewer general publications.

The RAI-TV, as a consequence of reforms passed in 1975–1976, has been reorganized on the basis of four television and six radio channels, all semi-independent and to some extent in competition with each other and with their own fairly distinct political orientation.[3] These organizations coexist within a single company, the RAI-TV, run by a board of directors made up of representatives of six political parties and tightly controlled by a parliamentary watchdog committee on which all nine political groups are represented. Until a few years ago, this company was run in a very centralized fashion by a small group of trusted politicians of the Christian Democratic party. One can easily understand how this new situation has led to almost daily conflict and tension and why the running of the RAI has been the cause of continual wrangling among the parties. What is more, a number of companies are dependent on RAI, including SIPRA, at present under a communist chairman, which holds the monopoly on advertising concessions for RAI, the largest element in the advertising market, and which also looks after advertising for newspapers and periodicals. The competition between the channels has, on the other hand, sharpened the wits of journalists and producers and has led to an often remarkable rise in audience figures, especially for television.

The situation is equally complex in the field of private radio and television. In 1976, the constitutional court declared the RAI's monopoly to be illegitimate, and in so doing, it permitted the establishment of private local radio and television stations. Since no agreement has been reached among the parties on this matter, no legislation has been passed to control the issue of licenses and the operation of such stations. In the last few years, there has been a race between groups of all kinds to open radio and television stations: a race between foreign television companies broadcasting from abroad, newspaper publishers, commercial companies, political groups, local authorities, trade unions and cooperatives, and, above all in radio, groups of young students. Practically the whole country is now covered by a dense network of radio and television antennas, especially in the largest cities, broadcasting around the clock, and often interfering with air traffic control, radio taxis, and police.

The programs of these stations contain a bit of everything. There is much improvisation and amateurism, but they do also tend to break away from the official conformity to which RAI-TV had accustomed Italian audiences. Local radios broadcast mainly music but also include local news, long neglected by RAI and the press, and reach a young and female audience mainly during the afternoon. Some of them are operated by extreme left-wing groups, feminists, homosexuals, or unemployed graduates broadcasting nonstop programs on topics of particular interest to their audience. Almost all of these stations make frequent use of live broadcasts and phone-in programs. In 1977 in particular, there was a veritable explosion in the use of these techniques.

The use of live and phone-in programs was introduced by RAI in the months following the reform (end of 1975 and 1976) as a reaction against the official conformism, which for so many years had characterized the state television service. For some time, the air was flooded with chatter, an indication, with all its inherent ambiguities, of the great vitality and dynamism of Italy, waking all at once, even if convulsively and confusedly, to democracy, politics, and participation.

There are now two kinds of television stations. The first, comprising Tele-Monte Carlo, Tele-Lugano, and Tele-Capodistria, are operated by large concerns from the borders of the country, broadcasting very varied programs and providing serious competition for RAI, since their transmitters cover a large part of the country. The second kind have a local radius and are variously constituted; some are highly commercial and semiprofessional, while others are more amateurish. The mainstay of all of these stations are movies, and these, together with the activities of clubs and associations specializing in the presentation of series of old movies in many Italian cities, have contributed to an extraordinary revival of interest in movies.

To complicate this situation still further, the intricate relationship between public and private sectors also extends to the other parts of the mass communication system (movies, book publishing, the record business, music, and theater), where the state exercises a triple function: owner and shareholder in companies, distributor of contributions and subsidies, and controller of the legislative machinery.

In Italy, when one mentions the state, one is talking above all of the party system. The development of mass communications in Italy has been more closely controlled by the political system and by its internal balances than in most other countries. Also, in some ways paradoxically, the interest of the political parties in controlling the largest possible audiences has increased with the widening of the market.

The ordering of mass communications has been an important theme in the political struggles of the last few years. The RAI-TV reform was passed in 1975, and its enactment is still a cause for continual tension between the parties. Among the reform bills that have been much discussed but have remained unpassed are those for newspaper publishing (a proposal agreed among the parties has been before Parliament for months) and local radio and television.

The most controversial points are those concerning the relationship between the public and private sectors and the spheres of influence of political parties.

The Christian Democratic party (which formerly controlled the RAI-TV and part of the local press and maintained good relations with the large private publishers but has now lost its supremacy over RAI and a large part of the press) favors solutions that would encourage private publishers who could be influenced by public subsidies. The Communist party (which because of its electoral successes in 1975 and 1976 has managed to gain sympathy among journalists, although this declined in the last months of 1978) favors solutions that would penalize private enterprise, is opposed to amalgamations, and favors placing RAI-TV in a dominant position in the system and strictly controlled by Parliament. The Socialist party, until recently close to the position of the Communists, has now completely changed its policy, coming out in favor of solutions that encourage the spirit of initiative and competition. This change in policy by the Socialist party has introduced a new element of dynamism, but of agitation too, into a situation that was already very volatile.

A rich and varied picture makes the present situation in Italy particularly lively and interesting to follow. In the late 1970s, there was an

231

explosion in mass communications in Italy, despite the economic and social crisis. There has been an enormous increase in audiences, especially for radio and television. There has been a break-up of traditional political balances, one of the consequences of which has been that mass communications have acquired a very visible and quite unprecedented centrality in the political debate. A keen struggle has thus developed first for control of an advertising market that remains quite small but is expected to increase with the changes in mass communications; second, to obtain state contributions, which are essential to balance the books or to reduce losses; third, for control of news space, until recently mainly controlled by the Christian Democrat party and its allies in government; and fourth, for the control of journalists and intellectuals who have become precious instruments in the organization of consensus, all the more precious now as the increase in audiences and competition has made them more autonomous and independent.

All of these elements form the background for strong tensions and lively debate on professionalism and on the objectivity, completeness, impartiality, and pluralism that are generally expected in the presentation of information. Currently, any buying and selling of shareholdings, any change of director, any change of job within a company structure, gives rise to negotiations between the parties and to a relatively large amount of public interest.

The present situation, though precarious and unstable, is the result of a very clear evolution in Italian politics during the course of the last few years, one that has been marked by strong tensions and conflicts affecting every aspect of social life, including mass communications.

Social, Political, and Cultural Evolution in Italy

For many years, newspapers and other mass media in Italy discussed everything but that which concerned them directly. Public debate and attention from scholars are quite recent phenomena, dating from the beginning of 1968. Until then, there were no more than ten or so books, and not all of great importance, dealing with the question of information, whether from a politicohistorical or psychosociological point of view. There had been some discussion of these problems in journals with small readerships or in small intellectual circles, but rarely had any cultural or political debate developed that went beyond a denunciation of the excessive power of the Christian Democracy or worries about the spread of the means of mass communication.

The Italian daily press has been a quality one from the start; a popular daily paper with wide circulation has never appeared. Circulation figures have thus remained relatively low (one copy for ten to twelve inhabitants) and have been basically stationary since the beginning of the century, with perhaps the highest figure being reached during the heyday of fascism (1934–1936). The circulation of the largest and most authoritative daily newspaper, the *Corriere della Sera,* has remained around 600,000 copies since World War I. In other countries, the popular daily was the first of the mass media to reach the population at large. In Italy, the masses were affected by the mass media only in the 1930s by means of radio and movies, which were almost totally controlled by the fascist regime. The circulation of American movies and songs, the most typical and popular aspects of the popular culture of the period, was forbidden.

In the years after World War I, movie theaters were filled with American films, and moviegoing had reached the height of its development by the middle of the 1950s. Television began in 1954 under a system of public monopoly strongly controlled by the Catholic party in power, the Christian Democrats. It developed rapidly, reaching the farthest corners of the country and spreading popular culture of American origin, though interspersed with and limited by programs on traditional and Catholic lines.

Today the press still reaches only the upper and upper-middle classes. In contrast to other industrialized capitalist countries, the working classes in Italy have been reached by the visual image first through movies and then through television, before coming under the influence of the written word. The broadcast media reached the majority of the population before formal education and the written press did.

This anomalous course can be understood if we bear in mind five elements in the structuring of modern Italy. First, Italy became one country only in 1870 and achieved social, political, and cultural unity only very recently. Second, industrial development began after World War II and is still incomplete. Third, there has never been on a national level a bourgeois ruling class with homogeneous values, aspirations, and style of life and government. Fourth, liberal representative democracy, which was successful only in the first decade of this century, failed and was replaced by fascism. Fifth, the cultural illiteracy of the people has persisted until very recently and is still more widespread than appears in statistics.[4]

The existence of these five elements and their interrelationship also helps to explain the particular interweaving of the public and private sectors. For decades, the level of income and culture of most of the population was so low as to prevent their participating at all in politics and culture. Until recent years, the material and cultural conditions necessary for the creation of a market for culture and information did not exist. The ruling class and the upper middle class were not large or homogeneous enough, given the great disparity among regions and between north and south, to constitute a market in themselves, as such classes had in European and North American countries since the eighteenth century, where the market had expanded to include first the middle and then the working classes. In Italy, therefore, all cultural undertakings were economically fragile, requiring, with some exceptions, help from the state or from private patrons in order to survive.

This had two important consequences: there were never many economically self-sufficient cultural or journalistic enterprises, and intellectuals and journalists, apart from the few who could depend on private family resources, always lived in a state of financial uncertainty and hence enjoyed little autonomy. The state, which was in control of this situation, always had ample opportunities for maneuver and interference, whether in cultural or journalistic enterprises or with individual intellectuals and journalists.

The fascist regime made great use of these opportunities during the almost twenty years it remained in power, creating authorities and laws that curbed any spirit of initiative. Most of these same laws and authorities remained after the fall of fascism and were used for many years afterward. They are still used to some extent by the party that has ruled Italy without interruption, alone or in coalition, since the war: the Christian Democrats.

Even so, the pattern has gradually changed and with it the Italian situation as a whole. Italy has become more integrated into the international economic and cultural world; economic development has created a home market large enough to allow the distribution and consumption of material goods at a popular level; the large internal migrations have altered the relationships among people of different regions and classes and have led to a great increase in urban populations; universal suffrage, introduced in 1945, and the existence of organized political parties have increased participation and democracy.

By the end of the 1960s, Italy was truly moving forward, having definitely embarked on the road to liberalization and modernization. The rigid monopolization of power by the Catholic party, which had characterized the postwar years, was gradually eroded, first by the center-left coalitions of the 1960s promoted by the Socialist party, which had broken with the Communists and was seen by the new social classes, the product of the economic expansion, as the embodiment of their desire for reform; and second by the existence of a greater pluralism in society demonstrated by a militant trade union movement and an ever-increasing number of other organizations, which altered the relationships among the parties and between the parties and society.

Until the mid-1960s, the political parties were the most important organizations in the country, being well organized and almost all powerful. Since then, they have slowly been transformed and no longer have the monopoly of power.

234

The student movement of the late 1960s provided Italy an incentive to change. The very intense phase of social, political, and cultural life, which then began, still continues. The country was overwhelmed with conflict and struggles, which have led to profound transformations in the customs and culture of the Italian people. Information and cultural institutions were among the structures most affected by this wave of dissent. Amid the confusion and ambition engendered by a strange mixture of economic interests and great ideological infatuations, organizations and institutions promoting participation spread: unions, associations, committees of all sorts, organizations that in the history of other countries had been spawned either by the slow evolution of democracy or in the violence of revolution.

Amid such tension and fear, such enthusiasm and disappointment, a profound sense of crisis was generated that still goes on. Educational levels have soared in all types of schools and universities, though without attaining those in the United States, England, France, and Germany. Through the initiative of young people, cultural projects have multiplied, on a cooperative or commercial basis, in book publishing and publication of information in films, theater, and music. A market has been created for culture and the mass media, subdivided into many different areas according to ideology, age group, sex, region, and so forth.

It is against this background of change that the Italian system of mass communications is developing. In it the reality of the country over the course of these years has been portrayed through words and images, and it has been the stage for clashes and struggles among different groups and opinions. The number of writings and scientific studies analyzing the role of mass communication has multiplied in recent years. It has become a subject in universities, and groups, centers, and institutes have been set up to examine it.

The Journalistic Profession

In Italy, journalism is organized by law. Although not all those who work in the mass media are journalists, the majority of those working in news agencies and on daily newspapers and periodicals (with the obvious exception of managers and printers) and of those employed in the news section of the RAI-TV are. All of these people belong to the National Order of Journalists, set up by the unanimous vote of all the parties in Parliament in 1963. Only those who are members of the order, which is similar to the professional organizations of doctors, lawyers, and architects, may work as journalists. This creation of the group simply perfected an already existing institution set up by the fascists in 1925, the Journalists' List, which in practice prevented those who were not members from practicing the profession. Those who wish to join go through a complicated procedure jointly administered by publishers and the administration of the order itself. New members are admitted through controlled entry and exams. There are two types of journalists belonging to the group: full-time professional journalists and freelance, part-time journalists working independently. In 1978, there were about eight thousand professional and about fifteen thousand freelance journalists; in 1951, there were about three thousand and five thousand, respectively, in each category. Few members of the order work in the privately owned free or local radio and television. There the majority of editorial staff and freelance part-timers are young people who are often poorly paid or even unpaid.

Elsewhere the earnings of professional journalists are high compared with average earnings, although with considerable differences between one newspaper and another and between individual journalists. These differences are the cause of fierce arguments, but precise facts about them are scarce. Journalists on the staff of RAI-TV earn, by contract, a salary approximately 20 percent above the average.

Besides commanding advantageous salaries, journalists enjoy further advantages and benefits, which are substantial but not easily quantifiable. They have an insurance and welfare association created by the fascists and heavily subsidized until recently by the state, which gives them a first-rate health service and high pensions. They have credit facilities for buying a house and substantial reductions for personal trips for themselves and their families on trains, airlines, and motorways. Furthermore, although their contracts stipulate that they work exclusively for the company which employs them, it is relatively easy for an enterprising journalist to accumulate extra work, and thus add a second or third job, or even more, to his principal one and so augment his income.

Italian journalists are certainly among the best treated and best paid in the world. Journalists rarely change profession, as may happen in other countries. Even those who are not successful still earn substantial incomes.

To enter this profession, which promises such good earnings and conditions, it is not necessary to possess particular intellectual or moral gifts or to have pursued particularly demanding studies. In recent years, indeed, it has not been uncommon for entrants to be quite young (twenty to twenty-five years of age). What is necessary, above all, is to belong to the milieu. According to recent estimates, 48 percent of the profession enter through family connections, friendships, or recommendations, though still formally respecting the procedures laid down for contracts and exams.[5] Clearly this form of admission to the profession is leading to tension, particularly because Italy is a country with severe youth employment problems. Indeed one of the reasons for the growth in local radio and television in recent years is this phenomenon of unemployment among the young, since young graduates, particularly in the south, hope to find jobs as journalists after an apprenticeship with one of these radio or television stations.

236

All professional and some freelance journalists belong to a single, autonomous national trade union, the Federazione Nazionale della Stampa Italiana (FNSI), which for many years was dominated by conservative or right-wing journalists and which since 1969 has been controlled by progressives. In practice, an agreement among Catholics, Socialists, and Communists allows the progressives to administer the union substantially unopposed, despite the presence, particularly among Roman and southern journalists, of many moderates and conservatives. This is a further example of the close relationship between journalists and the political parties. The existence of the national order controlled by moderates, and of a single trade union controlled by progressives, explains how journalists have managed to obtain such advantageous conditions of work and income, particularly since the national strike on December 5, 1958.

There are many other specialized associations of journalists, complicating the network of relationships between journalists themselves and with public and private institutions. The most influential of these is the association of Catholic journalists. Each year it holds a national convention chaired for many years by Signor Flaminio Piccoli, the present president of the Christian Democratic party, which has been in power since 1945. The existence of this complex network of associatons in a country traditionally short of corporate spirit greatly subdues the individualism typical of the journalistic profession and tends to resolve professional conflicts and rivalries by agreements and compromises that are to the advantage of all the members of the profession. These are the characteristic features of the Italian journalistic profession, which make it in many crucial respects like the other liberal professions such as medicine or law but unlike the journalistic profession in other countries.

Only in the last two or three years, as a result of the political evolution of the country, has the question been raised whether the great social responsibilities associated with journalism demand a more specialized training of journalists and a more open system of entry into the profession. The idea of schools of journalism and specialized university training has begun to be discussed without the usual contempt and complacency with which such questions have been treated until recently.

The way in which the profession functions, strongly conditioned as it was until a few years ago by the political and cultural systems of the country, demonstrates how greatly Italian journalism has been influenced by its special relationship with the political classes and with government.

The privileges and benefits enjoyed by journalists are greatly coveted by intellectuals working in similar fields, such as book publishing, and especially in RAI-TV, where it is often difficult to distinguish between the work of journalists and others. The existence of closely interconnected sectors, one protected by the political parties and subsidized by the state and the other free and dependent on demand, multiplies the possibilities for material advantage and prestige for those who work in the cultural industry.[6] The same intellectual can benefit both from the political protection that guarantees his security or from his own professionalism and competence, which he can use on the open market and thereby gain large financial rewards.

The Italian Model and Its Possible Developments

The Italian mass communication model is a liberal one, though both incomplete and postbourgeois. At its beginning it was cast in the classical liberal-bourgeois mold of the progressive and enlightened upper-middle class, which forged the unity of Italy in the mid-nineteenth century. It has been affected recently by some of the changes and developments in the United States, but not so as to change its basic character, which has always been determined by its relationship with the political parties. This was particularly evident and well publicized during the fascist years and, no less crucial though less obvious, in the central years of the Christian Democrat era.

The presence in Italy of a strong Communist party, opposed to Anglo-Saxon culture and the American way of life, and inspired by an ideology that envisages the state as the centralizer and controller of the social machinery, has greatly contributed toward the perpetuation of this pattern until recent years. What is more, the Communist party and Marxist culture have had some influence on Italian intellectuals and thus have reinforced their negative attitude toward the mass media. This explains why the left-wing parties have always joined with the Christian Democrats in defending the monopoly held by RAI-TV. However, in the last ten years a number of other liberal and libertarian elements have been introduced by the growth of the trade unions and of political awareness in the media, which is hardly at all due to the activities of the Communist party. The breakdown of the front for the defense of the monopoly, for instance, was brought about by a challenge from the extreme left-wing parties outside Parliament. In the same way, a number of publishing ventures have been started as a result of initiatives conceived in left-wing, though noncommunist, cultural and political circles. These liberal and libertarian elements introduced by new interests, which are not entirely under the control of the political system or of commercial factors, are the most significant development of recent years. In the near future, when the ideological impulse that set them in motion has died down, they will prove to be the main advocates of a seriously based professionalism in journalism. The diversity of interests in this media system makes it unstable and provisional. But it is inconceivable that it will develop, as in other countries, into a straightforward adaptation of any system already established elsewhere, be it the 'liberal' model of industrialized capitalist countries or the statist one of communist countries. Professional opinion within the media, as well as general public opinion, is well insulated against both in Italy, where the two classic models are held in great suspicion. With some slight modifications, the Italian model may retain its four essential features: liberal, politico-statist, American, and liberal-libertarian. For this reason the question of professionalism is likely to become a central point of discussion in Italy.

At present the Italian system has lost the sure legal focal point and stable basis previously provided by the state and the party system, though the positions of the parties relative to the state remains important. The new dominant force cannot be the market, though it has acquired a weight that it never before possessed, nor can the gap be filled by the appeal of direct access to the media and abolition of journalistic mediation, though this is an opinion held by some theorists of free radio and counterinformation.

Each of these positions, none of which is predominant at present, embodies a different model of professionalism. In the first, professionalism consists of the ability of the individual journalist or of the system, semidependent on the political parties, to comply with their directives. This is the professionalism to be found under all statist regimes, and its logical consequence is the end of freedom of the press and subordination to power.

In the second mode, professionalism consists of an ability to adapt to market pressures as measured in audience appreciation and sales indexes, which tend to smooth over differences of political opinion. This is the American model, the extreme consequences of which are illustrated, for example, in the movie *Network*. The end of press freedom and the subordination of journalism to the balances of power is the logical consequence of this system too.

In the third model, professionalism is denied inasmuch as it is considered that the actors on the social stage do not need the mediation of journalists in order to communicate; anyone can be a journalist. This is an extreme position, which may fulfill a positive function as a critique of the degeneracy of the first and second models and at a moment of liberation in a crisis situation, but it cannot become institutionalized.

There remains a fourth model, based on a conscious professionalism, which may be created by a general and specific training and a regulated professional apprenticeship. In such a case, the profession must be exercised in the context of journalistic companies run on commercial lines. There must be competition between them within limits, controlled and guaranteed by wide social and political participation and by a relatively homogeneous social structure with a widespread corporative spirit. In this last case, the market is in a position to act as a regulating and stabilizing factor. It is clear that this last position is an ideal type in the Weberian sense, but only by adhering to it can a freer and less subservient type of journalism be achieved.

I believe that the situation in Italy, despite its apparent paradoxes and startling contradictions, is one in which the conditions are now right for a development toward this ideal. This model has been affected by the fact that the newspaper industry was not able, as a whole, to become a real profit-making industry. Only for brief periods and only in certain parts of the industry has the making of profit been considered a goal in itself and a basis for editorial autonomy. This was true in the late years of the nineteenth century and in the beginning of the twentieth. Newspapers such as *La Stampa* of Turin, *Corriere della Sera* of

239

Milan, *La Nazione* in Florence, *Il Giornale d'Italia* and *Il Messagero* of Rome, and *Il Mattino* of Naples—all leading papers of the period—were managed in such a way as to be profitable consistently over a period. Top newspaper editors like Albertini (*Corriere della Sera*), Fonati (*La Stampa*), and Berganioni (*Il Giornale d'Italia*) succeeded in enlarging the audiences of their newspapers and thus establishing a basis for profit and for relatively autonomous editorial policies. But none of these papers (with the possible exception of *Corriere*) really succeeded as enterprises; the linkages with external financial and political groups always remained crucial. The reason for this phenomenon was structural; the potential market for newspapers was confined by the high level of illiteracy in the general population to the middle class. Just before World War I, the construction of a national newspaper industry was becoming viable, but the process was severely interrupted by the emergence of fascism, which reduced the freedom of the press almost to zero. Financial and political support for the press since that time has remained a major element in the newspaper business.

Newspapers in Italy were thus either created or aided or entirely financed not for the purpose of creating profits but in order to search for and sustain an element of consensus among that relatively small section of the population that contained those most influential within the political scene: mainly from the middle and upper social groups. Only in the 1960s did the arrival of a larger middle class and a prosperous working class create the basis for a wider circulation of newspapers, and at that moment the other mass media were developing rapidly, appealing to the population as a whole far more than Italy's daily press could do, highly traditional as it is both in the style of its news coverage and in its editorial comment, despite the minor concessions that have been made to popular taste.

Emerging Tendencies

All the elements which have been described developed even more intensively as the 1970s progressed. Italy appears to have emerged from the serious economic crisis that has paralyzed it in previous years. Even if this conclusion is not seemingly corroborated by the official figures, there are nonetheless many signs of a recovery in economic activity, especially among small and medium sized industries. According to authoritative sources, Italy recently has developed a large, unofficial, and profitable sector of the economy, making products both for the home market and for export.[7]

Politically a government was established that for the first time was supported by the Communist party and was able to command a large parliamentary majority. This fact, however, led to the emergence of divisions and tensions between and within the political parties. The new leadership of the Socialist party, victorious in the party conference

240

of March 1978, changed the line and image of the party, giving rise to fierce controversy with the Communist party. At the same time, the crisis in political participation deepened, leading many people to theorize about the fall of the myths and ideologies that had sustained the struggles of previous years. The results of certain by-elections in the spring and autumn of 1978 and of two referenda in June revealed new patterns in electoral behavior: decline of the Communist party, gains by the Socialist party, and the emergence of new political coalitions not identifying themselves with established national parties.

Against this background, three events demonstrated the character of the world of journalism and the mass media: the reactions to the kidnapping and assassination of Italy's most authoritative political leader, Aldo Moro; the Socialist proposal for a radical change in the law governing journalism and mass communications in November; and the introduction of new technologies in many daily newspapers.

Italian newspapers gave enormous coverage to the Moro case, a coverage that many considered excessive, mainly because until then the media had underestimated the extent of the phenomenon of terrorism and had supplied little and often inaccurate information about the Red Brigades and other similar terrorist organizations. What is more, a wide and intense debate developed after the kidnapping, which involved all newspapers in a discussion on the nature of terrorism and on the role of the press and the mass media.[8] The coverage of the Moro case and the debate it fired have revealed a substantial solidarity between journalists and the politically conscious social groups that has been challenged by intellectuals and critics from outside the political and journalistic system.

This event caused the newspapers to bring out many special editions, and there was a great increase in readership. Similar successes were achieved in connection with two other events: the resignation of the president of the Republic, Giovanni Leone, following accusations brought against him in the course of a virulent press campaign, and the death of two popes, the first of whom, Pope Paul VI, had exercised a great influence on Italian political life since the end of the war, having been the friend and inspiration of an important part of the Christian Democratic leadership, including Moro.

Increased circulation, the great debate on the role of the press, the controversy between Socialists and Communists, and the more direct and unscrupulous use of the media by the Socialists and by Prime Minister Andreotti led to the media's, especially the daily press, playing the most important role in the political debate.[9] If one then adds that the traditional means of political participation, debates in local party organizations, and assemblies in places of work have entered a period of crisis, one can conclude that a shift in the scene of political debate from direct participation to indirect participation through the media is occurring.

241

In the future, the media undoubtedly will have a much greater role to play in the determination of the political will than it has in the past. This prospect probably influenced the decision taken by the Socialist party in mid-November 1978, widely reported in the media, proposing a change in the relationship between the public and private sectors that would allow greater scope to the private sector. Regarding television, the new Socialist party official responsible for information, Claudio Martelli, has proposed a variation on the British system. Alongside RAI, a public company, a private company would be formed that would be run by a consortium of private publishers, though using public equipment. Furthermore Martelli has proposed that the pricing system of newspapers, which at present is kept at a fixed level, should be greatly liberalized. These proposals mark a radical change in the traditional stance adopted by the majority of Italian political parties in relation to the media.

Also of importance are technological developments. Many daily newspapers are changing their methods of composition and printing by introducing electronic equipment. These changes will bring about radical changes in methods of production and in the organization of work. Already they are provoking hostile reactions, including industrial action, by typographers and journalists.

Clearly the overall scene is changing. It may be that a market is being created for daily newspapers that could allow the information sector to run at a profit and without the financial support of the state. If this occurs, even if initially in a limited form, the media would enjoy greater autonomy from the political parties. The character of information would thus no longer be determined primarily by its privileged relationship with political parties but would also be influenced by its relationship with the market. It is no accident that the media scene at present is strongly influenced by the presence of two large private publishing concerns, Rizzoli and Mondadori, which, though only recently arrived in the field of newspaper publishing, are increasingly equipping themselves to run an integrated group of companies active in the various areas of the cultural industry (such as books, periodicals, films, radio, and television).

Notes

1. The Italian journalists' union does not belong to either of the two international journalists' associations, the Eastern and the Western.

2. In recent years, as many as three daily newspapers inspired by small extraparliamentary left-wing groups have been started and continue to appear: *Il Manifesto,* which for some time was very authoritative among the left-wing intelligentsia; *Lotta Continua,* the only daily paper that is read by and expresses the feelings of young and very young militants; and *Il Quotidiano dei Lavoratori,* with a smaller circulation than the other two but more tied to the working class. Two authoritative daily newspapers have also appeared: *Il Giornale Nuovo,* run by a group of moderate journalists who have broken away from the *Corriere della Sera,* and *La Repubblic,* a quality paper, without crime reporting, edited by Eugenio Scalfari, a prestigious journalist who is at present pro-Communist.

3. There have been three recent developments: the shutting down of the official organ of the Republic party, *La voce repubblicana,* which was formerly very influential; the birth of a popular daily from the Rizzoli stable; and the birth of a new daily of the extraparliamentary left.

4. It is calculated that at the time of the unification of Italy in 1870, less than 2 percent of the population spoke Italian and that in 1945 only 15 to 20 percent knew the language. Only in recent years has this figure reached 70 to 80 percent.

5. The rest enter the profession in the following proportion: 30 percent after an apprenticeship in news, sports, or as proofreaders; 10 percent after having been peripheral correspondents; 5 percent after having attended schools or institutes of journalism. Cf. U. Ronfani, "Le Scuole di Gornalismo," *L'ordine dei giornalisti* 5 (May–July 1978).

6. There are two television channels for news and current affairs and two channels for entertainment and fiction; three radio channels for news and current affairs and three channels for entertainment, fiction, and music. In 1979 other channels should start working, partially decentralized at the regional level.

7. The CENSIS, a private foundation that undertakes socioeconomical research on demand by public agencies, in its last annual report (November 1978) to the National Council of Economics and Work (CNEL) states that Italy is going through a new economic boom.

8. By the end of 1978, at least twenty books were published that analyzed the press, the origins and development of terrorism, and the political and cultural debate originating from the Moro case.

9. Recently there has been much more frequent use made by politicians, especially Socialists, of exclusive interviews in a variety of papers. Their purpose is not only to communicate with the broader public but also with their own colleagues. Thus Andreotti finally reached the point in September 1978 when he granted an exclusive interview to a daily of the extraparliamentary Left, *Il Quotidiano dei lavoratori,* in the course of which he made some important revelations on the Moro case.

IV

Editorial Content and Control

To newspaper readers (and to many editors), the change from the traditional newspaper to the modern, more consumer-oriented journal has taken place in imperceptible stages. Editors have tried to placate rather than rush readers by adding new ranges of material without too emphatically appearing to remove any. Leo Bogart's study of American editors' and readers' attitudes toward the content priorities of newspapers supports the argument that the traditional editorial purposes of newspapers have not been outmoded in modern times even though editors have to create a new and broader mixture of content. The elimination of competition among newspapers means that editors are obliged to maintain the support of an entire community and therefore balance the interest in local, sublocal, and trivial information with the continuing desire of readers to have their papers provide news on national and international affairs. The ending of competition has not, therefore, enabled editors suddenly to ignore areas of information that were previously found desirable by the same body of readers. The market for information is gradually changing as a whole, and the newspaper world has been turning increasingly to new sources of expertise to help grapple with it. The editorial quest that lies at the heart of the industry has been slowly transformed into a kind of constant sociological analysis.

The newspaper is a social system in itself, and the external changes in its market have exercised an important impact on its internal relationships. In the 1960s, there was a great deal of discussion in all countries on newsroom democracy or internal press freedoms and cooperative ownership. Very few of the countries discussed in this book have failed to produce at least one example of an attempt to save a threatened title through employee takeover either of management or of ownership. Sweden and Italy even offer special subsidies to newspapers taken over by their staff to prevent the ending of publication. *Le Monde* is the classic example of a newspaper in which the journalists exercise sovereign power. David Hart examines some of the politics of this new tension between publishers and editors (in the German sense of the term, which includes the whole range of senior journalists on a paper), which has evolved in the period in which internal press freedom has been under discussion. He shows how it has become important at a time when the external multiplicity of newspapers, which underlay the traditional internal structure of command, has disappeared. Without an array of competing titles, the newspaper adopts a different stance and new responsibilities toward the reader and, indeed, society as a whole. It is hard to maintain that publishers have the same wide-ranging rights over their businesses as in the past, since their industry plays so special and crucial a role in society's governance. The coming of new technology has reinforced the new awareness on the part of editors of their altered position in the world of information; a new sense has arisen of where the boundary marks of various rights and privileges should be placed. In Germany, with which Hart's article is mainly concerned, lawyers, moralists, political scientists, and politicians, as well as newspaper specialists, have been debating this new alignment of publisher and editor perhaps more intensely than in any other society.

Finally James Curran and his associates raise a fresh and disturbing question. The newspaper industry in many countries (Britain most conspicuously) during the last half-century has gradually divided itself into high and low information categories, into entertainment and serious groups of newspapers. But is the reader really free to choose between high politics and entertaining feature material? Is the entertainment paper not at root a subverted version of a political paper? This study starts with an examination of the content of British popular papers at ten-year intervals over the course of a half-century and argues that the genres of popular journalism are, historically, encoded transmutations of politics; the popular newspaper, in sum, is in many ways an illusion. Mass journalism as practiced in Britain is an apparatus of subtle social control, almost consciously manipulating mass consciousness and doing so as effectively as any newspaper conducting overt propaganda. According to this line of analysis, the reportorial ethic of objectivity goes nowhere toward guaranteeing the readership a systematic presentation of the significant events of the world, still less a version of those events that provide readers with the means to make up their own minds. Perhaps the greatest danger to which this chapter draws attention is that which results from a too complete polarization between what the British formally label "quality" and "popular." It is an increasing and widespread danger.

246

11

Editorial Ideals, Editorial Illusions

Leo Bogart

In the August 3, 1752, issue of the *New York Gazette,* the editor, James Parker earnestly entreats all those who are angry at him for printing things they don't like, calmly to consider the following particulars:

Being continually employed in serving all Parties, Printers naturally acquire a vast Unconcernedness as to right or wrong Opinions contain'd in what they print. . . . If they sometimes print vicious or Silly Things, not worth reading, it may not be, because they approve of such Things themselves, but because people are so viciously and corruptly educated, that good things are not encouraged. Thus I have known a large Edition of the story of an old Woman drowned at Ratcliff Highway sell here to good profit, whilst a Piece recommending Piety and Religion never sold at all.

Today's newspaper editors still face the same dilemma. On the one hand, they are moral agents, voicing the aspirations of their society, turning their lantern into its dark corners. But on the other, they are artisans, out to earn an innocuous dollar, and often finding that they can best do so by satisfying the people's meanest appetites. Their peculiar art is to balance these two requirements: to say what they want to say and to sell it to good profit as well. In arriving at this compromise, editors are continually testing the limits of the readers' attention to what they know to be important.

It is the moral underpinning, the ideals of editorial integrity, that distinguish journalism from mere print-

A shorter version of this paper was originally presented before the American Society of Newspaper Editors and appeared in the spring 1979 issue of the *Journal of Communications.* I gratefully acknowledge the contribution of Charles Lehman in the execution and analysis of the editors' survey.

ing. But mass media are profitable, which is to say they survive, when they give advertisers what they want; and advertisers want saturation coverage of their markets.

How do editors reconcile their professional mission with the need to attract the largest possible audiences they can? During the 1970s, this question acquired new urgency for the American press as it faced a complex assortment of changes in its internal economic structure, in its social environment, and in competitive pressures from other mass media.

Advertising represents about three-fourths of the revenues of American daily newspapers. If the press were exclusively dependent for its income upon readers, the price per copy would have to be three or four times what it is. This would be on the assumption that circulation would not drop off. Actually this is an impossible assumption, since there is evidence that in America price does affect the demand for newspapers and also that advertising represents a major attraction for readers.

In the American advertising marketplace, newspapers can remain competitive with other media only if they stay in line by the criterion of cost per thousand readers (CPM). If they raise their advertising rates without increasing their audiences, their CPM goes up even if their advertising rates stay the same. Newspaper publishers have had to juggle these considerations as they encountered massive rises in newsprint, ink, and energy costs, which far exceeded the general rate of inflation in the United States.

A 1973 survey of circulation executives found that price increases were blamed by three out of four whose papers had failed to show gains in readership. But there are more complex reasons why the daily press did not keep pace with the growth in population and households during the 1970s. In this decade, there was a vast migration of the white middle class out of the large central cities in which a substantial part of total newspaper circulation is concentrated. Retailers followed their customers to the suburbs, thereby weakening the advertising income of second and third papers in a number of metropolitan areas. The resulting failures and mergers reduced aggregate circulation figures, although the total number of dailies has stayed level for several decades (it was 1,764 in 1979), and the number of cities with their own dailies has actually increased (to 1,544).

248

At the same time, living patterns and interests were influenced by changes in family structures, increased participation of women in the work force, and greater population mobility, especially among young people. Also among the young there appeared to be, in the wake of Vietnam and Watergate, a new current of political apathy and alienation that diminished the appetite for news in any form.

The 1970s saw a great growth of alternative choices in print media; specialized and local magazines and weekly newspapers, both paid and free, proliferated. Television continued to be the principal leisure activity for most Americans, but television audiences had remained level for many years, and television news viewing seemed to be unrelated to the readership trends for individual newspapers. (In fact, during the New York City newspaper strike of 1978, the absence of newspapers appears to account for an actual decline in the viewing of the evening news.) All of these external forces were transforming both the conditions under which daily newspapers are sold and distributed and the very expectations and values of the reading public.

As James Parker lamented, editors have always sought to meet and even to anticipate readers' changing expectations. At the same time, it is in the nature of their calling to seek to mold readers' values. In producing a daily newspaper, these sometimes contradictory goals can be approached not in terms of any grand design but rather as the outcome of innumerable specific decisions on how to handle individual items of content. Each day a typical metropolitan newspaper receives and processes about ten times as many words as it eventually prints. This means that the assignment of stories, as well as their selection, reduction, synthesis, placement, and assemblage, takes place at great speed on the basis of assumptions, intuitions, and experiences that are virtually impossible to articulate or formalize into a theoretical framework.

A catch phrase among editors in the late 1970s was "Give the readers what they want." What they want, presumably, is what they report to interviewers in surveys designed to elicit their opinions on the various elements of the newspaper and on anything else that might be relevant (such as the interests now satisfied by other media). Some highlights from one such survey are reviewed later in this chapter. But since the perception of readers' attitudes represents only one horn of the editor's dilemma, we should first consider how they define their own professional objectives and how they reconcile these with the mundane requirements of the business they are in.

The Editors' Survey

Information on this subject comes from 746 questionnaires returned in March 1977 by working editors—56 percent of 1,300 sent to actively employed members of the American Society of Newspaper Editors and the Associated Press Managing Editors (after screening for dual membership).

The returns represented a good cross-section of the two organizations. Fifty-six percent of them were from editors and executive editors and 37 percent were from managing editors; the remainder were associate editors or held other titles. There are about the same proportions of bigger papers (over 50,000 circulation) represented by those who answered (42 percent) and those who did not (43 percent). However, the membership of ASNE and APME overrepresents the larger papers.

Seven percent of all the dailies, with 49 percent of all circulation, are over 100,000. But 24 percent of the replies are from these big city editors. At the other extreme, the small papers of less than 25,000 represent 70 percent of the newspapers, 21 percent of the circulation, and 32 percent of the replies. The editors of the largest papers are split evenly between morning and afternoon publications, while most of the smaller papers represented (83 percent) come out in the afternoon. Since they tend to be bigger, more of the morning papers responding are in competitive markets. Only one in four is in a town with no other daily, compared with seven in ten of the evening papers. These well-known differences must be mentioned because it is imperative to sort out the answers according to size. Executive editors of metropolitan papers must see their functions somewhat differently from managing editors of small-community dailies.

Big papers are fatter than smaller papers because they carry more advertising, which gives them a bigger newshole. But this means that their newshole is less as a percentage of total pages. For papers with circulation 100,000 and over, the newshole rate is 37 percent; for those between 50,000 and 100,000, it is 42 percent; for those between 25,000 and 50,000 it is 44 percent; and for those under 25,000, it is 49 percent.

Staff-written copy fills a higher proportion of big papers, as one would expect. In fact, the big city editors do not have much of a gap, on the average, between the percentage of staff-written copy they actually run (58 percent) and the proportion they would ideally like (61 percent). The small town editors are somewhat inclined to sense that they fall short of their own ideal and to take the big city paper as their model in this respect.

There are similar differences between editors of large and small papers when we consider the proportion of editorial content devoted to feature material, however each editor individually defines that. Editors of big papers carry a higher percentage than those on small papers (about 33 and 23 percent, respectively), and they generally feel they are at the ideal ratio right now. Editors of smaller papers would like to run somewhat more feature material than they do.

Building Circulation
Will newspapers increase their circulation mainly by changing their content or by improving the way that they promote, sell, and deliver? The answers editors give depend very much on how well their own papers are doing. Editors of papers whose circulations went up in 1976 split evenly between those who think the solution is primarily editorial and those who say it is primarily a matter of distribution. However, those editors whose papers lost circulation in 1976 vote overwhelmingly (57 percent) to put the onus on the circulation department.

A request for specific suggestions turned up rather unspecific responses. The big city editors offered the fewest proposals on content (perhaps simply because they were most impatient with the questioning procedure). The thought mentioned most often is to tailor the content to reader interest. Next (a low second) come references to writing or editorial quality. These turned out to be of comparatively greater concern to editors of smaller papers. It is worth noting that only a small proportion of editors regard changes in the appearance of their papers as a way to improve their reader appeal.

Are newspapers that do an outstanding professional editorial job also likely to be the most successful in building circulation? The editors' answers apparently depend in part on how well they are doing in circulation themselves. Of those whose papers gained circulation in 1976, 70 percent agree that good papers are successful in building circulation, while 26 percent think there is no clear relationship between quality and success, and 2 percent agree that papers that they admire professionally are actually least successful. Among those whose circulation went down, only 56 percent agree that good papers are successful, while 42 percent see no clear relationship.

Defining Quality

If editorial quality leads to circulation success, as a majority of editors think, the definition of quality is of more than passing importance. The editors were asked to rank seven attributes that might be associated with quality. Editors on all kinds of papers, big and small, competitive and noncompetitive, agreed on the first three: accuracy, impartiality in reporting, and investigative enterprise. The next four attributes of editorial quality were rated somewhat differently by editors on papers of different sizes. Among the editors of the biggest dailies with circulations of over a quarter of a million, fourth place is given to specialized staff skills, fifth is individuality of character, and sixth is literary style. Civic-mindedness is last on the list, perhaps because metropolitan editors might assume it to be a necessary by-product of accuracy and investigativeness.

Editors of the smallest papers give these four attributes quite a different ranking. Civic-mindedness is number four, then specialized staff skills and literary style. Individuality of character is less important to a small daily that reflects its whole community than to a big competitive paper that has to make its own special mark.

All of these attributes, like motherhood and the flag, are beyond discussion. Editors commonly use subjective criteria like these when they look at their own papers or at others. But although such values are important in judging editorial awards, they cannot very well be used on a large scale to relate editorial excellence to trends in circulation, advertising, profitability, or other criteria of success. To do that requires yardsticks that can be readily determined or actually measured.

The editors were given twenty-three such attributes to rate on a scale from +3 to −3. These criteria were by no means an exhaustive list, and a number of editors suggested additional ones. Their suggestions did not fall into any pattern that indicated that something critical had been left

251

out of the original selection. The other points they raised include the proportion of editorials on local subjects, the ratio of human-interest stories to total content, the presence of a column on personalities, a detailed weather report, a front-page photograph, a local editorial cartoon, a calendar of local events, and texts of statements and speeches.

One thoughtful critique was written on the back of a questionnaire: "If I were judging a paper from the outside, I'd look first at the obvious: looks, typos, general pattern of seeming to cover the kinds of things all good newspapers cover. Once past that hurdle, I'd look for writing style, variety, well-told [local] stories . . . and selection variety, judgment and editing of wire and syndicate stuff. And finally—and perhaps most important of all—I'd look for something in that newspaper every day that would, could, and should be a topic of conversation over the back fence or on the commuter train for every possible group of readers of the paper."

Comparing Quality and Reader Interest

These may well be the kinds of criteria that editors instinctively use as they look at other papers, but they do not lend themselves to any systematic effort to differentiate newspapers in the aggregate, which was the purpose of the study.[1]

The attributes of quality that editors put at the top of the list, when their ratings are averaged and ranked, begin with a high ratio of staff-written copy to wire service and feature service copy. Second, the total amount of nonadvertising or editorial content in the paper, like the preceding indicator, reflects a paper's circulation size, so in effect editors seem to feel that bigger papers are likely to be better. Third is a high ratio of news interpretation and backgrounders to spot news reports. Fourth is the number of letters to the editor. Fifth is the diversity of political columnists. This is worth noting because the number of political columnists is rated as having virtually no relation to quality at all. Sixth is a high readability score on a test of reading ease. Seventh is a high ratio of illustrations to text. Eighth is a high ratio of news, or nonadvertising, content to advertising. Paradoxically this contradicts the high value placed on the absolute size of the newshole, which generally goes up as the amount of advertising goes up, but not in exact proportion. Ninth is the number of staff-bylined features.

Most editors feel that editorial excellence is rewarded by success in circulation. Does that mean that the traits that make a newspaper good are also considered to make it popular? The answer is no. The three attributes that are ranked most highly on success with readers are not high on the list as attributes of quality. First is the presence of an action-line column; next, a high ratio of sports news and features to total news content; and third, the presence of a news summary. However the next four attributes rated high for reader interest also come up strongly rated on editorial quality: the number of letters to the editor, a high ratio of illustrations to text, a high ratio of staff-written copy, and a high readability score.

Consider the attributes that are rated much higher on reader interest that on editorial quality. The biggest gap between the two ratings is for the number of comic strips. An astrology column gets a slight negative on quality without being much of a plus for reader interest. The interest ascribed to action line and to a large sports section has already been noted. Their quality scores are positive, but there is still quite a gap between these and the assumed interest levels. Also rated higher on interest than on quality are the presence of a news summary and a high ratio of homemaking news and features to total news content.

On the opposite side of the equation, there are a number of points that editors rate higher for themselves than for readers. The number of wire services carried is considered moderately indicative of editorial quality but of absolutely no interest to the reader.

Readers were also assumed to be indifferent to a number of attributes that editors link to quality: a high proportion of staff-written copy, a high proportion of news interpretation, a diversity of political columnists, the total amount of editorial (nonadvertising) content, a high ratio of news to features, and the number of editorials per issue.

One attribute turned out to be unrelated either to quality or to reader interest: the length (as opposed to brevity) of the average front-page news story (including the jump). This suggests that there is a standoff in the continuing debate over whether newspapers overwhelm or underwhelm the reader with the number of front-page stories they present and the number they cover in depth.

Another way of examining the same data is to compare the ratings that individual editors give to each of twenty-three attributes for quality and reader interest. A substantial proportion, ranging from 27 percent to 58 percent, rated the items identically by both yardsticks. Those attributes that are generally considered to be much higher in reader interest than as indicators of quality tend to be entertaining rather than informative in character.

In filling out the questionnaire, one editor wrote in a comment that he would answer it differently if he were running a bigger paper. But in fact, it turns out that there is virtually total agreement between editors of small and big papers on the comparative ratios of quality to reader interest scores for all of the attributes. In both big and small towns, there was fairly high agreement among editors of both competitive and noncompetitive papers. This was also true for the rankings of the seven subjective attributes: accuracy, impartiality, and the like. That does not mean that the actual scores are always identical. For example, the presence of a news summary is rated higher on quality by editors of smaller papers but higher on interest by editors of larger ones. The same is true on the number of letters to the editor, on the readability score, and on the number of comic strips. But such differences in judg-

253

ment appear minor relative to the substantial differences in the conditions under which small town and metropolitan editors operate.

An important objective of this study was to find out whether editors whose papers have been losing circulation are using different standards of editorial judgment than are the majority whose circulations have been going up. In fact, there is very little difference both on quality and on interest scores. That does not mean that there are not important but subtle differences in the style of these two groups of papers, differences that sensitive editors might detect. But these differences are not of the kind that can be pointed out as guidelines to fame and fortune. Moreover, the actual editorial practices of the papers that are failing to gain circulation are in three important respects objectively identical with those of their more successful contemporaries in the same circulation size bracket. (The proportion who report gains is 67 percent among papers of over 100,000 and 77 percent for those of under 25,000.) Within each circulation-size group, gainers and losers are almost identical in the size of their newshole relative to advertising, the proportion of their editorial matter that is staff written, and the proportion that is feature material rather than news.

If the editors showing losses are using the same kinds of editorial standards as the rest and are producing rather similar papers on the whole, this finding provides some confirmation for their feeling that their losses are for the most part due to external conditions—problems of selling and promotion—and not to matters of content.

Editorial Consensus
This examination of editors' opinions suggests a number of conclusions. First, editing appears to be a profession whose members really have common values. There is a surprising degree of consensus as to what makes a newspaper good and what makes it attractive. For executive editors and managing editors, on big papers and on small ones, the variety of opinion within each group is greater than the differences between groups. Second, editors define quality in a newspaper, above all, as dedication to the truth: accuracy and fairness in reporting. Third, editors of small papers have to run them differently, but they would run them like big ones if they could. Fourth, editors seem to have a high degree of confidence in their readers. What they think is good in a newspaper is in most cases not too wildly different from what they think readers like. They must sugarcoat each day's bitter pill of news, but they do not seem torn by any great inner conflict about the need to do this. When they rate quality, there are few strong negative votes, even for features like comics and astrology columns that they consider to be moderately interesting to readers. What is surprising is that such established utilitarian features as business, culture, and homemaking do not rate strongly either on quality or reader interest. And finally, they think that an attractive paper also creates reader interest. They associate reader interest with participation (through letters and an

254

action line). They connect it to a strong sports section and to the kind of packaging that a news summary typifies. Amazingly they do not consider the total size of the newshole to be of any interest to readers.

What Interests Readers?

Editors' judgments are, by definition, impeccable in evaluating quality in journalism. Who else, after all, can set standards of excellence? But how accurately do editors perceive readers' interests? Even to ask this question invites editorial mistrust, for it suggests that the judgments that go into the creation of the newspaper can be second-guessed by readers reacting to out-of-context summary statements in an interview. Several studies have indeed shown a discrepancy between editors' and readers' ratings of the same subjects. In one such study, managing editors scored 11 percent better than chance in ranking the public's probable response to 120 news items, presented in summary form.[2]

The most commonplace method of comparing readers' responses to different elements of the paper is to go through an issue they have looked at to determine what specific items they remember having seen or read. This technique (the so-called recognition method) has the advantage of avoiding the kind of generalized reactions that people give to broad categories of content, like movie reviews or stories about local politicians. Its disadvantages relate to the fragility and selectivity of the memory processes and to the fact that since such interviews must be conducted among readers of the particular issue, there is no way of tapping the responses of the nonreaders whom the editor may be trying to attract.

A somewhat different approach was therefore used in a national study of newspaper reading conducted at the same time as the 1977 editors' survey. This study provided an opportunity to check assumptions regarding reader interests, even though no head-on comparisons were possible with editors' views. The study was conducted during the week of March 14 among a probability sample of three thousand adults aged eighteen and over. A variety of questioning methods were used to examine how newspaper content was regarded both by people who had read a given issue and by those who had not.[3]

Personal interviews covered a sampling of the editorial and advertising items (over seventy-five lines or five and one-half column inches) and advertisements on nine randomly selected pages of a local newspaper. The 109,331 items were classified into categories identical with those used in 1971 in a study that used the recognition method to obtain reported readership. The first column of table 11.1 shows the distribution of content, by categories.

Each item was rated twice by the respondent. First each was told, "When we look at a newspaper, we usually find some things more in-

Table 11.1 *Daily Newspaper Content and Reader Ratings of Content, 1977*

	Total Number of Items[a]	Reader Ratings	
		% Very Interested	% Very Important
General interest	66.6%	28	20
State and local news	12.4	21	17
General local news	7.3	19	13
State and local government	5.1	25	22
International news	6.3	29	24
Wars, rebellions	1.5	33	26
International, diplomatic	4.8	28	24
U.S. government, domestic	3.5	33	29
Other general interest	44.4	29	20
Crime	7.3	33	23
Education, school news	3.1	23	19
Cultural events, reviews	2.4	15	10
Public health, welfare	2.8	35	33
News in brief	2.4	32	23
Accidents, disasters, natural phenomena	1.9	39	26
Social problems, protest	1.6	36	29
Obituaries	1.2	26	21
Labor, wages	1.6	29	26
Environment	1.7	35	32
General nonlocal human interest	2.7	22	13
Energy problems	0.7	40	38
Racial news, minorities (peaceful)	0.6	28	22
Weather	1.7	37	27
Science, invention	0.7	32	22
Travel	1.0	25	20
Taxes	0.9	37	34
Religion	0.6	18	15
Comics	2.8	19	6
Editorial cartoons	1.0	24	14
Puzzles, horoscopes	2.9	16	7
TV/Radio logs	1.1	26	16
Entertainers, Hollywood	1.0	16	8
Letters to the editor	0.7	37	27
Men's interest	21.2	16	12
Sports	13.9	14	9
Business, finance	7.3	21	20

Table 11.1 (continued)

	Total Number of Items[a]	Reader Ratings	
		% Very Interested	% Very Important
Women's interest	3.3	18	9
Fashion, society	2.0	15	3
Food, home, garden	1.3	23	17
Columns			
Advice	1.7	28	19
Political	1.6	31	24
Humor	0.4	23	14
Gossip	0.2	19	13
Other items not classified elsewhere	5.0		

[a]Covers items of seventy-five lines or greater. The categories shown combine a larger number of classifications which were coded.

teresting than others. Now I'm going to show you some pages from yesterday's paper, and I would like to know whether you personally find the news stories and ads on that page very interesting, somewhat interesting, or not at all interesting. You don't have to read every word, but enough to decide whether you personally find each article or ad interesting."[4] (When respondents did not answer or could not provide an answer for a particular item, this itself was coded as a response, but in the analysis of the results, these answers were included with those of people who said the particular item had no interest or importance for them.) After the respondent had rated every item on each page in terms of interest, he or she was asked to go back and rate every news and feature article as follows: "Now I would like to consider just the articles and not the ads with something completely different in mind. I'd like you to tell me which articles have information that is really important for you yourself to know about, regardless of how interesting they are."

The adjectives *interesting* and *important* are, of course, only two of the many that can be applied to media content. They were selected as key dimensions in this analysis because they seemed to correspond both with the public's reading experience and with its expectations of the newspaper. They also reflected the two aspects of the dilemma in which we are interested: the compulsion of editors to make their papers appealing to the largest possible numbers of readers and their professional desire to be useful and informative at the same time.

Readers had a wide range of reactions to the individual items classified under a particular category of content. With all the variety of subjects that a newspaper must cover, many of them of a specialized nature, it is somewhat unexpected that a majority have at least some interest to the average person, whether or not he is actually a reader. Twenty-five percent of all items were classed very interesting by the average person; 30 percent as having some interest; 34 percent as of no interest; and for 11 percent no answer was given.

Overall there are not very large differences among various types of news categories in the interest and importance scores assigned to the average item. The range is from 75 percent for social welfare to 45 percent for international crime in the proportion with at least some interest. The proportion who attribute at least some importance runs from 72 percent for social welfare to 40 percent for miscellaneous human-interest stories. These results seem to suggest that the range of interest and importance attributed to individual items within many single categories is often greater than the differences in response to the various kinds of news as such.

As the second column of table 11.1 shows, the percentage "very interested" ranges from at least four of ten people for the average item under the headings of consumer safety, energy, national welfare, juvenile crime, and accidents down to a level of about one in seven in the case of fashion, cultural events, sports (when both men and women are counted), wedding announcements, and puzzles.

The broader the interest in a particular kind of content, the more intense that interest is also likely to be. That is, we can consider what proportion of stories in a particular content category are rated as being either somewhat or very interesting. To evaluate the intensity of interest, we can consider what proportion the very interested represent of all those who consider an item to be of at least some interest. The two go together.

The average item was ranked somewhat lower in importance than it was in interest. The third column in the table shows that 18 percent were rated as very important to the respondent personally, 26 percent as having some importance, and 34 percent as having no importance at all. Twenty-two percent were not rated on importance.

Interest and importance tend to be related, but by no means perfectly. (There was a 0.61 Spearman rank order correlation between the two measures.) Sixty-one percent of the items that were rated very interesting were also rated very important. Of items rated somewhat interesting, 61 percent were also rated as somewhat important. Of those rated as not at all interesting, 75 percent were rated not at all important. Similarly 85 percent of the items that were not rated on interest were also not rated in importance.

A prime concern of anyone concerned with increasing the frequency of newspaper readership is the possibility of modifying the mix of content to meet the needs of people who are not now reading the paper on a regular daily basis. Sixty-six percent of the public report reading the newspaper on at least four of the last five weekdays. These frequent readers may be compared with the less frequent readers, which class includes occasional readers and the 8 percent who have not read a daily paper in the last five weekdays or a Sunday paper on the last four Sundays. The infrequent readers greatly resemble the frequent readers in their levels of interest in specific kinds of subject matter. For many kinds of content, there is no difference at all. There is no type of content that is much more appealing to infrequent readers than to frequent ones.[5]

How do the findings of the national survey gibe with editors' expectations? Before answering that question, one observation is necessary: nineteenth-century American newspapers served audiences segmented along social class or political lines. With diminished competition, all but a few papers today must seek to win acceptance from their entire communities, offering something to everyone. The editors' task is to balance the heterogeneous needs of their many constituencies. A newspaper that contained only content of maximum general interest would probably be remarkably unsuccessful, for it would fail to meet the concerns of the assorted minorities who make up its readership. This premise may always have been correct, but it acquires special meaning in an era when the average half-hour television newscast covers only 10 percent of the stories that the typical newspaper carries.

The content of the newspaper is like a mosaic, and the individual pieces are meaningless unless they are seen as part of a pattern. The national survey found that there is no type of content in which every item is either of universal interest or of no interest to any one. And average levels of interest in a particular category of content can be deceptive. Consider, for example, the fact that the average item of sports news attracts at least some interest from only two readers in five. This last surprising result reflects the fact that the percentages are based on both men and women; this fact also accounts for the comparatively low readership of society news. A reader may be highly interested in the popular sport of the season and be uninterested in a great many other sports items that newspapers routinely cover.

Similarly there is a wide range of interest among different kinds of local news and among different kinds of world and national news. Where interest in a particular kind of news falls below average, it is usually obvious that it has a limited constituency. Educational news is an example. But for that constituency of pupils, their parents, and teachers, the school news may be of vital concern, and an edition would be foolish to minimize its value.

259

The Changing Importance of Local News

A key editorial tenet appears to be that a good paper reflects the work and effort of its own staff and is produced for its own community with a minimum of canned or boilerplate material. This gives rise to the further assumption that a good paper will carry a large proportion of local news, since that is the kind of copy that a newspaper's own staff is likely to generate. As we have noted, editors rank emphasis on local news high in reader interest as well. Few individual newspapers can afford the luxury of a Washington bureau, and only a handful have foreign correspondents. The ascendant power of television network news has led many editors to concentrate on local coverage, where the newspaper's preeminence is rarely challenged.

According to the editors, about half of the copy in their papers is staff written, somewhat less than the ideal proportion. Of the straight news items measured in the national survey, about three out of five were local in content and the remainder were general.

Still among the public the average item of local news has slightly fewer people who say they are interested in it, or very interested in it, than the average item of general (national or international) news. This runs counter to what was found in the editors' survey, and there may be a number of explanations. (1) Perhaps television news has steadily intensified public interest in the major national and international issues and news personalities. They are vivid, familiar, and meaningful to the average person in a way that was not true in the past. (2) In today's mobile society, people are more cosmopolitan and less parochial in orientation. They feel less rooted in their local communities and more closely connected to others with similar occupational or avocational interests in other parts of the country. (3) Over half of the metropolitan population now lives in suburban areas rather than in the central cities where big newspapers are published. American cities lost 8 percent of their white population between 1970 and 1977. Fewer of the metropolitan newspapers' readers live within the political jurisdiction that is a major source of its news. Local news is far more segmented than it used to be, and any particular event is likely to affect far fewer people.

Editors correctly perceive the public's concern with the big news story that is local, in contrast to events that seem remote and impersonal. But many local news stories come under the heading of minutiae. A high proportion of local news items are actually sublocal; they deal with events and people with whom the vast majority of readers can not identify. Even with regional editions, it is harder than ever for a metropolitan newspaper to give the kind of detailed coverage of neighborhood events, politics, and personalities that community weeklies cover as a matter of course.

260

News and Entertainment

The subject matter of the news is an infinitely more complicated business than it used to be. There are over twice as many sovereign countries in the world as there were thirty years ago. American government—federal, state, and local—has a budget in constant dollars over three times as big as it was then, and its structure is vastly more complex, with more different specialized agencies, all generating news. Thus vastly more news is being made in the area of public affairs: internationally, nationally, regionally, locally. Increasingly more of it is of specialized interest and requires complex background information to make it understandable. Government news involves a volatile cast of easily forgettable characters. Yet tedious as much of the news sometimes appears to be, it is, not surprisingly, the preoccupation of editors.

Editors have always wanted to meet the latest possible deadlines that their production and circulation departments could give them in order to present the very latest news. Broadcast news bulletins have eliminated the newspaper extra. In today's tangled traffic, the logistics of timely distribution are tougher than ever. The net effect may be to put more editorial emphasis on feature material as well as on news interpretation, both of which can be prepared at a more deliberate pace. The preference for features is strongest among younger people, whom newspapers are especially eager to attract as readers.

Greater use of features may also reflect newspaper editors' response to the challenge of television news. Television news on the local level makes considerable use of feature material, which can be filmed in advance. This comes off better as on-air entertainment than a talking head reeling off bulletins on fresh-breaking stories that remain unillustrated. It may well be that this has had an effect on the press. Whatever the reason, the non-news content of newspapers has recently had more visibility.

Guided by research findings interpreted to suggest the emergence of new life-styles, a number of major newspapers have introduced new sections that package utilitarian information of the kind formerly regarded as the province of specialized magazines. These sections have emerged as part of a wider process of editorial experimentation and innovation stimulated by new production technology (more flexible formatting and greater use of color, for example). In at least several successful cases, these sections have brought in enough new advertising to make possible an enlargement of the total number of pages of editorial matter. Although some critics have insisted that hard news has been reduced to make room for this kind of feature content, it is more reasonable to conclude that the main effect has been to change the overall balance of news and features in those papers.

It was noted earlier that about three-tenths of the average newshole represents features, according to what the editors report, and that they generally feel this proportion is right. (The definition of features was left to the editors' own judgment. Many features, such as political columns, undoubtedly are serious and informative in character, while many news items, such as those purveying personality gossip, are intended to be read for fun. Still it does not seem unreasonable to identify features with entertainment.) Feature or entertainment material also represents about one-eighth of the items measured in the national survey.[6] But it is hard to square the findings of that survey with the prevailing editorial assumption that entertaining features enjoy greater interest than most straight news items.

The first relevant finding is that a majority (59 percent) of the public would choose a paper entirely devoted to news rather than one which just provided a news summary and consisted mostly of entertaining features. This response might be dismissed as merely an expression of a socially acceptable attitude, yet it tells us that people hold expectations of a newspaper that go beyond their personal tastes. Because they recognize its larger social functions, they want and expect it to cover subjects that, individually, they would not normally read about.[7]

Similarly when people are asked to construct a personal newspaper from a list of subjects exclusive of general news, the formula they typically concoct for themselves gives considerable weight to informational material (like health and medical news) and rather little to pure amusements like comics or puzzles. At one time, the *New York Times* promoted circulation with the slogan, "You don't have to read it all, but it's nice to know it's all there." The survey findings suggest that this is a very genuine public sentiment.

But if these questions relate to the ideal notion of what a newspaper should be, the expressions of interest in individual items or articles provide a dispassionate measurement of public response to newspaper content as it actually is. (The classification of these items by subject matter took place during the processing of the survey results and was invisible to the respondents.)

Except for television and radio program listings, personal advice columns, and travel articles, entertainment features all score below average in reader interest. (Even when the more popular types of material just mentioned are combined with humor and gossip columns, comics, puzzles and horoscopes, and cultural and show business stories and reviews, the typical item is rated very interesting by 20 percent of the public, while the typical straight news story is rated very interesting by 31 percent.) Again it must be remembered that the minorities who follow a favorite comic strip, chess column, or concert notices may be intensely devoted to these features. Editors cannot deal with them lightly.

Editors indicate that they run entertainment features for business rather than professional reasons: to build audience rather than to enhance editorial quality. Yet much of what they run for this purpose turns out to be something less than ideally successful in achieving this objective.

Is this conclusion valid? The national survey findings can be questioned on the grounds that people distort their real feelings when they are interviewed, that they disguise their true interest in trivia, and that they claim to be interested in the subjects they ought to be interested in as good citizens. Indeed they do tend to rate articles as interesting if they consider them important. But it is hard to sustain

262

the argument that it is prestigious to admit interest in crime stories (which rate high) and déclassé to acknowledge interest in cultural reviews and events (which rate low).

When research findings contradict expert wisdom or prevailing assumptions, this does not necessarily mean that the experts are wrong. The trouble may lie with the research. This type of inconsistency is nonetheless useful to establish because it pinpoints areas of controversy for further discussion and investigation.

Editors and Research

American newspapers have maintained journalistic integrity by separating the news from the business function. The professional ethos of journalism, however vaguely defined this may be, rests on the principle of independence from commercial constraints. Still the constraints are always present, since newspapers operate within fixed limits of space more or less determined by advertising volume. To fill that space, editors must reconcile the public interest with the public's interests. This is the point at which the marketing perspective is apt to intervene, with its fundamental premise that a successful product is one designed to meet consumer desires and needs. And it is in the business office, with its concern about circulation and advertising revenues, that the marketing perspective arises.

Is it any wonder that editors have been warned to beware the market thinkers, those who abandon the traditional task of telling readers what they need to know in favor of the new philosophy of giving them what they want, or claim to want? What they claim to want is, of course, what they say in reader surveys, which have been on the scene since George Gallup started them at the *Des Moines Register* in 1932. The ascendancy of the much publicized "program doctors" in local television news has left many newspaper editors concerned about how research might be used to dictate editorial changes.[8] At the 1978 convention of the American Society of Newspaper Editors, hollow laughter greeted one speaker who suggested to his brethren that they might be replaced by the computer. His attempt at facetiousness masked a genuine anxiety. Some editors criticized our survey of their opinions as invalid apparently with the apprehension that what they rated as indicative of editorial quality could be quoted back to them as a true measure of quality.

Yet in spite of this suspicion, the same survey shows that there has never been a time when research was as widely used in the newspaper business as it is at present. And it appears to have won a high degree of acceptance from many editors. Naturally the first papers to call in the researchers have been the big ones, especially those that have failed to make circulation gains. A majority of editors on papers of over 50,000 circulation have used an outside research firm to survey their readers within the past two years; this is an overwhelming majority (83 percent) on papers of over 100,000. Even on dailies of less than 25,000, 13 percent have done reader surveys.

What is the value of this outside research? Only 6 percent find it not particularly useful; 37 percent find it very useful and 57 percent describe it as somewhat useful. The principal value of this considerable volume of research may well be that it gives editors a better understanding of who their readers are. But in the process of coming to use research, there is always the danger of overenthusiasm and overexpectation.

In consumer research, it is well understood that people cannot imagine what has not yet been invented; they can only comment on what is right or wrong with what they know and make choices among specific alternatives that are presented to them. They cannot ordinarily dream up the ideal alternatives themselves. And there is never any guarantee that they will really accept in practice what they say they want in theory. This is an important limitation to the marketing approach.

Marketers are great at identifying potential markets; they are fairly good at understanding consumer motivations; they are competent at testing proposed alternatives, but they are not exceptionally skilled at coming up with creative solutions. If they were, and in the newspaper business, they would be editors and not marketers.

The Organization of Victory

Comparable newspapers are regarded by their readers in remarkably different ways. Surveys show that high or low regard is reflected in reactions to all of the newspaper's ingredients. Subtle distinctions of style, treatment, and physical appearance may be much more significant to readers than the conventional subject matter categories of content analysis used in our national surveys. Readers seem to look at and react to newspapers as a whole rather than in terms of their component parts. They respond to the total package of what a paper represents rather than to the individual bits and pieces. The public's perception of what a newspaper is and what it stands for is inseparable from the self-image of those who produce it. This self-image is apt to be reflected throughout, in the paper's preoccupations, its writing style, its political stance.

264 In the survey of editors, those whose papers were gaining circulation and those who had failed to gain showed no visible differences either in their philosophies or their editorial practices. This does not mean that the characteristics of individual newspapers, or their guiding editorial philosophies, have no bearing on their success with readers in the marketplace. Rather it means that the effects of editorial content are extremely difficult to sort out from all of the social forces that bear on the newspaper reading habit.

The findings of the national survey tend to reinforce this conclusion. The analysis looked for differences in response to different elements of newspaper content by regular newspaper readers, occasional readers, and nonreaders. While such differences do exist, they turn out to be comparatively minor. If we were to invent an ideal newspaper to suit the interests of the people who are not reading one today, it would not be too different from the ones now being published; at the very least it would fall well within the existing range of variety.

The content of the newspapers that people buy at newsstands or from vending racks is identical with the content of the papers that are delivered by a home subscription. Yet the percentage of Americans who read a home-delivered newspaper has remained at a constant level, while the proportion reading an individually purchased copy is less than it was in 1970. Single-copy sales are concentrated in the major cities where competition has been most intense and social conditions have generally deteriorated. The inescapable conclusion is that the problems of distribution infinitely outweigh the deficiencies of content as explanations of the drop in single-copy readership.

Some years ago Nobel Prize winner Herbert Simon coined a new term that has found its place in modern econometric theory: to *satisfyce*. To satisfyce is to establish the optimum common denominator of acceptability that allows an institution to meet the competing and conflicting needs of many masters. In effect, newspaper editors do just this. They produce something less than the best product they can but one that the minimum number of people will turn away from. The danger of the marketing approach is that it makes this kind of compromise explicit. If editors have to worry in advance over how many people will read an article, they may decide not to run it at all. They become followers of public taste when they should be shaping it.

Yet it is precisely in the competitive environment that content makes a difference between success and failure. Certainly the newspapers in competitive cities tend to be more strongly differentiated in style, politics, and social class orientation than are those in markets where both a morning and an evening paper are published under the same ownership. When single-ownership papers have separate editorial leadership, their circulation, relative to the market potential, is as high as it is in competitive markets and higher than it is in cities where the two jointly owned papers are both produced by the same staff.

Thus the challenge to editors who take their social obligations seriously is perhaps greatest precisely where the circulation and business fortunes of their newspapers are most secure: where theirs is the only daily newspaper voice in town and where their constituency is the entire community rather than a particular segment of class or taste. These are the situations that foster complacency and lead to atrophy of editorial enterprise. Yet an inspection of newspapers of similar size in such cities shows an enormous variability in reader acceptance, as well as in the character and in the quality of the newspapers themselves. In part these differences arise from the histories and nature of the papers' home towns. But principally they reflect the energies and the guiding spirits of their editors.

Editors have a wide latitude of choices in handling content, if only because the activity of newspaper reading is profoundly influenced by pricing, delivery service, promotion, and civic conditions over which they have no control. Operating within this latitude of choice, editors may do better to exercise their own professional standards rather than to accept the dictates of what surveys represent to be the reader's choice. And yet they should ever keep in mind Hugh Chisholm's observation in his article, "Newspapers," in the authoritative eleventh edition of the *Encyclopedia Brittanica:* "The great journalist is he who makes the paper with which he is a success; and in days of competition the elements necessary for obtaining and keeping a hold on the public are so diverse, and the factors bearing on the financial success, the business side of the paper, are so many, that the organization of victory frequently depends on other considerations than those of its intrinsic literary excellence or sagacity of opinion, even if it cannot be wholly independent of these."

Notes

1. The actual application of our survey results to content analysis measurement is beyond the scope of this chapter.

2. Leo Bogart, "Changing News Interests and the News Media," *Public Opinion Quarterly* 32 (Winter 1968–1969): 560–574.

3. Each interviewer carried copies of the preceding day's issue of the three newspapers with the largest local circulations. A respondent who usually read one of the three was interviewed on that paper. If not, he or she was asked which of the three papers he or she would be most likely to read. Thus 73 percent of the interviews were carried out on papers selected by the respondents, whether or not they had read the particular issue. The remaining 27 percent were selected at random when the respondent was unable to express a preference.

4. The percentages very interested in different types of items turned out to be generally similar in level to recognition scores obtained in the comparable 1971 survey. In fact there was a 0.59 correlation between the two measures.

5. Infrequent readers are slightly more interested in food, religion, school news, science, health, television listings, war, and disarmament talks. They are less interested in social welfare, labor and wages, race, travel, comics, letters, political columns, taxes, and cultural news.

6. The proportions are not identical because editors in many cases may have had in mind feature articles pertaining to news subjects. For example, a personality profile on a baseball player might be considered a feature story but would have been classified under sports news in our national study.

7. This point is also supported by the disparity between the newspaper articles people rate as interesting and those they rate as important. For example, half of those who find the average sports item very interesting also rate it as not very important.

8. Research has been used to shape local television news programs exactly as it has been used for many years to evaluate entertainment programming content. The personality of the newscaster is a key determinant of what makes a television news program attractive, just as the personality of the performers is a primary ingredient in determining the attractiveness of any entertainment show. Research has been used to get newscasters to modify their speech, their form of delivery, their dress, haircuts, and makeup. It can also lead to decisions on hiring and firing. It has been used to put newscasters in uniform, change the sets on which they perform, and to set the number and length of items they use, with and without illustration. Research has suggested an emphasis on happy news and on action film clips of fires and crime scenes. All this has often made broadcast news professionals think of researchers as adversaries.

12

Changing Relationships between Publishers and Journalists: An Overview

David J. Hart

The newspaper, is a vehicle—one of several in our society—for informing, guiding, and entertaining. It therefore fulfills a public role, the social value of which is tied to our concept of democracy and the right of the public to be informed, freely and without bias or censorship. But publishing a newspaper is also a commercial undertaking and subject to the same profit-making goals as any other manufacturing venture. In addition to its public role, therefore, the newspaper is also a vehicle for making money. Within society, therefore, the press has a dual identity as an institution and an industry. The introduction of new technology and the new tensions that have arisen from it have to be seen inside the whole nexus of tensions which constitute the social system of the newspaper industry, and in terms of the primary functions of the newspaper in modern society, all of which are undergoing stress as the great technical transition proceeds.

The status of the press as a democratic institution depends upon the alertness of its journalists to current events and the freedom they have to interpret, criticize, and present their views for public scrutiny. In other words, the institutional value of the press depends on the freedom of journalists from constraint and influence by those who may have a vested political or economic interest in the fashioning of public opinion. In this sense, therefore, journalism is an industry within an industry. And the fact that newspaper journalists must practice within the framework of a commercial enterprise means that some degree of conflict between the ideological and commercial interests of the press is unavoidable. Thus, the relationship between journalist and publisher is one of caution and entails a constant search for peaceful coexistence and compromise. This is as much true in the daily contact between publishers and their editorial staff as it is collectively regarding the status of journalism as a profession and the safeguarding of its interests by journalists' unions and other forms of professional organization.

Most of the key issues of debate and negotiation between newspaper publishers and journalists stem from the journalists' desire to safeguard their editorial freedom and integrity and the publishers' concern that the journalists' desire be accommodated within the economic and political framework of the newspaper. In this respect, the policy of most European journalists' unions has been strongly influenced, though to varying extents, by three major issues: internal press freedom and the safeguarding of editorial responsibility and the right of codetermination, press concentration and its effects on the equilibrium of political opinion forming and the professional status and employment of newspaper journalists, and the implications of new editorial and production techniques.

The Division of Responsibility

A central theme in the debate concerning internal press freedom has been the delimitation of publishers' and editorial responsibility, through collective agreement or by legal definition, and the editorial right of codetermination in three basic issues: the control of mergers leading to group ownership or the establishment of policies of technical or editorial cooperation, the assignment of responsibility for editorial direction to the editorial staff of the newspaper, and the selection of editorial staff.

Publishers and journalists communicate through the chief editor and senior editorial staff of the newspaper. The chief editor is appointed by the publisher on the understanding that he shares the publisher's opinions on basic policy and is therefore usually assigned a high level of autonomy in day-to-day editorial decision making and the detailed editorial shaping of the newspaper. It is his responsibility to ensure that basic policy is adhered to but in such a way that neither he nor any journalists are called upon to write in conflict with their own principles or knowledge of the facts. Within the framework of a defined policy, therefore, the publisher must necessarily rely on the cooperation and discretion of his chief and senior editors.

269

A newspaper is controlled by the publisher because as its owner, or its owner's deputy, he is responsible for the financial position of the company and for the success of investment decisions in which large sums of private or public money may be involved. By the same token, the publisher bears the responsibility for whatever financial consequences (such as a decline in circulation or advertising income) may result if the editorial standards of the newspaper either fail to satisfy the needs of its market or threaten the credibility, and hence the sales potential, of the newspaper in the eyes of its readers.

The Question of Competence

Attempting to draw a clear dividing line between editorial and publishers' responsibility is tantamount to trying to dissociate the commercial from the editorial interests of the newspaper. To some extent this is and must be done; the concept of a free press requires this to be so. But what the protagonists of divided responsibility seemingly fail to realize is that there is no way that the two responsibilities can be fully separated that does not then replace the risk of abusive influence from an owner by that of abusive influence from within the journalists' own ranks. Given that producing a newspaper is something of a two-horse race, it is seldom the case that the two horses try to head in completely opposite directions. And if differences of opinion do arise as to which direction they should be headed in, this places still greater demands on the publisher and the editors to pull together in order to avoid collision with the rails on either side. The question is basically one of competence, and according to Johannes Binkowski, president of the German Newspaper Publishers Association, "We distinguish between three different competences, in basic rule, directions and detail."[1]

In Germany, as elsewhere, the right of the publisher to determine the basic principles and character of the newspaper is not in question. But just as it is his right to establish the basic policy of the newspaper, it is also his duty to make this policy known to his editorial staff. Neither is the right of the editor to assume responsibility for shaping the detailed editorial character of the newspaper held in question. It is mainly in the question as to whether the publisher or the editor should be responsible for direction that conflict arises.

The question of editorial direction must be resolved whenever an important news item arises, and the editorial policy and approach to it is not guided by the paper's basic policy. Generally questions of this kind are resolved by discussion and agreement between the publisher and his senior editors. But according to Binkowski, the German federations of journalists have sought a more formalistic delimitation of responsibility at this level because of a fear that "the [publishers'] right of giving directions might be misused for undermining the [editors'] competence of detail." To the publisher, on the other hand, the right of giving directions is seen as a "natural reflection of his competence of basic rule."[2]

Collective Agreement or Law?

In seeking ways to protect the independence of journalists, journalists' unions tend to agree that some form of machinery is required, but they vary in their opinions as to the form that this machinery should take. In most cases, they prefer a collective agreement between the publisher and journalist and clauses in contracts of employment relating to the declaration of the policy of the newspaper and acknowledgment of the professional codes of conduct of the journalist. In some countries, however, the call for the legislative definition and guarantee of internal press freedom has also been raised. Even the Executive Committee of the International Federation of Journalists (IFJ) recently declared "its belief in the need to write internal press freedom clauses into new contracts and, where practicable, to have any such rights guaranteed by law."[3] The problem with defining the borders of editorial responsibility legally is that any legislation must not conflict with existing rights of ownership, direction, and codetermination within private industry.

The press law that was being considered by the German Ministry of the Interior in the early 1970s would have provided for the legal division of editorial and publishing responsibility. It began as little more than a formal statement of the right of codetermination and then evolved into a more specific proposal that would have restricted publishers' rights solely to that of determining the basic policy of the newspaper, According to Binkowski, the publisher "is asked to be responsible for a product, upon the shaping of which he has no influence at all."[4]

In the German press, the question of editorial statutes and their administration by individuals whose legal title is "editorial adviser" has been hotly disputed for many years. It is not surprising that the publishers "are against editorial advisers with discretionary powers of their own. If the shop committee that represents the whole establishment has no decisive rights, how might it be possible to grant these rights to a section of the shop employees, the editors?"[5]

In a later attempt to introduce a law for the protection of the free information of opinion, all rights other than those of defining basic policy and eventually preventing publication likely to cause damage would have been assigned to the chief editor. From the publisher's point of view, such a division of responsibility caused a dilemma: since the chief editor could be dismissed only with the consent of a majority of the editorial advisers, the publisher not only relinquished his influence but also could not regain it by changing his senior editorial management.

The idea that the journalist should assume responsibility for the nature of the newspaper's policy while the publisher is confined to the commercial side of the business seems neither desirable nor realistic. Even the professional freedom of the individual journalist would seem to be better assured in a press structure that permits dialog and cooperation with the publisher rather than one in which editorial direction and detail are left to the sole discretion of a small and potentially radical group of editors.

271

The Economic Balance

The survival of the press as a democratic institution depends upon its ability to survive as an industry. For many newspapers, the balance between profit and loss is a delicate one. And during recent years, the effects of economic recession, inflation (especially regarding the price of labor and raw materials), and the stability of the advertising market have made the balance still more delicate and, for some, critical. Amalgamation and a reduction in the labor force have become the only alternatives to closure in many cases.

If the economic position of a newspaper is too weak, its existence is threatened. The publisher can consider one of three courses of action: to go out of business, to consider a redirection of its policy in order to secure a greater share of readership or advertising revenue in particular areas with greater profit potential, or to consider merger within an ownership group and thereby seek to benefit from the usually more favorable economies of large-scale production and business management.

It is generally true that, in a competitive market, larger newspapers with a well-established readership and share of advertising market are financially less vulnerable than the smaller and medium-sized newspapers. One of the conclusions that was drawn by the British Royal Commission on the Press (1961–1962) was that "within any class of competitive newspapers, the economies of large scale operation provide a natural tendency for a newspaper which already has a large circulation to flourish and attract still more readers, whilst a newspaper which has a small circulation is likely to be in difficulties. . . . the economic forces preventing the co-existence of more than a few newspapers in the class are very strong: the ones with a smaller circulation can survive only if they differentiate themselves in a way which will appeal to special types of readers and advertisers and so reduce the intensity of competition with their more powerful rivals."[6] Clearly press plurality like editorial independence, also has its roots in a sound economy.

Three main economic factors contribute to a stagnation or decline in the profitability of newspaper production and to the trend toward group ownership and other forms of press concentration: (1) fluctuations in advertising and sales revenue and the inability of individual newspapers to secure and control an adequate share of the market; (2) changes in the basic costs of newspaper production, particularly increases in the price of labor and raw materials; and (3) the introduction of new production machinery, often requiring large-scale financial investment, which may also increase profitability through technical cooperation or merger.

Publishing a newspaper is a costly business. Newspaper production is intensive in its demand for capital, labor, and materials, the price of each of which is highly sensitive to changes in the national, and to some extent even the international, economic climate. The largest item in the budget of a newspaper is payroll, which usually amounts to between 30 and 50 percent of the total costs. Next comes the cost of purchasing the newsprint. Depending on the size and circulation of the newspaper, this usually accounts for a further 20 to 30 percent of the total costs. For a multimillion circulation popular daily, the proportion can be as high as 40 percent.

A newspaper derives its main income from copy sales and advertising revenue, the proportions being decided by its circulation and the share of local advertising expenditure that it is able to control. Considering the dependence of the newspaper on advertising revenue, it is not difficult to appreciate why the economic position of a newspaper is prone to fluctuate with the status of the economy as a whole. In times of economic recession, advertising expenditure tends to stagnate, and advertisers tend to view the advertising potential of the media more critically. Whether as the result of a general economic recession or dwindling circulation, the threat of a reduction in advertising revenue to the individual newspaper is all the more marked if the newspaper is in an initially weak position in the advertising market. In times of recession, therefore, such newspapers are the first to suffer.

In most parts of Europe, the period between 1973 and 1975 proved to be critical for many newspapers. Inflation was at a high level, and newspaper advertising declined. At the same time, the cost of newsprint increased suddenly and dramatically. Throughout the 1960s, the price index of newsprint relative to other costs had tended to decline. Between 1970 and 1975, however, the price of newsprint more than doubled, and the price of labor very nearly kept pace.

The Struggle for Advertising

The structure of the British newspaper industry comprises a network of regional and local newspapers and a relatively large number of national popular and quality newspapers. Television and radio broadcasting are important advertising media, but their share of the advertising market seems to have little potential for growth and has tended to remain essentially constant. Competition for a greater share in the advertising market is within the newspaper industry itself, between the national and regional press.

According to the report issued by the Third Royal Commission on the Press in the United Kingdom, the advertising proportion of the total revenue of popular and national dailies has declined progressively since the mid-1960s. Additionally between 1969 and 1974, the proportion of the total advertising market that was controlled by the national newspaper industry showed a slight tendency to decline, while the share of advertising expenditures in the regional press showed a significant increase. According to the commission, "There has been a tendency for newspapers to specialise in different markets for readers and advertisers, and this has helped them to resist the competition from the larger selling papers."

Unlike the U.K. newspaper industry with its well-established and comprehensive national press, the German newspaper industry is very much more regionally and locally oriented. Television advertising is less well established than in some other European countries, and the time allocated for radio and television advertising is strictly controlled. Neither radio nor television caters to the needs of local or regional advertising markets.

In the FRG, competition for advertising revenue is fiercest between the newspaper and magazine publishing industries. One of the conclusions that was drawn in the Michel Report on the economic position of the press to the German Bundestag in 1967 was that "the economic situation [of the newspaper industry] is very much more dependent on the competition between newspapers and illustrated magazines than on the relatively slight competition with television advertising."[7] Following a decline in the early 1960s, the balance of advertising revenue to the newspaper and magazine publishing industries has tended to favor newspapers.

The structure of the U.S. newspaper industry provides an interesting comparison with the highly competitive situation between national magazine publishing and the predominantly regional press in the FRG and the more pronounced tripartite competition between the national and regional press and television advertising media in the United Kingdom. The U.S. newspaper industry is essentially locally and regionally based; a high proportion of newspapers—about 86 percent—have circulations of less than 50,000. Spending on newspaper advertising has continued to grow at a slightly faster rate than the general U.S. economy.[8] Between 1973 and 1976, advertising revenue increased at an average rate of about 9 percent, slightly less than twice the growth rate of advertising revenue in the German newspaper industry. According to a U.S. Department of Commerce report in 1969, "Newspaper advertising revenue today is almost as great as television, radio and magazine advertising revenue combined."[9] Because of the strong local nature of the U.S. newspaper industry and the apparent saturation of radio and television as advertising media, competition for an increased share of the advertising market is mainly with direct mail for local household coverage.

274

The Measure of Concentration

Although press concentration is a focal point of concern in political debate about the media in most countries, the discussion is often confused by the fact that neither the trend itself nor its effect on the equilibrium of political opinion forming is easy to measure. The final report of the Gunter Commission to the German Bundestag in 1967 on the effects of press concentration on the freedom of the press suggested that if the market share of a single publishing concern amounted to 20 percent of the total daily and Sunday newspaper circulation, this could be taken to constitute a "threat to the freedom of the press."[10] If the market share amounted to 40 percent, this could be regarded as an "encroachment on the freedom of the press."

Defining the effects of press concentration in terms of market share leads logically to the idea of limiting the market share of individual publishing concerns to a level at which a more favorable equilibrium for the expression of opinion is maintained, and this was indeed one of the proposals outlined in the Gunter report. The main drawback in so doing, however, is the fact that press concentration can take several forms, each with its own implications regarding the independence and diversity of the press.

It is possible to distinguish three basic types of concentration: group ownership, which results in fewer and larger publishing companies; market specialization, in which the greater proportion of a particular type of publication or a particular regional market is served by only one or very few publications; and *"publicistic" concentration,* the decline in the number of newspapers with their own "publicistic units"[11] (i.e., producers of independent editorial—particularly political editorial—content). There are many more newspaper titles than separate editorial teams.

The publicistic unit as defined here is an important indicator of multiplicity within the political sector of journalism in the national and regional press. Newspapers within the same publicistic unit can appear at least twice weekly and include current affairs features that are essentially the same in content and opinion. The only differences between newspapers within the unit may be in the presentation of local news and advertisements. In other words, it is a unit for a statistical index based solely on the presentation of political reportage and is independent of the publishing structure of the industry.[12]

Between 1954 and 1976, the number of such separate units in the German newspaper press decreased by 46.3 percent from 225 to 121, while the combined circulation of all newspapers rose from 13.4 million to 19.1 million copies. The trend toward concentration primarily affected the smaller regional newspapers and those in a less favorable economic position. The market share of the five largest newspaper concerns is currently about 45 percent. The ten largest, which together publish thirty-five titles, control about 55 percent.

275

A reduction in the number of publicistic units can come about for one of a number of reasons. If there seems little prospect of being able to rescue the ailing financial position of the company, the publisher may choose or be forced to suspend publication. He may, on the other hand, choose to merge within an ownership group or accept a direct takeover.

A more direct route toward greater political concentration is provided when newspapers lose their publicistic independence. This occurs when two or more merge under the same banner or when an editorial cooperative is formed with either another newspaper or an existing editorial cooperative. Publicistic concentration is also strengthened whenever an editorial cooperative is dissolved.

According to the 1978 report of the German government on the German press, press concentration between 1973 and 1976 continued, although at a slower rate than in previous years.[13] The number of publishing concerns was further reduced by thirty-five, bringing the total to 403 with 1,229 editorial publications. This compares with the loss of seventy-nine daily newspaper publishing concerns between 1969 and 1973. According to the same report, the decline in numbers of publicistic units was also less, falling from 124 to 119 between May 1974 and July 1978.

In France, competition between newspapers in the regional press has been reduced by two types of merger, described by Bouzinac as the horizontal type (the conclusion of advertising or editorial agreements between two or more papers) and the vertical type (in which one or more previously independent papers is absorbed by a more powerful publication group).[14] By 1967, most regional papers had concluded advertising agreements in order to resist competition from the periodicals and to withstand competition from television advertising more effectively. In some cases, agreements in the technical and editorial fields have followed advertising agreements.

A *Financial Times* commentary on the status of the Parisian press suggested that the difficulties facing the French national press have been as much due to the policy of the publishers, particularly in not having adapted to the changing needs of the French newspaper market, as to the changes that have taken place within the market itself.[15] In 1976, the 52 million population of France read fewer papers than did the 39 million population in 1945. It was suggested that the average French newspaper reader, being younger, more mobile, better educated, and more use than his predecessors to variety in the media, placed new and changing demands on the style and editorial structure of the newspaper. In the *Times's* opinion, many French metropolitan newspaper publishers have failed to realize this composition, with the result that the status of the metropolitan press has suffered while the provincial French press has grown stronger.

In the United Kingdom, there were nine national daily and seven national Sunday newspapers in 1975—one less than in 1961—with a total circulation of about 14 million copies during weekdays and about 20 million on Sundays. According to the Royal Commission, the readership in 1977 was roughly three times as large as in 1961. Competing against the nationally distributed newspapers in England and Wales are only twelve regional morning newspapers with a total circulation of less than a million copies. Along with the two London evening newspapers are 77 regional evening papers. Since 1961 nine titles have disappeared, eight of them in locations served by more than one evening newspaper. Seven of the national publishers also publish regional newspapers. Five of them, described by the Royal Commission as national chain publishers, together produce 52 daily newspapers and more than 200 weekly newspapers. As in the case of the German press, the trend toward greater press concentration is more noticeable in the reduction in the number of publishing concerns than in the number of titles. The 1961 Royal Commission on the Press recorded more than 490 independent newspaper publishers. By 1977, the number had been reduced to about 220.

In 1978, there were 1,762 daily newspapers in the United States, most of them—about 1,500—privately owned. Prior to the mid-1960s, the trend to press concentration in the U.S. newspaper industry was mainly toward local and regional concentration of press ownership. The establishment of larger national groups or chains of daily newspapers first became apparent during the 1960s. According to Raymond B. Nixon, by the end of 1975, 174 groups owned 1,038 daily newspapers.[16] In 1971 only 879 newspapers were under group ownership. The growth in number and size of national newspaper chains would seem to be due to the greater profitability and more favorable tax concessions to be gained from group ownership.

According to Jon G. Udell, "Considerable evidence supports the claim of group owners that their primary concern and control centres on efficient business management of their media enterprises, not on group editorial control . . . it is not unusual for individual dailies within a newspaper group to have very diverse editorial philosophies ranging from liberal to conservative."[17]

Concentration and Journalist Unemployment

Increasing concentration within the press brings with it the risk that increasing numbers of newspaper journalists may face with the prospect of unemployment, an unwelcome prospect to journalists' unions. With the reduction in the total number of job opportunities, displaced journalists may have considerable difficulty in finding new employment, particularly in their home area. There is also a risk that, in order to keep a position within the newspaper industry, displaced journalists might be forced, simply through lack of choice, to join a newspaper with some parts of whose policy they do not agree.

277   In an analysis of the status and causes of unemployment of journalists in the German press, it was estimated that between 1961 and 1971, 686 journalists lost their jobs as the result of concentration in one form or another.[18] Many were later able to find jobs within the industry, but few, if any, found their way into radio or television unless they had at some earlier time been connected with these sectors of the media.

The question of unemployment among journalists was also taken up in a recent government report on the status of the German press.[19] It was estimated that there were 956 unemployed journalists in Germany in September 1977, about 25 percent of whom had lost their jobs as a direct result of suspended publication, merger within an ownership group, or the establishment of some form of cooperation with another publication. The age group most affected was those under forty and not, as many had presumed, those over fifty.

New Technology

The majority of European newspapers are still using conventional hot-metal composing and stereo letterpress printing techniques, both of which have remained essentially unchanged since the beginning of the century. Many of them are well organized, profitable, and efficient from a productivity point of view. Nevertheless growing concern about the profitability of newspaper production and the general desire to avoid direct subsidy from external sources such as government has brought the need for economizing in the use of manpower and materials into sharp focus. In a well-run newspaper plant using conventional production techniques, however, the technical and organizational possibilities for further rationalization of the production process are very limited or, in most cases, exhausted. Even where further reductions in manpower may be technically feasible, union constraints often prohibit further rationalization.

During the past twenty years, the techniques and machinery of newspaper production have undergone major changes. The abandonment of the traditional hot metal technique of text composition in favor of photo composition is in the forefront of what is often referred to as the Era of New Technology. Parallel developments have taken place in most other sectors of production and administration. The introduction of computerized systems for commercial, administrative, and editorial work are all key ingredients of modern newspaper production technology. So too are the semiautomated and fully automated systems in publishing rooms, traditionally one of the most labor-intensive parts of newspaper production.

The utilization of new production and editorial techniques has progressed more rapidly in the United States than in Europe. For example, the American Newspaper Publishers Association estimated that in 1974, 84 percent of all U.S. daily newspapers were partially or wholly photocomposed, the trend being greatest among the regional newspapers. In Europe, it has been estimated that in 1977, 50 percent of all newspaper production plants were equipped with photocomposing equipment of varying degrees of sophistication, and only 7.4 percent had fully on-line composing room systems with video display terminals for input, proofreading, and correction.

The introduction of new editorial and composing room systems has been relatively unimpeded in the United States. In Europe, however,

278

new technology has become a key issue of debate and contention between publishers and the trade unions.

Since the mid-1970s, journalists' unions throughout Europe have been working on a policy for developing new technology that best fits into the framework of their national newspaper industry. There are some matters of specifically national interest, and there are also several key questions that concern unions throughout Europe:

■ The definition, and where necessary, the redefinition of job demarcation lines.

■ The right of participation in decisions about the selection and installation of new production machinery.

■ Editorial safeguards and the continued responsibility of journalists for the editorial content and presentation of the newspaper.

■ Staffing requirements, retraining, and redundancy among journalists and the more directly affected graphical workers.

■ Working conditions, wage scales, and questions related to health and safety.

Demarcation

The installation of a computerized editorial or composing room system implies a major change in the organizational structure of a newspaper plant. Insofar as many of the functions that were previously separate, associated with different skill and salary levels, and often performed by members of different unions become integrated within the computer, the traditional lines of job demarcation disappear or become less visible. From the union standpoint, therefore, demarcation is a crucial issue, going beyond the simple definition of which union does what work. It also implies the redefinition of required levels of skill and pay structure associated with them and with new tasks that may arise. The way in which these issues are dealt with and resolved depends to a very large extent on the existing in-house labor structure and division of work. It also depends on the sophistication of the system that is to be installed and the extent to which its design requires a change in labor structure. Both vary considerably from house to house, but generally the problems of demarcation are greatest among the larger newspaper.

The question of whether the journalist might actually take over the role of the compositor has never arisen although, from a purely technical point of view, the integration of on-line editorial and composing room systems makes this feasible. Without exception, journalists' unions throughout Europe adhere to the principle that the graphical workers' unions should remain in control of all work that is traditionally part of their domain. Any suggestion that now, or at some stage in the future, they might assume a broader role in the production of the newspaper tends, therefore, to be viewed with suspicion.

The major issue confronting the journalists' and graphical workers' unions is whether the traditionally defined lines of demarcation can

279

continue. This is primarily an interunion issue, but one that must be resolved in order to provide basic policy guidelines. In many countries, the lack of such a policy has been one of the major stumbling blocks to the success of union-management negotiations on the introduction of new techniques.

There seem to be two ways of considering the basic issue of demarcation. The first is essentially concerned with the task definitions of what constitutes editorial and graphical work. The role of the journalist is primarily that of a creative writer, producing and editing copy. The role of the compositor has traditionally been that of typesetting the material supplied by the editorial department and outside contributors and putting pages together under editorial supervision. This division of responsibility entails fundamental differences in the tasks of two groups. From a union standpoint, therefore, provided that these task distinctions can be maintained and provided also that the procedures involved in the direct inputting of text by journalists do not encroach upon those associated with the work of the compositor, many features of traditional task demarcation can be retained. In tackling the question of demarcation from this direction, the problem is reduced to one of defining, and where necessary redefining, the nature of editorial and graphical tasks.

The second approach is more concerned with the question of procedure. In this case, it is the basic right of journalists to input material using a VDT that becomes a central point in debate. It could be argued that, compared to a typewriter, the VDT is an integral part of a production system and that the right to operate it falls under the jurisdiction of graphical personnel. Such an agreement is very difficult to justify, however, since it fails to acknowledge that even the most integrated system serves a dual role with a clear, albeit invisible, interface between the input and editing facilities of the computer and the typographic and output facilities of the system. Once this role is acknowledged, the journalistic use of a VDT is in principle no different from the journalistic use of a typewriter.

In some countries, the joint attempts of journalists' and graphics unions to clarify the question of demarcation and to provide a national policy have been very successful. With few exceptions, these are based on task definintions, and interunion agreements of this kind have been reached in Finland, Sweden, Denmark, West Germany, and the Netherlands. The basic delineation of editorial and graphic task responsibility regarding the inputting of material is a central point in the agreement between the journalists' and the printing workers' unions in Finland, which states that "if a technical system renders direct input of editorial material possible, editorial staff may type their own creative material into the computer memory. . . . All other text fed into computer memories belongs to the printing workers' field of tasks. Texts transmitted to the editorial staff by telephone or otherwise received by it are typed by editorial staff in the first instance but feeding these texts into a computer memory is a part of printing workers' field of tasks."[20]

The question of demarcation is dealt with more explicitly in an agreement between the Swedish unions of journalists (SJF) and graphical workers (GF):

GF and SJF certify that the following tasks are to be attributed, by tradition and as per agreement, to the journalistic sphere of work: writing, editing, editorial layout work and drawings, editorial proofreading and check-reading, copy reception by telephone, photo reporting, journalistic evaluation and treatment of photos (by picture editors) and editorial filing.

The unions also agree that the following tasks are to be attributed, by tradition and as per agreement, to graphic work: preparation of finished copy and pictures, reproduction of copy and pictures directly on information carriers (such as punch tape, magnetic tape, etc.) preparations of graphic originals as well as graphic art work, preparation and reading of proof (non-editorial), preparation of repro copies, picture reproduction (photography, scanning, retouching), makeup/mounting, mounting/copying and other preparations of reproductions and print media.

Conflicts of interest may arise in situations where new technology brings graphic and journalistic tasks together. This may occur, for instance, with writing/feeding the copy on-line into VDT or other information carriers (ie. written copy simultaneously becoming graphic copy or rendering graphic copy input and/or coding superfluous) and with tele-reception/input to VDT on-line. Demarcation problems also occur in connection with proof-reading on VDT on-line editing/coding on VDT on-line, and layout/makeup on-line (pagination).[21]

But not all attempts to reach interunion accord on the question of new technology have been equally successful. In Norway, for example, the journalists' union declared itself willing to approve the editorial use of VDTs and entered into a unilateral agreement with the Newspaper Employers Federation.[22] In spite of an agreement in principle on policy between the journalists' and graphical unions, the graphical union in the end declined to sanction the agreement between the journalists and the employers, and the matter was referred to a court of arbitration. The issue at stake in this debate was the procedural right of journalists to operate a VDT in the light of existing interunion and management agreements, a right not upheld by the court. In reaching its decision, however, the court urged greater efforts on the part of the unions involved to settle their differences. This proved successful, and toward the end of 1978, both unions entered into an agreement that approved a "limited number of experiments" in newspaper plants.

There are, of course, many factors that determine the willingness of individual unions to enter into interunion policy negotiations on new technology. To the graphical unions, the introduction of new techniques and the disqualification of traditional demarcational boundaries brings with it the threat of large-scale redundancy. Other unions, however, may see an opportunity to improve their position, particularly in working conditions and salary levels. For example, the on-line use of VDTs in advertising, accounting, and other commercial departments may be

281

seen by the unions engaged in this side of the operation (clerical workers' unions, for example) as a step toward reducing existing wage differentials.

Editorial Safeguards

The union view on the question of editorial safeguards is primarily concerned with the safeguarding of editorial quality so that journalists and editors can do their jobs properly, usually taken to refer to the procedures and standards that they are at present able to maintain. Journalists are not happy with the thought that using any form of system might result in a deterioration of the editorial quality of the newspaper, either directly due to a basic inadequacy of the system as an editing tool or indirectly as the result of undesirable changes in copy handling procedure. Some journalists fear that their way of working may suffer or have to be adjusted for the convenience of a system, rather than vice versa, and are understandably reluctant to accept the whole idea of the new technology. For example, the fact that the facilities of an editorial system make it possible to dispense with proofreading, correction, and a certain amount of editing (journalists are able to spot and correct many of the errors that might otherwise have escaped detection until later) is not necessarily an advantage to journalists. On the other hand, it has been claimed that "it is a myth that reporters or feature writers are the best people to read their own copy for errors."[23]

Journalists also foresee certain practical difficulties if the introduction of a computer system is viewed as a step toward a paperless office. Even with the best-designed system, situations frequently arise in copy editing that are better coped with on paper than on screen. It does justice to neither the journalist nor the system if the use of an editorial system is viewed rigorously as a question of the old ways versus the new. Getting the best out of an editorial system means putting both to their best uses, a fact that makes it essential for those responsible for designing the system to understand fully the copy handling procedures required by journalists and editors.

The question of editorial safeguards also has a number of implications for the integrity of the individual journalist. For example, the facilities of a computer system make it possible to evaluate the productivity of each member of the editorial staff. But the right of management to exercise this form of control is challenged by all journalists' unions, a challenge that has been conceded by all.

282   New technology in which a third party can gain access to the work of a journalist once it has been edited and filed in the computer brings with it the risk that the content of a story could be tampered with in a way that was neither intended nor authorized by the journalist in question. If this were to occur and the article were to go to press, the reputation of the journalist might be jeopardized. Thus a number of ethical and copyright problems arise. To safeguard against such a possibility, some journalists' unions have emphasized the need to provide hard

copies of their articles, both for proofing and eventually as a means of self-defense.

Working Conditions, Health, and Safety

Any change in working methods or conditions that occurs as the result of technical development and the introduction of new techniques tends to be viewed by unions as an opportunity to reconsider the basic issues of working conditions, working hours, and rates of pay. The reaction of most, but not all, journalists' unions to the introduction of new editorial technology is no exception. But generally where they have arisen, claims for reduced working hours and higher rates of pay have not been due entirely to an opportunistic attitude on the part of the journalists' unions. They have been guided more by policy and strategic agreements in other sectors of the union movement and the desire to ensure parity.

There would seem to be nothing in the use of a VDT system—for example, greater difficulty of working or greater work load—that would justify shorter working hours or higher pay. But the contention that working with a visual display terminal might result in some form of health risk to its operator has complicated the issue and has led to a number of claims for reduced working hours at the VDT and for frequent and (in comparison to the norm) quite long rest pauses.

The suspicion that a VDT may emit some form of harmful radiation and that prolonged work with it may result in some form of damage to the eyes has understandably caused consternation among many who are either using or are faced with the prospect of having to use one. The difficulties that this has created in union-management negotiations, not only in the newspaper industry, but in industry in general, have stemmed from a lack of sufficient knowledge with which to judge whether a VDT does in fact pose a threat of this kind. During the past few years, therefore, a great deal of research has been undertaken to determine if, and if so under what conditions, working with a VDT poses a health risk to operators. Fortunately there is no evidence to suggest that there is anything inherently harmful in the use of a VDT, although certain short-term types of discomfort can occur if insufficient attention is paid to the design of the environment in which a VDT is to be used.[24] From the point of view of ensuring the comfort and well-being of a VDT operator, therefore, the problems of installing a computer system boil down to not what work is done but the way that it is performed.

283

Concern about the health and safety of VDT operators has led to a variety of demands from European journalists' unions, the most contentious of which has been that of restricting the amount of time in each day that a journalist may work with a VDT in order to safeguard against the risk of damage to eyesight. This was a major point of contest in the struggle between the German printing unions and employers prior to the signing of the collective agreement in 1978.[25] It appeared then, and subsequent research has not proved otherwise, that there was no plausible ground on which a claim such as this—in this case for a maximum of four hours—should be conceded, and even less so in the case of journalists, most of whom spend relatively little time working with the VDT and then usually in brief though intense periods during which more time is spent looking at the keyboard than at the screen. Very few journalists possess the skills of a trained typist with the ability to touch type. Nevertheless, in acknowledging that some types of VDT task are more arduous than others, a compromise agreement was reached in the German contract to the effect that "those activities requiring continual visual contact with a VDT screen for more than four consecutive hours must be provided with pauses to provide rest for the eyes, either five minutes every hour or fifteen minutes every two hours."

In a recent contest in the Australian newspaper press, a court of arbitration refused a claim from the journalists' union that journalists working with VDTs should be entitled to a fifteen-minute break every two hours, saying, among other things, that "the journalist works to a flexible routine with an absence of regimentation. There are some busy shifts involving close attention over long periods, but in such circumstances the journalist normally takes his own informal breaks to relieve the strain at times which he finds to be suitable."[26] At the same time, however, the court gave the journalists' union leave to appeal against the ruling subject to fresh evidence.

The German contract also includes an agreement to the effect that personnel required to work with a VDT should undergo ophthalmic examinations prior to starting work with VDTs and at yearly intervals thereafter. The need for some form of ophthalmological supervision has been a major point of concern to most European unions, and a procedure has recently been developed for this purpose. In conceding the need for a medical examination of this kind, however, the question naturally arises as to what course of action should be taken in respect of those who, for proven medical reasons, are deemed unfit to work with a VDT. In most agreements, including the German contract, the point is conceded that if for medical or any other testifiable reason any individual journalists find it intolerable to work with a VDT, they will not be forced to do so.

Newspaper management is severely handicapped in any contest with the trade unions. Disputes that lead to a stoppage of production have a much greater impact than in most other manufacturing industries simply because a stoppage cannot be prepared for in advance. Neither can the loss of revenue and credibility in the eyes of the public that is caused by repeated strikes be made up for later. For this reason, there has always existed a strong need for a well-defined and authoritative machinery for negotiation and the settlement of dispute at local and national levels within the newspaper industry. The introduction of new production techniques and the demarcational issues that stem from it

284

have increased the need for such a machinery and for improved lines of communication and authority.

Procedures for negotiation and the settlement of disputes are dealt with in most collective agreements between individual unions and employers' federations. In practice, however, the effectiveness of such a machinery depends on the authority vested in the senior executives of the labor and publishers' organizations and the extent to which this authority is respected at local level. One of the biggest hindrances to the improvement of union-management relations in some countries is the defiance of official union policy at house or local level. Lines of communication and authority within some unions are too segmented to provide sufficient safeguards against unofficial action. In cases such as this, the managment of a newspaper is placed in a very difficult bargaining position.

Perhaps the biggest challenge that faces the newspaper industry in many parts of Europe is the need to develop better and more authoritative lines of communication between unions and management and also within the trade unions. At a time when the newspaper industry, like so many others, is undergoing a technical upheaval that requires clearheadedness on the part of management and unions alike, there is an obvious need for dialogue. Even though improved communications will not make the business of negotiation any the less rugged, no other single step can contribute so much to improved labor relations within the industry.

Notes

1. J. Binkowski, *Fiej-Bulletin,* 89 (1971):34–41.

2. Ibid.

3. International Federation of Journalist, Executive Committee, May 1975.

4. J. Binkowski, *Fiej-Bulletin* 94 (1972):19–25.

5. J. Binkowski, *Fiej-Bulletin* 89 (1971):34–41.

6. Royal Commission on the Press, 1961–1962 (Shawcross Commission), Cmnd. 1811 (London: Her Majesty's Stationery Office, 1962).

7. *Bericht der Kommission zur Untersuchung der Wettbewerbsgleichheit von Presse, Funk, Fernsehen und Film* (Bonn: Michel, 1967).

8. Jon G. Udell, *The Economics of the American Newspaper* (New York: Hastings House, 1978).

9. U.S. Department of Commerce, Business and Defense Services Administration, *U.S. Industrial Outlook* (Washington, D.C.: Government Printing Office, 1969).

10. *Bericht der Kommission zur Untersuchung der Gefahrdung der wirtsschaftlichen Existenz von Presseunternehmen und der Folgen der Konzentration fur die Meinungsfreiheit in der Bundesrepublik* (Bonn: Gunter, 1967).

11. *'Publizistische Einheiten.'*

12. W. J. Schutz, *Media Perspektiven* 5 (1976).

13. *Bericht der Bundesregierung über die Lage von Presse und Rundfunk in der Bundesrepublik Deutschland* (Bonn, 1978).

14. R. Bouzinac, FIEJ Congress (Tel Aviv, 1967).

15. *London Financial Times,* July 13, 1976.

16. Allan Wells, ed., *Trends in U.S. Newspaper Ownership: Concentration in Competition, Mass Media and Society,* 2d ed. (Palo Alto, Calif.: Mayfield Publishing Co., 1975).

17. Udell, *Economics.*

18. W. R. Langenbucher, O. B. Roegele, and F. Schumacher, *Pressekonzentration und Journalistenfreiheit, AfK-Studien* (Berlin, 1976), vol. 4.

19. *Bericht der Bundesregierung über die Lage von Presse und Rundfunk in der Bundesrepublik Deutschland* (Bonn, 1978).

20. The agreement between the unions of journalists and printing workers in Finland, "Recommendations on the Adaptation Principles for New Technology," was signed in May 1976.

21. "Cooperation Agreement between the Union of Graphical Workers and the Swedish Union of Journalists (June 1977).

22. "Agreement between the Norwegian Union of Journalists and the Newspaper Employers Federation" (April 1975).

23. *Journalists and New Technology* (London: National Union of Journalists, 1977).

24. D. J. Hart et al., *The Human Aspects of Working with Visual Display Terminals* (Darmstadt: 1979); A. Cakir et al., *Anpassung von Bildschirmarbeitsplatzen an die physische und psychische Funktionsweise des Menschen* (Bonn: Bericht des Bundesministeriums fur Arbeit und Sozialordnung, 1978).

25. *Tarifvertrag uber Einfuhrung und Anwendung rechnergesteuerter Textsysteme, BVD, BDZV, VDZ, IDP, DAG, DJV, EHBV* (Bonn, 1978).

26. Mr. Justice Alley, Australian Conciliation and Arbitration Commission, in *AJA* v. *John Fairfax & Sons Ltd.* (July 1978).

13

The Political Economy of the Human-Interest Story

James Curran, Angus Douglas, and Garry Whannel

Studies of the British press have been characterized by an incomplete, partial approach to the nature of the papers being examined. Students of the British press (save for those engaged in the mass culture debate) have tended to focus almost exclusively on its explicit political content.[1] News and current affairs coverage has been seen as the solid substance, the core of the press, and hence the part of the newspaper that reveals its nature and significance most clearly. Insofar as acknowledgment is given to entertainment features in the press, this tends to be grudging and dismissive, as if such content detracts from the central political role and purpose of the press.

This selective view of the press reflects the powerful and enduring influence of classical liberal political theory, which conceives of the newspaper primarily as a political medium with important functions within a liberal democracy. This has provided the frame of reference of all major enquiries into the British press, which have evaluated the press primarily in terms of its functioning within the political system and assessed its performance almost exclusively in terms of its political context.[2] Classical liberal theory has also provided the dominant framework of analysis in press history in which newspapers are characteristically portrayed as channels of political information and ideas, a check on the executive, a fourth estate, and so on within a liberal analytic perspective.[3] Even in sociological research into the British press, classical liberal theory (sometimes updated in the form of functional theory) has had a remarkably tenacious hold. Many studies portray the press simply as a system of political communication and tacitly portray its overtly political content as its sole constitutive element.[4]

This conventional perspective of the press as a political agency, common to historical, sociological, and political analysis, is seriously misleading and ignores the basic reality of the press as an entertainment industry subject to the economic pressures of commodity production for the mass market. It provides a totally misleading impression of what is published in newspapers and what people actually read. And it sometimes implies a false dichotomy between current affairs coverage and entertainment by representing one as being politically significant and the other as being mere diversion. As a consequence of this imagined dichotomy, the ideological significance of what most people read in newspapers most of the time has been largely ignored.

This study is intended to offer an alternative perspective. It will attempt to put the academic preoccupation with the current affairs coverage of the press into proportion by examining the allocation of space in national newspapers during the last fifty years as well as survey evidence about what people have read in newspapers; it will consider the economic forces that have shaped the editorial content of the press during this period; and it will attempt to assess, in a contemporary context, the wider significance of non-current-affairs coverage in the press, which tends to be overlooked or discounted. This is necessarily an exploratory study, and we hope it will indicate the need for a shift in orientation in British press research.

The Interwar Period

Economic Pressures of the Mass Market

During the interwar period, there was an important change in the content and market orientation of an important section of the British popular press, largely brought about by the interplay of economic forces operating within the press industry. The interwar national press achieved large economies of scale as a result of its high fixed costs in relation to variable costs.[5] Heavy expenditure was incurred in making the first copy irrespective of the number of copies produced. The more copies that were sold, therefore, the cheaper each copy cost, since heavy fixed costs could be spread over more copies. There were also a number of other costs that did not rise proportionately in relation to increased output. There was thus a strong economic incentive for national publishers to adopt editorial strategies maximizing circulation in order to reduce unit costs.

This economic incentive was powerfully reinforced by the non-price-competitive strategies adopted by leading publishers during the interwar period. A 41 percent increase in national newspaper circulation between 1920 and 1941 produced substantial increases in scale economies, accruing most to publishers who gained the biggest increases in circulation.[6] There was also a massive increase in press

289

advertising, which benefited some papers disproportionately.[7] The increased resources, generated by larger advertising receipts and scale economies, were largely reinvested by leading publishers into heavier editorial expenditure (reflected in a higher level of editorial load in relation to advertising), larger and better-paid staffs, better terms to distributors and, above all, massive promotion in a circulation war that became notorious.

Less successful competitors were forced to follow suit by spending more, if on a more modest basis, in order to stay competitive. The resulting increase in costs contributed to the closure of eight national newspapers between 1921 and 1939 and squeezed even the most successful papers. The *Daily Herald,* for instance, was running at a loss of £10,000 to £20,000 a week when it was the largest-circulation daily newspaper in the world in 1933.[8] The *Daily Express,* when it overtook the *Daily Herald* to become the top selling daily, was nonetheless making only an estimated £150,000 profit on a turnover of £10.2 million in 1936 and 1937, even though this was a good year for advertising.[9]

This enormous increase in costs had the effect of exerting strong pressure on popular newspaper publishers to universalize their papers' appeal. This pressure was combined with opportunity to expand into three overlapping markets that had not been fully exploited, particularly by national daily publishers. In the early 1920s, the circulation of the London-based national dailies was concentrated very heavily in the home counties, the south, and, to a lesser extent, the midlands.[10] Their readership among women was very much lower than among men.[11] And their penetration of the working-class market was very much less than among the middle and upper classes.[12] Northern and Celtic regions, housewives, and the working class thus represented the most accessible markets along with young people for recruiting new readers.

Market opportunity and cost pressure coincided with changes in the needs and priorities of advertisers, a crucial point since newspapers were sold at prices that did not cover costs.[13] The difference between sales returns and costs, and any surplus, was made up by advertising receipts. The pattern of advertising patronage thus determined which markets it was profitable to expand into.

The continued development of large-scale enterprise and brand marketing gave rise to continuing substantial increases in national advertising during the interwar period, further reinforcing advertisers' patronage of media that had a nationwide distribution and were (because of scale economies) able to undercut the regional press. There were thus growing advertising rewards for the achievement of a more extensive and evenly distributed national circulation.

290

There was also a major expansion in the home market, with total consumer expenditure growing (at constant 1938 prices) from £3,343 million in 1920 to £4,416 million in 1939.[14] This very large increase reflected not merely a growth in the size of the domestic market but, among other factors, a significant increase in consumption by some sections of the working class, particularly during the 1930s.[15] It was the growth in working-class purchasing power (notwithstanding significant differences between regions, occupations, and, in terms of discretionary spending, age) that partly accounted for a large increase in consumption of certain product categories, such as women's clothes, motorbikes, furnishings, and cosmetics.[16] The effect of this growth in consumption was to upgrade the advertising value of media penetrating working-class markets and consequently to reinforce the attraction to publishers of expanding circulation among the working class.

The third major change in marketing during this period was the development of new techniques of market investigation. In the early 1920s, market study of consumer purchasing behavior and attitudes was extremely primitive, being based largely on sales records, unsystematic sounding of opinion from a small number of consumers, and reports from retailers and commercial salesmen.[17] The development of modern market research during the late 1920s and early 1930s had the effect of stressing the importance of women as consumers. The first British textbook on market research stressed, for instance, that "women purchase 80% of the goods sold in retail shops in the country."[18] This reorientation toward the market resulted in a reclassification of newspaper audiences. Whereas before readership had been defined in official readership surveys in terms of households, in 1939 readers were classified in terms of their sex, an innovation introduced earlier by the more progressive agencies.[19] This change was symptomatic of the increased importance given by advertisers to reaching women, a shift mirrored in the promotional literature of newspapers in the 1930s.[20]

There were thus mounting advertising incentives to expand circulation in certain ways. These incentives were tempered, however, by continuing inequalities of wealth and purchasing power. Although there were powerful economic inducements to recruit more working-class readers and, in particular, more working-class women readers, there was a strong disincentive to become an exclusively working-class newspaper. This was because the working class constituted a less affluent market and generated less advertising revenue per copy than the middle class. Advertising literature throughout the interwar period strongly emphasized that the low-paid were able to buy only a limited range of products.[21] Indeed official readership surveys actually excluded the poor from their samples until 1936 as being not worth bothering about.[22] The result of this commercially inspired discrimination was that popular newspapers that had a strong working-class appeal received much less advertising revenue than did papers with a more middle-class readership. For instance, the *Daily Mail,* which had a middle-market readership, obtained in 1936 just over double the advertising revenue per copy of the unprofitable *Daily Herald,* with an overwhelmingly working-class readership.[23] This meant that it was commercially inadvisable for a paper to become too closely identified with a working-class audience. Significantly, when the *Daily Mirror* moved gradually downmarket during the late 1930s, it published reassuring advertisements in the trade press that it was a good medium for reaching the wealthiest 7 percent of the population.[24]

There were thus strong economic pressures on popular publishers to move into the middle ground by building bigger but less differentiated audiences through editorial strategies that appealed equally to men and women, that were attractive to families in all regions of the country, and that appealed to people of all social classes.[25] In developing strategies for recruiting new readers, publishers also had to take care not to alienate their traditional readers. This also tended to encourage a middle-market orientation among papers that had been situated at the upper end of the mass market.

These commercial pressures did not necessarily conflict with non-revenue goals within newspaper organizations catering for the mass market. Tunstall has argued, in a different context, that "a coalition audience goal" tends to emerge as the dominant goal within news organizations since it contains elements to which all can assent. During the interwar period, audience maximization within certain parameters offered a way of increasing both sales and advertising revenue and, at the same time, of fulfilling the nonrevenue goals of political influence and prestige. Leading publishers and editors of popular papers in the interwar period clearly regarded large circulations as an indicator both of their political influence and, in a more intangible sense, of their success.[26]

The impact of these economic pressures can be briefly illustrated in relation to the relaunch of the *Daily Mirror* between 1933 and 1936, which is rightly regarded as a major landmark in popular journalism. The *Daily Mirror* during the early 1930s was a middle-market paper with a double liability: its circulation was steadily declining in the face of intensified competition, and it received less advertising revenue per copy than any daily paper apart from the *Daily Sketch* (another tabloid), partly because many advertisers believed that illustrated papers received only limited attention from readers. The *Daily Mirror* was consequently denied the advertising bounty that its middle-market readership would normally command. Faced with the prospect of closure, the *Daily Mirror* was deliberately pointed downmarket in an attempt to recruit new readers. The principal target market was young working women (in the words of one of the journalists closely involved in the change, "Working girls, hundreds of thousands of them working over typewriters and ledgers and reading in many cases nothing more enlightening than Peg's Paper.")[27] and young working people generally, although care was also taken not to alienate too many traditional *Mirror* readers. The marketing strategy, according to the advertising director, was decisively influenced by an assessment of where market opportunities were greatest and what advertisers wanted.[28] The guiding principle of the paper's relaunch was, in the words of one of its best-known journalists, to fill the paper with "items of maximum interest to the maximum number of people." This orientation was to produce a very different sort of daily newspaper.

Different pressures operated on "quality" papers. Their prosperity depended upon the receipt of a large volume of advertising, charged at very high rates, based on their ability to deliver elite markets without dilution by nonelite readers. As one advertising consultant succinctly put it, "A publication may have a small circulation, but its readers may be of so select a class that every one of them is a probable customer for certain advertisers. If they used a more popular paper, they would have to pay for addressing an enormous preponderance of useless readers. The high rates, relative to sale . . . are considered to be justified by their select circulation.[29] Economic pressures thus encouraged quality papers to increase their current type of audience and positively discouraged them from attracting readers that advertisers aiming at elite markets did not want to reach. This economic deterrent against the indiscriminate maximization of audiences complemented the commitment of many people working on quality newspapers to prestige goals incompatible with editorial strategies designed to build mass circulations.[30]

These very different sets of pressures on the popular and the quality press were crucial in contributing to cultural polarization between the popular and the quality press. Popular newspapers came under mounting pressure to maximize circulation by increasing features that were of universal appeal to larger and less differentiated audiences. At the same time, quality newspapers were economically restrained by advertising pressure from expanding features that would attract large audiences that advertisers did not want. But while advertising pressure induced an increasingly divergent target definition of audiences between quality and popular papers, there was one sense in which it encouraged a growing convergence. The growth of press advertising during the interwar period generated further pressure on publishers to segregate their readers into groups that could be readily identified and picked out by specialist advertisers and to provide an editorial environment that would enhance the sale of the products or services being advertised.[31] This pressure was greatest on the quality press since quality publishers relied more heavily on advertising.

Pattern of Consumer Demand

Market research commissioned by leading publishers provides an interesting insight into the development of editorial planning strategies during the interwar period, for they reveal what features different groups among the newspaper reading public read most, thereby indicating the editorial implications of maximizing circulation among different segments of the newspaper market.

Market research was first commissioned by leading publishers on a significant scale in the early 1930s. Major studies into what people read, using research techniques pioneered in the United States, were commissioned, among others, by three major publishing groups between 1932 and 1934.[32] Only one of these probably numerous reports[33] has survived; it is a survey, based on a sample of twenty-thousand respondents, of what people read in national daily and London evening papers in 1933 conducted by the London Press Exchange for the *News Chronicle*. Its findings largely vindicate the intuitive assessments of how best to maximize circulations made by a number of leading popular journalists during the interwar period.

The survey shows that certain categories of news, most notably human-interest stories, and certain categories of features, most notably letters, serials, and gossip articles, had above-average appeal to the readers of the popular press, and international politics, industry and commerce, sports, and foreign politics had below-average appeal (table 13.1, appendix). But averages conceal important differences among subgroups of readers. For instance, parliamentary and domestic political reports had a strong appeal among a significant section of male readers, but they attained only an average complete readership score because of their weaker appeal to women. The principal strength of all the high-ranking categories of editorial content—news stories about accidents, crime, divorce, calamities, personal gossip and gossip features about personalities, serials, and letters—is that they were of universal appeal: they transcended differences between sex and class.[34]

The amount of space that was devoted to this common-denominator material enormously increased during the interwar period in the paper that symbolized the new journalism, the *Daily Mirror* (table 13.2). The categories employed by the first Royal Commission on the Press in its content analysis of two popular daily papers (*Daily Mirror* and *Daily Mail*) are not strictly comparable with the categories used in the London Press Exchange survey, but it is clear from the commission's content analysis that there was a massive and disproportionate increase in human-interest stories devoted to accidents, crime, and divorce, as well as in letters and gossip features in the *Daily Mirror*. The trend was very much less pronounced, however, in the case of the *Daily Mail*. It had been a pioneer at the turn of the century in popularizing the national daily press by greatly increasing human-interest material but by the 1930s had been superseded by a new and still more commercially oriented innovator in the form of the *Daily Mirror*. Indeed the space devoted by the *Daily Mail* to some categories of human-interest story with a universal appeal (such as accidents) actually declined as a proportion of editorial space, between 1927 and 1937, though this was offset by increases in the proportion given to other content with a wide appeal (such as social and gossip columns).

This disproportionate increase in common-denominator material, particularly in the *Daily Mirror,* was accompanied by an increase in news and feature material with a particularly strong appeal to certain subgroups whose importance could not be ignored, particularly in view of the mounting economic pressure to attract women readers, working-class readers, and minorities who were particularly attractive to advertisers. This is reflected in the disproportionate growth of women's features in the *Daily Mirror*, the disproportionate increase in sports coverage with a particularly strong appeal to working-class men, the rapid growth of financial coverage for a small minority that advertisers particularly wanted to reach, and the growth of both minority and common-denominator features that were included in the commission's omnibus categories of "other features" (such as radio listings, obituaries, and horoscopes) and "arts and entertainment."

In seeking to maximize circulation, popular newspaper publishers were also forced to reconcile regional differences.[35] This was achieved, in the case of the *Daily Mail*, by establishing a northern edition produced in Manchester as early as 1900. This precedent was followed by eight national newspapers during the interwar period, which established regional production centers in Manchester, Glasgow, or Leeds.[36]

The pursuit of bigger and less differentiated audiences was achieved at a price. The expansion of common-denominator material and of editorial content aimed at selected subgroups occurred largely at the expense of public-affairs coverage (table 13.3). The *Daily Mail* and the *Daily Mirror*, taken as representative by the first press commission of the two basic types of popular national daily, reduced coverage of political, social, and economic affairs during the interwar period. Most strikingly, the *Daily Mirror* almost halved its public-affairs coverage as a proportion of space in 1937 compared with 1927.[37]

There was no change in the content of the *Times* comparable to that in the *Daily Mail* and *Daily Mirror* between 1927 and 1937. Although there was a small reduction in the proportion of its space given to public affairs, this was largely due to a big expansion of its financial coverage linked to the growth of financial advertising.[38] This contrast between the development of representative popular and quality dailies reflects the divergent pressure exerted by advertising.

The extent to which this growing difference between quality and popular journalism was the product of economic forces is underlined by the pattern of reader interest in the quality press. The most read items in the quality dailies in 1933 were news stories about crime and divorce. There is a similarity in news items most and least read in the quality daily press with those in the popular daily press (table 13.4): court and divorce news, parliamentary reports, and government policy articles had the highest readership, followed by international politics, gossip, and other foreign news and sports. The trailing categories were foreign politics and industry and commerce. It should be borne in mind, however, that a comparison is being made between average readership of different quantities of material. Publishers of quality papers did not greatly expand features with a common-denominator appeal at the expense of public-affairs coverage, both for reasons of personal commitment and because it would have meant destroying the economic base of the quality press, its utility to advertisers as a means of reaching specialized, wealthy audiences.

The consequences of this increased polarization between popular and quality papers are illustrated in table 13.5. By 1937 the *Daily Mirror* devoted only 8 percent of its total editorial space to political, social, and economic affairs—less than half the proportion of the much larger *Times*. The *Daily Mirror*'s sports coverage was over double that of its public-affairs coverage; its other news, consisting mainly of human-interest stories, also dwarfed its coverage of current affairs. A new style of journalism had developed, remarkable not so much (as its architects now proclaim[39]) for its vaguely left-wing politics as for the relative lack of attention it gave to politics in any form. A new commodity had been processed for the mass market with the widest possible appeal to the widest possible audience, extending the trend initiated in the national daily press by the *Daily Mail* at the turn of the century.

The Easing of Competitive Pressures in the 1940s

During the 1940s, the balance of content in the popular press was transformed. Between 1936 and 1946, the proportion of space devoted to news and comment about public affairs doubled or nearly doubled in the majority of popular papers in our sample.[40] Public-affairs coverage increased to constitute more than a third of editorial space in three out of four national dailies in our sample of popular dailies and accounted for a quarter or more of the editorial space of the three popular Sunday papers that were examined. Although there were also substantial increases in the proportion of space given over to current affairs in the *Daily Telegraph* and the *Observer,* the two quality papers in our sample, the contrast between the human-interest-oriented popular press and the current-affairs-oriented quality press was substantially reduced. The extent of this conversion of the popular press was, however, uneven: three papers (*Daily Mirror, People,* and *Sunday Pictorial*) switched their emphasis to current affairs to a smaller extent than did their rivals. Human-interest news and sports coverage, both with a large circulation appeal, held their own in most popular papers. The relative shift to current-affairs coverage was largely at the expense of human-interest features (with a reduction of photos), women's, consumer, financial, arts, and entertainment features (table 13.6).

296

The main cause of this shift was newsprint rationing, which was first introduced in 1939. Newsprint controls caused the editorial content of popular newspapers to be only about a third of their size in 1946 compared with ten years before. The limitations of space encouraged a shift to current-affairs coverage at the expense of feature material at a time when major events at home and abroad called for detailed news reports and analysis.

The change in the balance of newspaper content clearly also reflected the easing of competitive pressures in the mass market. The reduction in the size of newspapers significantly reduced newspapers' costs. Indeed the total costs of national daily and London evening newspapers fell from £19,808,000 in 1937 to £17,274,000 in 1946, notwithstanding the increase in aggregate circulation during this period.[41] This cost saving resulted in what the Royal Commission on the Press of 1947–1949 called "guaranteed prosperity"[42] since it was not accompanied by a reduction in prices charged to the public. The threat of closure, which had galvanized the management of the *Daily Mirror,* for instance, into a relaunch[43] and which had prompted a number of desperate circulation-hunting editorial strategies during the interwar period, was lifted. All national newspapers (with the possible exception of the communist *Daily Worker*) made a profit. The level of profitability was also very much higher than before the war.[44] The economic incentive to maximize circulation among popular newspaper publishers was consequently greatly reduced.

Publishers also had no way of gauging public response in the normal way by a rise or fall in circulation returns, since newspaper circulations were pegged for much of the 1940s by newsprint restrictions. They were thus insulated—psychologically as well as economically—from the consequences of pursuing the editorial strategies that they did. Even when a brief spell of free sale was permitted from September 1946 through February 1947, the effect of free competition was cushioned to some extent by extremely buoyant demand. The press had recruited a substantial number of new readers during the war, and public demand was further inflated by the reduced size of newspapers, which led some households to compensate by buying more newspaper titles.[45] During the period of free sale, by far the largest gains among our sample of papers were made by the three papers (*Daily Mirror, Sunday Pictorial,* and *People*) that increased their current-affairs coverage least. They increased their circulation by more than a million copies each in 1946 and 1947. But these massive increases were not made at the expense of their rivals, all of which made modest gains in a rapidly expanding market.[46]

Another unintended consequence of government economic controls was to reduce competition for advertising. The reduction in costs reduced newspapers' need for advertising; two mass circulation national newspapers even made a profit on their sales alone in 1946.[47] Official limits were also imposed on the amount of advertising that could be carried in newspapers between 1942 and 1946, and the effect of these limitations was further reinforced by newsprint rationing. The resulting space shortage meant that most national newspaper publishers had more applications for advertising than they could accept.[48] This temporary emancipation from advertising pressure had important consequences that our content categories were not designed to identify. For instance, it enabled the *Daily Mirror* to become a much more working-class and radical tabloid, without fear of the consequences in terms of lost advertising revenue.[49] In terms of space allocation, however, its most important effect was perhaps to reduce advertising sponsorship, editorial matter linked by topic or subject to advertising on the same or opposite page. The decline of advertising sponsorship in a space sellers' market led to a marked reduction in the proportion of space taken up by sponsored features, most notably city and consumer features (table 13.7).

It is difficult to assess whether changes in space allocation reflected (as well as affected) changes in reading behavior. A study by Mass-Observation relating to this period uses methodology so inadequate that it provides a totally unreliable guide.[50] A series of studies conducted by Odhams into what people read in the *Daily Herald* between 1947 and 1950 uses slightly different techniques and a much smaller sample of stories than did the *News Chronicle* survey of 1933 and is therefore not strictly comparable.[51] It does not suggest, however, a significant change in what people read by comparison with the 1930s. There is nothing with which to compare a series of studies of what was read in the *People* during the late 1940s,[52] since the London Press Exchange survey of 1933 covered only dailies. But the pattern of reader interest in the *People* during the late 1940s seems merely to be a less serious version of the pattern revealed in comparison with daily papers during the 1930s.

In short, the transformation of the balance of content in the popular press would seem mainly to reflect the physical reduction in its size and the temporary suspension of mass marketing pressures brought about by newsprint rationing. It also seems probable that this change reflected a marked increase of interest in public affairs during the war, but the available evidence does not suggest that this is true of the postwar period.[53]

The Postwar Years

The Resumption of Competition

Free sale of newspapers was resumed on a permanent basis in 1949, while statutory newsprint controls were progressively eased after 1950 and finally abolished in 1956. The relaxation and eventual lifting of government economic controls led to the progressive reemergence of competitive pressures on the press in a form that was broadly comparable with the interwar period.

Close competition without economic restrictions led to a sustained increase in costs as leading papers exploited the advantage of their larger advertising receipts and greater scale economies to spend more on editorial outlay and promotion. The number of pages progressively increased, with the pace usually being set by the leading papers, so that the total average issue print size of popular daily papers, in our sample, increased by 266 percent between 1946 and 1976, and the total average issue print space of popular Sunday papers in our sample increased by 235 percent during the same period. This enormous increase in paging was the principal cause of rapidly escalating costs. It was reinforced by other factors, of which the most important was the rising level of inflation, especially in newsprint costs, which doubled between 1972 and 1973.[54] Consequently the annual costs of the average London daily (excluding the *Daily Worker/Morning Star*) rose from £1,570,363 in 1946 to £28,140,111 in 1974.[55]

Escalating costs exerted a strong pressure on publishers to achieve an offsetting increase in revenue through increased circulation. The pressure to maximize circulation occurred, however, at a time when circulation levels were steadily declining. Between 1950 and 1976, national Sunday paper circulation fell by 44 percent and national daily circulation by 28 percent.[56] Although this decline was inflated by newspaper closures and reflected a fall in multiple newspaper purchase rather than a decline in newspaper purchasers,[57] it still meant that newspaper managements were under increasing pressure to expand sales while the market was contracting. Squeezed in both directions— needing to increase circulation yet confronted by falling demand— many inevitably adopted increasingly frantic expedients to enhance their papers' reader appeal.

The pursuit of circulation was dictated by the need to attract advertising as well as sales revenue. Rising costs ensured that all national newspapers cost more to produce and market by the 1950s than the prices at which they were sold.[58] Changes in advertising media planning and the growth of working-class consumption during the postwar period provided an added incentive for popular newspapers to expand their sales in the mass market in order to attract advertising.

There continued, nonetheless, to be differences in the advertising generated by different segments of the market. As competition for advertising intensified, some publishers sought to maximize their circulation by means that appealed disproportionately to women, middle-class, and young readers on the grounds that these subgroups were particularly sought after by advertisers. The orientation of some newspaper managements to youth also reflected the belief that young people had less entrenched newspaper loyalties than did their parents and consequently constituted a more accessible market. During the 1970s, however, some popular-newspaper managements paid less disproportionate attention to attracting middle-class readers. This shift reflected the declining real value of advertising as advertising rates failed to keep up with rising costs. Indeed some newspaper publishers actually published advertisements at a loss in 1975. The reduction in advertising profits meant increased reliance on sales as a source of revenue, so publishers have become increasingly anxious to draw readers from any direction they can. In practice, this has meant a shift on the part of some newspaper managements from a middle- to a more downmarket strategy, since the bottom end of the market was not exploited fully during the 1960s.

The cumulative economic pressure on publishers of popular papers to expand their mass appeal has been reinforced by the overall deterioration in the economic structure of the press industry. Costs have risen faster than revenue as competition has grown fiercer. This deterioration is documented with admirable lucidity and detail by the Economist Intelligence Unit in the crucial period, 1957–1963.[59] A further deterioration continued during the mid-1960s. The National Board for Prices and Incomes reported, for instance, that five of eight national dailies suffered losses amounting to £4.329 million in 1966.[60] In the downturn of the economic cycle during the 1970s, the plight of the national press became even more perilous. In 1975, only four of eight national dailies and only one of seven national Sunday papers made a profit.[61] During the postwar period, six national newspapers have closed, and a number of other titles have made substantial losses and remain in jeopardy. The pressure on publishers to universalize their commodities' appeal has become overwhelming in the growing struggle for survival.

Economic pressures on quality newspaper publishers, although every bit as acute as on the popular press, have taken a rather different form. Quality papers have continued to derive over two-thirds of their revenue from advertising.[62] Moreover the profit margins from this advertising have not been eroded in the same way as in the popular press.[63] Their survival has continued to depend mainly upon their ability to charge high advertising rates for reaching small but select audiences. Any significant dilution of their readership undermines their utility to advertisers and, consequently, their economic viability.

Pattern of Reader Interest

The full implications of these economic pressures on the popular press can be adequately understood only in relation to survey evidence on what people read. Studies using comparable techniques examining every year what articles were read in the *Daily Herald/Sun* and the *People/Sunday People* between 1947 and 1970, and what was read in the *Daily Mirror* and *Sunday Mirror* between 1962 and 1970, as well as additional investigations into the readership of other papers, reveal an extraordinary consistency in the pattern of reader interest in the postwar press.[64] This pattern can be briefly illustrated by one study, conducted for internal purposes by Odhams into what people read in nineteen issues of popular daily papers in 1963, based on a representative sample of 7,752 respondents.

300

The 1963 survey of reader interest in popular national dailies shows that human-interest content, letters, horoscopes, and cartoons were read significantly above average, with home politics (as in 1933) scoring slightly above average, and sports, international affairs, the city, and consumer features being read significantly below average (table

13.8). There is, indeed, a striking similarity between the pattern of reader interest in 1963 and that of thirty years before. This similarity is even greater when differences in classifying content between the two surveys are taken into account.

The differences in reading behavior between major demographic subgroups in the postwar period is also strikingly similar to that revealed by the 1933 survey (table 13.9). Survey evidence shows that human-interest stories continued to cross the barriers of sex, class, and age, appealing almost equally to all types of reader. Sports coverage has a very strong appeal to men, particularly working-class men. The appeal of women's features is not correspondingly high for women, but women's features generate editorially linked advertising.[65] Consumer features and city features have a generally low readership, but they also generate editorially linked advertising.[66]

Current-affairs coverage poses a special problem. Some aspects of current-affairs coverage have a strong appeal to subgroups across the broad range of popular newspapers. Coverage of home politics, for instance, is read well above average by a number of overlapping groups: men, those over thirty-five, and the middle class. Industrial stories are also read above average by men. But these only constitute elements in the mass aggregation of demand that popular newspaper managements must cater for in processing commodities for the mass market. Furthermore current-affairs coverage does not attract advertising linked to editorial content and does not enable advertisers to pick out particular groups of consumers in a suitable editorial milieu in the way that features about the city, property, travel, motoring, beauty, and so on do. Current-affairs coverage, although appealing to millions of readers, is a minority interest in mass marketing terms and is not directly sponsored by advertisers.[67]

Content Changes

The interaction between economic pressures to maximize circulation and the pattern of reader demand led inevitably to a transformation of the newspaper in postwar Britain. Between 1946 and 1976, the proportion of editorial space devoted to current affairs declined by at least half in all sample popular papers, and in the case of three papers (the *Daily Herald/Sun,* the *Sunday Pictorial/Sunday Mirror,* and *People/Sunday People*) by two-thirds. Public-affairs content in all of the sample popular papers in 1976 was dwarfed by human-interest material and indeed occupied less space than sports did in all seven papers. The proportion of editorial space given over to public affairs, including both news and features, shrank to less than 15 percent in four papers (table 13.10). In effect, popular newspapers in 1976 had reverted to the pattern of the interwar years in response to a similar set of economic and market pressures, although there was a small shift from news to feature material in public-affairs coverage[68] which can perhaps be attributed, in part, to the introduction of television. Other significant

301

shifts over the forty-year period of 1936 to 1976 include the growth of sports news, with its strong, working-class male audience appeal; a relative decline of space devoted to human-interest features (largely due to a decline of accompanying photographs) but not a decline of human-interest news; a relative decline of advertising-linked features reflecting the declining advertising orientation of popular newspapers; and a relative growth of arts and entertainment content largely due to features devoted to television. Most of these changes have been relatively small (table 13.11).

The only striking exceptions to this broad pattern of continuity are three papers: the *Sunday Pictorial/Sunday Mirror, People/Sunday People,* and the *Daily Herald/Sun.* These papers have drastically reduced their public-affairs coverage—most strikingly in the case of the *Daily Herald/Sun,* from 33 percent of its editorial space in 1936 to 13 percent in 1976. Coverage of social, political, and economic issues in all three papers has given way to coverage of sports and human-interest content. The change in the *Sunday Pictorial/Sunday Mirror* and *People/Sunday People* dates back to the late 1930s when they responded to the commercial success of the *Daily Mirror* by applying the same strategy in the Sunday newspaper market.[69] Their transformation should be viewed, therefore, as part of the journalistic change of the interwar period. The transformation of the *Daily Herald/Sun* is a more recent phenomenon. Acquired by News International in 1969, the *Sun* developed a new style of journalism that effectively updated and extended the tabloid revolution of the 1930s by carrying it one stage further. The new *Sun* published yet more photographs, more human-interest stories, and more sports with a broad audience appeal and more than doubled its circulation. Now the largest-circulation daily in Britain, it has compelled an editorial adjustment by its principal competitors, forcing them to make significant changes since 1976, the most recent year of our content analysis.[70]

After allowing for the distortions caused by government economic controls, the shift away from public affairs toward other types of content during the last fifty years would seem to have occurred in two waves, during the 1930s and during the 1970s, with the *Daily Mirror* and *Sun* as the two main innovators among the dailies. A small supplementary analysis also reveals important changes in the presentation of public affairs in the national daily press. Coverage of public affairs was given less prominence in all four national dailies that were examined in 1936 and 1976 in the sense that they were less often selected as lead stories. Human-interest stories, on the other hand, received much greater prominence (table 13.12).

Headlines have also grown much bigger in order to grab readers' attention. As a result, there has been a marked reduction between 1936 and 1976 in the space taken up by text (as opposed to headlines and pictures) concerned with public-affairs news (table 13.13). This contraction in the main body of the text of public-affairs news (and other news items) has coincided with an overall contraction in the editorial content of newspapers between 1936 and 1976. All of the popular papers in our sample experienced a fall in the total space occupied by editorial content ranging from 27 percent (*Daily Express, Daily Herald/Sun*) to 12 percent (*Daily Mirror*) between 1936 and 1976. This has resulted in a universal reduction in the absolute space given to public affairs in all the papers that were studied, even when the shrinkage in the main body of the text is not taken into account (table 13.14).

The range of public-affairs coverage as reflected in the number of news items has also declined, part of a general trend toward carrying fewer news stories, which can be explained only partly in terms of the overall contraction in editorial size. The reduction in the number of stories is much greater than the overall reduction in the editorial contents of popular newspapers and has resulted in less comprehensive public-affairs coverage in terms of the number of news stories published (table 13.15).

We also obtained a strong impression that the treatment of public-affairs coverage in the popular press has become more personalized and less contextualized than it was. A recurrent finding of editorial research carried out by publishers is that a human-interest angle gives stories a wider audience appeal, particularly among women and young people who tend to be light readers of public-affairs content. To take only one example, Odhams research department found that a story about a raid by the Irish Republican Army gained a high readership by focusing upon the "guard who only had a stick": it was commended as a model to the editorial department as a way of exploiting public affairs to obtain a higher readership.[71] This process of personalization—with all the distortion and trivialization that it implies—has become a recognized and approved strategy for building circulation. The result is that coverage of public affairs has increasingly been reduced to the level of human-interest stories.

Cultural Polarization between the Quality and Popular Press

The trend toward trivialization by the popular press has widened the gap between elite and mass-consumption papers. Changes in our two sample quality papers—the *Daily Telegraph* and *Observer*—did not correspond to changes in a large section of the popular press between 1936 and 1976. Indeed the proportion of space devoted to public affairs in both quality papers was actually higher in 1976 than in 1936. Perhaps the most significant change was the decline of arts and entertainment features in the *Observer*, due largely to a marked reduction in book advertising and consequently of book reviews (table 13.16).

It would be wrong, however, to assume that the difference between quality and popular journalism reflects a pronounced difference in the reading preferences of the elite and mass publics. One of the most striking and unexpected findings of unpublished survey research into what people read in newspapers is how similar is the pattern of reader interest between readers of quality and popular papers. This is not to suggest that statistics based on average readership of categories of articles provide an index of consumption in the popular and quality press. They do not take into account differences in the proportion of space devoted to different categories of content between quality and popular papers and hence what is actually read. They also tend to understate the level of reading intensity among quality-paper readers for two reasons: quality papers carry longer articles and consequently fare worst on readership statistics based on thorough readership of articles (those read from beginning to end), and quality papers are also much larger than popular papers, so that a lower average thorough readership score does not mean that less is read. In short, average thorough readership statistics are a misleading guide to what is actually read, but they do provide a valuable insight into the pattern of reader interest: what categories of content different groups of people read.[72] A comparison of the pattern of reader interest in popular daily papers and the *Daily Telegraph* is illuminating in this respect, since the results derive from the same survey using a comparable sample of items checked and comparable techniques of measurement. It shows that the most-read category of article in the *Daily Telegraph,* as in the popular national dailies, was human-interest tragedy stories. Also although male readers of the *Daily Telegraph* did have more interest in the leader and home politics (though not in industrial news) than readers of popular daily papers, they nonetheless also showed a high level of interest in human interest content. Women readers of the *Daily Telegraph* were still more comparable in their reading preferences to women readers of the popular daily press: the items they favored were human-interest tragedy stories, women's features, and stories about celebrities. Differences in reading preferences not only between men and women but also between young and old were also common to both the *Daily Telegraph* and popular daily papers. (See table 13.17.)

A similar pattern of reader interest emerged in research undertaken by the Thomson Organisation into what people read in quality Sunday papers. It shows that the most-read stories in the *Sunday Times, Sunday Telegraph,* and *Observer* were stories about sex, love, romance, court, crime, accidents, and other human-interest themes. Favorite among women were women's features and human-interest stories about celebrities. Only among male readers of the Sunday quality press was there a relatively high level of preference for home affairs news and comment, leavened by lighter material. (See table 13.18.)

This pattern of reader interest is reflected time and again in research into quality paper readership.[73] Any lingering belief that there is a fundamental difference in the pattern of reader preference between quality and popular paper readers is confounded by evidence of the high proportion of quality paper readers regularly reading popular papers.[74]

The difference between quality and popular journalism in Britain thus derives not so much from market demand as from the economic pressures that determine the way in which this demand is catered to. There is strong economic pressure on the quality press not to maximize their appeal since this would jeopardize their advertising value. In contrast, popular newspapers catering to the mass market have to produce contents with mass aggregate appeal in order to survive.

The contrast can be briefly illustrated by the success of two papers, the *Times* and the *Daily Herald.* The *Times* increased its circulation by 69 percent between 1965 and 1969 by an aggressive promotion campaign and by including more editorial material with a wider audience appeal. Its additional readers included a number of lower-middle-class and even working-class readers whom advertisers did not wish to pay the high advertising rates charged by the *Times* to reach. Consequently the *Times* failed to recoup the losses made on increased sales of uneconomically priced copies with a comparable increase in advertising revenue. The management of the *Times* then pursued an editorial policy deliberately designed to jettison some of its new readers by reducing its editorial content with a broad audience appeal and by changing its promotion policy.[75]

In marked contrast, the *Daily Herald* closed with over five times the readership of the *Times* in 1964. It appealed to a predominantly working-class readership, which did not generate elite advertising. Its heavy emphasis on public affairs, although read thoroughly by a substantial section of its readership, deterred the recruitment of a larger audience necessary for its survival. It was relaunched as the *Sun,* increasingly filled with human-interest content of a universal appeal and with, by 1976, only 8 percent of its editorial space devoted to public-affairs news.[76]

Human Interest and Ideology

National quality newspapers accounted for only 17 percent of national newspaper circulation in 1977.[77] Mass circulation papers dominate the market and contain very little about home and international news in the traditional meaning of the word *news.* Discussion of the national press should begin, therefore, by breaking with the concept of a *news* paper and instead considering the press as a broader form of cultural production, involving the construction of messages, the ideological significance of which is not limited to the narrowly and overtly political.

Indeed the common assumption that one section of a newspaper— that dealing with public affairs—is political, whereas the rest is apolitical, seems to us to be profoundly misleading. It is precisely where content offers itself as apolitical (in such areas as sports, human interest, and gossip) that ideological significance is most successfully concealed and therefore most demands analysis. If the media are seen as providing a major fund of images and a key repository of available meanings,[78] the importance of examining human-interest and other entertainment content becomes clear[79] because it is not simply a neutral window on a multifaceted and diverse world but embodies a particular way of seeing the world.

The non-current-affairs sections of the national popular press may seem diverse and random. It is, however, also possible to detect an underlying unity, based upon a partial and selective mode of seeing the world and representing it to the readers. There is first a rejection of any attempt to explain events as having a relation to social, economic, or political forces. Instead events are portrayed in terms of the actions and interactions of individuals, strongly governed by luck, fate, and chance, within a given, naturalized world, which merely forms an unchanging background. Real and fundamental structural inequalities and deep-rooted social antagonisms remain masked.

Second, this varied, diverse, multifaceted panorama of individuals is reunited in the form of a community that shares common universal experiences: birth, love, death, accident, illness, and, crucially, the experience of consuming. Individuals are symbolically reunited within a "passive community of consumers."[80] This community is further given focus by the stock of commonsense assumptions about the world implicit in human-interest stories, paralleling and complementing the construction and reproduction of consensus that takes place in current-affairs coverage. Identification is also invited with symbols of national unity presented as above narrow political differences.

This underlying ideological structuring of human-interest content should not be seen as the result of a conscious strategy but rather as the outcome of routine practices of press production and the professional ideology they generate. The demands of regular news production create organizational routines that tend to promote the continued reproduction of the various categories of news.[81] In the case of human interest, the various news values embodied in this professional ideology are particularly important. Prime among these is personalization. The marking off of current affairs stories as the domain of politics suggests an implicit depoliticization of the rest of the paper, which is further reinforced by the individualized nature of non-current-affairs coverage. It is, above all, personalization that the fragmented view of the world is built upon.

This fragmented picture of the world has two aspects. First it is atomized, broken down into an aggregation of discrete events based on individual interactions. Events are lifted out of their broader context and presented in isolation. Second, it is randomized; events are presented as caused by unpredictable factors (luck and fate) or by eternal human drives, such as fear, love, hate, and greed.

This form of presentation gives human-interest stories their characteristic appearance of being unusual, trivial, not typifying any broader

306

social events or trends, but drawing instead on classic elements of gossip, voyeurism and titillation:

POLICE WAKE DIANE, THE FAST ASLEEP WALKER
Student nurse Diane Cooley went for a late night stroll around town yesterday—in her nightie, dressing gown and slippers. Police were called after a passer-by saw 22 year old Diane sleepwalking at 2 am.

Daily Mail, August 23, 1978

But at the same time their place in the paper suggests a certain significance. As messages about the world, they generate, contribute to, and reinforce the stock of stereotypical images of life, drawing here for instance on the innuendo of the housewife-milkman mythology:

BIKINI WIFE AND THE WINDOW CLEANER
An amorous wife slipped up when she took a shine to a window cleaner. For her husband returned home one day to find her taking guitar lessons from him when she was wearing nothing but her bikini.

Daily Mirror, July 8, 1978

Human-interest stories are clearly distinct from current affairs; they are presented as having no broader social or political dimension. Instead their implicit significance is of a more universal nature. A story like "Sweethearts Die in Car Cliff Tragedy" invites audience identification based on the instant familiarity of *sweethearts, car, cliff,* and *tragedy.* The atomized, individualized view of the world is reinforced by the typical opposition presented between individual humans and the cold, inhuman bureaucracies:

GIRL, 17, DIES AT DENTIST
A beauty queen who collapsed and died in a dentist's chair was rushed to hospital. But her mother sat in the waiting room for 35 minutes without being told, it was claimed last night.

Daily Express, August 1, 1976

RED TAPE WRECKERS. BIG TOWN HALL
BUGLES ARE HURTING NEEDY.
Red-tape wreckers are ruining the lives of some
needy people, a Tory MP claims today. The
wreckers think they can do better than volunteer
workers. But, says MP Lynda Chalker, they just
make a mess of things.

Daily Mirror, June 27, 1978

Everyone brushes with Big Brother from time to
time . . . over mistaken meter readings, the actions of over-zealous officials, perhaps on a point
in the regulations so readily quoted by those in
authority, but so rarely actually seen.

Daily Mail, April 1, 1978

The generalized view of bureaucracies presented here has clear links
to bourgeois notions of freedom and the danger of excessive state intru-
sion into private life, a theme sometimes raised explicitly in editorials
but also deeply embedded in the human-interest approach to the world.
Human-interest stories represent the world of experience, the world of
individuals, as opposed to the impersonal abstractions of institutions.

Events are presented in terms of human emotion, frequently taking
the form of personalized drama. Characteristically the drama involves
sexual jealousy and situations newsworthy in part by virtue of their
transgression of the normal, happy couple relationship:

TELL TALE GASP THAT SNOOKERED
A HUSBAND
Window cleaner Arthur Charlton was really
snookered the night he claimed to be potting the
black in his bedroom. For his wife Iris was watching from outside. The room was in darkness and
she recognised the gasp he gave as the sound he
made when making love.

Sun, July 13, 1978

308

STABLE LAD STABBED BROTHER IN ROW
OVER LOVE FOR LIZA
Passion for a pretty Swedish au pair girl drove
stable lad William Holmes to kill the brother he
had always loved, a court was told yesterday.

Sun, July 13, 1978

Within the frame of individual human emotion, there is a focus upon the presumed high spots and crisis moments—birth, love, sickness, accident, death—the elements of shared universal experience:

THE ONE IN A MILLION BABY

A woman who was told by doctors that there was one chance in a million of her having a baby has given birth to a 10lb girl.

Sunday Express, August 22, 1976

DEATH ENDS A LOVE STORY

Footballer Alan Groves, who was involved in a child-bride storm in 1976 died suddenly yesterday. His 17 year old wife Debbie awoke to find him struggling for breath beside her.

Daily Mirror, June 16, 1978

The causes of these events are presented as random and unpredictable. Accident, sickness, and death are seen as not only tragic but also as mysterious, as the outcome of fate:

MYSTERY VIRUS KILLS BOY, 3

A boy of three died in his sleep after complaining that he was tired—but the infection that killed him remains a mystery.

Daily Mail, August 23, 1978

THE BAMBOO SPINE DEATH

Builder Arthur Preston was proud of his strength. He was well over 6 feet tall and weighed 18 stone. But he died after a struggle with police. The reason, a coroner was told yesterday, was that Mr. Preston had a disease commonly known as "bamboo spine."

Daily Mirror, June 8, 1978

Fate, of course, is not only random and mysterious but socially impartial; it strikes at both poor and rich:

COLD BATH KILLED THE SOCIETY WIFE

Society hostess Susan Stanley fell asleep in her bath and slowly died of cold. With the water getting cooler and cooler she became a victim of hypothermia.

Daily Mail, March 4, 1976

This constant emphasis on fate is a form of naturalization of the world, concealing the connections between events and their social and material context. Fate and tragedy are forces beyond and separate from human intervention. While the lives of individuals are shown as ultimately subject to fate, they are also blessed with good fortune:

HOW THE SUN PUT A £100 SMILE ON BRIDES FACE

Bride Shirley Hill and her groom Michael Phillips were feeling really lucky on their wedding day. So during the reception, Michael, aged 25, and 4 others slipped out to a betting shop, and following tips in the Sun for Saturdays races they won nearly £100 between them.

Sun, September 6, 1976

A SQUIRES LAST GIFT

Shy tycoon William Hunt loved nothing more than the peace and quiet of village life. . . . But yesterday the elderly bachelor who talked mainly to children was firmly in the limelight. For it was revealed that he has left nearly £500,000 to the village where he lived. . . . The windfall works out at nearly £200 a head for every man, woman and child.

Daily Mirror, June 8, 1978

The presentation of events in terms of good luck and bad luck, winners and losers, emphasizes life as a gamble, a lottery, with success and failure governed by chance.[82] The importance of good luck to success is a characteristic feature of the rags-to-riches format of star biographies, carrying the implicit message that anyone can make it:

310

Eventually Carol [Royle] went to a drama school. She finished two years ago. "Then", she said, "I was tremendously lucky. A producer had seen me acting at drama school and when I left I got the part of Laura Collins in The Cedar Tree."

Daily Mirror, July 8, 1978

WHO'S AFRAID OF BIG BAD BRONSON?
"Ten or fifteen years ago, mine was not the sort of face anybody wanted to see in the movies. Not being worn by the good guy anyway. But times have changed, I seem to have the right face at the right time."

Sun, September 6, 1976

The effect of the personalized approach is to produce a fragmented representation of the world. Individual events appear in atomized form, severed from their social context. The world is seen as a panorama of separate human dramas. The causes of these events are portrayed as random and unpredictable. They are either individual and hence emotional, or rooted in fate, luck and chance, and hence beyond control, irrational. Social structure is concealed. The world merely forms a fixed, given background.

But this is only half of the ideological process. The atomized, randomized world is at the same time given a coherence, brought together in an imaginary unity. This unification is implicit in the nature of the audience appeal of human-interest stories. Audience identification with these personal dramas is constructed around universal and eternal elements of experience.

In this sense human-interest stories offer themselves as tokens of the real world of individual human experience as opposed to the arena of public affairs and its cast of actors. Identification with this world also encourages identification with the sets of implicit commonsense assumptions that structure its portrayal.[83]

Further contributing to this imaginary unity is the emphasis in the press on a particular experience: the experience of consumption. Participation in the sphere of consumption is emphasized as a central common experience, while structured inequalities tend to be ignored or downplayed. Quite apart from the large part of the national press devoted to advertising, much of the editorial content celebrates consumption. Specialized features about travel, gardening, motoring, fashion, even financial coverage tend to address the reader as potential consumer. Reviews of films, records, concerts, books, and other forms of entertainment similarly promote the concept of consumption. Televi-

311

sion and radio pages usually include guides to viewing and listening. The guide to weekend television programs often occupies five pages of the Saturday *Daily Mirror*. Preview and buildup articles are an important part of sports coverage. Consumption is also highlighted in less obvious areas, such as horoscopes: "Some of you could be thinking of buying a car or caravan, and will be planning weekends away, or holidays" (*Daily Mirror*, July 25, 1978). The introduction of features like the Mirror Pop Club serves not only to preview and hence promote concerts but helps to promote the *Mirror* and also symbolizes the concept of a community of consumers, a club. The frequent competitions link together the concepts of consumption and luck:

WIN YOURSELF A DREAM
Your last chance to win a dream sports car plus £1000 in the boot. Now the Daily Express offers you a chance to win a prize you'll never forget, Leyland's latest—the TR7.

Daily Express, June 4, 1976

These competitions also serve to promote continuing consumption of the paper: "There's more to the *Mirror* tomorrow—Super Skateboard Gear must be won" (*Daily Mirror*, July 25, 1978). Even love is best expressed through commodities, as this advertisement suggests: "Look at all these things for Dad—just in time for Father's Day. And look at the prices too. It doesn't take much to tell Dad you love him—at Boots (*Daily Mirror*, June 7, 1978). The press does not simply promote the consumption of specific objects but symbolically affirms the concept of consumption generally, inviting everyone to participate. Consumption is emphasized as a central unifying experience, common to all.

The community is further given identity in the form of symbols of national unity. These symbols are clearly distinct from the world of politics and are offered with an assumption of universal approval. Everyone, it is assumed, takes pride in British success in competition: "No-one who saw last year's British Grand Prix will forget the roar of the crowd as they greeted a home victory (*Sun,* July 13, 1978).

Achievements in the industrial and scientific field also emerge as symbols of national identity—even Concorde, despite being an economic disaster and only half-British anyway: "It was hailed as the greatest thing since steam engines—Britain's most prestigious stroke since we let the Beatles loose on the world market" (*Daily Mail,* October 12, 1976).

Central symbols are the royal family, who are clearly presented as embodying a national unity above politics and as universally approved of. In this example, the diving instructor, offered as a "man of experience," certifies Prince Charles's competence to lead:

312

HRH ACTION MAN
His chief diving instructor was struck by the young officer's coolness. He recalled, "I thought to myself, if he's to be the next King of England, he'll do for me."

Sunday People, October 5, 1975

By implication, he will do for the rest of us. The consensual appeal of national unity symbolism is also evoked by advertising:

GUESS WHICH OIL COMPANY IS WORKING HARDER FOR EVERYONE?
BP Oil is a new 100% British Company. As a new company we have a new slogan: "Working Harder for Everyone". It's not advertising puffery! We actually mean it.

Daily Express, June 2, 1976

A bid is clearly being made here for the kind of universal approval invited by things British. This strategy in advertising often attempts to link the product to some other symbol of national identity: "Finally you might be wondering what the Avenger has in common with the members of the Scottish World Cup pool shown above. They're both stylish, tough, great performers. And they're both proven winners. Great British winners"[84] (*Daily Mirror,* June 8, 1978).

The evocation of symbols of national identity in a sense completes the process of unification by giving the passive community of consumers a positive focus of identity. It also provides, in an apparently apolitical form, a view of the world that powerfully reinforces the consensual themes of much of the current-affairs section of the press: the general interest, the common good, the need for management and unions to work together for national recovery, the common battle against inflation, and so on.[85]

The whole process of individualized presentation, portrayal of events from a human-interest standpoint, unification around the point of consumption, and the generation of symbols of national identity can be illustrated by reference to the portrayal of celebrities in the press. The individual-centered presentation of the world aids the emergence of stars, personalities whose regular appearance in the press results in their becoming celebrities in their own right. Celebrities emerge from all areas of the paper—not just the obvious areas of sport and show business but also from the arts world and from human interest.

Alberoni has argued that stars constitute a powerless elite, a group of people who are admired but do not incite envy or jealousy. Their rise to fame is not seen as giving witness to fundamental social inequalities

313

but is rather seen as being based upon a combination of talent and luck.[86] It is significant that people who personify the very dynamics of power, top people in the business and financial world, tend to be absent from the world of celebrities, emerging from the shadows only at a point of collapse or as aberrant mavericks. Their rise to celebrity status involves a degree of separation from the origins of the fame. Well known for being well known, celebrities become presented from a human-interest standpoint: "Robin Day is human after all. And there are pictures that prove it. The face that launched a thousand TV interviews is not, contrary to some rumours, a relentless computer that is wheeled out of a studio cupboard whenever a politician needs deflating. He is unmasked today as just a big softy in the hands of Daniel his six month old son" (*Daily Mail,* April 1, 1976).

The private lives of stars become a focus of interest, so that while remaining glamorous, they are also seen as "just like us." Increasingly celebrities from different fields enter the same world: rock stars party with politicians, film stars hobnob with sports stars:

NASTY PLAYS IT NICE FOR ALI
Tempestuous tennis star Ilie Nastase was making scenes at Wimbledon again yesterday . . . and showing that he's a good guy at heart. His reward: a kiss from actress Ali McGraw.

Daily Mirror, July 7, 1978

The fascination David Steel has for pop stars continues. . . . Yesterday he entertained Steve Harley for lunch at the Commons. To the amusement of Labour MPs, Harley appeared in the Distinguished Strangers Gallery (to listen to agricultural questions) wearing a bright red suit, while Steel, friend of Rod Stewart, pretended not to notice.

Daily Mail, March 18, 1977

The gossip columns further serve to draw together celebrities, who appear to inhabit a generalized, unified world. This world is predominately one of leisure, and more particularly of consumption: "Francis Lee is one of nature's winners. The sideboard full of trophies, a cupboard full of caps, the flourishing paper business, the big Mercedes . . . all the trappings of success" (*Sunday People,* October 12, 1975).

Examined in terms of the processes of fragmenting and uniting, the construction of celebrity stories can be seen as symbolizing both the individualized view of the world and the universal identification of everyone within the sphere of leisure and consumption. Ordinary

314

people cannot emulate the life-style of the celebrities, but as well as signifying the good life, the celebrity life-style offers a unity based around the concept of happiness linked to consumption, and the experience, as Lowenthal characterized it, of "being at one with the lofty and great in the sphere of consumption."[87] As well as representing the individual as consumer, celebrities are also offered up as the commodity: "Watch TV with Bogey behind you and Kojak tucked in the small of your back . . . these Freelance cushions from America are 14 ins square in natural coloured cotton canvas photo-printed with images of screen tough guys Humphrey Bogart and Telly Savalas" (Daily Mail, April 5, 1976). The styles adopted by celebrities are offered up as styles for consumption: "Fedora fever is sweeping South London. Copies of Malcolm Allison's hat are being snapped up by Crystal Palace fans as fast as a Southend firm can produce them. Palace have sold 3,500 of the red and blue fedoras so far during their FA Cup run" (Daily Mail, April 1, 1976).

Advertisers frequently link their products to celebrities as tokens of success: "Meeting of Today's Champions: Bjorn Borg and Wilkinson Sword" (Sun, July 13, 1978). The success of celebrities, particularly in the sports field, can be used to evoke the national identity theme. An article on the athlete Steve Ovett comments: "The record shows that this Blue Riband race is where the British excel. The 1500 metres, like the mile, requires not only speed and strength, but flair, and it is a quality which cannot be conjured up easily in the sports factories of East Germany and Russia" (Daily Mail, August 23, 1978). It links characteristics of Ovett's running to national characteristics generally, but also implicitly compares free enterprise flair with communist uniformity. Within the modes of presentation of celebrities in the press, the various elements of the process—individualized presentation, portrayal of events from a human-interest standpoint, unification around the concept of consumption, and the representation of national identity—can be clearly detected.

The non-current-affairs content of the press does not simply fit the skeletal explanation offered here; it has a far more complex and contradictory nature that requires analysis in depth. But we have demonstrated that although non-current-affairs coverage offers itself as apolitical, and has indeed characteristically been seen as multifaceted, diverse, and trivial, it nevertheless has an ideological dimension of some significance. Despite the varied forms of this content, underlying structures that give the field a certain unity can be identified.

This unity is rooted in a particular way of representing the world, which can be seen as having two elements. First, the world is divided into a diverse collection of individual interractions, separate from broader social determination, whereby social structure is concealed and hence naturalized. But second, the fragmented world is given an imaginary unity. This coherence is built upon the universality of individual experience, the sets of commonsense assumptions about this experience, the common experience of consumption, and the overall frame of national identity and common interest. The world of human interest offers itself as the world of real human, individual experience, as distinct from the abstract divisiveness of social and political structures and institutions.

Conclusion

Most of what is published and read in newspapers has very little to do with what they are generally considered to be significant for by historians, sociologists, and policy makers concerned with the press. Less than one-eighth of popular national newspapers in Britain is devoted to current affairs,[88] and the average reader spends less than a fifth of his time when reading a popular national paper on current-affairs content.

There has been a large reduction in the proportion of space devoted to current affairs in popular newspapers during the last fifty years. This has not been accompanied by a corresponding reduction in the quality press during the same period. This growing polarization has not been due to a growing divergence between elite and mass audiences but to economic forces operating within the press industry. There is, in fact, surprisingly little difference in the pattern of reader interest between quality and popular papers. Publishers of popular newspapers have merely been under mounting economic pressure to maximize their circulation by providing more material with a universal appeal to mass, undifferentiated audiences, whereas publishers of quality papers have continued to be under strong pressure not to expand into the mass market by publishing a large amount of material with a mass market appeal.

This domination of non-current-affairs material in the popular press calls for a reassessment of its nature and role in society. This should not prompt, however, the simple conclusion that its political role has been replaced by that of entertainer. Its apparently diverse and apolitical human-interest content represents reality in a form that powerfully reinforces and complements the dominant political consensus articulated in its current-affairs coverage. Indeed much of the persuasive power of this human-interest content derives from its apparent neutrality, its abstract from the world of politics and, not least, its genuine entertainment value.

316

Appendix to Chapter 13

Table 13.1 *Average Complete Readership of Selected Categories of News and Features in the British National Daily Popular Press*

Above Average		Approximately Average	
Accidents	(46%)	Parliamentary reports and	
Court and divorce	(44%)	government policy	(41%)
Personal gossip	(43%)	Social issues	(40%)
		Foreign general[a]	(40%)
Letters	(44%)	Editorials	(36%)
Serials	(40%)		
Gossip articles	(39%)		

Source: Derived from *A Survey of the Reader Interest in the National Morning and London Evening Newspapers 1934* (London: London Press Exchange/News Chronicle), vol. 2, which reported an average of 40.5% of all news stories being read completely in the popular national daily press and an average complete readership of 35% for features. All figures presented in this table are based on complete-readership scores, estimated where necessary by applying the average complete readership in each paper to the aggregated reader-interest score ("glanced at," "partly read," and "completely read") for each category of content. Categories are common to all popular national dailies. Estimates have been calculated on the basis of average-complete-readership scores for the following papers: *Daily Express, Daily Mail, Daily Herald, Daily Mirror, News Chronicle,* and *Daily Sketch.*

a. Includes a large number of human-interest stories, most notably in the *Daily Mirror.*

Below Average	
International politics	(39%)
Industry and commerce	(37%)
Sports	(36%)
Foreign politics	(36%)
Special articles	(31%)
Sports features	(26%)
Principal women's articles	(15%)

Table 13.2 *Changes in Space Allocated to Content with Diverse Appeal in Daily Mail and Daily Mirror, 1927–1937*

	Daily Mail	
	Editorial Space in 1937 as % of Editorial Space in 1927	Change in Content Categories 1927–1937 Compared with Change in Total Editorial Space[a]
Total editorial space (index)	135%	100%
Domestic		
Law, police, accidents	92	68
Personality, court news[b]	123	91
Other[c]	100	74
Other international news[d]	93	70
Other special articles[e]	192	142
Light columns[f]	181	134
Letters	135	100
Puzzles, contests, cartoons, fiction, etc.	135	100
Pictures[g]	173	128

Source: Derived from Royal Commission on the Press *1947–9 Report* (London: HMSO, 1949), appendix VII, tables 1–5.

a. These two columns show how content categories changed in relation to the overall increase in editorial space. For instance, "puzzles, contests, etc." in the *Daily Mail* increased in size in exact relation to the increase in the overall editorial space of the paper, and hence is tabulated as 100%.

b. "Personalities, court news" includes promotions, appointments, news of social functions when the guest is the main interest of the news item, and biographical notes on people in the news.

c. "Other domestic news" is defined as domestic news in brief, accidents not involving injury or loss of life, and all other home news not classified elsewhere.

d. All international news that is not social, political, or economic.

e. "Other special articles" are those related to topics other than politics.

f. "Light columns" consist mainly of gossip.

g. Pictures, it seems, were classified as a separate item, without regard for content.

Daily Mirror	
Editorial Space in 1937 as % of Editorial Space in 1927	Change in Content Categories 1927–1937 Compared with Change in Total Editorial Space[a]
148%	100%
242	163
245	165
196	132
245	165
231	156
157	106
219	148
174	118
96	64

Table 13.3 *Changes in Space Allocated to Public-Affairs Coverage in Daily Mail and Daily Mirror, 1927–1937*

	Daily Mail		Daily Mirror	
	Editorial Space in 1937 as % of Editorial Space in 1927	Change in Content Categories 1927–1937 Compared with Change in Total Editorial Space[a]	Editorial Space in 1937 as % of Editorial Space in 1927	Change in Content Categories 1927–1937 Compared with Change in Total Editorial Space[a]
Total editorial space (index)	135%	100%	148%	100%
Domestic news (political, social, economic)	73	54	91	61
International news (political, social, economic)	135	100	92	62
Editorials	68	50	72	49
Special political articles	93	69	233	157
Total	99	73	97	66

Source: Derived from Royal Commission on the Press *1947–9 Report*, appendix VII, tables 1–5.
a. See table 13.2, note a.

Table 13.4 *Average Complete Readership of Selected Categories of News in British National "Quality" Dailies, 1934*

Above Average[a]		Approximately Average		Below Average	
Court and divorce	(40%)	International politics	(34%)	Foreign politics	(30%)
Parliamentary reports and government policy	(37%)	Personal gossip	(33%)	Industry and commerce	(30%)
		Foreign general	(32%)		
		Sports[b]	(32%)		

Source: Derived from *A Survey of the Reader Interest in the National Morning and London Evening Papers 1934* (London: London Press Exchange/News Chronicle), part IV, section A, appendix. The newspapers included in the survey were the *Times*, the *Daily Telegraph*, and the *Morning Post*.

a. The average complete readership of all news for all readers, 33.2%, is the average between newspaper titles. The basis on which items have been selected and average complete readership scores have been calculated is the same as in table 13.1.

b. The readership figure for sports is only for the *Daily Telegraph*.

Table 13.5 *Allocation of Space in Three National Dailies, 1937*

	Public Affairs News and Features	Other News	Sports	Finance	Puzzles, Contests, Cartoons, and Fiction	Other Features[a]	Pictures
Times	21%	15%	15%	24%	3%	17%	6%
Daily Mail	11	16	19	9	7	20	18
Daily Mirror	5	19	13	2	13	24	24

Source: Royal Commission on the Press, *1947–9 Report* (London: HMSO, 1949), pp. 247–251.

a. Includes gossip columns, women's features, entertainment, and arts criticism.

Table 13.6 Editorial Contents of Selected National Daily and Sunday Newspapers, 1936–1946 (168 Issues Sampled)

	Daily										Sunday							
	Daily Express		Daily Herald		Daily Mail		Daily Mirror		Daily Telegraph		Sunday Express		The People		Sunday Pictorial		The Observer	
	1936	1946	1936	1946	1936	1946	1936	1946	1936	1946	1936	1946	1936	1946	1936	1946	1936	1946
Advertising	43%	18%	42%	17%	46%	18%	29%	16%	47%	35%	51%	16%	38%	22%	24%	25%	46%	36%
Editorial content	57	82	58	83	54	82	71	84	53	64	49	84	62	78	76	75	54	64
Photographs	13	7	9	5	15	7	21	8	8	2	14	4	11	4	26	25	3	3
Illustrations	4	4	2	4	5	4	7	15	1	1	4	6	2	2	6	6	1	*
Domestic public-affairs news																		
Social, political, economic	6	10	9	12	5	10	4	6	7	12	1	6	3	4	2	6	4	7
Industrial	1	4	3	5	1	2	1	3	2	5	1	3	1	2	1	*	1	3
Other	1	2	2	4	2	3	2	4	2	2	2	4	1	1	1	1	3	1
International public-affairs news	6	13	9	13	7	12	3	5	8	21	4	7	5	8	3	3	12	17
All public-affairs news	14	29	23	34	15	27	10	18	19	40	8	20	10	15	7	10	20	28
Public-affairs features	4	10	10	11	4	12	2	7	3	9	10	19	4	11	10	16	6	19
Total, public affairs	18	39	33	45	19	39	12	25	22	49	18	39	14	26	17	26	26	47
Finance	10	4	6	1	9	3	4	*	20	8	5	2	1	1	2	*	7	2
Sports	22	18	19	20	20	19	15	9	14	11	21	20	25	28	18	20	17	12
Human-interest news																		
Sex, love, romance	1	*ᵍ	1	1	1	1	2	1	*	*	1	*	1	1	1	5	1	*
Court, crime, accidents	10	11	9	9	9	11	11	15	8	8	6	6	10	7	3	3	2	2

	1	2	3	4	5	6	7	8	9	10	11	12	13	14	15	16	17	18
Other celebrity news[a]	5	4	1	1	3	3	3	3	3	3	3	2	3	2	4	3	2	1
Other	4	5	3	3	1	4	5	9	3	1	5	3	4	5	3	3	2	2
All human-interest news	20	20	14	14	14	19	21	29	14	12	15	11	18	15	11	14	7	5
Human-interest features																		
Sex, love, romance	*	*	*	*	2	*	7	*	*	*	*	*	5	3	1	5	*	*
Court, crime, accidents	3	*	1	*	1	*	*	*	*	*	2	1	3	1	*	1	*	*
Other celebrity features[c]	3	2	1	2	4	1	6	*	8	9	13	1	6	6	1	10	2	3
Other human-interest features[d]	4	4	6	2	8	2	14	5	2	1	8	7	9	7	13	10	4	4
All human-interest features	10	6	8	4	15	3	27	5	10	10	23	9	23	17	15	26	6	7
Consumer features[e]	2	1	2	1	4	1	1	1	1	*	1	2	*	1	4	1	3	1
Women's features	5	1	3	2	4	1	5	3	2	1	3	*	3	2	4	4	1	1
Arts, entertainment features[f]	6	4	6	4	5	5	4	1	6	3	3	4	3	2	7	3	25	20
Letters	1	1	1	2	1	1	2	5	3	3	*	3	*	*	*	1	3	1
Horoscopes, contests, quizzes, puzzles, cartoons, strips	4	3	3	3	3	4	6	16	1	1	4	6	8	8	14	3	3	5
Other features	4	4	5	2	6	5	5	5	4	4	8	4	6	2	3	2	2	3

a. "Other celebrity news" includes all news stories involving celebrities not coded in "sex, love, romance news" and "court, crime, accident news."
b. "Other human-interest news" includes all human-interest news stories not coded elsewhere.
c. "Other celebrity features" are defined as in note a.
d. "Other human-interest features" are defined as in note b.
e. "Consumer features" includes gardening, property, jobs, travel and motoring.
f. "Arts, entertainment features" includes books, films, theatre, broadcasting, art, museums, etc.
g. Asterisk denotes <0.5%.

Table 13.7 *Percentage of Editorial Space Allocated to Advertising-Sponsored Features, 1936–1947 (132 Issues Sampled)*

	Daily Express		Daily Mail		Daily Mirror		Daily Telegraph		Sunday Express		Sunday Pictorial		The Observer	
	1936	1946	1936	1946	1936	1946	1936	1946	1936	1946	1936	1946	1936	1946
Total editorial space sponsored by advertising	13.5%	4.6%	15.8%	5.6%	4.6%	2.8%	22.0%	3.0%	17.3%	2.5%	5.1%	6.0%	30.9%	12.9%
Finance	5.6	3.6	7.2	1.6	0.7	–	12.7	1.2	4.9	–	1.0	–	6.2	1.0
Books	0.3	–	–	–	0.6	–	1.3	0.8	–	–	–	–	13.7	10.6
Other arts and entertainment features	0.6	–	1.4	3.3	1.1	–	2.3	0.7	5.9	2.1	0.7	3.1	6.3	0.3
Women's features	3.8	0.6	3.1	0.3	1.9	2.3	2.5	0.3	2.0	–	2.5	2.6	1.7	1.0
Other consumer features	3.2	0.4	4.1	0.4	0.3	0.5	3.2	–	4.5	0.4	0.9	0.3	3.0	–

Table 13.8 *Average Thorough Readership (Percentage of Readers Who Read Items from Beginning to End) of Selected Categories of News and Features in the British National Daily Popular Press, 1963*

Above Average[a]		Approximately Average		Below Average	
"Tragic" human-interest stories concerning ordinary people	(53%)	Domestic politics	(37%)	Sports	(32%)
Human-interest stories concerning celebrities	(50%)	Television columns	(35%)	Main columnists	(32%)
Cartoons	(50%)	Special news[b]	(35%)	Special features[c]	(31%)
Letters	(44%)	Industrial news	(35%)	Social problems	(31%)
"Light" human-interest stories concerning ordinary people	(42%)	Editorials	(34%)	International affairs	(29%)
Sex, love, romance stories concerning ordinary people	(41%)			Women's features	(26%)
Horoscopes	(41%)			Entertainment features[d]	(24%)
Crime and court stories concerning ordinary people	(39%)			Finance (city)	(17%)

Source: Odhams Research Department, *Feature Readership in National Dailies* (1964). It was not possible to distinguish between news and features to ensure greater comparability with table 1, because of the way in which the data in the Odhams report were classified. All figures relate to the average scores among the titles (*Daily Express, Daily Mail, Daily Mirror,* and *Daily Herald*) included in the survey.

a. Average = 35%.

b. "Special news" includes assorted items that would have been classified under a number of different categories in our content analysis (both human-interest and public-affairs stories).

c. "Special features" includes nonrecurrent articles usually appearing on the editorial page.

d. "Entertainment features" includes features about entertainment, recreation, and other leisure pursuits.

Table 13.9 *Average Thorough Readership of Selected Items in Selected British National Dailies by Demographic Subgroups, 1963*

	Daily Express							Daily Herald						
	All readers	Men	Women	Middle class	Working class	Under 35	Over 35	All readers	Men	Women	Middle class	Working class	Under 35	Over 35
Human Interest														
"Tragic"/Ordinary people	45%	42%	48%	43%	46%	40%	46%	59%	57%	62%	57%	60%	55%	60%
Crime, court/Ordinary people	34	34	35	32	36	31	35	44	44	44	45	44	37	46
"Light"/Ordinary people	45	47	42	44	46	x	48	41	40	44	33	43	34	44
Love, romance, divorce	42	x	x	x	x	x	x	41	x	x	x	x	x	x
Celebrities	50	49	51	52	47	49	50	43	43	43	38	44	38	44
Public Affairs														
Domestic politics	37	42	30	40	34	24	41	39	43	31	42	38	22	44
International	27	27	27	28	27	21	29	28	32	20	25	29	21	30
Industrial	33	39	24	30	35	25	35	37	41	29	41	36	15	43
Social problems	31	29	34	33	29	27	32	33	33	32	26	34	26	35
Special news	35	35	36	36	35	32	36	38	34	43	43	37	20	43
Finance (city)	15	22	6	17	14	8	18	15	20	7	13	16	11	17
Features														
Editorials	32	37	29	35	29	14	38	38	44	28	44	37	25	43
Letters	36	30	44	36	37	29	39	40	38	45	35	41	24	44
Cartoons	43	46	39	45	39	46	43	53	51	56	52	56	46	55
Horoscopes	37	21	58	35	39	35	38	38	30	55	25	42	37	39
Sports	34	47	8	24	42	31	33	43	59	13	23	47	26	38
Women's features	30	11	42	26	26	23	28	30	19	47	27	33	23	31
Entertainment	19	19	20	19	20	16	21	25	24	26	25	26	17	28
Television	x	x	x	x	x	x	x	32	28	40	31	33	18	37
Main columnist	34	27	45	37	32	25	38	27	26	28	35	25	17	30
Special features	23	23	22	23	22	17	26	32	33	30	33	30	17	35
Average thorough readership of editorial contents	33	35	30	32	34	28	36	36	39	30	29	37	25	39

Source: Odhams Research Department, *Feature Readership in National Dailies* (1964), appendix. Thorough readership is defined as reading an item from beginning to end. All content categories are defined as in table 13.8. x indicates either that the appropriate content was not published in the paper or that the number of items in the issues checked was too small to yield reliable results.

Daily Mail							Daily Mirror						
All readers	Men	Women	Middle class	Working class	Under 35	Over 35	All readers	Men	Women	Middle class	Working class	Under 35	Over 35
54%	54%	54%	52%	56%	53%	54%	52%	47%	57%	56%	50%	47%	55%
35	35	35	36	34	38	34	44	42	47	42	45	39	47
x	x	x	x	x	x	x	41	38	45	41	41	39	43
41	x	x	x	x	x	x	40	34	46	37	40	35	43
52	50	54	56	47	59	50	53	51	53	50	53	48	56
39	43	36	40	38	29	42	34	35	33	40	33	22	44
23	25	20	25	21	25	22	36	x	x	x	x	x	x
32	40	24	32	33	37	31	38	34	42	34	39	31	43
18	21	15	18	20	x	18	41	37	45	38	42	38	43
34	33	36	34	34	x	36	31	x	x	x	x	x	x
15	19	11	20	10	14	16	24	x	x	x	x	x	x
39	41	36	43	34	25	43	28	31	25	34	26	18	33
43	35	53	41	45	26	47	56	47	60	53	53	45	57
43	45	41	44	41	47	42	59	64	54	62	54	61	58
40	28	55	35	46	34	42	49	34	65	41	51	44	53
22	37	8	16	31	26	22	28	46	9	26	28	26	29
20	10	31	24	15	21	18	28	17	40	22	30	23	31
22	20	24	21	24	26	21	30	31	28	31	28	27	32
32	37	25	31	32	x	x	40	37	42	44	39	36	42
36	27	48	38	34	38	37	30	31	25	41	27	21	37
29	25	33	27	33	22	31	40	39	41	40	41	34	44
31	31	31	30	31	31	31	38	39	37	39	38	33	42

Table 13.10 *Percentage of Editorial Space Allocated to Selected Categories of News and Features in Selected British National Popular Newspapers, 1946 and 1976 (132 Issues Sampled)*

	Daily Express		Daily Herald/Sun		Daily Mail	
	1946	1976	1946	1976	1946	1976
Total public affairs (news and features)[a]	39	18	45	13	39	20
Total human interest (news and features)	26	28	18	34	22	27
Finance	4	7	1	1	3	10
Sports	18	27	20	30	19	23
Consumer, women's, arts, entertainment features	6	11	7	9	7	14
Other features[b]	8	10	7	15	10	8

a. All items related to social, political, industrial, and economic affairs.
b. Letters, horoscopes, quizzes, contests, cartoons, pet features, children's features, editorials, etc.

	Daily Mirror		Sunday Express		The People/ Sunday People		Sunday Pictorial Sunday Mirror	
	1946	1976	1946	1976	1946	1976	1946	1976
	25	13	39	17	26	8	26	11
	34	33	20	29	32	35	40	41
	x	1	2	2	1	1	x	2
	9	28	20	25	28	30	20	27
	5	10	6	16	5	11	8	11
	26	15	13	10	11	16	6	9

Table 13.11 Contents of Selected British National Popular Daily and Sunday Newspapers, 1936 and 1976

	Daily Express		Daily Herald/Sun		Daily Mail		Daily Mirror		Sunday Express		The People/ Sunday People		Sunday Pictorial/ Sunday Mirror	
	1936	1976	1936	1976	1936	1976	1936	1976	1936	1976	1936	1976	1936	1976
Advertising	43%	44%	42%	40%	46%	36%	29%	42%	51%	56%	38%	44%	24%	46%
Editorial content	57	56	58	60	54	64	71	58	49	44	62	56	76	54
Photographs	13	13	9	16	15	14	21	18	14	13	11	21	26	20
Illustrations	4	5	2	6	5	5	7	8	4	9	2	2	6	6
Domestic public-affairs news														
Social, political, economic	6	6	9	5	5	5	4	5	1	2	3	1	2	3
Industrial	1	1	3	1	1	2	1	1	1	1	1	1	1	1
Other	1	1	2	x	2	2	2	1	2	x	1	x	1	x
International public-affairs news	6	4	9	2	7	3	3	2	4	2	5	x	3	1
All public-affairs news	14	12	23	8	15	12	10	9	8	5	10	2	7	5
Public-affairs features	4	6	10	6	4	8	2	4	10	12	4	6	10	6
Total, public affairs	18	18	33	13	19	20	12	13	18	17	14	8	17	11
Finance	10	7	6	1	9	10	4	1	5	2	1	1	2	2

	27	18	30	25	25	21	28	15	23	20	30	19	27	22
Sports	3	1	3	1	1	1	3	2	1	1	1	1	1	1
Human-interest news														
Sex, love, romance	5	3	3	10	6	6	8	11	11	9	9	9	9	10
Court, crime, accidents	2	4	2	3	2	3	2	3	2	3	1	1	2	5
Other celebrity news	3	3	5	4	3	5	4	5	3	1	3	3	4	4
Other	3	1	3	1	1	1	3	2	1	1	1	1	1	1
All human-interest news	13	11	13	18	12	15	17	21	17	14	14	14	16	20
Human-interest features														
Sex, love, romance	8	1	3	5	1	×	3	7	1	2	8	×	1	×
Court, crime, accidents	3	×	1	3	×	2	3	×	×	1	1	1	1	3
Other celebrity features	11	1	11	6	9	13	8	6	5	4	5	1	8	3
Other	6	13	7	9	7	8	2	14	4	8	6	6	2	4
All human-interest features	28	15	22	23	17	23	16	27	10	15	20	8	12	10
Consumer features	2	4	3	×	6	1	1	1	3	4	1	2	2	2
Women's features	3	4	2	3	4	3	1	5	2	4	1	3	2	5
Arts, entertainment features	6	7	6	3	6	3	8	4	9	5	7	6	7	6
Letters	2	×	5	×	1	×	2	2	2	1	2	1	1	1
Horoscopes, contests, Quizzes, cartoons, strips	5	14	6	8	6	4	10	6	5	3	8	3	6	4
Other features	2	9	5	6	3	8	3	5	1	6	5	5	3	4

Table 13.12 *Percentage of News Stories Devoted to Three Types of News In Four British National Popular Dailies, 1936 and 1976 (48 Issues Sampled)*

	Daily Mail		Daily Express		Daily Mirror		Daily Herald/Sun	
	1936	1976	1936	1976	1936	1976	1936	1976
Public affairs	73	51	52	48	45	30	80	22
Court, crime, accidents	25	28	32	25	28	30	17	33
Other human-interest news[a]	2	20	16	27	27	40	3	44

a. News of sex, love, and romance; celebrities; and other human-interest news not included in "court, crime, accidents" category.

Table 13.13 *Percentage of "Public Affairs" News Space Devoted to Headlines, Pictures, and Body Text In Three British National Popular Dailies, 1936 and 1976 (36 Issues Sampled)*

	Daily Express		Daily Mirror		Daily Herald/Sun	
	1936	1976	1936	1976	1936	1976
Headlines	33%	46%	34%	51%	29%	47%
Pictures and captions	3	5	20	18	8	4
Body text	64	49	46	31	63	49

Table 13.14 *The Decline of Public-Affairs News and Features: 1976 Content as Percentage of 1936 Content in Selected Papers (132 Issues Sampled)*

Daily Express	Daily Herald/Sun	Daily Mail	Daily Mirror	Sunday Express	People/Sunday People	Sunday Pictorial/Mirror
71%	31%	83%	97%	74%	51%	57%

Table 13.15 *Number of News Items Devoted to Three Categories of News in Selected Dailies, 1936 and 1976 (48 Issues Sampled)*

Average No. Items Per Issue	Daily Mail		Daily Express		Daily Mirror		Daily Herald/Sun	
	1936	1976	1936	1976	1936	1976	1936	1976
Total, news	54	35	71	38	48	35	88	34
Public-affairs news	29	18	35	19	18	14	51	13
Court, crime, accidents news	14	11	18	10	11	10	18	9
Other human-interest news	11	6	18	9	19	11	19	12

Table 13.16 *Contents of Selected British National "Quality" Daily and Sunday Papers, 1936 and 1976 (36 Issues Sampled)*

	Daily Telegraph		The Observer	
	1936	1976	1936	1976
Advertising	47%	48%	46%	49%
Editorial content	53	52	54	51
Photographs	8	9	3	12
Illustrations	1	1	1	3
Domestic public-affairs news				
Social, political, economic	7	10	4	5
Industrial	2	3	1	1
Other	2	3	3	2
International public-affairs news	8	10	12	8
All public-affairs news	19	26	20	16
Public-affairs features	3	4	6	14
Total, public affairs	22	30	26	30
Finance	20	20	7	10
Sports	14	18	17	16
Human-interest news				
Sex, love, romance	x	1	1	x
Court, crime, accidents	8	8	2	2
Other celebrity news	3	2	2	1
Other	3	2	2	2
All human-interest news	14	13	7	5
Human-interest features				
Sex, love, romance	x	x	x	x
Court, crime, accidents	x	x	x	x
Other celebrity features	8	1	2	5
Other	2	1	4	3
All human-interest features	10	2	6	3
Consumer features	1	2	3	7
Women's features	2	3	1	4
Arts, entertainment features	x	10	25	15
Letters	3	2	3	2
Horoscopes, contests, quizzes, etc.	1	1	3	1
Other features	x	1	2	3

Table 13.17 *Average Thorough Readership of Daily Telegraph Compared with Four Popular Dailies, 1963*

	Average, Popular Dailies[a]						
	All readers	Men	Women	Middle class	Working class	Under 35	Over 35
Human interest							
"Tragic"/Ordinary people	53	50	55	52	53	49	54
Crime, court/Ordinary people	39	39	40	39	40	36	41
"Light"/Ordinary people[b]	42	42	44	39	43	37	45
Love, romance, divorce/							
Ordinary people	41	33	52	40	41	NA	NA
Celebrities	50	48	50	49	48	49	50
Public affairs							
Domestic politics	37	41	25	41	36	24	42
International	29	28	22	26	26	22	27
Industrial	35	39	30	34	36	27	38
Social problems	31	30	32	29	31	30	32
Special news	35	34	38	38	35	26	38
Finance (city)	17	20	8	17	13	11	17
Features							
Editorials	34	38	30	39	32	21	39
Letters	44	38	51	42	44	31	47
Cartoons	50	52	48	51	48	50	50
Horoscopes	41	28	58	34	45	38	43
Sports	32	47	10	22	37	27	31
Women's features	26	14	40	25	19	23	27
Entertainment	24	24	25	24	25	22	26
Television[c]	35	34	36	35	35	27	40
Main columnist	31	28	38	38	30	25	36
Special features	31	30	32	31	32	23	34
Whole paper	35	36	32	33	35	29	37

Source: Odhams Research Department, *Feature Readership in National Dailies* (1964), appendix. For definition of categories see Table 8.
a. *Daily Express, Daily Mirror, Daily Herald, Daily Mail.*
b. There were no data on "light human-interest" items for the *Daily Mail.*
c. There was no television column in the *Daily Express.*

Daily Telegraph

All readers	Men	Women	Middle class	Working class	Under 35	Over 35
54	53	55	51	73	52	55
37	46	27	36	45	34	38
X	X	X	X	X	X	X
X	X	X	X	X	X	X
40	35	46	43	27	27	45
43	49	36	43	41	34	46
28	32	23	28	26	24	29
28	35	20	26	31	22	30
X	X	X	X	X	X	X
30	31	29	31	24	29	30
15	23	6	16	9	7	17
41	48	33	43	27	27	45
32	34	30	33	27	22	36
X	X	X	X	X	X	X
X	X	X	X	X	X	X
17	25	7	15	26	20	16
30	9	53	29	33	35	27
19	19	19	19	19	16	21
X	X	X	X	X	X	X
42	40	43	43	36	31	45
28	32	23	31	23	25	30
28	30	25	28	28	25	30

Table 13.18 Readership of Selected Categories of Articles in British Sunday "Quality" Papers by Sex, 1969–1971

Men			Women		
Above Average	Approximately Average	Below Average	Above Average	Approximately Average	Below Average
Domestic affairs news (34%)	Letters (22%)	Sports (18%)	Women's features (35%)	Letters (20%)	Domestic affairs features (15%)
Human interest (ordinary people) (31%)	International affairs features (20%)	Consumer features (15%)	Human interest (celebrities) (31%)	Domestic affairs news (20%)	Consumer features (14%)
Main review article[a] (31%)		Finance (city) (14%)	Human interest (ordinary people) (30%)		International affairs news (14%)
Editorials (27%)		Arts and entertainment features (12%)	Main review article[a] (30%)		Editorials (14%)
Domestic affairs features (26%)		Women's features (7%)			Arts and entertainment features (14%)
Human interest (celebrities) (26%)					International affairs features (9%)
International affairs news (25%)					Finance (city) (4%)
					Sports (2%)

Source: Sunday Times, Ltd., Marketing Research Readership Studes (1969–1971). The figures are based on 3 issues of the *Sunday Times*, 5 issues of the *Sunday Telegraph*, and 5 issues of *The Observer*. The average thorough readership scores (22% for men, 19% for women) are averages for these three papers. The number of items checked per issue for Sunday quality newspapers in our analysis of the Sunday Times survey is 48 items. The average thorough readership scores for quality Sunday newspapers are therefore somewhat lower than those for the *Daily Telegraph*, which, in the Odhams survey, was based on a check of 27 more prominent items.

a. Main review articles appear only in *Observer* and *Sunday Times*, and tend to deal with celebrities in the cultural field.

Notes

1. For examples of critical essays on the British press in the mass culture tradition that consider the non-current-affairs content of the press, see some of the essays in R. Hoggart, ed., *Your Sunday Paper* (London: University of London Press, 1967); R. Boston, ed., *The Press We Deserve* (London: Routledge and Kegan Paul, 1970); and D. Thompson, ed., *Discrimination and Popular Culture* (Harmondsworth: Penguin, 1964). In addition, some aspects of the broad range of contents of the press are considered in studies that have emerged out of the sociology of deviance that consider the media construction of images of deviant behavior, notably Stanley Cohen, ed., *Images of Deviance* (Harmondsworth: Penguin, 1971), and Stanley Cohen and Jack Young, eds., *Manufacture of News* (London: Constable, 1973). But the main influence of this tradition so far has been on the study of crime news, an area of press content that straddles the boundaries between human interest and public affairs; see Stanley Cohen, *Folk Devils and Moral Panics* (London: Paladin, 1971); Steve Chibnall, *Law-and-Order News* (London: Tavistock, 1977); and Stuart Hall et al., *Policing the Crisis* (London: Macmillan, 1978). There has also been some work on sex role portrayals in the press, although this has been largely restricted to magazines and advertisements. See, in particular, Trevor Millum, *Images of Women* (London: Chatto and Windus, 1975); Helen Butcher et al., *Images of Women in the Media*, Birmingham Centre of Contemporary Cultural Studies Stencilled Paper 31 (1974); Josephine King and Mary Stott, eds., *Is This Your Life?* (London: Virago, 1977); and Janice Winship, "A Woman's World," in *Women Take Issue* (London: Hutchinson, 1978). All of these studies are, with the exception of the mass culture critiques, only peripherally concerned with the bulk of newspaper content and do not constitute a counterweight to the almost exclusive concern of most of the literature with the overtly political content of the press.

2. Royal Commission on the Press, *1947–9 Report* (London: HMSO, 1949), esp. pp. 100–122; Royal Commission on the Press, *1961–2 Report* (London: HMSO, 1962), esp. pp. 14–21; and Royal Commission on the Press, *Final Report* (London: HMSO, 1977), esp. pp. 8–11, 75–100. The last commission (p. 8) also made explicit the conventional distinction between the political and entertainment roles of the press in a particularly simplistic form.

3. For a useful bibliography of British press history, see G. Boyce, J. Curran, and P. Wingate, eds., *Newspaper History* (Beverly Hills: Sage, 1978), pp. 399–406. Ironically although a number of essays in *Newspaper History* seek to contest the dominant Whig interpretation of press history, most of them persist in portraying the press primarily as a political agency within a conventional liberal framework of analysis.

4. This one-sided view of the press is not only a reflection of the enduring influence of liberal political theory but perhaps is also due to the political science orientation of many of those who have shown an interest in the press (both in Britain and America). For a valuable survey of the literature see D. McQuail, *Review of Sociological Writing on the Press*, Royal Commission on the Press Working Paper No. 2 (London: HMSO, 1976).

5. Perhaps the most useful theoretical exposition, drawing upon empirical evidence relating to the British national press, is provided by W. Reddaway, "The Economics of Newspapers," *Economic Journal* (1963). For an analysis of newspaper costs during the interwar period, see *Report on the British Press* (London:

Political and Economic Planning, 1938), and Royal Commission, *1947–9 Report*.

6. Calculated from N. Kaldor and R. Silverman, *A Statistical Analysis of Advertising Expenditure and of the Revenue of the Press* (Cambridge: At the Press, 1948), table 45, which includes provincial Sunday papers. This growth in production was sustained by fewer production units since the number of national papers declined from twenty-six to nineteen titles between 1921 and 1939 (Royal Commission on the Press, *1947–9 Report,* app. 2, table 2) without closures being offset by new launches. The increase in fixed costs during the period probably ensured that the leading publishers were able to renew the advantages of scale economies.

7. R. A. Critchley, *UK Advertising Statistics* (London: Advertising Association, 1972), p. 1, estimates that total media advertising expenditure in the United Kingdom increased from £45 million to £56 million between 1924 and 1938.

8. R. J. Minney, *Viscount Southwood* (London: Odhams, 1954), p. 243.

9. P.E.P., *op. cit.,* 1938, p. 73.

10. *Press Circulations Analysed 1928* (London: London Research Bureau, 1928).

11. London Press Exchange, "Report of an Investigation Made in Relation to the Consumption of Breakfast Cereals in General and Grape Nuts in Particular in the British Isles," app. I, London Press Exchange Ltd. records, London.

12. *Press Circulations Analysed.*

13. Royal Commission on the Press, *1947–9 Report,* p. 82, and *Report on the British Press,* p. 74.

14. C. H. Feinstein, *Statistical Tables of National Income, Expenditure and Output of the UK. 1855–1965* (Cambridge: At the Press, 1976), p. 65.

15. J. Stevenson and C. Cook, *The Slump: Society and Politics During the Depression* (London: Cape, 1977), pp. 16–39; S. Pollard, *The Development of the British Economy, 1914–67* (London: Arnold, 1969), pp. 268–277; N. Branson, *Britain in the Nineteen Twenties* (London: Weidenfeld and Nicholson, 1975), pp. 152–165; N. Branson and M. Heinemann, *Britain in the Nineteen Thirties* (London: Weidenfeld and Nicholson, 1971), pp. 133–147.

16. R. Stone and D. A. Rowe, *The Measurement of Consumers' Expenditure and Behaviour in the United Kingdom, 1920–1938* (Cambridge: At the Press, 1966), pp. 8, 12.

17. See, for instance, C. Chisholm, *Marketing and Merchandising* (London: Modern Business Institute, 1924).

18. P. Redmayne and H. Weeks, *Market Research* (London: Butterworth, 1931), p. 163.

19. *Survey of Press Readership* (London: Institute of Incorporated Practitioners in Advertising, 1939). Progressive advertising agencies like London Press Exchange and J. Walter Thompson introduced sex classifications on their readership surveys during the period 1934–1936.

20. See, for instance, advertisements placed in the *Statistical Review of Press Advertising* 2, nos. 2, 3 (1934) by national newspaper publishers.

21. For instance, Cyril Freer, *The Inner Side of Advertising* (London: Library Press, 1921); G. Harrison and F. C. Mitchell, *The Home Market* (London: Allen and Unwin, 1936).

22. *An Analysis of Press Circulations* (London: Institute of Incorporated Practitioners in Advertising, 1930, 1932, 1933, 1934).

23. "A Statistical Survey of Press Advertising During 1936," London Press Exchange Ltd. Archives, 1937.

24. *Statistical Review of Press Advertising* 6, 3 (1938): 35.

25. For a further discussion of the impact of advertising on the interwar press, see James Curran, "Advertising as a Patronage System," *Sociological Review* Monograph 29 (1980).

26. See, for instance, Lord Beaverbrook, cited in C. Seymour-Ure, *The Press, Politics and the Public* (London: Methuen, 1968), p. 95; H. Cudlipp (editor of the *Sunday Pictorial* in 1938), *Walking on the Water* (London: Bodley Head, 1976), p. 90.

27. H. Cudlipp, cited in A. C. H. Smith, E. Immirzi, and T. Blackwell, *Paper Voices: The Popular Press and Social Change, 1935–1965* (London: Chatto and Windus, 1975), p. 83.

28. C. King, *Strictly Personal* (London: Weidenfeld and Nicholson, 1969), p. 101.

29. J. Russell, *A Working Text-Book of Advertising* (London: Russell-Hart, 1925), p. 102.

30. For portraits of quality newspaper editors, revealing their commitment to prestige goals, see, for instance, J. E. Wrench, *Geoffrey Dawson and Our Times* (London: Hutchinson, 1955), and John Stubbs, "Appearance and Reality: A Case Study of the Observer and J. L. Garvin, 1914–42," in Boyce, Curran, and Wingate, *Newspaper History.*

31. The nature of this pressure is graphically illustrated in the advice given in the standard advertising textbooks during the interwar period about the value to advertisers of the editorial context. See, for instance, N. Hunter, *Advertising Through the Press* (London: Pitman, 1921), and H. W. Eley, *Advertising Media* (London: Butterworth, 1932).

32. *Daily Sketch* (1933), *News Chronicle* (1934), and *Daily Herald* (1936).

33. *A Survey of the Reader Interest in the National Morning and London Evening Press 1934* (London: London Press Exchange/News Chronicle, 1934). Despite its title, the survey was conducted in 1933.

34. Ibid., 2:pts. 3–5.

35. Survey investigation in the postwar period suggests that regional variations in terms of readership of categories of editorial content (such as sports, leaders, and letters) are very small, although there are regional differences in terms of specific items of content (for example, which football match reports readers are interested in) that regional editions are designed to cater to.

36. *Daily News*, 1921; *Daily Chronicle*, 1925; *Daily Express*, 1927; *Sunday Express*, 1927; *Daily Herald*, 1930; *Sunday Dispatch*, 1930; *News Chronicle*, 1930; and *Sunday Graphic*, 1932.

37. Royal Commission on the Press, *1947–9 Report*, pp. 257–258. There was not, however, a corresponding reduction in the space devoted to public affairs due to the *Daily Mirror*'s increased size.

38. Ibid., pp. 247–251. For the connection between the amount of space allocated to financial coverage and the volume of financial advertising, see James Curran, "Advertising and the Press," in J. Curran, ed., *The British Press: A Manifesto* (London: Macmillan, 1978).

39. King,·*Strictly Personal*, and Cudlipp, *Walking on the Water*.

40. The contents of seven popular and two quality national newspapers, based on a sample of twelve issues in the case of dailies and six issues in the case of Sunday papers per year (selected on a rotational principle so as to be representative of different days and weeks as well as months within the year), were examined in 1936, 1946, and 1976. The papers selected were the *Daily Express, Daily Herald/Sun, Daily Mail, Daily Mirror, Daily Telegraph, Sunday Express, People, Sunday People, Sunday Pictorial, Sunday Mirror*, and the *Observer*. A code-recode analysis of 1,491 items published in a sample of all nine papers that were examined, covering the three sampling years, by the two coders working on the project (Angus Douglas and Garry Whannel), produced a 16.5 percent divergence in the classification of the results.

41. Royal Commission on the Press, *1947–9 Report*, p. 82.

42. Ibid., p. 81.

43. The relaunch of the *Daily Mirror* was spurred by the prospect of closure; indeed its principal shareholder, Lord Rothermere, secretly sold his shares, expecting the paper to close. See M. Edelman, *The Mirror: A Political History* (London: Hamish Hamilton, 1966).

44. Royal Commission on the Press, *1947–9 Report*, p. 82.

45. P. Kimble, *Newspaper Reading in the Third Year of the War* (London: Allen and Unwin, 1942).

46. J. Curran, "The Impact of TV on the Audience for National Newspapers 1945–68," in J. Tunstall, ed., *Media Sociology* (London: Constable, London, 1970).

47. Royal Commission on the Press, *1947–9 Report*.

48. J. E. Gerald, *The British Press Under Government Economic Controls* (Minneapolis: University of Minnesota Press, 1958).

49. For a very interesting account of the editorial change in the *Daily Mirror*, though not adequately related to changes within the press industry, see A. C. H. Smith, E. Immirzi, and T. Blackwell, *Paper Voices: The Popular Press and Social Change, 1933–1965* (London: Chatto and Windus, 1966).

50. Mass Observation, *Press and Its Readers* (London: Art and Technics, 1949).

51. *Daily Herald and Daily Mail Readership Survey* (Odhams Research Department [ORD], DH5, 1946); *Report on Reading the Daily Herald* (ORD, DH8, 1948); *Daily Herald and Daily Mail Feature Readership* (ORD, DH8, 1949).

52. *Report of an Investigation into the Readership of the People*, Series ORD (1947).

53. This is the impression strongly conveyed by the Ministry of Information home intelligence reports, which indicate a strong degree of interest not only in the prosecution of the war but also in a wide range of domestic political and social issues during the early 1940s. For a detailed analysis of these reports, see I. McLaine, *Ministry of Morale* (London: Allen and Unwin, 1979).

54. For detailed assessments of the causes of increased costs, see *The Survey of the National Newspaper Industry* (London: Economist Intelligence Unit, 1966); Royal Commission on the Press, *1961–2 Report; Costs and Revenue of National Daily Newspapers*, National Board for Prices and Incomes Report No. 43 (London: HMSO, 1967); *Costs and Revenues of National Newspapers*, National Board for Prices and Incomes Report No. 141 (London: HMSO, 1970); Royal Commis-

sion on the Press, *Interim Report* (London: HMSO, 1976); Royal Commission on the Press, *1974–7 Final Report* (London: HMSO, 1977); G. Cleverley, *The Fleet Street Disaster* (Beverly Hills: Sage, 1976); K. Sisson, *Industrial Relations in Fleet Street* (Oxford: Blackwells, 1975); and *Industrial Relations in the National Newspaper Industry,* Royal Commission on the Press Research Series 1 (London: HMSO, 1975).

55. Estimated from Royal Commission on the Press, *1947–9 Report,* p. 82, and third Royal Commission on the Press, *Interim Report,* p. 96.

56. Curran, op cit.

57. *Survey of the National Newspaper Industry,* Tables 43–48; Royal Commission on the Press, *1961–62 Report,* pp. 23, 187; *Costs and Revenues of National Newspapers,* pp. 4, 34; Royal Commission on the Press, *Interim Report,* pp. 99–100.

58. Royal Commission on the Press, *Final Report,* p. 39. The reorientation down market was particularly marked in the case of the *Sun, Daily Mirror,* and, to some extent, the *Daily Express* during the 1970s.

59. *Survey of the National Newspaper Industry.*

60. *Costs and Revenues of National Daily Newspapers,* p. 7.

61. Royal Commission on the Press, *Interim Report,* p. 5.

62. Ibid., pp. 99–100.

63. Royal Commission on the Press, *Final Report,* p. 39.

64. This is revealed particularly clearly by the regular survey investigations, using comparable techniques, undertaken by Odhams/IPC during the postwar period. These included investigations into all mass circulation national dailies and Sundays at some point during the postwar period, as well as the papers owned by Odhams/IPC monitored on a more regular basis.

65. Curran, "Advertising and the Press," pp. 232–237.

66. Ibid.

67. The minority rating gained by current affairs with only about a third of popular newspaper readers reading thoroughly a typical current affairs article in the popular press still means that such articles are read by well over a million readers of each popular paper.

68. This was largely due to the much greater reduction of foreign news compared with features. This reduction may have been encouraged by the decline in the number of foreign correspondents employed by the national press mainly due to reasons of cost; see Oliver Boyd-Barrett, "The Collection of Foreign News in the National Press," in *Studies on the Press,* Royal Commission on the Press Working Paper Number 3 (London: HMSO, 1977). The shift from news to features may also reflect the popular belief among many newspapermen that television has reduced interest in news but increased interest in comment and analysis in the form of features. There is no evidence, however, that television viewing has reduced interest in news. For an assessment, see Curran, "The Impact of TV" and J. Curran and J. Tunstall, "Mass Media and Leisure," in M. Smith, S. Parker, and C. Smith, eds., *Leisure and Society in Britain* (London: Allen Lane, 1973).

69. For a description of the transformation of the *Sunday Pictorial,* see Hugh Cudlipp, *At Your Peril* (London: Weidenfeld and Nicholson, 1962), p. 41.

70. An unsystematic examination suggests that both the *Daily Mirror* and *Daily Express* have cut back still further on their current-affairs coverage since

1976 and that the new daily launched in 1978, the *Daily Star,* has even less current-affairs content than any other rival paper.

71. *People Readership Interest Survey* (London: Odhams Research Department, 1955).

72. For a useful assessment of research techniques in measuring reading behavior, see R. Fletcher, "Reading Behaviour Reconsidered," *Journal of the Market Research Society* 12, no. 1 (1970).

73. A closely similar pattern of reader interest is revealed in research undertaken by Odhams and by the *Daily Telegraph* group.

74. *Hulton Readership Surveys* (London: Hulton, 1947–1955); Institute of Practitioners in Advertising (IPA), *National Readership Surveys* (London: IPA, 1956–1967); *JICNARS* (London: IPA, 1968–1978).

75. For a fuller description, see Fred Hirsch and David Gordon, *Newspaper Money* (London: Hutchinson, 1975).

76. A more detailed examination of the market pressures that destroyed the *Daily Herald* is provided in Curran, "Advertising and the Press."

77. Derived from the Audit Bureau of Circulations.

78. Graham Murdock, "Mass Communication and the Construction of Meaning," in N. Armistead, *Reconstructing Social Psychology* (Harmondsworth: Penguin, 1974).

79. For a pioneering and important examination of human-interest content in the American press that is written from a different ideological perspective to our own, see Helen Hughes, *News and the Human Interest Story* (Chicago: University of Chicago Press, 1940).

80. For an interesting development of this theme in a general context, see Stuart Hall, "Culture, Media and the Ideological Effect," in J. Curran, M. Gurevitch, and J. Woollacott, eds., *Mass Communication and Society* (Beverly Hills: Sage, 1979).

81. This is well documented in relation to crime reporting by Chibnall, *Law-and-Order News.*

82. For an interesting discussion of the belief in luck and associated concepts in the value systems of subordinate classes and its importance in encouraging an accommodation to subordinate status, see F. Parkin, *Class Inequality and Political Order* (London: Paladin, 1972), p. 76.

83. Space does not permit a discussion of the commonsense assumptions embedded in apparently apolitical human-interest stories and their wider ideological implications. But for a particularly insightful commentary on the relationship between commonsense ideas, expressed in an apparently apolitical form, and political debates bout law and order, see S. Hall et al., *Policing the Crisis* (London: Macmillan, 1978).

84. This appropriation of the Scotland team as "British," common to both advertisement and sports commentary when Scotland made the finals of the 1978 World Cup, was rapidly dropped when the Scotland team flopped in Argentina.

85. For a particularly interesting exposition of the consensual themes that underly and inform coverage of industrial relations, see Dave Morley, "Industrial Conflict and the Mass Media," *Sociological Review* (1976).

86. Francesco Alberoni, "The Powerless Elite," in D. McQuail, ed., *Sociology of Mass Communications* (Harmondsworth: Penguin, 1972).

87. Leo Lowenthal, "The Triumph of Mass Idols," in *Literature, Popular Culture and Society* (Englewood Cliffs, N.J.: Prentice-Hall, 1961).

88. This estimate is based on the total content of popular national newspapers, including their advertisements. As we have seen, current-affairs content accounts for less than one-fifth of their editorial content.

About the Contributors

Giovanni Bechelloni is among the best known of Italian students of mass communications with special interests in the political system. He has undertaken a great deal of research and has been active as editor and publisher. In the 1970s he was chief editor of the review *Tempi Moderni* and later founded CESDI, a research center specializing in sociology and culture. He currently teaches sociology at the University of Naples, is chief editor of the review *Rassegna Italiana di Sociologia,* and is coeditor of the quarterly *Problemi dell'Informazione.* He has published numerous essays and books, among them, *The Italian Cultural Machine, Information and Power,* and *Culture and Ideology in the New Left.*

Leo Bogart is executive vice-president and general manager of the Newspaper Advertising Bureau, Inc. He joined the bureau in 1960 as vice-president of marketing planning and research. Formerly he directed public opinion research for Standard Oil Company (New Jersey), marketing research for Revlon, and international research (among other responsibilities) at McCann-Erickson, where he was vice-president of the Market Planning Corporation Division. He has taught at the Illinois Institute of Technology, New York University, and Columbia University. He is the author or editor of numerous books and articles in the fields of public opinion, communications, and marketing research.

Hans Dahl, a historian, is the author of several books on modern history and communication topics. His main work is a two-volume history of broadcasting in Norway. He is currently cultural editor of the daily paper *Dagbladet,* in Oslo.

James Curran graduated in history at Cambridge University, where he also did postgraduate research on the post-1945 British press. He was appointed a research fellow at the Social Sciences Faculty of the Open University before becoming a senior lecturer at the School of Communication, Polytechnic of Central London. An academic adviser to the Royal Commission on the Press, 1974–1977, he has published widely in the fields of media sociology and press history. He is editor or coeditor of *Mass Communication and Society; Newspaper History;* and *British Press: A Manifesto.* He is also a founding editor of the academic journal *Media, Culture and Society,* started in 1979.

Angus Douglas and **Garry Whannel** were among the first class of students to graduate in media studies in Britain—at the School of Communication, Polytechnic of Central London, in 1978. The former is now working as an assistant stage manager and the latter is now doing postgraduate research at the Centre for Contemporary Cultural Studies at Birmingham University.

Karl Erik Gustafsson is associate professor of business economics, University of Gothenburg, Sweden. He has served as expert on a number of government commissions on mass media, among them the Commission on Advertising and the 1972 Parliamentary Commission on the Press. He is currently principal secretary of the fourth government Commission on the Press.

David J. Hart graduated with a degree in engineering from the University of Leicester in England in 1965. He has worked in the aircraft and mining equipment industries. In 1975, he was appointed research director of the Inca-Fiej Research Association in Darmstadt, Federal Republic of Germany, an affiliation of daily newspaper publishers and materials and equipment manufacturers engaged in a program of training, information, and applied research aimed at providing technical support to the newspaper industry.

William Horsley took a B.A. in Japanese studies at Oxford University in 1971 and then joined the British Broadcasting Corporation. From 1974 to 1977 he worked in Japan, first as a producer and announcer on secondment from the BBC to the Japan Broadcasting Corporation, and later as a freelance writer and reporter. A book of his collected translations from the *Asahi Shimbun* was published by the *Asahi Evening News.* He has written many articles on Japanese politics and society for *The Listener* and other publications in the United Kingdom and Japan and now works for BBC Radio Current Affairs.

Ben Pimlott is a lecturer in politics at the University of Newcastle upon Tyne. He has held the British Academy Thank Offering to British Fellowship and a Nuffield Foundation Social Science Research Fellowship. He is the author of *Labour and the Left in the 1930s* and of articles on British parties and political history and contemporary Portuguese politics.

Jean Seaton is a lecturer in sociology in the Polytechnic of the South Bank, London. She has written on the sociology and politics of the mass media in Britain and Portugal and currently is writing a history of the press and broadcasting industries in Britain.

Anthony Smith is the Director of the British Film Institute, a television producer, and a former fellow of St. Antony's College, Oxford. His main publications are *The Shadow in the Cave: The Broadcaster, the Audience and the State; Subsidies and the Press in Western Europe; The Politics of Information: Problems of Policy in Modern Media; The Newspaper: An International History; Television and Political Life: Studies in Six European Societies;* the companion volume to the current study commissioned by the German Marshall Fund of the United States, *Goodbye Gutenberg;* and *The Geopolitics of Information.*

José Antonio Martinez Soler during the last years of the Franco regime participated in the launching of independent and critical publications, among them the banned daily paper *Nivel.* He was the first managing editor of the popular political weekly *Cambio 16,* and later founding editor of the critical political and economic weekly magazine *Doblon* and the monthly *Historia Internacional.* During this period he had the dubious honor of being one of the journalists with the greatest number of judicial prosecutions and indictments. While editor of *Doblon,* a few months after the death of Franco he was kidnapped, tortured, and interrogated about his sources by a paramilitary armed group of the extreme right. He became a Nieman fellow at Harvard University and later foreign editor in Madrid of the newspaper *El Pais.* At present he is adviser to José Luis Leal, the secretary of state for economic affairs.

Antoine de Tarlé has worked on the staff of the French parliament since 1965 and has for the last ten years been the National Assembly's chief adviser on media matters (press and broadcasting). He is currently in charge of a seminar on the future of the French broadcasting system at Ecole Nationale d'Administration and a member of the editing board of the monthly *Les Etudes;* and he was a contributor to *Television and Politics in Western Europe.*

351

Tetsuro Tomita was graduated from the law faculty of Tokyo University in 1957. He has held positions in Japan's Ministry of Posts and Telecommunications and Defense Agency, and has been Assistant Director of Communications Policy Division (MPT) and Counselor of Telecommunications. At present he is Director of the MPT Communications

Policy Division. His publications include "The Volume of Information Flow and Quantum Evaluation of Media" and "Information and Communication Policies in an Age Oversupplied with Information."

Pauline Wingate is an Oxford-trained historian, a freelance researcher, editor, and writer. She has worked with, among others, the Acton Society Trust, the National Prices and Incomes Board, and the Oxford Centre for Management Studies on subjects as diverse as investment patterns, industrial mergers, and management structures. She is secretary of the Acton Society Press group and edited, with George Boyce and James Curran, *Newspaper History*.